GODS AND MEN

" . . . the religion which Greek tragic poets explored and which Greek tragedy served was not what we understand by religion; unless we realize that it was not, we miss the meaning of Greek tragedy . . . The world of gods and the world of men were quite apart; gods were not primarily concerned with regulating men, nor men with emulating gods. Each followed his own nature; for the gods two plus two might equal five, but men must continue making it four. If, making it four, man is tripped up by a system he cannot control or even understand which makes it five, the result is tragedy. So far from being a punishment for error tragedy may therefore be proof of the sufferer's merits and demonstration that he deserves the status of hero."

From the Editor's Introduction

MOSES HADAS, late Jay Professor of Greek at Columbia University, was the author of the authoritative **History of Greek Literature,** the companion **History of Latin Literature,** and **Hellenistic Culture: Fusion and Diffusion.** Bantam Books edited by Professor Hadas include **The Complete Plays of Aristophanes, Ten Plays by Euripides, The Aeneid,** and **The Essential Works of Stoicism,** in addition to his **Introduction to Classical Drama.**

D0724827

Classics in Drama from Bantam Books
Ask your bookseller for the books you have missed

AESCHYLUS: THE ORESTEIA Translated by Robert Fagles
ARMS AND THE MAN by George Bernard Shaw
THE COMPLETE PLAYS OF ARISTOPHANES
    Edited by Moses Hadas
THE COMPLETE PLAYS OF SOPHOCLES Edited by Moses Hadas
THE CRUCIBLE by Arthur Miller
CYRANO DE BERGERAC by Edmond Rostand
FOUR GREAT PLAYS by Henrik Ibsen
FOUR GREAT PLAYS BY CHEKHOV
GREEK DRAMA Edited by Moses Hadas
MEDIEVAL AND TUDOR DRAMA Edited by John Gassner
TEN GREAT ONE ACT PLAYS Edited by Morris Sweetkind
TEN PLAYS BY EURIPIDES Edited by Moses Hadas

GREEK DRAMA

Edited by
MOSES HADAS

BANTAM BOOKS · TORONTO · NEW YORK · LONDON

RL 9, IL 10-up

GREEK DRAMA

A Bantam Classic | December 1965
2nd printing .... February 1967
Bantam World Drama edition | August 1968
4th printing ...... January 1969   5th printing .. November 1970
Bantam edition | November 1971
7th printing .. September 1972   10th printing .... July 1976
8th printing .... April 1973   11th printing . November 1978
9th printing .... March 1975   12th printing .... June 1980

Front-cover photograph by Roberto Kechler

Library of Congress Catalog Card Number: 65-26668

Frogs: © *Copyright, 1962, by the University of Virginia Press,*
translated by Robert H. Webb and included in this volume by
permission of the University of Virginia Press.

Medea, Hippolytus, Trojan Women: *Copyright 1936, by the*
Dial Press, Inc. © *Copyright, 1960, by Bantam Books, Inc.*

Bantam Books are published by Bantam Books, Inc. Its trade-
mark, consisting of the words "Bantam Books" and the por-
trayal of a bantam, is Registered in U.S. Patent and Trademark
Office and in other countries. Marca Registrada. Bantam
Books, Inc., 666 Fifth Avenue, New York, New York 10019.

PRINTED IN THE UNITED STATES OF AMERICA

21 20 19 18 17 16 15 14 13 12

CONTENTS

THE LEGACY OF GREECE

by John Gassner

PROFESSOR HADAS' useful summary of essential facts in the Introduction that follows obviates the necessity of encumbering this preface with information on the plays in the present collection. But since it is a volume in Bantam Books' Library of World Drama it is appropriate to advert here to the place of the classic drama in the world's theater. The subject, moreover, is by no means of purely antiquarian interest; it has engaged us for many years as a distinctly modern, if not indeed avant-garde, topic.

It is true enough that the Roman world revered Greek drama to the point of both direct imitation and adaptation. But in the case of tragedy, the imitations seem to have been early academic exercises which failed to survive. If plays by the Stoic philosopher Seneca exerted a literary influence in the sixteenth century, they reflected classic Greek tragedy only remotely in structure, style, and theatrical viability. And if Greek comedy had a more direct continuity and more salutary influence through the Romans Plautus and Terence (their influence has been considerable ever since the Renaissance), a substantial qualification must be made; we know too little about their immediate Greek models written by the famous Menander and other fourth-century B.C. playwrights. Roman comedy, like the so-called New Comedy of fourth-century Athens, is primarily domestic and romantic, comedy of "manners," whereas the Old, or Aristophanic, Comedy is, on the one hand, critical and satirical, and, on the other hand, lyrical and fantastic. With a few distinguished exceptions (one may cite Molière's *The Imaginary Invalid* and John Gay's *The Beggar's Opera*), it commands attention again only as a modern phenomenon. We can identify and appreciate it best in such guises as Shavian and Brechtian comedy, topical revues, and musical comedies like *Of Thee I Sing!, Finian's Rainbow,* and *Oh, What a Lovely War!*

In the case of Greek tragedy, too, we are most apt to be concerned in the theater with the modern possibilities. The purely historical interest has greatly receded. Today there can be but little concern with virtually forgotten Renaissance imitations and with misleading commentaries on Aristotle's *Poetics* that foisted the cult of the unities of time, place and action on playwrights for approximately three centuries. (Aristotle himself had actually insisted on only *one* unity— that of dramatic action.)

Theater historians may take note of Milton's great dramatic poem *Samson Agonistes* (1673), composed like a Greek tragedy with alternating dramatic scenes and choral recitations, but only to observe that the author's interest was literary rather than theatrical since he did not intend this work to be performed. The historian can come to more than a brief pause only in arriving at the neo-classic period in France climaxed by the tragedies of Racine (1639-1699) in which the emphasis on inner cohesion, consistent with the author's focus on character, accounted for essential classicality of form, whether or not he employed the formal Greek structure of alternate scenes and choral passages. But Racine's achievement is but an interlude in a long and dreary chronicle of neo-classical sterility in a dozen languages which even the literary genius of Voltaire could not alleviate. And even the later classical German drama, exemplified by Schiller's *Wallenstein's Death* and *The Bride of Messina* and Goethe's *Iphigenia in Tauris,* was only another brief interval.

It is, of course, a high compliment to Greek drama to be able to cite as examples of its influence such altitudes of European tragedy as the dramatic writings of Racine, Goethe, and Schiller. But for our own time it is more useful to observe some of the direct and indirect affiliations and parallels, as well as contrasts, that have engaged the modern theater.

We must certainly take note of the tendencies to translate the classic theme of guilt and retribution into strikingly modern terms. Thus in Ibsen's *Ghosts,* and in other modern plays, guilt often consists in conformity to, rather than defiance of, convention. (Ibsen's Mrs. Alving "sinned" in *returning* to her husband rather than in leaving him.) Punishment in *Ghosts* is not for *hubris* but for lack of that self-respect and self-regard. Ibsen calls for self-realization and requires independence of judgment. Later, existentialist drama makes the same point imaginatively, in Sartre's *No Exit* and *The Flies,* and in Anouilh's *Antigone.* Euripidean scepticism has filled the modern theater with much questioning of accepted values and with many anti-heroic or deflationary treatments of once generally accepted values; with concepts of moral relativity (*The Wild Duck* is one example, and another is Shaw's *The Doctor's Dilemma*); and with more or less dialectical interpretations of history as exemplified by *The Cherry Orchard* and *Saint Joan.*

Today we can look upon the Greek classics from the vantage point of modern drama of "ideas." We can appreciate much of the extant work of Aeschylus and Euripides as distinguished, if not indeed the most memorable, examples of this genre, since they possess the imaginativeness and power of poetic drama in addition to developing an argument or demonstrating a problem. Neither social criticism nor philosophical and religious inquiry suffers from this sublimation and universalization of reality by means of myth, choral song, and ritualism. This is amply apparent in the social dramas of Euripides (the best known example is *The Trojan Women*) and the trilogies of Aeschylus. The religious background of the Greek tragedies and the ritualistic occasion of their production in Athens' Theatre of Dionysus only enhance the intensity and depth of the work. And if notions of Fate have been translated into concepts of determinism (heredity, instinct, and environment) in modern literature, it is still true that the tragic experience is supra-rational; it belongs to poetry rather than to debate and to passion rather than to scientific or sociological argument.

William Arrowsmith defined the "Greek theater of ideas" instructively when, in differentiating it from "a theater of intellectual *sententiae,*" he described it as "a theater of dramatists whose medium of thought was the stage, who used the whole machinery of the theater as a way of thinking, critically and constructively, about their world." *

Another, and equally modern development—that of "psychological" or character drama—is no less prefigured in the work of Sophocles and Euripides. It is most plainly observable in the latter's plunge into anti-heroic realism with *Electra* and *Orestes* (the latter is largely an exercise in

* "A Greek Theater of Ideas," *Ideas in the Drama,* ed. by John Gassner. New York: Columbia University Press, 1964.

pathology) and in his symbolical use of myth in such masterpieces as his *Hippolytus* and *The Bacchae,* which O'Neill
would probably have selected as prime early examples of the
genre he called "super-realism." The proper study of man,
begun by Sophocles, interests us especially wherever we find
Euripides anticipating the naturalists and the Freudians who
have flourished since the last quarter of the nineteenth century. When Ibsen and Strindberg focus attention on their
divided, destructive and self-destructive characters (as in
Hedda Gabler and *Miss Julie*) they establish a kinship with
the Greek tragic poets despite differences of style and dramatic form. When these and other modernists (such as
Hauptmann, Wedekind and Schnitzler) deal with the destructive compulsions of the sexual instinct, or with "the duel of
the sexes," they are decisively closer to the Greek masters
than to the writers of typical eighteenth- and nineteenth-
century dramatic literature.

I believe we can understand Euripides' *Electra* and *Medea*
better today than Euripides' audience could have done in
fifth-century Athens. And Euripides would have had no difficulty in understanding what Strindberg was about when he
translated the husband-and-wife conflict of Aeschylus' *Agamemnon* into a modern war of the sexes in *The Father.*
Euripides would have also understood and probably approved
Eugene O'Neill's effort in *Mourning Becomes Electra* to
translate the *Oresteia* into Freudian terms.

Moving, moreover, from subject matter to dramatic form
and style, we can only conclude that our advanced playwrights, designers, and stage directors have felt closer to the
Greek theater than to any other, with the possible exception of
the Elizabethan. Their consuming desire has been to recover
or, better still, to recreate the poetic theater with a presenta-
tional rather than representational type of drama. This effort has been successful in such radically different experiments as the plays of Eliot, Lorca, and Brecht. And, under-
standably, some of the most impressive endeavors have actually been modernistic versions of the Greek tragedies themselves, such as Giraudoux' *Electra*, Anouilh's *Antigone*, and
Cocteau's Oedipus-drama, *The Infernal Machine.* In a number of modern experiments with or without a classic subject,
playwrights have even adopted or adapted the formal features of the classic chorus, the Messenger, and the Narrator.

(O'Neill went further and adopted the formal feature of the mask in *The Great God Brown*.)

With the employment of classical strategies, we have recovered in our century the *theatrical* resources of the drama. Progress has consisted largely in a re-theatricalization of the theater that the advent of nineteenth-century realism had deprived of open and expressive theatricality. In this modernist effort no example has been more potent than that afforded by the art of Aeschylus, Sophocles, Euripides, and Aristophanes.

INTRODUCTION

THE INTELLECTUAL AND artistic achievements of the Greeks claim our attention not only for their own sake, as the art and literature of other advanced peoples do, but also because they have had a substantial role in shaping outlooks and taste for all Western civilization. Of all the various cultural productions of the Greeks their tragedy offers the most convenient approach to their spiritual contributions because tragedy combines high art with profound thought and because drama is a form generally familiar. Everyone has seen or read plays and knows their general techniques and aims, so that reading a Greek play is not exploring territory wholly uncharted. But to judge ancient tragedy by gauges appropriate to modern drama can be misleading, for the premises and objectives of the Greek plays are different from those of the modern.

The basic difference is that whereas our theater is secular, Greek drama grew out of religious ritual and was presented as part of a religious cult. The religious association is indicated by the place and occasion of presentation, and it controls the structure of the plays and the mode of their presentation, the choice of subjects and themes, the attitude of the playwright and of his audience. The theater of Dionysus at Athens, where the plays were presented, was part of the sacred precinct of that divinity. The theater itself was a large open-air structure consisting of three parts. Its original and central element was a level circle, some ninety feet in diameter, called the *orchestra* (which means "dancing place"), where the chorus performed. Outside one arc of the circle was a low rectangular building, with uncovered passages at either end. From and into this building, called *skene* or tent, the actors usually made their entrances and exits and in it they changed their costumes and masks; eventually its front was decorated with simple painting—whence our word "scenery." Rising from the circle of the orchestra (except for the arc occupied by the skene) was an auditorium of many tiers of stone seats, in sections divided by transverse passages. The theater at Athens accommodated some 17,000 spectators; others held as many as 40,000. The audience was not, then, a privileged elite but comprised a good part of the total population. The fact that they saw the performance virtually in the round, not frontally as in a picture-frame stage, helped make them participants in what was enacted, rather than eavesdroppers as modern spectators tend to be. The Greek spectator was not expected to imagine that he was watching real people going through real crises in a real living room. He knew that what he saw was a stylized reenactment of an ancient story as distilled through the mind of the poet. The ritualistic character of the performance was underscored by the circumstance that plays were presented only during annual religious festivals. If a man were allowed to attend the theater whenever he was inclined to seek entertainment, the plays could not have effected the spiritual purgation Aristotle said they were meant to produce.

The plays were not only all in verse, which is not a natural medium of conversation, but the actors' conversations were periodically interrupted by a chorus which sang and danced to express their comments and reflections on the action. The structure of the plays, in its developed form, was as rigidly prescribed as the design of a Doric temple. The *prologue* contained a dialogue which informed the audience of the circumstances of the play. The chorus entered, with a chant in a marching rhythm, and then sang their first fixed choral ode, or *stasimon*. They performed other stasima between *episodes*, equivalent to acts, when the scene was bare of actors, and at the end of the play marched out in an *exodus*. The choral lyrics are built in elaborate triads of *strophe, antistrophe,* and *epode,* and in early tragedy must have taken as long in performance as the "spoken" parts of the play. Tragedy started with choral lyric, to which actors' dialogue was added; and even after the role of the chorus was diminished it retained certain archaic wordforms. Tragedy was more conservative in form than in content.

The actors, three in number and all men, could play several roles by changing masks; there are never more than three speaking roles in a single episode. In their costume as in their speech the actors were removed from ordinary humanity. Their masks had a swelling at the top (*onkos*) to enhance their dignity; the tragic buskin (*cothurnus*) raised their stature; and their robes, unlike any that could be seen in ordinary life, were like priestly vestments. Actors were incapable of violent movements or gesticulation; their only instrument of expression was the voice. Scenes of violence, and especially of bloodshed, were not enacted on the stage but reported by a messenger. The motive for this restraint may have been religious, but it may also have been a matter of taste. Turmoil like that in the closing scene of *Hamlet* would seem to the Greeks childish and not as convincing as a dramatic oral description. Similarly, there was no attempt at realism in representing scenery; such indication of locality as there was amounted to little more than asking the audience, "Please imagine that this is Argos"—or Athens, or Delphi.

The plots of the tragedies were almost all drawn from the great body of traditional myth, which was esteemed almost as a species of scripture. In the source only the bare bones of a story might be given, with no how or why or therefore—for example a Clytemnestra murders an Agamemnon, who is then avenged by an Orestes. The poet proceeds to show the character and motivation of personages who could so behave, and what their behavior can mean to the rest of us. Because the personages were familiar to the audience from childhood, the poet did not need to build them up by explaining that Agamemnon was the commander of the Greek expedition in the Trojan War or that Clytemnestra was born of a goddess. All the principal personages must be of heroic stature; the fate of little men may be very sad, but it cannot be tragic. And because the bare story was capable of more than one interpretation, it could be used repeatedly by different poets. It was not the outcome of the story (which everyone knew) that the audience came to discover, but rather how the new poet would handle the plot. With the essentials of the story he could not tamper, but he could add intrigue and even minor personages, provided they were convincing and contributed to understanding. The themes, broadly speaking, had to do with the precarious situation of man vis-à-vis external forces, whether these derive from the society of which he is a part or, more usually, from the unintelligible supernatural powers which impinge upon his life. The poet was in fact a religious teacher as

well as artist, with a status somewhat analogous to that of a
prophet in Israel.

But the religion which Greek tragic poets explored and
which Greek tragedy served was not what we understand by
religion; unless we realize that it was not, we miss the meaning of Greek tragedy. The Greeks did not have a single all-
powerful and benevolent deity and a prescribed code of
rights and wrongs, but many gods with specialized, sometimes
conflicting, powers and demands. Except that they were immortal and ever-glorious, gods were like men in shape and
emotions and lived their own lives. The world of gods and
the world of men were quite apart; gods were not primarily
concerned with regulating men, nor men with emulating gods.
Each followed his own nature; for the gods two plus two
might equal five, but men must continue making it four. If,
making it four, he is tripped up by a system he cannot control or even understand which makes it five, the result is
tragedy. So far from being a punishment for error tragedy
may therefore be proof of the sufferer's merits and demonstration that he deserves the status of hero.

Hero in the technical Greek sense is not merely the principal figure in a work of literature but a man whose career
has somehow enlarged the horizons of what is possible for
humanity and who has therefore, after his death, been
deemed worthy of religious commemoration. It is not expected that the hero should be without flaw; often, like
Achilles or Ajax or Oedipus, he is a self-willed brute. But
then a flawless man is not apt to possess the determined
energy heroism requires. Men like coins must be taken as
wholes; we cannot choose to accept the heads and reject
the tails. An issue between an obvious white and an obvious black may be appropriate for melodrama; it is not a
subject for tragedy.

The presentation of plays was a state function, in the
form of a prize contest under the supervision of the chief
magistrates of the state. The magistrate chose three among
the playwrights who submitted their work, to whom he "gave
a chorus." Each entry was a tetralogy, or group of four plays
—a trilogy of tragedies, not necessarily related in subject,
plus a ribald satyr play to serve as afterpiece. The duty and
expense of mounting each poet's work was assigned to a
rich citizen as a *liturgy,* or form of income tax; another
liturgy (or *choregia*) was to fit out a battleship. Judges

were drawn by lot from a large panel previously selected. The names of the victorious choregus, poet, and actor were inscribed on tablets; our knowledge of the subject derives from abstracts or remains of these records.

In the fifth century B.C., apparently, only new plays were presented, but after the death of the Great Three it was enacted that a choregus who wished might revive one of their plays. Revivals tempt virtuoso actors to "fatten" their parts; to prevent corruption of the text, a magistrate with script in hand stood ready to stop the play if an actor deviated from the official text. In the third century B.C. King Ptolemy Philadelphus of Egypt is said to have borrowed the state texts against a huge deposit to make copies of them for the great Alexandrian Library and then to have sent the copies to Athens, forfeiting his deposit in order to keep the originals. The plays which have come down to us, only a small fraction of those that were written, have survived because they were included in anthologies for teaching. The titles and some portions of many plays that have not survived are known from lists and quotations and allusions in later books; in recent years bits of plays have turned up on scraps of Egyptian papyrus.

At the first official presentation of drama at Athens, in 534 B.C., the prize was won by Thespis, after whom actors are still sometimes called "thespians." Thespis is said to have "invented one actor." This means that instead of merely giving the chorus an opening by asking "What happened next?" Thespis *impersonated* a character in dialogue with the chorus, and so invented true drama. The revolutionary nature of this innovation, and incidentally the sobriety expected of Greek literature, is illustrated by a story told of Solon. After he witnessed his first play Solon reproached Thespis for telling the assembly lies, and when Thespis replied that deception was proper in a play, Solon argued that the habit of persuading people that imaginary things are true might be carried into politics. Of the several playwrights between Thespis and Aeschylus of whom we have some knowledge, the most important was Phrynichus. At the presentation of Phrynichus' *The Sack of Miletus* (an allied city in Asia Minor which the Athenians failed to save from the Persians), Herodotus tells us, "the whole theater burst into tears and the people sentenced him to pay a fine of a thousand drachmas for recalling to them their own misfortunes. They

likewise made a law that no one should ever again exhibit
that piece."

The few other playwrights of whom we know little and
the many of whom we know nothing at all were eclipsed in
popular vogue and critical esteem by Aeschylus, Sophocles,
and Euripides, and there can be little doubt that these three
were in fact the best in their kind. Whether the plays
chosen by schoolmasters in later antiquity to represent each
of the poets are those we should choose today if we had the
complete works before us is another matter; the seven plays
each of Aeschylus and Sophocles which have survived are
less than a tenth of those they wrote, and the nineteen of
Euripides little more than a fifth of his total.

The two significant facts in the life of Aeschylus (ca.
525–456 B.C.) are that he was born in Eleusis, the suburb
where Athenians went for the solemn rites of the Eleusinian
Mysteries, and that he fought for the Athenian democracy in
the Persian War. The first may have influenced his profound
religious speculations, the second his attachment to democratic values. His great technical innovation was the introduction of the second actor, which made true drama, in the
sense of conflict of wills, possible. Later in his career, when
Sophocles had introduced a third actor, Aeschylus employed
three actors also. The plays in a trilogy of Aeschylus were in-
terrelated, so that while each play was complete in itself, it
was at the same time one act in a larger composition. This
scale made it possible to carry the story, and the examination
of problems which it involved, over several generations of
the same family. It was the problem, more than the person-
alities of the figures who illustrate it, that was Aeschylus'
chief concern. The characters are indeed so far individual-
ized as to make their conduct intelligible and plausible, but
their ultimate function is as a kind of mathematical symbol
to make the argument meaningful. Usually the argument involves moral choices, between courses each of which has its
own sanctions. The highest sanction is Zeus'; Aeschylus has a
loftier conception of Zeus' power and justice than any other
classical poet. His language, elaborately wrought in vocabu-
lary and syntax and imagery, matches the grandeur of his
conceptions. His plays are not versified prose; the mode of
his thought as of his expression is the subtle mode of lyric,
not only in the stately choral odes but also in the "spoken"
parts.

The seven surviving tragedies of Aeschylus are *Persians,* which celebrates the Athenian victory over the Persian invaders at the battle of Salamis; *Seven Against Thebes,* which deals with the strife between the sons of Oedipus, in that part of the Theban legend which occupies the interval between Sophocles' *Oedipus at Colonus* and *Antigone; Suppliants,* which tells how the fifty Danaids, fleeing marriage with their Egyptian cousins, were given asylum at Argos; the *Oresteia* trilogy (including *Agamemnon, Choephoroe,* and *Eumenides*), and *Prometheus* which tells of Prometheus' championship of man and his punishment by Zeus.

The long life of Sophocles (496–406 B.C.) coincides with the great period of Athenian glory. He came to manhood amid the surging political and cultural activity after the victory over Persia, and died just before the fall of Athens at the end of the Peloponnesian War. He was rich, handsome, and popular, he held high offices of state and won many dramatic prizes. He retained his extraordinary powers until the end of his life, and (an important matter for a Greek) left a son who was also a successful playwright. Yet despite so happy a career Sophocles' view of life was very somber; he "saw life steadily, and saw it whole" (in Matthew Arnold's phrase) and decided that it was better for man not to have been born. In almost all of his plays there is one stark self-willed character whose conduct is deplored by the chorus and lesser characters but who marches steadfastly on his course to his ultimate destruction, achieving thereby a heroism which enriches lesser people but of which lesser people are themselves incapable. The greater the hero, the more he is exposed to the forces beyond his control; it is his own heroism which gives dignity and meaning to the precariousness of life. It is the individual hero rather than the forces outside him to which Sophocles gives his attention, and the individual can best be studied in a single play. That is why the plays in Sophocles' trilogies were unconnected, not part of a larger whole as they were in Aeschylus'. Other innovations of Sophocles were his introduction of the third actor, which multiplied opportunities for intrigue, and of scene painting. His sense of theater is much more sophisticated than Aeschylus'; for example, to heighten pathos he will place a scene of jubilant optimism just before the fall, or he will have a character leave on some errand and then return, after he has been forgotten, to a completely new situation.

The seven extant tragedies of Sophocles are *Ajax,* in which the hero who had attempted to murder his generals in a fit of madness commits suicide but is yet granted honorable burial; *Antigone,* who dies because she has disregarded the king's edict against burying her brother; *Trachinian Women,* on the career and death of Heracles; *Oedipus the King,* whose persistence in discovering his own unintentional guilt causes his downfall; *Electra,* which is parallel to Aeschylus' *Choephoroe* and Euripides' *Electra; Philoctetes,* in which the hero, unjustly marooned, resolves to abjure his society and is then persuaded to rejoin it; and *Oedipus at Colonus,* which recounts the death and transfiguration of the aged hero. The longest of the fragments recovered from papyri is a portion of the *Ichneutai* or *Trackers,* a satyr play on the childhood of Hermes.

Instead of representing men as they should be, as Sophocles is reported to have said, Euripides (485–406 B.C.) represented men as they are. Superficially Euripides' plays are like his predecessors': the plots derive from the same body of myth and the names of the personages are familiar; the structure, with iambic episodes alternating with lyric choral odes, is the same. But there are significant differences in form and even more in outlook. The language of the "spoken" parts is almost as simple as colloquial prose; the choral portions are not closely interwoven with the rest but almost detachable interludes. The plots are complicated and enriched by new matter, frequently drawn from folk motifs. Hence the prologue, sometimes spoken by a personage who does not appear elsewhere in the play, often outlines the plot to enable the audience to follow its intricacies. Often the traditional endings are not those Euripides' treatment would naturally lead to; the traditional but illogical ending may then be imposed by a "god out of the machine." By looking at their persons and problems as if they were contemporary, Euripides brings the stark stories of the heroic age down to a bourgeois level, often with happy instead of "tragic" endings. By applying contemporary gauges, furthermore, Euripides can expose inadequacies in traditional ideals and conventions, as for example in the glorification of war and the legal and social disabilities imposed on women and foreigners. Euripides is a great poet, but he is also a reforming pamphleteer. That is why a conservative like the comic playwright Aristophanes repeatedly attacks Euripides for his shabby heroes and his other flouting of established decencies. That is also doubtless why Euripides was awarded so few victories during his lifetime. After his death, however, audiences found the style and outlook of his plays more sympathetic than those of his older rivals, and they appear to have been revived and copied more frequently. That is why we have more plays of Euripides than of Aeschylus and Sophocles together.

Surviving out of some hundred plays which Euripides wrote are the following nineteen: *Alcestis:* A decent man finds it proper for his wife to die in his stead; she is restored to life by a ribald Heracles. *Medea:* A non-Greek woman rejected by her husband murders his fiancee and his and her own children. *Heracleidae:* The children of Heracles are persecuted in their father's absence and then avenged. *Hippolytus:* A young man of illegitimate birth resolves to avoid love and is destroyed through the agency of Aphrodite. *Andromache:* Written at the beginning of the Peloponnesian War, this is an attack on Spartan cruelty and deception. *Hecuba* and the *Suppliants:* Antiwar plays. [*Mad*] *Heracles:* In a fit of madness induced by abuse of his family during his absence Heracles kills his own children; he then caps his career of benevolent heroism by consenting to live on instead of taking his own life. *Ion:* An ingenuous foundling at Delphi whom the queen of Athens believes to be her son by Apollo and the king his by a Delphian girl reluctantly becomes heir to their throne. This play and others which are virtual parodies of legend come very near comedy. *Trojan Women:* This heartrending pacifist play shows that even victors in a war are demoralized. *Electra:* This shows that the slaying of Aegisthus and Clytemnestra by Orestes, glorified in Aeschylus and Sophocles, is in fact dastardly and unnecessary murder. *Iphigenia Among the Taurians:* A romance involving recognition between brother and sister in a faraway place, loyalty of friends, adventurous escape. In *Helen* too, which reads like a burlesque of *Iphigenia Among the Taurians,* clever but unprincipled Greeks overreach a naive barbarian. *Phoenician Women:* Deals with the Theban cycle; includes parts of the story dealt with in Aeschylus' *Seven Against Thebes* and Sophocles' *Antigone, Oedipus the King,* and *Oedipus at Colonus.*

Orestes: Carries the story of Orestes and Electra on from the end of *Electra. Bacchants:* Tells of Dionysus' reception in Thebes; shows the power of the irrational in human life. *Iphigenia at Aulis:* An unheroic treatment of the purported sacrifice of Iphigenia by her father Agamemnon to raise the winds for the becalmed Greek fleet. The Euripidean authorship of *Rhesus,* which is an inferior treatment of an episode in the *Iliad,* is doubtful. *Cyclops:* The only complete satyr play to survive; a ribald treatment of Odysseus' adventure with Polyphemus.

Comedy too had its origin in religious ritual, doubtless as part of a fertility cult, and its form—dialogue interspersed with song and dance—is analogous to the form of tragedy. Despite its exuberance and its obscenity comedy too aimed to teach, not about the relations of man to external forces but about politics and education and manners. An essential distinction between the two genres, out of which other differences stemmed, is that whereas the tragic poet expatiated upon a traditional story with fixed dramatis personae, the comic poet could use contemporary or invented personages and construct plots with little regard for history or probability. The striking thing about the plots of Aristophanes (and presumably of his rivals) is a rich fantasy which turned the world topsyturvy. War is tiresome? Make a private treaty with the enemy, or go to heaven to release the goddess Peace, or call a sex strike to bring jingoes to their senses. Life in Athens is tiresome? Build a better city in the sky. Contemporary poets are trifling? Fetch an old one back from hell. The fantastic scheme is set forth in the prologue, and the remainder of the play assumes, straightfaced, that it is actually carried out. The chorus (of twenty-four, in comedy) often divide into two parts, each espousing one side of a dispute. At one point in the play the chorus deliver a *parabasis,* a direct address to the audience in the poet's own name, frequently mentioning his merits and his claims for the prize. At the end of the play the representative of the undesirable viewpoint is discomfited and the "hero" goes off for a bout of merrymaking. Though the structure of comedy is necessarily looser than that of tragedy, its various parts follow a regular pattern, with songs of a particular kind inserted in particular places.

Aristophanes (ca. 445–ca. 388 B.C.) is the only representative of Old Comedy whose work has survived. His three outstanding characteristics, which the modern reader may find strange in combination, are his gross obscenity, his exquisite lyricism, and his serious concern for old-fashioned decency and morality. Comedy was presented at Dionysiac festivals which entailed release from the restraints of normal behavior. Such a period of release might better preserve propriety during the remainder of the year than attempting to maintain a rigorous level throughout could do. But, especially in a play like the *Birds*, Aristophanes can produce delicate and refined poetry. And also, with his bawdiness and his gaiety Aristophanes shows a mature concern for public and private morality. His position is consistently conservative. He opposes modernism in philosophy and education, in poetry and music, and most of all measures favoring a welfare state. He is tireless in his criticism of Euripides because Euripides embodied all the new outlooks which he deplored. It is a mark of his courage, and of Athenian liberalism, that in the midst of the Peloponnesian War he could dare criticize the policies and leaders of his own state and show sympathy for the views of the state's enemies.

Eleven plays of Aristophanes are extant. In *Acharnians*, presented in 425 B.C. when the author was barely twenty, a farmer weary of the war makes an individual treaty with the enemy. *Knights* (424) attacks Cleon, the democratic leader of the state, as an unprincipled demagogue. *Clouds* (423) is an attack on the Sophists and the new education they favored; Socrates is represented, most unfairly, as a typical Sophist. *Wasps* (422) is another attack on Cleon's demagogic measures, particularly his introduction of payment for public service. In *Peace* (421) an Athenian ascends to heaven to release the goddess of peace from imprisonment. *Birds* (414) is a charming fantasy in which a pair of men, weary of the tensions and nuisances in Athens, build an ideal city in the clouds. In *Lysistrata* (411) the women of Greece conspire to refuse conjugal relations to their menfolk unless they end the war. *Thesmophoriazusae* (411) represents a convention of women trying Euripides for his abuses. Euripides is again attacked in *Frogs* (405), which contrasts his work with Aeschylus'. In *Ecclesiazusae* (392) the women of Athens take over the assembly to enact a species of communism, which Aristophanes ridicules. *Plutus* (388) shows how property might be redistributed if the blinded god of wealth recovered his sight.

Of Middle Comedy, which formed a transition between Old and New, we know little. Of New Comedy, whose great master was Menander (342–291 B.C.), we have one complete play (*Dyskolos*) and considerable fragments of others, all recovered from papyri, and some twenty-five Latin adaptations by Plautus and Terence. New Comedy is less like the slashing farce of Aristophanes than like the later plays of Euripides, being thoughtful treatments of ordinary people in ordinary situations, with elements of romance and intrigue. Its more rational materials and outlooks replaced the heroic legends and ideals which had become too artificial and remote for vital drama. Tragedies composed in the fourth and succeeding centuries B.C. seem to have been little more than literary exercises. The only ancient tragedies we possess, aside from those of Aeschylus, Sophocles, and Euripides, are Latin adaptations of them made by Seneca (4 B.C.–A.D. 65). These are highly rhetorical and sensational versions of Greek masterpieces, without the intellectual depth of the Greeks. Seneca's tragedies were in turn emulated, after the Renaissance, in the various languages of Europe; but what the adapters learned, again, was form rather than content. Twentieth-century dramatic treatments of ancient materials are less bound by traditional form but often truer reflections of the Greeks in representing the quandary of the individual poised between the competing claims of his own nature and of the external world.

For the modern reader, who must work with translations, the full import of a Greek play is hard to comprehend. What is most accessible to him, and what is apt to concern him most, is not so much the refinement of the poet's art as the substance of his thought, and for this a prose version is a safer and easier guide than one in verse. Except for Aristophanes, then, of whom the best prose versions are intolerably flat and often disgusting, the versions offered in this collection are all in straightforward prose. The editor has taken the liberty of modernizing certain archaisms—especially in Jebb's admirable Sophocles—except in choral passages, whose texture is different from that of the "spoken" portions. To make the difference obvious to the eye lyric portions are printed in italic type.

For collateral reading the following list (all available in paperback) is suggested:

C. E. Robinson, *Hellas: A Short History of Ancient Greece* (Beacon)

M. Hadas, *History of Greek Literature* (Columbia University Press)

G. Norwood, *Greek Tragedy* (Hill and Wang)

H. D. F. Kitto, *Greek Tragedy* (Anchor)

AESCHYLUS

Agamemnon

THE TRILOGY CALLED *Oresteia*, of which *Agamemnon* is the first play, deals with the succession of crimes and their retribution in the house of Atreus. The series had started, before the action of *Agamemnon* begins, when Atreus had unfairly kept his brother Thyestes from the throne of Argos. In *Agamemnon* Thyestes' son Aegisthus and Agamemnon's wife Clytemnestra murder Agamemnon and seize his throne. In *Choephoroe,* the second play of the trilogy, Orestes avenges his father Agamemnon's murder by murdering Clytemnestra and Aegisthus. In *Eumenides,* the third play, hereditary blood vengeance is ended when a newly instituted court acquits Orestes. Other crimes antecedent to its action are involved in the problems of *Agamemnon:* the abduction of Helen, the war of reprisal against Troy, Agamemnon's sacrifice of his daughter Iphigenia to raise the winds for the Greek fleet becalmed at Aulis. It was during Agamemnon's absence at Troy that Aegisthus and Clytemnestra formed their illicit relationship and plotted his murder.

The tragedy of *Agamemnon* involves war and politics as well as a domestic triangle, and in none of its aspects is an unqualified right opposed to an unqualified wrong. It was wrong for Trojan Paris to abduct Helen, and right for the crime to be punished; but Helen was an evil woman, and Argives murmured at the slaughter of their young men in a war for an evil woman's sake. The chorus, consistently loyal to Agamemnon, elaborate on the horror of the sacrifice of

14

Iphigenia, the waywardness of Helen, and the cost of the war in Argive blood. The dissatisfaction of the Argives as well as his hereditary claim provide at least the appearance of justification for Aegisthus' usurpation. Nor is the behavior of Clytemnestra, who is at once described as a woman with the temper of a man, wholly without justification. Agamemnon had earned her hatred, she says, when he wantonly sacrificed her first-born; he had been unfaithful to her in his stay at Troy, and had even brought Cassandra home with him as a concubine; and finally, she was not herself the murderer but only the instrument of fate. In the end she hopes for a peaceful rule for herself and Aegisthus.

The rich and subtle poetry of *Agamemnon* is a perfect medium for its problems and insights. Recurrent images and verbal patterns create implicit connections in themes separate in time and place and provide psychological background for the action in hand. The tone of foreboding is set by the nameless watchman speaking on the roof of the palace at dawn, and the old men of the chorus weave a psychological backdrop in their majestic ode on the moral implications of the Trojan War and the sacrifice of Iphigenia, a backdrop elaborated by subsequent lyrics on the curse of Helen and the horrors of war and by Cassandra's prophetic *danse macabre* when she steps from Agamemnon's chariot. The swiftness and the drama of the action is introduced by the beacon speech. Spectacle itself produced high drama in the carpet scene, which not only supplies full and complete characterization of Agamemnon and Clytemnestra but communicates utter doom when Agamemnon treads the blood-colored carpet across the wide orchestra and into the palace doors which close behind him.

CHARACTERS

WATCHMAN

CHORUS OF ARGIVE ELDERS

CLYTEMNESTRA, *wife of Agamemnon*

HERALD

AGAMEMNON, *King of Argos*

CASSANDRA, *daughter of Priam
and slave of Agamemnon*

AEGISTHUS, *son of Thyestes
and cousin of Agamemnon*

ATTENDANTS

SCENE: Palace at Argos

Translated by A. W. VERRALL

WATCHMAN (*on palace roof*): A whole long year of watch
have I prayed heaven for release, a year that, like a dog, I
have made my bed in the embrace of this palace roof, till
I know all the nightly company of the stars, and chiefly
those chief signs that, marked by their brightness for the
princes of the sky, bring summer and winter to man, all
their wanings and their risings. And still I am watching for
the token-flame, the beacon-blaze which is to carry the
news from Troy, the tidings of the capture! This it is to be
commanded by a woman, who brings her quick hopes into
the business of men! When I have found my bed, rain-
wetted, restless, and safer than some are from the visit of
dreams (for instead of sleep comes the fear that sleeping
might close my eyes forever), and when the fancy comes
to whistle or sing by way of a salve for drowsiness, then
tears arise of sorrow for what has befallen this house,
now put to no such good work as in the old days. But ah,
this time may the blessed release be given, the blessed
beacon dawn with its message from the dark.

O joy! O welcome blaze, that shows in night as it were a
dawn, you harbinger of many a dance, that shall be set in
Argos for this good fortune! What ho! What ho! Lady of
Agamemnon, I cry you loud: Up from the dark couch,

quick, up, and raise the morning-hymn of your house in honor of yonder fire, if, as the signal manifestly announces, Troy town is taken indeed. Aye, and myself at least will prelude the dancing; for my score shall profit by my master's game, the treble-six, thrown me by yonder fire-signal.

Well, may the king return, may I clasp his welcome hand in mine. The rest shall be unspoken (my tongue has upon it an ox-foot weight), though the house itself, if it could find a voice, might declare it plain enough; for I mean to be, for my part, clear to who knows and to him who knows not blind. (*Exit.*)

(*Enter* CHORUS.)

CHORUS: *'Tis now the tenth year since, to urge their powerful right against Priam, King Menelaus and King Agamemnon, the mighty sons of Atreus, paired in the honor of throne and scepter derived from Zeus, put forth from this land with an Argive armament, a thousand crews of fighting men, summoned to their aid.*

Loud rang their angry battle-cry, as the scream of vultures who, vexed by boys in the supreme solitudes where they nest, wheel with beating pinions round and round, when they miss the young brood whose bed it was their care to watch. And the shrill sad cry of the birds is heard by ears supreme, by Apollo belike or Pan or Zeus, who to avenge the licensed sojourners of their dwelling-place, sends soon or late on the offenders the ministers of punishment. Even such ministers are the sons of Atreus, sent to punish the triumph of Paris by their mightier Zeus, guardian of hospitality, that so for a woman whom many could win there should be wrestlings many and weary, where the knee is pressed in the dust and the shaft, the spousal shaft, is snapped, between suffering Greek and Trojan suffering too.

The cause is this day no further: the end will be as it must. By no increase of fuel or libation, and by no tears, shalt thou overcome the stubbornness of a sacrifice that will not burn.

As for us, whose worn thews could not render their service, that martial gathering left us behind, and here we bide, on guiding-staves supporting our childish strength. For if the young breast, where the sap is rising, is no better than eld but in this, that the spirit of war is not there, oh what is man, when he is more than old? His leaf is withered, and with his three feet he wanders, weak as a child, a day-lit dream.

But what of thee, daughter of Tyndareus, Queen Clytemnestra? What chance? What news? On what intelligence, what convincing report are thy messengers gone round bidding sacrifice? To all the gods that dwell in Argos, upper and nether gods, the high gods and the low, the altars blaze with gifts, while on all sides the flames soar up to the sky, yielding to the innocent spell and soft persuasion of hallowed oil, rich from the store of kings. All this (so far as thou canst and mayest consent) do thou explain, and thus cure my present care, which vexes me now anon, although at whiles the sacrifices call up a kindly hope and drive from my mind the unsated thought that still returns to the prey.

It is my right to tell—it is an encouragement upon their way permitted to them whose vigor is past, that still at their years they draw from heaven that winning inspiration, which is the strength of song—how the twin-throned Achaean Kings, concordant leaders of Hellas' youth, were sped with avenging arm and spear to the Teucrian land by a gallant omen, when to the kings of ships appeared the black king of birds and the white-backed king together, seen near the palace on the spear-hand in conspicuous place, feasting on hares, then full of young, stayed one course short of home.

Be sorrow, sorrow spoken, but still let the good prevail!

Then the good seer, who followed the host, when he saw how the two brave Atridae were in temper twain, took cognizance of those hare-devouring birds and of the princely captains, and thus he spake interpreting: After long time they that here go forth must win King Priam's town, though ere they pass the wall all their cattle, their public store, shall perforce be divided and consumed. Only may no divine displeasure foresmite and overcloud the gathering of the host, whose might should bridle Troy. For the wrath of holy Artemis rests on the house of those winged coursers of her sire, who sacrifice a trembling mother with all her young unborn. She loathes such a feast of eagles.

Be sorrow, sorrow spoken, but still let the good prevail.

Yea, fair one, loving though thou art unto the uncouth whelps of many a fierce breed, and sweet to the suckling young of all that roam the field, yet to this sign thou art prayed to let the event accord. Auspicious are these eagle-omens, but not without a flaw. But oh, in the blessed name of the Healer, raise thou not hindering winds, long to delay from the seas the Argive fleet; urge not a second sacrifice, foul offering of forbidden meat, which shall put hate between flesh and bone and break marital awe. For patient, terrible, never to be laid, is the wrath of the wife still plotting at home revenge for the unforgotten child.

Thus Calchas crossed his chant of high promise to the royal house from the omens of the march: and so with according burden

Be sorrow, sorrow spoken, but still let the good prevail!

Zeus—power unknown, whom, since so to be called is his own pleasure, I by that name address. When I ponder upon all things, I can conjecture nought but Zeus to fit the need, if the burden of vanity is in very truth to be cast from the soul. Not he, who perhaps was strong of yore and flushed with victorious pride, could now be so much as proved to have had being: and he that came next hath found his conqueror and is gone. But whoso to Zeus by forethought giveth titles of victory, the guess of his thought shall be right. And Zeus it is who leadeth men to under-standing under this law, that they learn a truth by the smart thereof. The wound, where it lies dormant, will bleed, and its aching keep before the mind the memory of the hurt, so that wisdom comes to them without their will. And it is perhaps a mercy from a Power, who came by struggle to his majestic seat.

Thus it was with the Achaean admiral, the elder of the twain. A prophet, thought he, is not to blame, so he bent before the blast. But when his folk began to weary of hindering wind and empty cask, still lying over against

Chalcis, where the tides of Aulis rush to and fro, while still the gales blew thwart from Strymon, stayed them and starved them, and penned them in port, grinding the men and making of ship and tackle a prodigal waste, and with lapse of time, doubled over and over, still withering the flower of Argos away; then at last, when the prophet's voice pointed to Artemis and told of yet one more means to cure the tempest's bane, a means pressing more on the princes, which made the sons of Atreus beat their staves upon the ground and let the tear roll down—the elder then of the twain found voice and said:

"Sore is my fate if I obey not, and sore if I must slay my child, the jewel of my home, staining paternal hands with virgin stream from the victim at the altar's side. Are not the two ways woeful both? How can I fail my fleet and lose my soldiery? For eager is their craving that to stay the winds her virgin blood should be offered up, and well they may desire it. May it be for the best!"

So, having put on his neck the harness of Necessity, his spirit set to the new quarter, impious, wicked, unholy, and from that moment he took to his heart unflinching resolve. For to put faith in the shedding of blood is an obstinate delusion, whose base suggestion is the beginning of sin. Howsoever he did not shrink from slaying a victim daughter in aid of war waged for a stolen wife, a spousal-rite to bind unto him his fleet!

Her prayers, her cries to her father, mere life-breath of a girl, the spectators, eager for war, regarded not at all. Her father, after prayer, gave word to the ministers, while casting her robes about her she bowed herself desperately down, to lift her, as it were a kid, over the altar, and, for prevention of her beautiful lips, to stop the voice that might curse his house with the dumb cruel violence of the gag.

And she, as she let fall to earth her saffron robe, smote each one of the sacrificers with glance of eye that sought their pity, and seemed like as in a painting, fain to speak: for oft had she sung where men were met at her father's noble board, with pure voice virginally doing dear honor to the grace and blessing that crowned her father's feast.

What followed I saw not, neither do I tell. The rede of Calchas doth not lack fulfillment. Yet it is the law that only to experience knowledge should fall: when the future

*comes, then thou mayest hear of it; ere that, I care not for
the hearing, which is but anticipating sorrows; it will come
clear enough, and with it the proof of the rede itself.
Enough: let us pray for such immediate good, as the present matter needs. Here is our nearest concern, this fortress,
sole protection of the Argive land.*

(*Enter* CLYTEMNESTRA.)

I am come, Clytemnestra, in observance of your command. It is right to render obedience to the sovereign and
queen, when the husband's throne is empty. Now whether
tidings good or not good have moved you by this ceremony
to announce good hope, I would gladly learn from you:
though if you would keep the secret, I am content.

CLYTEMNESTRA: For "good," as says the proverb, may the
kind morn announce it from her kind mother night. But
"hope" is something short of the joy you will hear. The
Argive army has taken Priam's town.

CHORUS: How say you? I scarce caught the words, so incredible they were.

CLYTEMNESTRA: I said that Troy is ours. Do I speak clear?

CHORUS: It is joy that surprises me and commands its tear.

CLYTEMNESTRA: Yes, it is a loyal gladness of which your
eye accuses you.

CHORUS: And what then is the proof? Have you evidence
of this?

CLYTEMNESTRA: I have indeed, if miracle deceive me not.

CHORUS: Is it a dream-sign that commands your easy credence?

CLYTEMNESTRA: Not sight-proof would I accept from a brain
bemused.

CHORUS: Yet can you have taken cheer from some uncer-
tified presage?

CLYTEMNESTRA: You hold my sense as low as it were a
babe's.

CHORUS: And what sort of time is it since the city fell?

CLYTEMNESTRA: It fell, I say, in the night whence yonder
light is this moment born.

CHORUS: But what messenger could arrive so quick?

CLYTEMNESTRA: The fire-god was the messenger. From Ida
he sped forth the bright blaze, which beacon after beacon
by courier flame passed on to us. Ida sent it first to Hermes'
rock in Lemnos; and to the great bonfire on Lemnos' isle
succeeded third Zeus' mountain of Athos, with such a soar-

ing pile of wood upon it as might strengthen the traveling
torch to pass joyously over the wide main; and this, with
the golden light as it were of a sun, blazed on the message
to the outlook on Makistos. Nor he for any delay or for over-
coming sleep neglected heedlessly his messenger-part. Far
over Euripus' stream came his beacon-light and gave the
sign to the watchers of Messapius. These raised an answer-
ing light to pass the signal far away, with pile of withered
heath which they kindled up. And the torch thus strength-
ened flagged not yet, but leaping, broad as a moon, over
Asopus' plain to Cithaeron's scar, roused in turn the next
herald of the fiery train; nor there did the sentinels refuse
the far-heralded light, but made a bonfire higher than was
bid, whose flying brightness lit beyond Gorgopis' water,
and reaching the mount of Aegiplanctus, eagerly bade
them not to slack the commanded fire. They sped it on,
throwing high with force unstinted a flame like a great
beard, which could even overpass, so far it flamed, the
headland that looks down upon the Saronic gulf, and thus
alight then, and only then, when it reached the outlook,
nigh to our city, upon the Arachnaean peak; whence next
it lighted (at last!) here upon our royal roof, yonder light,
which shows a pedigree from the fire of Ida. Such are the
torch-bearers which I have ordained, by succession one to
another completing the course—of whom the victor is he
who ran first and last. Such is the evidence and token I
give you, my husband's message sped out of Troy to me.

CHORUS: My thanksgiving, lady, to heaven shall be presently paid; but first this story—I would satisfy my wonder
by hearing it repeated, in your way of telling, from point
to point.

CLYTEMNESTRA: Troy is this day in the hands of the
Achaeans! There must be sound there of voices that will
not blend. Pour with the same vessel vinegar and oil, and
you will exclaim at their unfriendly parting. Even so their
tones, the conqueror and the conquered, fall different as
their fortunes upon the ear. These on the ground clasping
the dead, their husbands, brothers, fathers, sons, young
children weeping for gray sires, themselves enslaved, are
wailing for their beloved. Those the hungry weariness of
fighting and a restless night have set to break their fast
upon what is in the town, not billeted orderly, but lodging
themselves by such chance as falls to each eager hand, in

the captured houses of Troy, to escape as they may the miseries of the open air, the frosts and the dews. With no watch to keep they will sleep the whole night long.

Now must they pay due respect to the gods that inhabit the town, the gods of the conquered land, or their victory may end in their own destruction after all. Too soon for their safety, the soldiery, seized with greed, may yield to their covetousness and lay hands on forbidden spoil. They have still to bring themselves home, have still the backward arm of the double course to make. And if no sin against heaven rest on the returning host, there is the wrong of the dead that watches. Evil may find accomplishment, although it fall not at once.

But for all these my womanish words, may the good prevail, plainly, I say, and undoubtfully; for choosing so, I choose more blessings than one.

CHORUS: Lady, no man could speak more kindly wisdom than you. For my part, after the sure proof heard from you, my purpose is now to give our thanks to the gods, who have wrought a return in full for all the pains.

(*Exit* CLYTEMNESTRA.)

Hail, sovereign Zeus, hail, gracious night, high is the glory thou hast won, thou night, that hast cast over the towers of Troy meshes so close, that none full-grown, nay, nor any young could pass the wide enslaving net, one capture taking them all. Zeus, god of host and guest, I confess him great, who hath wrought this vengeance for Paris' sin, though long he bent his bow, that so neither heaven-high the bolt might go, nor short of the mark might fall.

Zeus' stroke it is which they dare proclaim. This thought we may follow out. As he determines, so he accomplishes. It was said by one that the gods deign not to regard sinners, when they trample upon the grace of sacredness. But impiously was it said. It is manifested, how pregnant is the insolence of a too defiant pride, when the fullness of the house grossly exceedeth the best. And this best shall be so much, as will let a man blest with sense live of it undistressed.

For there is no defense for that man, who in the pride of wealth doth haughtily spurn the fixed foundation of Right, whereby he may be unseen: though strong is that obstinate persuasion, servant of Blindness and shaper of her decree. Remedy is all vain. Unhidden the mischief

*glows with a baleful light. Like base metal beneath the
rub and touch, he shows the black grain under justification (for his pursuit is idle as the boy's who follows the
flying bird), and leaves upon his people a fatal mark of
the touching. Deaf to supplication, the gods condemn for
wicked whosoever is conversant with such.*

*Such was the sin of Paris, who came to that house of
the Atridae and dishonored the hospitable board by theft
of the wife. Leaving to her countrymen the din of shield
and spear and the arming of fleets, and bringing to Ilium
ruin for her dower, she had passed with light step, careless of sin, through the gates. And oft they sighed, the
interpreters of the home, as they said, "Ah for the home!
aha, for the home! Aha, and ah, for the princes thereof,
for the husband's bed yet printed with her embrace." We
can see him there, his curses mocked with silence, the
parted spouse, the sweetest sight of them all! He shall
pine for her that is far beyond sea, till he seems but a
phantom lord of the house. Grace of beautiful statues the
husband hateth: with the want of the eyes all the passion is gone. Dream-forms stay with him a while, convincing semblances, and offer delight in vain; for lo, when
vainly he thinks to grasp the phantom, the vision escapes
through his arms and is gone that instant on wings that
follow the passing of sleep.*

*Such was the home-sorrow ere they parted hence; and
other woes they have, woes surpassing yet beyond these.
And in every home of those who set forth together from
Hellas' land the hearts of their womenfolk ache, as ache
they must, with all they have to wound them. Whom they
sped forth, them they know; but it is not the man they
know that comes to his home; it is but an urn and ashes.
A merchant in gold is Ares, and bodies of men are his
gold: in battle he holdeth his scale. He sends from Ilium
dust out of his fire, a heavy gold to weeping love, powder
that once was a man, now pressed into the compass of a
jar.*

*And they lament them, telling their praises, how skilled
was the dead in battle, or how bravely he shed his blood—
"And all through another's wife," snarls someone in a whisper: and so there spreads a resentful anger against the
quarrel of the sons of Atreus.*

Others there by the town, in their own shapes, possess

graves in Trojan earth, which hating them doth hide its fair possessors away.

Now when one anger moves a people, there is danger in their talk; it is a bond no less than a covenant sworn. And I am waiting in fear for a voice from the darkness of my thoughts.

For whosoever are guilty of lives, upon them god's eyes are fixed. The time comes when fortune unmerited turns to misfortune at a touch, when the dark Chastisers take the man's strength away: and once he is gone, no help for him. Glory too high is dangerous; it is upon the peak that the thunder strikes. Nay, let my happiness challenge no jealousy: and let me be no conqueror, nor see myself a conquered slave.

The beacon has spoken fair, and the report is spreading swiftly among the folk; but has it spoken true? Who knows? It is indeed miraculous—if not false.

How can one be so childish, so crazed of wit, to fire with hope at a sudden message of flame, and risk the pain of altered news?

With woman's impulse it is natural to give indulgent credit before the proof.

She is too ready of belief, a boundary quickly passed and encroached upon; but quick to pass away is the rumor that women cry.

LEADER: It will not be long before we know of this line of torch-bearers, this beacon chain of succeeding fires, whether they be true, or whether this gladding light, a dreamlike visitor, has beguiled the sense. Yonder herald comes from the shore, I see, with his shade of olive boughs. And the information of the thirsty Dust, sister and neighbor to the Mire, assures me of this, that with something more than dumb signals of fire-smoke, more than a bonfire of wood burnt upon a hill, he with a plain word will either explicitly bid us rejoice, or else—but the other word, for the sake of these, shall remain unspoken. May the fair appearance receive a like addition! If there be any that agrees not in this patriot prayer, let him reap himself the consequence of his mistake.

(*Enter* HERALD.)

HERALD: O native earth, O Argos, my country, hail! With the dawn of this tenth year I am come to you, at last. Many a hope has broken, but one I have grasped. For I

never thought I should die here, in this land of Argos,
and have my plot in her well-beloved soil. But now I bless
the land, I bless the bright sun, blessed be our Zeus supreme, and blessed he, the lord of Pytho; may he shoot his
shafts not upon us anymore. Long enough he came in enmity to Scamander's plain. But now be Savior, O King
Apollo, and Healer again! And the gods assembled here,
I salute them all, him too, my own protector, Hermes the
Herald, whom heralds love and revere, and all the deified,
they who sent forth the host, I bid them now receive it, so
much as the spear has spared. Hail royal palace, mansion beloved, and solemn seats, and deities eastward looking (and oh, how long you have looked!); with this bright
gladness in your eyes welcome fitly the king so long away.
For our prince is returned, bringing light in darkness to
impart to all that are here, even Agamemnon our king.

But you must greet him observantly, as is his due, having dug Troy out of the earth with the mattock of Zeus
the Avenger, which has broken her soil to dust. Her foundations cannot be found, or her fixed religious fanes, and
all she might grow from is perishing out of the ground.
So strong compulsion has the elder son of royal Atreus
put upon Troy, and happiest of mankind he comes home.
None has such claim to requital, not one in the live world.
As for Paris and his people, bound with him to payment,
they cannot boast a balance of damage done. Sentenced
for theft and rapine too, he has not only lost the reprisal
but also has ruined and razed his very father's house, it
and the place together. Twofold the loss the sons of Priam
have paid.

CHORUS: Joy to you, herald of the coming Achaean host!
Have you longed for your native land with a torturing
love?

HERALD: Aye, so that for joy my eyes weep tears upon it.

CHORUS: Then learn that it is a sweet languishing you have
taken.

HERALD: How so? I need a lesson to master your saying.

CHORUS: As being struck with a passion not unreturned.

HERALD: Argos, you say, pined for her pining soldiers.

CHORUS: So pined, as often to sigh for you from a weary
heart.

HERALD: Whence this melancholy? Was there yet this distress reserved for us that have fought?

CHORUS: For long past I have used silence to prevent hurt.

HERALD: But how so? Were you, the kings being away, in fear of someone?

CHORUS: So much that now, as you say, even death were grateful.

HERALD: Yes, we have done well every way, well, for the length of time. A man must speak well of his fortune, though part be not so good. Only a god can be without trouble all his time. For were I to count our sufferings in bad quarters, the narrow and comfortless berths (and in the daytime miserable for want of everything), and other miseries by land (and there it was worse, our camp being close to the enemy's wall), how the sky rained, and the dews from the marshy ground, rotting our garments and breeding foul life upon us: or were one to count the winter's cold, made so intolerable by the snows of Ida that the birds fell dead, or the heat, when in his noonday rest the sea sank windless and waveless to sleep—but what need to grieve for these things? The pain is past; so past for the dead, that they care not so much as to rise up any more. Ah, why should we count the number of the slain, when the living suffer by fortune's persistency? A full release from chance is also, say I, something worth. And for us who are left of the Argive host, the gain on the balance overweighs the hurt, seeing that yonder bright sun may proclaim in our honor, winging our fame over land and sea, "Troy in old time was won by an Argive armament: and these are the spoils which, to the glory of the gods throughout Hellas, they nailed upon the temples for a monumental pride." Hearing this, men must needs praise Argos and them that led her host; and the grace of Zeus that wrought it all shall be paid with thanks. And so I have said my say.

CHORUS: Defeat in argument I do not deny. To be teachable is a thing that ages not with age. But the household and Clytemnestra, whom this news should most nearly interest, must share the gain with me.

(*Enter* CLYTEMNESTRA.)

CLYTEMNESTRA: My joy was uttered some while ago, when the first fiery messenger came in the night, telling that Ilium was taken and destroyed. Then there were some who found fault with me, and said, "Are you by a beacon persuaded to think that Troy is taken now? How like a woman's heart

to fly up so high!" Thus they argued, proving my error.
But for all that I would sacrifice; and by womanly ordinance the townsfolk one and all took up the loud cry of
holy gladness and in the sacred temples stilled with feeding incense the fragrant flame.

And now, for the fuller tale, what need I to take it from
you? From the king himself I shall learn it all. Rather,
that I may bring my revered lord with swift return to my
loving reception—what light more sweet to the eyes of a
wife than this, when she opens the gate to her husband,
restored by heaven safe from war?—take back to my lord
this message: let him come with all speed to the people
that love him, come to find in his home the wife faithful,
even such as he left her, a very house-dog, loyal to one
and an enemy to his foes; aye, and in all else unchanged,
having never broken seal at all in this long while. I know
of pleasure or scandalous address from any other no more
than of dyeing bronze.   (*Exit.*)

HERALD: Self-praise like this, filled full with its truth, it does
    not misbeseem a noble wife to sound.

CHORUS: She speaks thus to teach you; to those who clearly
    can discern, her words are hypocrisy.
    But herald, speak: I would know of Menelaus, our well-
    loved king, this only, whether he has returned safe and will
    arrive with you.

HERALD: It were impossible, if I told a false tale fair, that as
    time goes on, your love should enjoy it still!

CHORUS: Oh, that your true tale might be happily told! It
    is not easy to hide, when good and true are parted.

HERALD: The prince is gone from the Achaean host, himself
    and his ship also. It is the truth.

CHORUS: Did he put forth in your sight from Ilium? Or was
    he snatched from the rest by a storm which fell upon all?

HERALD: You have, like a master bowman, hit the mark, and
    put a length of trouble in a brief phrase.

CHORUS: What then of the prince? Did the general rumor
    of the voyagers declare him living or dead?

HERALD: None can tell that for certain, save one only, the
    Sun that sustains life over all the earth.

CHORUS: And what from first to last was the story of the
    storm, thus sent on the fleet by angry gods?

HERALD: A day sacred to joy should not be fouled by the
    tongue of evil tidings. Religion sunders the two. When one

with sad countenance brings to a people heavy tidings of an army fallen, the state wounded with one great national grief and many a home robbed of its single victim by Ares' fork, his weapon beloved, twoheaded, horrible, red in both prongs with blood; he that bears such a pack of woe may well say a hymn to those who punish. But when one comes with tidings of deliverance to a folk rejoicing in happiness—how shall I mingle this good with that ill, with a tale of storm, at which our national gods must needs be displeased?

A conspiracy there was between two that had been utter foes, between fire and sea, and for pledge and proof of their league they destroyed the unfortunate men of Argos. In darkness it was done, which swelled the agony to its height; for the ships were dashed one against another by Thracian winds, till butting violently beneath the storm of the hurricane and the beating rain of the surge they fled away and away, lashed round by their cruel driver. And when the bright dawn rose, we saw on the Aegean corpses thick as flowers, our dead and wreck of our ships. As for ourselves and our ship, yet whole in hull, we were stolen away or, maybe, were begged off by someone more than human, who took her helm. Fortune, to save us, was pleased to ride aboard her, and keep her alike from taking in the surging water between her planks and from running upon rocks. So having escaped a watery grave, there in the white day, scarce sure of our good fortune, we brooded melancholy upon our altered case, our host undone and utterly dashed to pieces. And at this moment if any of them live and draw breath, they are doubtless speaking of us as lost, while we imagine the same case for them. But let us hope the best.

For Menelaus then, be it first supposed and soonest, that he got home. And at worst, if anywhere the sun's ray is discovering him, Zeus, we may hope, who cannot mean to destroy his offspring quite, will contrive to bring him alive and well to his home again. So much is all I can warrant you for fact. (*Exit.*)

CHORUS: *Who can have given that name, so to the very letter true? Was it some unseen power, who by foreknowledge of fate guided his tongue aright, that named the woman wooed with battle and spear by the name of Helen? She proved her name indeed upon ship and men and peoples, when from the delicate veils of her costly bower she passed over sea before the gale of the felon West, and after her a great hunt of shielded soldiers, following by the vanished track of the oar a quarry landed on Simois' banks, whose woods were to be wasted by their bloody fray.*

A bride? A sorrowful bride she was to Ilium, pursued by sure-remembering wrath, destined one day to avenge the dishonor of the board, and of Zeus the sanctifier of the feast, upon those that gave significant honor to that bridal music, the marriage-hymn of the groomsmen, their vantage of an hour. The aged city of Priam hath learnt an altered song, a burden surely of loud lamentation, and finds for the wedded Paris an evil name; for burdened with lamentation have been all her weary days till this for the miserable slaughter of her people.

A shepherd man in his house brought up a lion's whelp, weaned from the teat, a hungry suckling. Gentle it was in its infant days of love, made friends with youth, drew smiles from gravity's self. And many a thing it got when, like a nursing-child embraced, it fixed a bright eye on the hand and fawned for its belly's need. But after a time it showed the way that was born in it; for it paid thanks for its rearing by bloody ravage of the flock, making a feast unbidden; and the house was dabbled with gore, and the housefolk helpless in agony, and wide was the murderous waste. God sent it to that dwelling with a mission of ravage therein.

Even so came, would I say, to Ilium what seemed to fancy a windless calm, a darling of rich indolence, whose gentle eye shot that soft bolt, which pricks from the heart the flower of love. But swerving from that, she made them rue in the end that she was won, blasting with her companionship the ruined house of Priam's sons, whither the god of guest-plight sped and conducted her, a fiend to wed and repent.

It is an ancient maxim, made long ago among men, that wealth of man, grown big, gets offspring of its body before it die, and that of good fortune the natural scion is unappeasable woe. But I think not with the generality. It is in truth the impious deed, which after begetteth more, and like to its own kind. The house that keepeth righteousness, fair is the generation thereof forever. But it is the

*way of old pride to beget in the wicked soon or late,
when the destined hour arrives for the youthful birth, a
young pride and the kindred spirit of insolence, godless,
resistless, masterless, black curses both to the mansion and
like their parents both.*

*But righteousness shineth in sooty dwellings and prizeth
the modest man. If the palace is gilt but foul the hands,
with eyes averted she goes thence to the pure home, dis-
daining the might of wealth misstamped with praise. And
she guideth all to the goal.*

(*Enter* AGAMEMNON *with* CASSANDRA, *in a chariot.*)

*See now, O sovereign, Troy's conqueror, Atreus' son, how
shall I address thee? How pay thee homage neither above
nor short of due complaisance?*

*Many rate semblance above reality, and do injustice so.
Sighs for the suffering all have ready, although of the outward grief none touches the heart; they copy the looks of
him that laughs, putting force upon faces where no smile
is. But he that knoweth the points of a man is sure to
detect when the human eyes, which pretend to glisten with
kindness, are flattering him with a love that is but water.*

*Thou in past time, while warring still for Helen's sake
(frankly be it said) didst make an ungracious figure in
mine eyes, didst seem an undexterous steersman to thy
wits, that thou for a willing wanton would'st spend the
lives of men. But now we contemplate thee with riper
judgment and less unkind. Happy the labor that is happily
done. Thou wilt learn by inquisition hereafter, who here at
home hath done his duty, and who hath misspent the time.*

AGAMEMNON: To Argos first my salutation is due, and to the
gods that inhabit here, who have aided me to my homecoming and the justice which I have taken of Priam's
town. For they, having heard the mortal argument which
with main force we pleaded for Troy's destroying, put their
votes undivided into the vase for blood, while to the opposite urn hope of the hand came nigh, yet it was not
filled. By her smoke the conquered city is conspicuous
even yet. Life in the ruin pants, and from the expiring ash
is breathed a reek of richness. For all this there must be
paid to the gods a memorable return, even as the fine is
great, which our wrath has taken, since for one woman
stolen a city has been laid level by the fierce beast of
Argos, the foal of the horse, the folk of the shield, that

launched himself with a leap in the season of the Pleiads'
fall. Over the wall he sprang and, like a lion fleshed,
lapped his fill of proud princes' blood.

Now, having given to religion this ample precedence, I
come to you and your feelings. I remember what I have
heard. I am with you, and support your accusation. Rare
among men are they to whom it is natural to love and
admire the fortunate without envying. The poison of illwill settles to the heart and doubles the load of him that
has aught amiss: at once his own sorrows press upon him
and he sighs to see the other's happiness. I may speak with
knowledge, having learned thoroughly that mirror of friendship, image of a shadow, the hypocrites' semblance of devotion to me. Ulysses only, Ulysses, who joined the fleet
against his will, I found, being once in harness, my own
right horse. That I will say for him living or dead.

And for the rest, the affairs of state and religion too in
general assembly summoned together we will debate; where
we must take such counsel that what is well may endure
so and abide, while as for what must have medicinal remedy, we will do our kind endeavor with lancet or cautery
to defeat the mischief of the sore.

For the moment, I go to my house and private chambers,
where my hand's first greeting must be to the gods, who
sent me forth and have brought me back. May victory,
as she has attended me, constantly abide with me still!

(*Enter* CLYTEMNESTRA.)

CLYTEMNESTRA: Townsmen of Argos, her noblest present
here, what love I have practiced toward my husband my
modesty will let me declare to you. With time men lose
their fear.

Upon no witness but my own I can say, how weary
were my days all the long while my lord lay before Ilium.
A sore grief it is in itself, for a woman without a man
to sit in the empty throne of the house, with ever per-
sistent flatteries at her ear, and one coming after another
with loud tidings of woe to the house each worse than
the last. As for wounds, if my lord was wounded as often
as the conduits of fame brought news of it, he has holes in
him more in number than a net. And had he died, as report thereof multiplied, he might, with three bodies like
another Geryon, have boasted many times three—not beds,
but coverlets rather of earth taken on to him, if he had

had one death for each of his shapes. Such, ever present at my ear, were the rumors that put me many times to the hanging noose, while others, preventing my eagerness, loosed from my neck.

This is indeed why the boy Orestes, he who might best make confidence between you and me, is not, as he should be, here; be not surprised. He is in the special care of our ally, Strophius of Phocis, who warned me of double mischief, the peril first of you before Ilium, and the chance that noisy rebellion from below might risk a plot against us, as it is native to man to spurn the more him that is down. The excuse however is such as cannot have guile in it.

But as for me, the fountains of my tears have run themselves dry, and there is no drop there. With watching late my eyes are sore, with weeping for your attendance of torch-bearers neglected still. The droning gnat with lightest flutter would wake me from dreams, in which I saw you pass through more than the time of my sleep.

Now, after all this misery, in the relief of my soul, I would hail this my husband as a watchdog to the fold, the ship's securing stay, the high roof's grounded pillar, the father's sole-born child; or as a land espied by mariners in despair, dawn as it looks most beautiful after storm, a flowing spring to the thirsty wayfarer—but everywhere escape from distress is sweet; let these then stand for types of my salutation. And let jealousy refrain, seeing how much was the woe we endured before.

But now, I pray you, beloved, step from this car—but not on the earth, King, set that foot of yours, which has humbled Troy. Slaves, why delay to do your commanded office, and strew the ground of his way with coverings? In a moment let the laid path be turned to purple, that to a home unexpected he may have conduct due. And for the rest, a vigilance never laid asleep shall order it as just providence, I trust, intends.

AGAMEMNON: Daughter of Leda, who has my house in charge, if to the measure of my absence you have stretched the length of your address, still, for a modest praise, the honor should proceed from some other lips. For the rest, offer no womanish luxuries to me, nor before me, as before a king of the East, grovel with open-mouthed acclaim, nor with vestures strown draw jealous eyes upon

my path. To the gods these honors belong. To tread, a
mortal, upon fair fineries is to my poor thoughts a thing
of fear. Give me I say the worship not of your god but of
your lord. No foot-cloths, no false refinements, need proclaim what rumor cries. An unpresumptuous mind is God's
greatest gift: happy let him be called, who has come
prosperously to the end. And that such will be ever my
rule is the confidence for me.

CLYTEMNESTRA: Come answer, saving your judgment, one
question from me——

AGAMEMNON: My judgment, be assured, is fixed beyond
change by me.

CLYTEMNESTRA: Did you bind yourself, in some hour of terror, to this observance?

AGAMEMNON: Never was last word spoken on better re-
flexion than this.

CLYTEMNESTRA: What had Priam done, think you, if he had
achieved the same?

AGAMEMNON: He had made him a fine fair path, I am very
sure.

CLYTEMNESTRA: Then let not blame of men make you
ashamed.

AGAMEMNON: But the voice of the multitude is a mighty
thing.

CLYTEMNESTRA: Aye, but who moves no jealousy wins no
envy.

AGAMEMNON: To love contention is not a woman's part.

CLYTEMNESTRA: Nay, but the great may even yield a point
with grace.

AGAMEMNON: You plainly, no less than I, think the point
worth fight.

CLYTEMNESTRA: Yield: I constrain you; let it be with consent.

AGAMEMNON: Then, if this be your will, quick, let one loose
my shoes, these trodden slaves to the serving foot. —Even
with these bare soles, as I walk the sacred purple, I hope no
distant eye may give me an evil glance. It is shame enough
to stain with the stain of human feet textures of price,
purchased for silver.

Of this enough. But here is one, whom you must receive
into the house with kindness. A gentle master wins from
the distant eye of God an approving glance; for none takes
willingly to the yoke of a slave. This damsel was the

choice flower of a rich treasure, bestowed by the soldiers upon me, with whom she goes.

And now, since I am reduced to obey you herein, I will proceed to the palace along your purple path.

CLYTEMNESTRA: There is a sea (and who shall drain it dry?) which has in it purple enough, precious as silver, oozing fresh and fresh, to dye vestures withal. And we have, O King, I trust, a chamber of such from which to take thereof, our house being unacquainted with poverty. Vestures plenty would I have devoted to the trampling, had it been proposed to me in some temple of divination, when I was devising means to bring this dear life back. It is the root of the house, whereby the leaves arrive that make a shade overhead against the dog-star. Yes, now, at your coming to the familiar hearth, your winter-coming betokens warmth, and when Zeus from the grape's sourness is making wine, then it is to the home like a sudden coolness to be visited by the crowned lord thereof. Zeus, Zeus, who crowns all, crown but my prayer and let your providence do what you will.

(*Exeunt* AGAMEMNON *and* CLYTEMNESTRA.)

CHORUS: *Why is it that so constantly my auguring soul shows at the door this fluttering sign, and the prophet-chant offers itself without bidding or fee? Canst thou not spit it away, like an unexplainable dream, and reach such willing trust as the mind is glad to rest upon? Yet time hath heaped the sands of the shore upon the anchor-stones, since the naval host set forth to Troy: and they are returned, mine own eyes tell me so. But yet, as without the lyre, my bosom repeats that dirge of Doom, unlearned and self-inspired, unable to grasp in full the welcome assurance of hope. It cannot be for naught, the throb that with meaning recurrence the heart repeats to the unmistaken breast. But I pray my false expectation may lose itself in void.*

Too true it is, that the health which abounds encroaches; for sickness is its neighbor right up to the wall: and human fortune, running straight, will strike on a hidden reef. And as to the saving of goods, fear, discharging the measured scale, may keep the whole house from sinking under an over-freight of riches, and the boat from going down. (Rich we know and abundant is the gift of Zeus, and rids the plague of hunger out of the annual field.) But as

*for a man's red blood, once shed from his dying body upon
the ground, who with incantation may call it back? Nay,
not the straitest in virtue may be called from the dead
without sin!*

*And were it not that one god's purpose doth check and
limit another's decree, my heart outrunning my tongue
would have poured these bodings forth: but now she
mutters in darkness, vexed and hopeless ever to wind off
her task in time, and stirring the fire within me.*

(*Enter* CLYTEMNESTRA.)

CLYTEMNESTRA: Come in with you, you also, Cassandra, you:
since Zeus of his mercy has set you in a house, where you
may share the holy water in your place with the crowd of
slaves at the altar of stead and store. Descend from the
car, and be not proud. They say that Alcmene's son himself was sold and still bore up in spite of the slave's low
fare. If it so fall that one needs must take that state,
masters not new to wealth are a thing to be thankful for.
They to whom a rich pile has come by surprise are to their
slaves cruel always and overstrict. From us you are receiving what custom bids.

CHORUS: It is to you she speaks, and plainly. She waits for
you. And maybe, since you are in the toils of fate, you
should obey, if it may be—though, maybe, you will not.

CLYTEMNESTRA: Nay, if her foreign tongue is anything less
unintelligible than a swallow's twitter, my reason urged is
spoken within her understanding.

CHORUS: Go with her. She urges what, as things are, is best.
Obey, arise, and leave the chariot.

CLYTEMNESTRA: I have no leisure, you may know, to be thus
dallying abroad. For at the hearth, the central hearth,
there are victims standing already for the sacrifice of the
fire—since of the present joy there was no expectation! And
you, if you will take part in this, must not delay. If for
want of understanding you take not what I say, then with
your foreign hand converse instead of voice.

CHORUS: An interpreter, and a plain one, the strange lady
does indeed seem to want. She has the air of a beast new-
taken.

CLYTEMNESTRA: Aye, mad she is, and listens to her folly.
She comes here from a new-taken town, and yet she has
not the sense to bear the bridle, until she foam her humor

away in blood! But I will waste words no more, to be so
scorned! (*Exit.*)

CHORUS: And I, for I pity her, will not be angry. Come now,
unhappy, come down from where you ride and take on
you willingly the new yoke of hard fate.

CASSANDRA: *Ah! . . . O God! . . . Apollo, O Apollo!*

CHORUS: What means this sad cry on the name of Loxias?
It suits him not to meet a singer so melancholy.

CASSANDRA: *Ah! . . . O God! . . . Apollo, O Apollo!*

CHORUS: Once more the ill-omened cry, and upon that god,
one all unfit for a scene of lamentation!

CASSANDRA: *Apollo, god of the Gate, a very Apollo to me!
You have more than proved your name, before and now
again.*

CHORUS: She will prophesy upon her own miseries. The soul
retains that gift, when all but that is slave.

CASSANDRA: *Apollo, god of the Gate, a very Apollo to me!
Ah, where, where have you led me? Oh, what house
should this be?*

CHORUS: The palace of Atreus sure it is. That, if you conceive it not, I tell you: and you cannot say it is false.

CASSANDRA: *Ah no, ah no, an abominable place, full of
guilty secrets . . . yea, of unnatural murderers . . . aye,
truly, a place of human sacrifice, sprinkled with blood of
babes!*

CHORUS: The strange woman does indeed seem keen as a
hound upon a scent. She is on a track of murder where
she will find.

CASSANDRA: *Yes, there is the evidence that I trust upon!
See yonder babes, weeping their sacrifice, their flesh
roasted and eaten by their sire!*

CHORUS: We had heard of your fame as prophetess, had
heard of it: we seek none to speak for you.

CASSANDRA: *O God! . . . What is this, what purpose of
strange woe, horrible, horrible, that she purposes here
within? The fate of her nearest, fate beyond remedy,
and no help nigh!*

CHORUS: This prophesying is beyond my knowledge. The
other knew, for all the town is loud with it.

CASSANDRA: *O cruel! Will you do it? The partner of your
bed, will you cleanse him with lustration, and then—O,
how can I say it? Aye, soon it will be done. She is reaching forth, she is stretching hand after hand!*

CHORUS: I understand not yet. Then hints, now oracles blind perplex me still.

CASSANDRA: *Ah! . . .*

What appears now? Surely a net of Death? Nay, rather the snare is she, who shared the bed, who shares the crime. Now let the Chorus of Death, who thirst for the blood of the race, raise their ritual cry over their victim stoned.

CHORUS: What fiend is this, whom you bid sing triumph over this house? You look not glad yourself at the word. Pale is the drop that runs to your heart, even such as from a mortal wound drips slow and slower when life's light sets and death is coming quick.

CASSANDRA: *Ah! Ah! See, see! . . .*

Keep the bull from the cow! She has caught him in a vesture and gores him with her black, crafty horn. He falls in a vessel of water. In a treacherous murderous caldron is done the thing I tell you.

CHORUS: I cannot boast high skill in judging words inspired; but these I judge to figure some ill. But by this way what good word ever is sent to man? It is all ill, a skill of manifold phrases, offering for knowledge a terrifying chant.

CASSANDRA: *Alas, alas, for the unfortunate doom of a wretch, for my own fate! It shall have its drop in the lament.*

Where is this you have brought me, a hopeless wretch, just only to die with you, and nothing more?

CHORUS: You are in some sort crazed by the god who hurries your thoughts, and you wail in a wild tune, like some brown nightingale, that with singing never sated laments, alas, heart-sore, for Itys, Itys all her sorrow-filled days.

CASSANDRA: *Ah, the fate of the musical nightingale! For her the gods did clothe in a winged form, a sweet passage and a tearless, while I must be parted by the steel's sharp edge.*

CHORUS: *Whence sent, by what power imposed, is thy vain agony, that thou shapest that fearful song with words so hard and harsh and yet with a march so clear? How findest thou the terms of woe which guide thine inspired way?*

CASSANDRA: *Alas, for the bridal of Paris, the doom of his kin! Ah, sweet Scamander, my native stream! Once on your*

banks, ah me, was I nursed and grew. But now by the
River of Wailing, aye, and of Woe, my prophet-voice will
be uttered soon.

CHORUS: *What is this word thou hast spoken, only too plain?
A man new-born might understand. I bleed beneath the
wound of the piteous singer's breaking misery, which shat-
ters me to hear it.*

CASSANDRA: *Alas, for the labor of Troy, Troy destroyed utterly! Alas, for my father's sacrifices in her behalf, so
many grazing victims slain! They served not at all to
save the town from such fate as now it has; and I, the sick-
brained, I shall soon be sent after the wise.*

CHORUS: *Thy latter words go along with those before. Some
power there is who with overbearing press maddens thee
to sing of sorrows tending to death, though the end I
cannot see.*

CASSANDRA: See now, my prophecy shall not any more be
like a bride new-wed looking forth from a veil. It shall
come in bright as a fresh wind blowing toward sunrise
and rolling wavelike against the light a woe far higher
than this now. My teaching shall be by riddles no longer.
And be you witnesses with how close a scent I run in the
track of the crimes done long ago.

For out of that house there never departs a choir of
voices in unison not sweet, for the words are not fair. Aye,
and they have drunk, to be the bolder, of human blood,
and in the house they abide, hard to be turned away, a
rout of sister-fiends. They besiege the chambers and sing
their song, with still-repeated burden denouncing the hated
sin of him who defiled a brother's bed.

Have I missed? Or do I at all take observation like one
that aims a shot? Or am I a false prophet, who babbles
from door to door? Bear witness, swearing first, that I do
truly know the ancient sins in the story of this house.

CHORUS: *And how could an oath do good, being framed
in its nature to hurt? But I find it strange in you, that
bred beyond the sea you should be as right about an alien
city, as if you had been there present.*

CASSANDRA: The prophet-god it was who gave me this power,
for . . . The time has been when I dared not speak of it.

CHORUS: *For Apollo's self desired you. Was it so? We are
all more delicate in prosperity.*

CASSANDRA: Yea, then, he wrought with me, and mighty was his charm.

CHORUS: And came you too to the deed of kind in natural course?

CASSANDRA: I promised, but kept not faith with Loxias.

CHORUS: And had he won you with inspiration already given?

CASSANDRA: Yes, already I prophesied to my people all that befell them.

CHORUS: And how could the wrath of Loxias reach you then?

CASSANDRA: After I did that wrong, I could never make any believe me.

CHORUS: To us however you seem a prophet worthy belief.

CASSANDRA: *Ah! . . . Oh agony!*

Again the fearful pangs of present vision grow on me, whirling my soul in a confused beginning of—There! . . . Sitting there! . . . Do you see them? Sitting before the house! . . . Young children, like forms in a dream.

As infants slain by their parents they appear, their hands full of that meat of which he ate, whose own flesh it was, carrying, oh pitiable burden! the hearts and inward parts, of which their father tasted.

And hence the vengeance, plotted, I tell you, now by a certain lion of a craven sort, who haunting the couch has watched at home for him, alas, who is come, who is lord —for the slave must bear the yoke—of me. Little he knows, the destroyer of Ilium, captain of a lost fleet, how the tongue of that lewd creature has spoke and "stretched," with joyful thoughts her "plea" (her cast!) of treacherous death, and fatally shall reach him! So bold the crime, a woman to slay the man!

She is—ah what should the loveless monster be fitly called? A dragon, a Scylla, housed in the rocks, the mariner's bane, offering her fell sacrifices, like a priestess of Death, even while in the prayer of her soul her husband has no part. And how the bold wretch raised her cheer, as at the turn of battle, pretending to be glad of the safe coming-home!

And of this how much is believed, it matters not. What is to be will come, nay, soon you present yourselves will say with compassion, "A prophet only too true!"

CHORUS: Thyestes' feast of children's flesh I understood, and shuddered. Truly it is more than semblance, and it makes me afraid to hear it. But in what else was said I am thrown out of the track.

CASSANDRA: I say that you will see Agamemnon dead.

CHORUS: O hush, poor creature, hush your profane lips!

CASSANDRA: Nay, it is not as a Savior that he directs this sentence.

CHORUS: No indeed, if he will be present; but I trust it shall not be so.

CASSANDRA: While you pray against them, they are busy to slay.

CHORUS: Who is the man contriving this woe?

CASSANDRA: You must indeed have looked far wide of what I showed.

CHORUS: It is that I understand not the plan of him who should do it.

CASSANDRA: See now, I know the speech of Hellas, only too well.

CHORUS: Greek are the Pythian oracles, and yet hard to understand.

CASSANDRA: *Oh, this burning fire! . . . It is creeping over me! . . . Ah mercy, Apollo Lyceus, mercy upon me!*

See the lioness two-footed, that couches with the wolf while the noble lion is away! She will slay me, wretch that I am! Brewing as it were a medicine for her wrath, she will add to it also the recompense for me. She vows as she sharpens her man-slaying sword, to take of him for the bringing of me a bloody revenge.

Why then in derision of myself do I bear these, and the scepter of divination, and the stole about my neck?

You at least I will destroy ere I perish myself!

Down, cursed things, to the ground, where thus I take vengeance upon you! Because you have been my ruin, die too, so as you may.

But see, Apollo himself, stripping from me the prophet's vesture! He has had the spectacle of me exposed, even in and along with this sacred garb, to the derision of friend and foe alike, and in vain—yes, "mountebank, beggar, starveling" were the names, alas, that vagabondlike I had to bear: and now the Seer has finished my seership and brought me to die like this, where there awaits me not the altar of my home but a butcherly block for a victim struck before the last blood is cold.

Yet not unregarded of heaven shall we die. For there shall come another yet to requite for us, one born to slay his mother, to avenge his sire. Exiled from this land, a wanderer disowned, he shall return, to put on this tower of unnatural crimes that pinnacle, whereto his father's death is the leading spire.

I am come to my "home," and why thus wail? Since I saw first Ilium meet the fate it has, and now they, who were her captors, are brought by the gods of their choice to their present pass, I will go meet fate, will take death patiently, because the gods with a mighty oath have sworn it!

Only I greet this door as the portal of Death, and my prayer is to receive a mortal stroke, that the bloodstream may flow easy, and I may not struggle but close mine eyes.

CHORUS: O woman patient as miserable! When all this is spoken, yet now, if truly you know your own death, why do you go to it, stubbornly as the ox, which the god moves toward the altar?

CASSANDRA: There is no escape, friends, none, when the time is full.

CHORUS: Yea, but the last of the time is best.

CASSANDRA: The day is come. Little shall I gain by flight.

CHORUS: Then be assured, that you have a stubborn patience!

CASSANDRA: So praised is never any save the unhappy.

CHORUS: Yet a mortal may be glad to die with honor.

CASSANDRA: Ah father, to think of you and those, your genuine children! . . .

CHORUS: What is it? What horror turns thee back?

CASSANDRA: O foul, O foul!

CHORUS: What do you call foul, if the loathing be not in your fancy?

CASSANDRA: It is the horror of dripping blood, that the house exhales.

CHORUS: Nay, nay: it is the scent of the hearth-sacrifice.

CASSANDRA: It is such a reek as might come out of a grave.

CHORUS: You cannot mean the sweet incense of the palace.

CASSANDRA: Yet I will go, and within, as here, will wail the fate of me and of Agamemnon. Enough of life!

Oh friends, my friends!

I do not clamor for naught as a bird that dreads a bush. Bear this witness to me dead, when some day for my

death another woman shall die, and for the unfortunate
husband another fall. This office I ask of you at the
point to die.

CHORUS: Ah miserable, I pity you for your death foretold!

CASSANDRA: I would speak one speech more—or is it my
own dirge? To the sun I call, unto the last I see, that
those my avengers may take of these my enemies a bloody
vengeance also for the easy conquest of a poor slain slave.

Alas for the state of man! If happiness may be changed
as it were by a shade, misery is a picture which at the
dash of the wet sponge is gone. And this I say is the more
pitiable by far.   (*Exit.*)

CHORUS: *Prosperity in all men doth naturally crave more.*
Though the palace be pointed at by jealous fingers, none
forbidding shuts fortune out with these words: "Enter no
more."

And so to the king the gods have given to take the town
of Priam, and he comes honored of heaven to his home:
yet now if he must pay for the blood of those before, if
adding death to deaths he is to crown the pile with yet
other deaths in revenge, who hearing this could affirm that
any mortal is born with fortune beyond harm?

AGAMEMNON (*within*): Oh, I am struck, deep-struck and
mortally!

CHORUS: Silence! Who shrieks as wounded with a mortal
stroke?

AGAMEMNON: Again, oh again! Another stroke!

CHORUS: The deed, I doubt, is done, from the cries of the
king. But let us give each other safe counsel, if we may.

(*The members of the* CHORUS *speak individually.*)

I give you my own judgment, that we summon a rescue
of the townsfolk to the palace.

Nay, I think we had best dash in at once, and prove the
deed by the dripping sword.

And I too am with this judgment so far, that my vote is
for action. It is no moment for delay.

There is occasion to beware. Their beginning betokens
a plan to enslave the city.

Yes, because we linger! They, while she hesitates, tread
her honor down and work unresting.

I know not what advice I may find to say. To a doer it
belongs to advise about the doing.

I too am of like mind, for I see not how with words to raise up again the dead.

Are we to make death of life, thus yielding to the rule of those that have thus defiled a house?

Nay, it is intolerable, nay, death is better. It is a milder fate than to be enslaved.

Are we then indeed by inference from a cry to divine that the prince has perished?

Best know the facts before we hear each other talk. Guessing and knowing are two things.

All sides support me in assenting to this, to have clear knowledge how it is with Atreus' son.

(CLYTEMNESTRA *is revealed standing over the bodies of* AGAMEMNON *and* CASSANDRA.)

CLYTEMNESTRA: If now I contradict all that to suit the moment I said before, I shall feel no shame. What shame should he feel, who plots as a foe against a foe? With the semblance of friendship let him make his dangerous snare too high to be overleaped.

For me, I have had long enough to prepare this wrestle for victory, though it has come at last. I stand where I struck, over the finished work. And such I made the death (I will own this also) as to forbid escape or resistance, a net unpassable, like the fisherman's round a shoal, a rich robe deadly dyed. Twice I smote him, and with two shrieks he let himself sink down. And when he had fallen, I gave him yet a third stroke, an offering of thanks to the nether god, to Hades, safe keeper of the dead. With that he lay and himself gasped away his breath. And as he blew the spurts of his running blood, he rained upon me a crimson gory dew, and I rejoiced no less than beneath the sweet rain of heaven does the corn when it bursts from the laboring sheath.

So stands the case, nobles of Argos here; be glad of it, if you will; for me, I triumph upon it. And could there be case fit for a libation over the dead, justly and more than justly now would it be. With so many imprecations of suffering homes this man has filled the bowl which himself returning has drained.

CHORUS: We are astonished that your mouth bears so bold a tongue, to boast over your dead lord in such terms.

CLYTEMNESTRA: You challenge me, supposed an unthinking woman. But I speak with unshaken courage to those who know, indifferent whether you choose to praise or blame. This is Agamemnon, my husband, wrought to death by the just handicraft of this my hand. So stands the case.

CHORUS: What poison have you taken, woman, what drug born of the earth or draught from the great water, that you have brought on yourself the fury and the loud curses of yonder folk? You have cut off, cast off: and cast from communion shall you be, as a load on the people's hate.

CLYTEMNESTRA: Yes, now you would award to me exile from my country, the hate of the people and their loud curses to bear. You do not join in laying that reproach against him who lies here, against him who, caring no more than for the death of a beast, though his fleecy herds had sheep enough, sacrificed his own child, the darling born of my pains, to charm the winds of Thrace. Is it not he whom you should banish from Argive soil for his foul crime? No, it is in judgment of me that you are an auditor severe! But I warn you, threatening thus, to think that I am prepared, ready that he who conquers me in fair fight should rule me; but if fate intends the contrary, you will be taught, too late, the lesson of prudence.

CHORUS: You are proud of thought, and presumptuous is your note, for indeed the murderous stroke is maddening you. The blood-fleck in your eyes is right natural. For all this, you shall find yourself friendless and pay retaliatory stroke for stroke.

CLYTEMNESTRA: This also for your hearing I solemnly swear. By the accomplished Justice for my child, by Doom and Revenge, to whom I offered this dead man up, my hope does not set foot in the house of fear, so long as fire be kindled for the lighting of my hearths by Aegisthus, still devoted as ever to me.

For there, as our broad shield of confidence, lies, outraging his wife, my husband—the darling of each Chryseis in the Trojan camp!—and with him his captive, his auguress, his oracle-monger mistress, who shared with him faithfully even the ship's bench and the canvas! But they did it not unpunished! For he lies as you see, and she, having sung swanlike her last sad song of death, lies by him lovably, adding to the sweet of my triumph a spice of sex.

CHORUS: *Ah, could some death come quick, which without agony, without pillowed watch, might bring to us endless sleep, now that our kindest protector is laid low, who hav-*

ing much endured for a woman's sin, hath by a woman lost his life!

Oh . . . Helen, who didst alone destroy that multitude, that great multitude of lives at Troy, now, for thy final crown, thou hast destroyed one, the stain of whose murder shall not be washed away! Surely there hath been in this house a hard-fought rivalry of fatal wives.

CLYTEMNESTRA: *Nay, pray not for death in indignation at this. Nor turn your anger on Helen, as if alone in destruction she had destroyed that multitude of Argive lives and wrought incomparable woe.*

CHORUS: *O curse, how hast thou fallen on Tantalus' house in either branch, and shared between two women a life-destroying victory for which my heart is sore! Lo, on the body like a foul bird of prey he stands, boasting to celebrate a triumph lawful and just.*

CLYTEMNESTRA: *Nay, now you have mended the judgment of your lips, in that you call upon the fat-fed curse of this race. For therefrom is bred this craving of the maw for blood to lick, ever new gore, before the old woe be done.*

CHORUS: *Truly mighty he is and malignant, the curse of this house, of whose never-sated cruelty thou dost, alas, so grievously testify. And oh, and oh, it cometh by Zeus, the cause of all, the doer of all! For what without him is accomplished upon men? What of all this is not of divine appointment?*

O King, O King, how shall I weep for thee? Out of my heart's love what shall I say? And thou didst lie in this spider-web, dying by a wicked death, ah me, on this couch of slavery, struck down by a crafty arm with a weapon of double edge!

CLYTEMNESTRA: *Dare you say this deed was mine? Imagine not that I am Agamemnon's spouse. No, in the shape of this dead man's wife, the bitter fiend, long since provoked by Atreus the cruel feaster, has made by this full-grown victim payment for those slain babes.*

CHORUS: *That thou art guiltless of this murder, who shall aver? It cannot, cannot be: though perchance the fiend of his sire might be thy helper. He riots in fresh streams of kindred blood, the red Manslayer, drawn to the infant blood-slot of the child-flesh served for meat.*

O King, O King, how shall I weep for thee? Out of my heart's love what shall I say? And thou didst lie in this spider-web, dying by a wicked death, ah me, on this couch of slavery, struck down by a crafty arm with a weapon of double edge!

CLYTEMNESTRA: *And did he not then himself do a crafty crime against his house? Nay, for the thing he did to the blossom born of me and him, my long-wept Iphigenia, justice is done upon him! Let him not boast in Hades, for he has paid, as he sinned, with death.*

CHORUS: *My mind is blank and I find no ready thought, which way to fly from the tottering house. The storm will strike it, I fear, and wreck it quite, the storm of blood. The rain is ceasing, yet Justice is but whetting once more on the whetstone of hindrance her sword to punish again.*

O earth, earth, would that thou hadst received me, before I had seen my lord laid thus low in the silver-sided bath! Who shall bury him? Who sing his dirge? Wilt thou dare to do it, thou, that hast slain thy husband, dare to lament his parted soul? The compensation will scarce atone the offense! But who will stand over the hero's grave and pour forth the tearful praise with heart that truly aches?

CLYTEMNESTRA: *It belongs not to you to regard this care. By us he fell, he died, and we will bury him, not with weeping of his household, no, but Iphigenia his daughter, as is fit, will meet her father with joy at the swift passage of the sorrowful ford, and fling her arms around him, and give him a kiss.*

CHORUS: *Thus is reproach answered with other reproach! 'Tis a hard case to judge. The spoiler spoiled, the slayer slain! And it abides, while Zeus abides on his throne, that to him that doeth it shall be done: for lawful is it. Who can expel the cursed breed from the house? It is a kind that sticketh fast.*

O earth, earth, would that thou hadst received me, before I had seen my lord laid thus low in the silver-sided bath! Who shall bury him? Who sing his dirge? Wilt thou dare to do it, thou, that hast slain thy husband, dare to lament his parted soul? The compensation will scarce atone the offense! But who will stand over the hero's grave and pour forth the tearful praise with heart that truly aches?

CLYTEMNESTRA: *Up to this death it has truly followed prophecy, but I now am ready to swear a compact with the*

Fortune of the house of Pleisthenes, that we accept, hard though it be, what is done, if henceforth he will leave this house and harass with kin-murder some other race. A part of the wealth is not much to me who have it all, and moreover I am content if I but rid the palace of this internecine frenzy.

(*Enter* AEGISTHUS.)

AEGISTHUS: Hail, kindly dawn of the day that brings justice! This hour I will confess that from above earth gods look upon and avenge the woes of men, now that I see in a robe of the Furies' weaving this man lying as I would, and paying for what the hands of his father devised.

For Atreus, ruling in Argos, this man's father, being question in his sovereignty by Thyestes, who was (to make all clear) father to me and brother to Atreus himself, banished him from his house and from the country also. And Thyestes, having returned as a suppliant to the hearth, found, unhappy man, safety so far, that his life-blood was not shed upon his father's floor. But taking the very occasion of his arrival, Atreus, the impious father of this slain man, pretending, with eagerness little welcome to my father, to hold a glad day of festival, served him a banquet of his children's flesh. Of the extremities, the footparts and fingered hands, he put a mince on the top, sitting down with tables apart. And not knowing it at the moment for what it was, he took of the meat disguised, and ate of a meal, which, as you see, his race have found unwholesome. And when he perceived the monstrous thing he had done, he shrieked and fell back vomiting the sacrifice, and called a terrible doom on the house of Pelops, aiding his imprecation by the spurning of the banquet, that thus might perish all the race of Pleisthenes.

This is the cause which has laid this man where you may see. And it is a justice that I am the maker of this murder. Me whom, for my miserable sire's "just third," he sent, a swaddled babe, into exile along with him, that justice has brought back again as a man. Even from beyond the border I reached my victim, contriving and combining the whole hard plan. And now I can even die with honor, having seen him in the toils of this just revenge.

CHORUS: Aegisthus, I care not to insult distress; but do you confess unasked to be this man's slayer, the sole contriver of this pitiable murder? I say that you before justice will not escape, be sure, the people's dangerous imprecation of stones.

AEGISTHUS: Speak you so, you, whose place is at the lower oar, while they of the deck are masters of the ship? Your age will learn how grievous it is for one of your years to be schooled in the dictate of prudence. Yet the pains of bonds and the pains of hunger are most surpassing mediciners to school the oldest mind. Does not this sight warn you? Kick not against the pricks, lest hitting you hurt yourself.

CHORUS: You woman! You, who abode at home, helping to defile a brave man's bed! And shall then warriors fresh returned from battle—? It is a captain of soldiers whose death you have thus "contrived."

AEGISTHUS: These words again will prove the fathers of weeping. Your tongue is the opposite of Orpheus': for whereas he drew all things along with the joy of his voice, your soothing bark will provoke, till yourself are drawn along. But once mastered you will prove tamer.

CHORUS: And shall I think that you shall be despot of the Argives, who, being the "contriver" of the king's death, did not dare to do the deed of murder?

AEGISTHUS: The part of deceit fell manifestly to the wife: I, as a hereditary foe, was open to suspicion. In the wealth of the dead man I shall seek the means of control. On the disobedient subject I shall lay a heavy yoke, and give him, I warrant you, less than a racer's provender. Yes, hunger, which does not mate peaceably with high spirit, will not leave him till he is mild.

CHORUS: Why then of your cowardice did you not butcher the victim alone? Why, to the defilement of our country and our country's gods, join the wife with you in the murder? Oh, does Orestes haply live, that by grace of fortune he may return to this land and slay this pair victoriously?

AEGISTHUS: Nay then, if you will so say and do, you shall have a lesson at once!

CHORUS: Come on, comrades! Our work is not far off now.

AEGISTHUS: Come on! Make ready! Draw every man his sword!

CHORUS: Nay, I too, sword in hand, am prepared to die.

AEGISTHUS: "To die"! An acceptable word! We take the moment.

CLYTEMNESTRA: Nay, dearest, let us do no more ill. What is done is much to reap, a bitter harvest. Begin pain with enough; but let us have no bloodshed. Go you at once and confine these old men to their destined dwelling-place before they come to harm. What we arranged should have stood. And if we should find that enough has been inflicted, there we will stop, sore smitten as we have been by the heavy heel of fate.

AEGISTHUS: And must they thus flaunt the folly of their tongues against me, and tempt fate with a fling of such high words?

CLYTEMNESTRA: And when they lose their senses, must he who is master of them do the like?

CHORUS: It is not the way in Argos to fawn upon a villain!

AEGISTHUS: Well, I will come up with you one of these days yet.

CHORUS: Not if heaven guide Orestes back to the land.

AEGISTHUS: I know myself how exiles feed upon hopes.

CHORUS: Go on, make you fat, and befoul the good cause, as you can.

AEGISTHUS: Be sure you shall make me amends for this kind insolence!

CHORUS: Brag, brag with boldness, like a cock beside his hen!

CLYTEMNESTRA: Care not for this idle barking. I and you will make good order, being masters in this house.

SUMMARY OF
Choephoroe

AS BEFITS THE central member of a triptych, *Choephoroe* is a static play. It contains only one great action, the slaying of Clytemnestra by her son Orestes to avenge her murder of his father Agamemnon. To prepare the emotions of both participants and spectators for the horror of matricide there are long lyric exchanges of prayers and invocations, and these are difficult in Greek and lame in translation. For following the movement of the trilogy as a whole, therefore, an outline of *Choephoroe* will suffice.

When Clytemnestra murdered Agamemnon, Orestes had been sent out of the country for safety. Now grown to manhood and attended by his friend Pylades he returns to Argos, at Apollo's bidding, to avenge the murder. Upon his arrival he deposits a lock of his hair on his father's tomb as a pious offering, and then withdraws. Electra, Orestes' elder sister, emerges with the chorus; she has been sent with offerings for the tomb of Agamemnon by Clytemnestra, who has been troubled by a dream of a serpent whom she has nursed and who then attacks her. The lock of hair and the footsteps at the tomb raise Electra's hope that Orestes has returned, and Orestes himself steps forward to confirm the identification by a piece of clothing Electra has woven. Brother and sister rejoice at the reunion, and devise a scheme for slaying Aegisthus and Clytemnestra. Orestes gains access to the palace by pretending that he is a messenger bringing news of his own death. Clytemnestra welcomes him and offers him a hot bath. (We remember that it was in the same bath that Agamemnon was killed.) A Cilician servant who had been Orestes' nurse in his infancy is sent by Clytemnestra to summon Aegisthus and his guards to receive the news. The nurse laments the "death" of her charge, complains that Clytemnestra's show of grief was hypocritical, and is persuaded by the chorus to change the message to Aegisthus:

he is to come *without* his guards. Aegisthus enters the palace
and is killed by Orestes. A servant cries to Clytemnestra, "The
dead are killing the living!" Clytemnestra understands and
demands "the man-slaying ax." When Orestes confronts his
mother, who begs mercy on grounds of filial duty, he is ap-
palled by what he must do and appeals to Pylades for advice. Pylades' only line in the play is, "What will then become of the oracle of Apollo?" Orestes drives Clytemnestra
into the palace and there kills her. He emerges from the
deed distraught; his speech becomes increasingly delirious,
and finally he sees or imagines he sees the Furies pursuing
him. "You cannot see them," he cries, and flies from the
scene.

Orestes is the classic example of the tragic hero caught
between conflicting sanctions; whichever alternative he
chooses to follow renders him liable to reprisals on the part
of the other. Apollo, who fosters orderly government and
favors the masculine over the feminine, could not tolerate
the murder of a king, and that by a woman, and therefore
commanded the murdered man's heir to exact vengeance. But
to carry out the Olympian's behest Orestes finds himself
obliged to kill his own mother, and to the older deities
(called *chthonian*) whom the Furies represent, matricide is
the most heinous of all crimes. It was through no fault of his
that Orestes was forced to choose between the disparate sanctions, but he could evade neither the choice nor its consequences. The conflict between chthonian and Olympian
ideals becomes increasingly important in the course of the
trilogy; in *Eumenides* it is the subject of an explicit debate.

Eumenides

"EUMENIDES" OR **"Kindly Ones"** was a euphemism for
Erinyes or Furies. The play so named shows how the Furies
were in fact transformed into beneficent powers. The Erinyes
belonged to the old irrational order of deities; they were
feminine in nature and particularly concerned with blood
and kinship, and their function was to exact blood for blood.
No degrees of guilt were recognized: even if the original
bloodshed was accidental or justifiable it had to be requited
by shedding the blood of the slayer or of his blood kin. The
new Olympian gods introduced rationality: bloodshed, even of
one's own mother, does not automatically entail blood vengeance; each case must be judged separately. The introduction of trial by jury to replace the mechanical law of the
vendetta is a great advance in civilization, and it is this
which *Eumenides* celebrates. By the old order the series of
murders in the house of Tantalus must have gone on end-
lessly; now, with the acquittal of Orestes, the curse is laid to
rest. The Furies are not evil witches; in their own view the
fear which they inspired maintained order in society. Even
rational people, furthermore, find matricide more shocking
than other kinds of murder. The power of the Erinyes represents a legitimate human sentiment; they are not therefore
abolished when the new order is introduced, but sublimated
into a more civilized kind of function. Along with their mechanical retribution the Erinyes also represented the chthonic
primacy of the feminine principle over the masculine. The
transformation to the masculine principle of the Olympians

is another theme in *Eumenides*. That is why Apollo offers the absurd argument that not the mother but the father is the true parent of the child, and that is why he holds that the murder of a king by a dominating queen is particularly heinous.

A priestess establishes the serene sanctity of Delphi with her prayers opening the play, enters the shrine, and rushes out with a shriek. Inside she has seen a bloodstained man clinging to the sacred navel stone and around him, sleeping fitfully, a band of loathsome black-swathed females. The scene is revealed, with Apollo encouraging Orestes and bidding Hermes escort him to Athens. The ghost of Clytemnestra rises to spur the Furies on to pursuit. They sniff their way out, and when they return the scene is changed to Athens, with Orestes clasping a statue of Athena. They circle about him with a fearful "binding song." Athena appears, hears the dispute, and decrees that the issue must be decided by a court; in case of a tie she herself will decide. A jury comes forward, hears both sides, and casts ballots. These are tied, and Athena decides in favor of Orestes. The case is after all not simple black and white. The Furies object to the decision but are pacified by Athena's promises that they will be given a new and more beneficent function. All go off in procession escorting the Furies—who turn their black capes inside out to show white—to their permanent shrine on the declivity of the Acropolis.

CHARACTERS

PYTHIAN PROPHETESS
CHORUS OF FURIES
ORESTES
APOLLO
GHOST OF CLYTEMNESTRA
ATHENA

SCENE: First Delphi, then Athens

Translated by **F. A. PALEY**

(*Enter* PROPHETESS.)

PROPHETESS: In the first place, I address before all other gods, in this my prayer, the primeval prophetess Earth; and after her Themis, who next in succession occupied this oracular seat of her mother's, as is the common story: and in the third turn, with the full consent of Themis, and doing despite to no one, another Titanian goddess, child of Earth, took her seat there, Phoebe; *she* presents it as a birth-day-gift to Phoebus, and he retains Phoebe's name adapted to himself as the grandson. He, leaving the lake and low rocky isle of Delos, put-to at the shores of Pallas, where there was way for a ship, and so came to this (Delphian) land and the settlements near Parnassus. Thence he is escorted with solemn worship by roadmakers descended from Hephaestus, who caused the uncleared land to be opened for him by a highway. And on his arrival he is greatly honored by the people, and by Delphus the ruling sovereign of this land. Him then, inspired in mind with the prophetic art, Zeus appoints, fourth in order, to be the present occupant of the oracular seat; and Loxias acts as the interpreter of his father. These are the gods whom I address in my opening prayers: but Pallas, enshrined before the temple, claims the first right to be honorably mentioned; and I venerate also the Nymphs of the grotto in the Corycian cliff, frequented by birds, the haunt of deities. Bromius also claims the spot as his own, nor do I forget him, ever since the god led his Bacchanalian crew and

55

planned a death for Pentheus like that of a hunted hare. I invoke also the sources of the river Plistus, the majesty of Poseidon, and the supreme god of all, Zeus the Consummator. This being done, I go to take my seat as prophetess. And now may they grant that I may obtain far more favorable responses than from any former entrances! And if there are any deputies from the Hellenes, let them come forward, after determining their turns by lot, as is the established custom: for I give my answers just as the god may dictate.

(*Enters shrine and then emerges shrieking.*)

Truly a sight terrible to describe and terrible to behold with mortal eyes sent me back from out the shrine of Loxias, so that my steps neither have firm tread nor bear me erect; and I run by the aid of my hands, not by speed of my feet. For an old woman when alarmed is good for nothing; rather she is like a mere child. I on my part was going to the bay-crowned recess, when I saw at the central altar a man accursed of the gods taking refuge there from a deed of guilt, his hands all dripping with gore, and holding a newly-drawn sword and the top-branch of an olive-tree, duly tufted with very large fillets of wool, a white fleece; for on that point I shall speak with certainty. And in front of this man there sleeps a wondrous troop of women reposing on seats: women indeed I call them not, but Gorgons; and yet again I cannot compare them to Gorgon forms. I saw once pictured figures carrying off the victuals of Phineus: *these* however are wingless to behold, black, and altogether loathsome in their manners. They snore with labored breathings not to be approached, and from their eyes they dribble a noxious rheum. As for their dress, it is not fit to be carried to the statues of the gods, nor into the abodes of men. The tribe to which this sisterhood belongs I have seen not, nor know I what land can aver that it rears such a race with impunity, and has not afterward to repent of its pains. What is to be done now must be the care of the lord of this temple, the powerful Loxias himself: and he is both physician-prophet and portent-seer, as well as a purifier of houses for others.

(*The scene opens to reveal* APOLLO, ORESTES, *and the sleeping* FURIES.)

APOLLO: Be assured I will not abandon you; but having you

in my keeping to the end, either standing close by your side or removed to a distance from you, I will not be lenient to your enemies. And accordingly now you see these rampant witches overtaken by sleep; they have fallen down in slumber, these abhorred virgins, hoary hags, children of ancient birth; with whom no god consorts, nor any mortal, nor even beast, at any time. It was on account of foul deeds that they came into existence at all; for dismal darkness is their home, even Tartarus below the earth, detested both by men on earth and by the gods in Olympus. Nevertheless fly and turn not faint; for they will chase you even across the long continent, wandering ever wearily up and down the land and over the sea and island-cities. And do not forestall your woes by brooding anxiously over this toil; but go to the city of Pallas, and take your suppliant seat there, grasping in your arms her ancient statue; and there having judges to decide on these matters and arguments in palliation of your crime, we will find means to rid you effectually of these troubles: for it was even in obedience to me that you slew that body which gave you birth.

ORESTES: King Apollo, you already know what it is not to act with injustice; and as you know it, learn also not to be neglectful. And your power is sufficient in itself to serve me well.

APOLLO: Remember! let not fear overcome your resolution. And do you, my own brother born of a common father, Hermes, guard him, and, true to your name, be his conductor, tending with care this suppliant at my temple. Know that Zeus holds in honor the respect due to those out of the pale of the law, when it comes to mortals through safe convoy.

(*The Ghost of* CLYTEMNESTRA *rises.*)

CLYTEMNESTRA: Sleep on, ho there! yet what need have I of sleepers? I tell you that I, thus slighted by you among other dead, am unceasingly reproached among the shades with being a murderess, and am left to wander in disgrace; and I tell you that I have to bear the greatest blame from them. Yet, though I have endured so dreadful a fate at the hands of those dearest to me, none of the gods is indignant in my behoof, for being slain by matricidal hands. See these sword-wounds of my heart, from whom they came. For the mind in sleep is clear in its eyesight, though in the daytime the fate of mortals is hidden

from their ken. Assuredly, many presents of mine have
you lapped up: and wineless libations, sober drink-offerings,
and banquets in the solemn hour of the night I consecrated to you at the burning altar, at an hour common to
none other of the gods. And all these gifts I now see
spurned and trampled on: for *he* has escaped from you
and gone off like a fawn; yea, even from the middle of
the hunting-toils he has nimbly bounded, with gibes and
great mockery of you. Hear me, for I plead in defense of
my own life: be roused to consciousness, ye goddesses below the earth: for though in a dream, it is I Clytemnestra
that summon you.

(*A low moaning is heard.*)

Moan on; but the man is gone far away in flight: for
there are those who protect as suppliants my relations,
though not myself.

(*A moaning again.*)

Too deeply do you slumber, and do not compassionate
my sufferings: here is Orestes, the murderer of his own
mother, allowed to escape!

(*A stifled cry is heard.*)

Do you cry out? do you slumber still? Get up instantly!
What has been accomplished by you—except to cause harm?

(*A low cry again.*)

Sleep and toil, powerful conspirators, have taken out of
our fell she-dragon all her strength.

(*A twice-repeated cry, shrill in tone.*)

CHORUS: Seize, seize him, there, there, there! Mark him!

CLYTEMNESTRA: You are as one that pursues a quarry in a
dream, and idly give tongue like a dog that never ceases
thinking about its toil. What are you doing? Get up! Let
not fatigue overcome you, nor be unaware of your loss, having your fierceness tamed by sleep. Be pained in your heart
with just reproaches; for to the wise they are as goads to
the feelings. And do *you*, directing against him your gory
breath, withering him with the hot blast, the fire of your
inmost breast, pursue, wear him down with a second chase.

(*Exit.*)

CHORUS: Rouse, rouse up *her*, as I rouse you. Are you asleep?
Get up, cast off sleep, and let us see if any word of our
opening song is uttered in vain.

(*The* FURIES *speak individually.*)

Oh woe, alas! We have suffered, friends—

Much indeed and undeservedly have I endured——

Suffered (I say) a calamity deeply grievous, an intolerable evil.

The wild beast has escaped from the nets and is gone: while overcome by sleep I lost my prey.

Fie! son of Zeus; a thief's part you are acting.

And a young god you overrode us aged deities——

By paying regard to one who was your suppliant, an impious man, and cruel to his parents.

And one that was a matricide you stealthily took out of our hands, though you are a god. Which of these acts will anyone say is right?

But to me a reproach came in my dreams, and smote me, like a chariot-driver with a goad grasped by the middle, under the heart, under the liver.

One may feel what is the severe, the very severe smart of the fierce public executioner's lash.

This is what your younger gods do, holding authority altogether beyond what is right.

A blood-dripping gout round the head and the foot—

One may perceive Earth's central altar to have taken upon itself, so as to endure a terrible pollution of gore.

And though you call yourself a prophet, by a defilement of your own altar-stone you polluted the oracular recess self-impelled, self-invited, contrary to the law of the gods doing honor to human claims, and having brought to nought the goddesses of ancient birth.

Yea, and while to me he gives toil and trouble, yet him he shall not release; and even when he has fled beneath the earth he is no more free.

But as a guilty culprit he shall get another foul demon to alight on his head after me.

APOLLO: Out with you, I insist, out of this temple go at once! be off from the prophetic recess, lest you receive in your vitals a winged glistening serpent speeding from the golden bowstring, and disgorge through pain the black froth sucked from men, vomiting the gouts of gore which you have drained from them. Not to *these* abodes is it fitting that ye should approach: but rather where there are punishments of striking off heads and scooping-out eyes and the cutting of throats, and by the destroying of the seed the vigor of boys is impaired, and mutilation of extremities and deaths by stoning, and where men moan forth their horrid misery impaled below the backbone—do ye hear the sort of feast ye have a fondness for, and so become objects of disgust to the gods? Why, the whole fashion of your forms suggests it. The den of a blood-lapping lion such as *you* should inhabit, and not inflict a lasting pollution on the temple here close by. Go, ye that are tended without a keeper: for to such a flock as yours no god has friendly feelings.

CHORUS: King Apollo, hear our answer in turn. You yourself are not partly concerned in this, but you alone did it all, as the sole and entire author of it.

APOLLO: How was that? Prolong your account to that extent.

CHORUS: You delivered an oracle for the stranger to slay his mother.

APOLLO: I did enjoin that he should exact vengeance for his father: of course I did.

CHORUS: And then you engaged to take on yourself the guilt of recent blood.

APOLLO: Yes, and I enjoined him to take refuge at this temple.

CHORUS: And then you abuse us who attended him thither.

APOLLO: Yes, for it is not fitting that you should come to this sacred temple.

CHORUS: But on us this duty has been specially imposed.

APOLLO: What kind of honor is that? Boast of a prerogative that is creditable.

CHORUS: We drive matricides from out their homes.

APOLLO: What! The slayer of a wife who has killed her husband?

CHORUS: That would not be kindred blood shed by the hand of a relation.

APOLLO: Truly you make of no effect and of no importance the solemn pledges of Hera and Zeus the gods of Marriage; Cypris too is cast away without honor by this argument, source as she is of the dearest joys to mortals. For the marriage-bed appointed by fate for husband and wife is greater than a mere oath, guarded as it is by Justice. If then you are lax toward man and wife, when one slays the other, so that it does not happen that you regard the deed with any anger at all, then I say that you do not justly persecute Orestes. For in his case I know that you are greatly enraged against him; in hers, that you openly act with more leniency. But the goddess Pallas will see that justice is done at the trial of this matter.

CHORUS: That man I will never, never leave.

APOLLO: Then go on chasing him—and give yourself trouble still further.

CHORUS: Do not *you* attempt to abridge *my* prerogatives by your words.

APOLLO: *Your* prerogatives! I would not even accept them as a present.

CHORUS: No, for even without them you are held to be great by the throne of Zeus. But I—for the blood of a mother leads me on—shall pursue this man with vengeance, and here I put myself on his track.

(*Exeunt* FURIES *in pursuit.*)

APOLLO: Then *I* shall assist him, and rescue my own suppliant: for terrible both among men and gods is the wrath of a refugee, when one abandons him with intent.

(*Exit.*)

(*The scene changes to Athens.* ORESTES *is discovered clinging to the statue of Athena. Enter* FURIES.)

ORESTES: Athena my queen, by the commands of Loxias I here come; and do you receive favorably a wretch, not now with the guilt of blood upon him, nor unpurified in hand; but by this time blunted and worn down at other houses and ways of men, passing alike over dry land and sea, in obedience to the oracular behests of Loxias I am here at thy temple and thy statue, O Goddess. Here I will keep my post awaiting the issue of the trial.

CHORUS: So! Here is a clear trace of the man: follow the tellings of a voiceless informer. For as a hound does a wounded fawn, so do we track out our prey by blood and its droppings. And with my long toils to wear out the man in the chase my heart pants: for every spot of earth has been carefully gone over, and across the sea with wingless flight have I come plying my course, not at all behind a ship in speed. And now he is somewhere about here crouching down: the smell of human gore greets my senses.

(*The* FURIES *speak individually.*)

Look out, look out again, cast your eyes in every direction, lest the matricide should have escaped us by stealthy flight and should go unpunished.

Here we find him again having a safe asylum; with arms clasped round the statue of the immortal goddess——

He is willing enough to give himself up for justice into our hands!

But that cannot be: the blood of a mother is on the ground, not to be taken up again, alas!

The life-blood once shed on the ground is gone.

But you have yet to give me in return to suck the crimson draught from your limbs even in life.

Yea, from you would I fain get the feeding on a blood-draught by others loathed.

And after draining you dry I will take you alive to the regions below——

To pay just retribution for the pangs of a slaughtered mother.

And you shall there see if any other mortal sinned——

By impious conduct to a god, or a stranger, or to his parents dear——

Having each the punishment that Justice requires of him.

For Hades is a mighty corrector of mortals beneath the earth.

And notices all crimes in his recording mind.

ORESTES: Trained as I have been in the school of misfortune, I know many purifications, and to speak where it is proper, and to be silent alike; but in the present case I was ordered to plead by a wise instructor. For the blood sleeps, and is fading away from my hand; and the guilt of killing a mother is washed out. For while yet fresh it was driven off at the altar of the god Phoebus by purifications made with the blood of slaughtered swine. Long indeed would be my account from the beginning, of how many houses I visited with harmless intercourse. Time purifies all things, as it grows old along with them. And so now with guiltless voice I can invoke in a holy prayer the queen of this land, Athena, to come as my patroness; and she shall gain without war myself and my country and the Argive host, disinterestedly faithful and forever her ally. Whether then in the confines of the Libyan land, by Triton's stream, the river of her birth, she is setting her foot upright or draped in her peplus, in defense of her friends—or whether, like a bold general in his ranks, she is surveying the Phlegraean plain—may she come—and a god can hear even from a distance—that she may prove to me a deliverer from these my troubles.

CHORUS: Think not that Apollo or even Athena's might can save you from perishing in utter neglect, without one lingering joy left in your heart, the bloodless victim of us deities, a mere shadow. What! not a word of reply? Do you spurn my words, fattened as you have been and consecrated for my victim? Yea, alive you shall make me a meal, and not slaughtered at the altar. And now you shall hear a song that will bind you unto us.

Come now, let us e'en join hands in the dance, since it has been resolved to show the power of our weird strain, and to declare how our sisterhood distributes the fortunes that prevail among man: and we profess to exercise upright justice. Against the man who holds out pure hands no anger from us proceeds; he goes through life unharmed by us: but when a guilty wretch like this man hides under his robe his gory hands, we come forward as upright witnesses for the dead, and he finds that we exact from him to the full the price of blood.

Mother who didst bring me forth, O mother Night, that I might be a punishment to the living and the dead, hear me! For the son of Latona makes me dishonored in taking from me this crouching hind, this my own rightful victim for expiating a mother's murder. Such is the strain we sing over a victim that has been sacrificed, a maddening, a mind-destroying distraction, a hymn of the Furies that holds spellbound the reason, not chanted to by the lute, a blighting to mortals. For this office hath all-pervading Destiny allotted to us to hold forever; whensoever any mortals have been concerned in the wanton murders of kin, that we should follow them closely till they go under the earth; and when dead they are far from free. It was at our birth that these offices were solemnly confirmed to us: the part of the immortals is not to interfere with us; nor is any one of them a partaker with us of a common banquet. In snow-white robes too I was born to have no share, no allotted right: for I undertake the overthrow of houses, whenever domestic feuds have caused the death of a relation. Him, oh! do we closely pursue, strong runner though he be, and dim the crimson of the fresh blood. (Yet am I anxious to remove others from these cares;

*for the gods can only cause the nonfulfillment of prayers
offered to me, but they may not come to a quarrel with
me. For Zeus has deemed unworthy of his converse this
blood-dropping company, deserving only of his hatred.) For,
as I said, I take a spring from far above, and bear down
on him the heavy-falling force of my foot, my limbs which
trip up even runners in the long heat, a check hard to
endure. And people who are thought great and grand under
the light of heaven fall off and become little and of no
account on the earth, when we sisters of the sable robes
come suddenly upon them, and move our feet in the hateful dance. But when he falls he is unconscious of it through
his fatal folly: such a dark cloud of guilt hovers over the
man, and such a murky mist over his house does report
speak of with many a sigh.*

*Yea, 'tis a fixed and abiding law; for we Furies are ready
in resource and able to carry out our ends, and ever mindful of crimes; nor are we easily talked over by mortals,
while we silently pursue our dishonored and uncared-for
office, kept apart from the gods, with a torch that sees
not the light of the sun, chasing over rough roads both the
living and the dead alike. What mortal man is there then
who does not fear and stand in awe of this our office,
when he hears from me the rule which has been ratified
by fate, and assigned to us with full powers from the gods?
For I bear upon me an ancient prerogative, and I meet
not with dishonor even though I have a post beneath the
earth, and a sunless gloom.*

ATHENA: From afar I heard the sound of your call for help,
even from the Scamander, as I was taking possession of
a land which (be it known) the leaders and chiefs of the
Achaeans assigned to me as a large portion of the captured Trojan property, to be wholly mine with all the trees
upon it, a chosen present for the children of Theseus.
Thence came I plying my unwearied foot, not with wings,
but flapping in the breeze the folds of my aegis, having at-
tached this car of mine to strong young steeds. And now,
when I see these visitors to my land, I do not indeed feel
fear, but only wonder at the sight, who in the world ye
are: and I address myself to all in common, including the
stranger who is seated here at my image. But as for you,
who are like no race of creatures born, neither seen by
gods among goddesses, nor resembling human forms—

however, to speak ill of others when one has no cause for complaint, is far from right, and justice revolts from it.

CHORUS: You shall hear all in a few words, daughter of Zeus: we are the children of Eternal Night. In the abodes below the earth we are called *Spirits invoked for Evil*.

ATHENA: Your origin I know, and the titles you are called by.

CHORUS: But the duties which are properly mine you shall learn forthwith.

ATHENA: I might understand them if one of you would give me a clear account.

CHORUS: We chase homicides from their homes.

ATHENA: And where does the murderer find an end to the pursuit?

CHORUS: Where absence of all joy is the law of the place.

ATHENA: Are you urging this man also to the like flight?

CHORUS: Yes; he thought proper to be the murderer of his mother.

ATHENA: But was there not some other constraint—some threatened wrath he had to fear?

CHORUS: Why, what motive is sufficient to goad a man to murder his own mother?

ATHENA: There are two parties, but the statements of only one side are before us.

CHORUS: But he will neither take nor tender the legal oaths for a trial.

ATHENA: You are more willing to be called just than to act justly.

CHORUS: How is that? Inform me, for you are not deficient in wisdom.

ATHENA: I bid you not try to carry an unjust cause by oaths.

CHORUS: Proceed then to cross-questioning, and decide by a direct process.

ATHENA: Would you commit to me the decision of the cause?

CHORUS: Certainly, as holding in proper regard the worthy daughter of a worthy sire.

ATHENA: What do you wish to say, stranger, in your turn in answer to these charges? Tell first your country, your family, and your adventures, and then clear yourself of this slur on your fame, since it is in reliance on the justice of your cause that you sit clasping this my statue close to my altar, a sacred suppliant after the manner of Ixion. To all these questions give me an intelligible reply.

ORESTES: Queen Athena, I will begin by removing a great anxiety expressed in the latter words of your address. I am not a *guilty* suppliant: nor did I take my seat at your statue with pollution on my hand. And I will mention to you a great proof of this. It is the custom that the murderer should not speak nor be spoken to, until, by the ministration of some man who performs expiations for murder, the spurted blood of a slain sucking-pig shall have sprinkled him. Long ago have we had these cleansing rites performed on us at the houses of others, both by slain victims and by running streams. This care then I thus remove by my assurance. But what my family is, you shall hear forthwith. I am an Argive, and my father you know well, Agamemnon, ruler of the naval host; for with him you made Troy, the capital of Ilium, desolate; he perished, on return to his home, not indeed by an honorable death, but my gloomy-minded mother slew him by covering him over with embroidered toils, which bare witness after his death to the murder in the bath. And I returning, an exile hitherto, slew my mother, I will not deny it, by a revenge that required her blood for that of my dearest father. And of this deed Loxias shares the blame with myself, for predicting woes that would be as goads to my heart, if I omitted to do any of these things to those who were in fault. And do you, whether I acted rightly or not, decide the cause: for however I shall have fared before you in this matter, I shall acquiesce.

ATHENA: The case is too serious, if any mortal being thinks to decide it; nor is it lawful for me, a goddess, to act as judge in a suit about a murder that was caused by keen resentment. Besides, *you* have come to my temple as a suppliant, a broken-down wanderer, purified and incapable of causing harm by your converse: so that (though originally guilty) I receive you to my acropolis as if free from blame. On their parts, these Furies have a duty to perform which makes it hard to dismiss them: and if they should fail to gain their cause in this suit, hereafter poison falling on the ground in consequence of their anger will be a lasting disease causing barrenness to the land. Such then is the case in this matter: both courses, for them to remain here and for me to dismiss them, are harmful to the land, and perplexing to me. But, as this matter has devolved on me, *I* will appoint judges of murder, bound by oaths, to be an institution for all time: and do you, Furies, call on testimonies and evidences, the depositions on oath for forwarding the cause of justice. When I have selected the best-born of my citizens I will return, that they may decide this cause according to its real merits, having pledged themselves on oath to give no unfair decision.

(*Exit.*)

CHORUS: *Now there will be a revolution that brings in new laws: if the wrongful cause of this matricide is to prevail, then the deed will henceforth reconcile all mortals to an indifference for sin. And many cases of death, no mere fictions, inflicted by children on parents are in store for ages yet to come. For, as no wrath against these deeds is now to proceed from the weird sisters who watch the actions of man, I shall give free scope to every kind of death. And one shall hear from another, while he is predicting the misfortunes of his neighbor, that he is himself obtaining and harboring in his house the like evils; and the unhappy man speaks in vain of remedies that are no longer to be relied on. And let no one invoke our aid, when smitten by calamity, uttering words of this kind, "O Justice," "O thrones of the Furies." In this strain perhaps a father or a mother who has recently suffered may lament, because the temple of Justice is being overthrown. There are cases where it is right that awe should remain enthroned, keeping a salutary watch even over men's minds. It is expedient that they should be taught discretion by suffering. For who, if he kept no feeling of awe in gaiety of heart—whether city or individual—would equally continue to respect justice? Approve neither of a life that is free from all control, nor of one under the thrall of a despot: the god gives the superiority to the middle course in everything; but other things he regards differently. And I tell you a saying that agrees with this: of impiety bold daring is the offspring in very truth; but from soberness of mind comes that prosperity that is dear to and prayed for by all. And under all circumstances I give you these maxims: Respect the altar of Justice; do not, at sight of gain, spurn and trample on it with godless foot; for punishment will surely follow it. The rightful end is in store for all. Wherefore let people duly put in the first place of honor the respect due to parents, and have regard to a guest-honoring hospitality in their homes. A man who is just without con-*

straint will not be unprosperous: completely ruined he will never be. But I say that the transgressor who dares in defiance of these laws, and who acts in most things with random recklessness apart from justice, will in time haul down by force his mainsail, when trouble has overtaken him, and his yard-arm is breaking. And then he calls upon powers who hear him not, and struggles desperately for his life in the midst of the eddy. But the god laughs at the rash man, when he sees him powerless from helpless perplexities, unable even to weather the point, though he was so sure that he should never come to this: and so, having dashed against the sunken reef of justice all his former prosperity, he vanishes forever from sight, and perishes unlamented.

(*Enter* ATHENA *and* APOLLO.)

ATHENA: Make proclamation, herald, and keep back the people; and let the heaven-piercing Tyrrhenian trumpet, filled with human breath, sound forth to the host its loudest tones. For while this my council is assembling, it is to the interest of the people to keep silence, and that my institutions for all time be explained to the whole city, and especially to the culprit here, that the suit may be rightly decided against the guilty party.

CHORUS: King Apollo, be master of what belongs to yourself. What have *you* to do with this cause? Tell me.

APOLLO: Both to bear witness I come—for this man is a suppliant at my temple and a refugee at my altar, and it was I who purified him from the guilt of blood—and to be his advocate in person. I am thus responsible for the murder of this man's mother. But do you now open the case, whoever intends to lend his name to the present action.

ATHENA: It is for you, Furies, to specify the charge; for I open the suit. The pursuer, speaking first and describing the case from the beginning, will become rightly our instructor in the matter.

CHORUS: We are many in number, but we will speak concisely. Do you reply by giving line for line in your turn. And first say whether you slew your mother.

ORESTES: I did slay her: of that there is no denial.

CHORUS: This already is one of the three points of contention.

ORESTES: You make this boast over one who is not yet finally thrown.

CHORUS: But you must further say *how* you killed her.

ORESTES: I tell you: it was by stabbing her near the neck with a drawn sword in my hand.

CHORUS: But by whom were you persuaded, and by whose counsels did you do the deed?

ORESTES: By the oracles of Apollo here; and he is my witness.

CHORUS: What! One who is a seer gave you instructions to kill a mother?

ORESTES: Yes, and up to this time I have no reason to complain of my lot.

CHORUS: But if the vote shall convict you, you will soon speak differently.

ORESTES: I have faith, and my father will send me aid from the tomb.

CHORUS: That's right—trust to the dead, after killing your mother.

ORESTES: For she united in herself two crimes.

CHORUS: How was that? Inform the judges on that point.

ORESTES: In killing her husband she also killed my father.

CHORUS: Then the case stands thus: you live, but she has atoned for her crime by being slain.

ORESTES: Then why did you not chase her in flight while she was alive?

CHORUS: Because she was no blood-relation of the man whom she slew.

ORESTES: Do you call *me* related by blood to my mother?

CHORUS: Why, in what other way did she nurse you, you miscreant, within her girdle? Do you disown the dearest blood of a mother?

ORESTES: At this point put in *your* evidence, and explain for me, Apollo, whether I slew her with justice. For that I did the deed, as it has been done, I do not deny. But whether this murder seems to your mind to have been justly or unjustly executed, decide, that I may put the matter clearly before the judges.

APOLLO: I will address myself to you, the great institute of Athena here present, in the spirit of truth, and being a seer I will not deal in falsehoods. I never yet spoke on my prophetic seat, concerning any man, woman, or city, anything but what Zeus the father of the Olympian gods had ordered me. What weight this plea has, I bid you consider, and to fall in with the counsels of my father. For surely an oath has not more authority than Zeus.

CHORUS: Zeus, as *you* assert, gave you this oracle to deliver to Orestes here, that he must avenge his father's murder and set at nought the honor due to his mother.

APOLLO: For it is by no means the same thing, that a man of noble birth should die—one exalted by royalty conferred on him from Zeus—and that too by the hands of a woman, not by the far-darting war-bow, like that of an Amazon, but as you shall hear, Pallas, and you, judges, who have taken your seats to decide about this cause. For, after receiving him with kindly words of praise on his return from the army where he had made more gains than losses, she extended a garment like a canopy along the side of the laver, as he was going through the bath, even to the very foot of it, and struck down her husband entangled in an endless embroidered robe. Of a husband, I say, the fate was such as I have described to you—but it was also the fate of one who was held in awe by all, and the admiral of the fleet. And such I have shown her to be, that the people may be stung with indignation, who have been commissioned to decide with authority this cause.

CHORUS: Zeus holds in especial regard the fate of a father, according to your account; yet he himself imprisoned his aged father Cronus. Is not that which you say contradictory to this? And I call on you judges to take notice of his answer.

APOLLO: Why, you creatures universally detested, and abhorred even by the gods, fetters might be unloosed by Zeus; there is a remedy for that, and ample means of getting free from them; but when the dust has drunk up the blood of a man, there is no recalling to life one who is once dead. For *that* my father has not made any charm; but all other things he appoints now in this way now in that, by no certain rule, without exhausting himself by the effort.

CHORUS: Well, beware how you advocate this man's cause to procure an acquittal. After shedding on the ground the blood of a mother, from whence he derived his own, shall he still inhabit his father's house in Argos? What altars shall he use to which the public have access? What lustral-water of clansmen will admit him to sacrifice?

APOLLO: This point also I will explain; and take notice how

rightly I will expound it. The bearer of the so-called off-spring is not the mother of it, but only the nurse of the newly-conceived fetus. It is the male who is the author of its being; while she, as a stranger for a stranger, preserves the young plant for those for whom the god has not blighted it in the bud. And I will show you a proof of this assertion: one *may* become a father without a mother: there stands by a witness of this in the daughter of Olympian Zeus, who was not even nursed in the darkness of the womb, but is so fair a bud that no god could be her natural parent. But I, Pallas, in other respects, as I well know how, will make your city and your people great; indeed, I sent this man to the altar of your temple, that he might become a faithful friend to all time, and that you might gain him as a new ally, and those destined to succeed him; and that it might remain a law forever, that the posterity of this people should adhere to these treaties.

ATHENA: I now bid the court to give an impartial vote according to the best of their judgment, enough having been said.

CHORUS: *We* indeed have by this time discharged all our arrows; and I only wait to hear how the trial will be decided.

ATHENA: Well, how shall I settle the matter so as to incur no blame from you? (*To* JURY.) You have heard what you have heard; and when you give in your votes, strangers, respect your oath in your hearts.

Hear now my institution, ye Attic people, on holding this first trial for bloodshed. And for future time also this court of dicasts shall ever remain in force for the people of Aegeus. But this hill of Ares, once the seat and camping-ground of the Amazons, when they came through jealousy of Theseus on a hostile expedition, and fortified to a towering height, as a counterwork to the Acropolis on that special occasion, this newly-built part of the city—when they sacrificed to Ares, from which event the rock and hill of Ares derived their present name—in this hill, I repeat, a court held in respect by the citizens, and fear allied with awe shall restrain them from injustice both by day and by night, so long as the citizens themselves make no innovations in the laws. If you sully clear water by foul sewage and mud, you will never procure drink. The mean between anarchy and despotism I advise my citizens to embrace and hold in their regard, and not to cast all restraint of fear out of the city. For what mortal man, if he has nothing to fear, acts with honesty? Be assured that, if you hold in proper respect such an object of your awe, you will find in it both a bulwark of the land and a safeguard of the city, such as no human beings possess either among the Scythians or in the region of the Peloponnesus. Thus then do I appoint this court, untouched by bribes, inspiring awe, keen and prompt in vengeance, for a wakeful guardian of this land in behalf of those who are asleep. Such is the exhortation for their future conduct that I have given at length to my citizens. 'Tis for you now to rise, and each take his ballot and decide the cause with due reverence for your oaths. And now I have done.

(*The* JURORS *come forward to cast their ballots.*)

CHORUS: But my advice to you is, by no means to slight this our sisterhood, who can manifest their anger against the land.

APOLLO: Yes, and *I* bid you to fear oracles which are not only from me, but from Zeus, and not to make them fruitless.

CHORUS: But you are showing regard for a cause of blood, though that is not your prerogative, and the responses you give, while you continue on the prophetic seat, will no longer be pure and undefiled.

APOLLO: Was my father too at all mistaken in his counsels in the matter of Ixion, the first applicant for purification from murder?

CHORUS: You talk: but I, if I fail to obtain justice, will visit this land hereafter with my heavy wrath.

APOLLO: But among the young and the older gods alike *you* are scouted: *I* shall prevail in the cause.

CHORUS: That is what you did in the house of Pheres: you persuaded the fates to make mortals immortal.

APOLLO: And was it not right for me to benefit one who reverenced me, especially when he happened to want it?

CHORUS: *You* know that you did away with the old appointments, and cheated the ancient goddesses with wine.

APOLLO: And *you*, let me tell you, when you have failed to get a verdict in this cause, shall spit your poison that will be harmless to your enemies.

CHORUS: Since you, a young god, are overriding me an ancient goddess, I only wait to hear the issue of this trial, as having half a mind to be angry with the city.

ATHENA: 'Tis my part now to decide the suit by the remaining vote: and I shall give this ballot to Orestes; for there is no mother who gave me birth, and I approve of the male side—except that I do not marry—in all respects with my whole heart, and am entirely in favor of the father's cause. Thus I shall not pay undue regard to the death of a wife who slew her husband, the manager of her house; but Orestes wins the cause, even though he should have equal votes in the trial. Turn out immediately the ballots from the urns, you judges to whom that office has been enjoined.

ORESTES: O Phoebus Apollo, how will the trial be decided?

CHORUS: O sable mother Night, see you these things?

ORESTES: Now the matter will end for me either in a noose, or in my continuing to live.

CHORUS: Yes, and it will end for *us* in coming to naught, or exercising our prerogatives still further.

APOLLO: Count out correctly the ballots turned out from the urns, strangers, with due regard to fairness in the division. For, as serious harm results from the absence of a vote, so a single voter by giving his ballot sets up a household.

ATHENA: This man is acquitted in the action for murder; for the counting-up of the votes is equal.

ORESTES: O Pallas! O savior of my house! You, even you, when I was deprived of my paternal land, have reinstated me, and every man in Hellas will now say, "The noble fellow is an Argive once more, and lives on his hereditary wealth by favor of Pallas and Loxias, and that mighty consummator of all things, the saving Third, who, in compassion for the death of a father, is his preserver, on seeing that these Furies were advocates of his mother." And now I shall depart for my home, after pledging a solemn compact with this land and with your people, to last for the uttermost end of time, that no sovereign ruler of the Argive land shall ever invade this country, or bring against it a well-marshaled host; for we ourselves, being then in the tomb, will contrive for all who may transgress these present treaties, by perplexing disasters, and by making their expedition hopeless and their route discouraged by bad omens, that they shall repent of their trouble. But, if the treaties be uprightly observed, and if they honor the city

of Pallas in all times by their allied spear, we will be to the
citizens themselves more propitious. And now farewell, both
you and the people who protect your acropolis: may you
retain the art of fighting that allows your enemies no escape, bringing safety to you and victory in the contest.

(*Exeunt* APOLLO *and* ORESTES.)

CHORUS: *Ye younger gods, ye have overridden the old laws,
and have taken him out of my hands. But I, dishonored
(unhappy that I am), who show my heavy wrath by letting fall from my heart a poison on this land, a poison in
return for what I have suffered, a drop causing sterility to
the soil—for from it a blight destroying the leaves, killing
the young offspring (O revenge!), falling on the ground,
will cast throughout the country stains destructive of human life—what, I ask, must I do? Should I become a
grievous scourge to the citizens for what I have suffered?
For oh! terrible it is, ye unhappy daughters of Night,
who have to bewail your lot unhonored.*

ATHENA: Be persuaded by me not to bear your fate with
impatient grief; for you have not been beaten in the contest, but the trial came off with equal votes in all fairness,
and not to your discredit. The case was this—a clear testimony from Zeus was given in favor of Orestes: and the
god himself who urged him to the deed gave also evidence in person, so that Orestes, by taking this course,
suffers no harm. But do you not visit this country with
the weight of your anger, by discharging venom-drops
from your hearts, unkindly influences consuming the seed.
For I engage in good faith for you, that you shall occupy
seats in the cavernous recesses of a land made just by
your presence, seated at altars that shall be your glittering
thrones, and held in honor by the citizens of this land.

CHORUS: *Ye younger gods, ye have overridden the old
laws, and have taken him out of my hands. But I, dishonored (unhappy that I am), who show my heavy wrath
by letting fall from my heart a poison on this land, yea a
return for what I have suffered, a drop causing sterility to
the soil—for from it a blight destroying the leaves, killing
the young offspring (O revenge!), falling on the ground,
will cast throughout the country stains destructive of human life—what, I ask, must I do? Should I become a
grievous scourge to the citizens for what I have suffered?*

For oh! terrible it is, ye unhappy daughters of Night, who have to bewail your lot unhonored.

ATHENA: Ye are *not* dishonored: and do not in the excess of your anger, goddesses that ye are, make the land of mortal men unkindly to them. I too have trust in Zeus—but I need not speak about that—and I am the only one of the gods who knows the keys of the storehouses wherein the thunderbolt is sealed up. But we need it not; and so do you, in ready obedience to my request, cast not over the land the fruit of a rash curse, causing everything to do badly. Lull the angry force of the dark wave, as being held in solemn honor and an indweller of the land in common with myself. The time shall come when, enjoying the firstfruits of this great land, as offerings for offspring and for the marriage-rite, you shall find reason to praise forever these my terms.

CHORUS: *That I should be treated thus, alas! I of the ancient views, and should have an abode in the land, forsooth, unhonored and detested! Thereat I breathe out my fury and my full resentment. O Earth, woe is me! What pang is this that enters my side? Hear the cause of my wrath, mother Night! Dispossessed of my ancient honors, the baffling wiles of these gods have made me of no account.*

ATHENA: I will bear with your tempers, for you are older than myself: and in that respect indeed you are doubtless wiser than I; yet to me also Zeus hath granted to be not destitute of sense. But you, if you go off to the land of some other tribe, will some day be enamored of mine: I forewarn you of this. For the time that is coming on will bring greater honor to these citizens: and you, possessing an honored abode by the temple of Erectheus, shall receive from men and from companies of women privileges more numerous than you are ever likely to have from other mortals. But do not you throw upon my territories incitements to blood, the bane of young hearts, impassioned by fits of rage not caused by wine; nor, as if you had taken out the hearts of fighting-cocks, set to dwell among my citizens a demon of war, waged between citizens and marked by mutual cruelty. Let war be far away from my confines, coming with no stinted measure to him who may be possessed by a strong passion for glory—however, I say no more about the fighting of the domestic bird. Such then are the privileges you may receive from me; doing well, you shall be treated well, honored well, and have a stake in this land which is most favored by heaven.

CHORUS: *That I should be treated thus, alas! I of the ancient views, and should have an abode in the land, forsooth, unhonored and detested! Thereat I breathe out my fury and my full resentment. Oh Earth, woe is me! What pang is this that enters my side? Hear the cause of my wrath, mother Night! Dispossessed of my ancient honors, the baffling wiles of these gods have made me of no account.*

ATHENA: Be assured I shall not weary of telling you the good you will get; that you may never say that you, an elder goddess, have been made a dishonored outcast by me who am younger, and by the people my citizens, and have been banished from this land. But if you hold in devout reverence the power of Persuasion, and if the honeyed eloquence of my tongue can calm your wrath, then by all means stay: but if you choose not to remain, certainly you would not in fairness make to bear heavily on this city any lasting anger or resentment or harm to the people. For it is in your power to be a landowner in this country on fair terms, with full honors.

CHORUS: And what settlement, queen Athena, do you say that I shall have?

ATHENA: One unharmed by a single grief; and do you accept it.

CHORUS: Suppose that I do accept it; what special prerogative is in store for me?

ATHENA: That no family may thrive without your favor.

CHORUS: Will *you* effect this, that I shall have so much power?

ATHENA: Yes; for we shall direct aright the fortunes of him who reveres you.

CHORUS: And will you give me a warrant for all future time?

ATHENA: Yes; for I am not bound to promise what I shall not perform.

CHORUS: It seems that I must yield to your entreaties; and I desist from my anger.

ATHENA. Then you shall stay in this land and win for yourself new friends.

CHORUS: What then do you desire me to chant in favor of this land?

ATHENA: Such prayers as are directed to a victory that brings no disaster . . . and that too from the earth and from the dews of ocean, and from the sky; and that the breezes of the winds may shed their serene airs as they go over the land. That the produce of the earth and the flocks in teeming plenty may not fail to abound for the citizens for all time; and that there may be a safe rearing of human progeny. But the impious may you be more disposed to root out of the city: for I feel an affection—even as a gardener for his plants—for the family of this just people, spared from mourning. Such are the terms offered you: and I for my part will not rest content without giving honor among men to this city, renowned for national victories in the glorious contests of war.

CHORUS: *I will accept the offer of living with Pallas, and will not reject the worship of a city which even Zeus the all-powerful and Ares rule as the stronghold of the gods, the pride of the Hellenic divinities and the protector of their altars. For her I now pray, no longer with wrathful bodings, that the bright beams of the sun may send up from the earth in boundless profusion the blessings that give enjoyment to life.*

ATHENA: *This care I undertake in kindly regard for my citizens, in establishing among them the powerful and hardly-appeased deities; for it is their appointed office to direct all that happens among men; and he who has not met with adverse fortune knows not from what source the scourges of life suddenly fall upon him. For the sins of his ancestors bring him into the power of the Furies, a silent destruction, and in the midst of his high boastings level him even with the dust through their anger and hatred.*

CHORUS: *But may no evil airs blow causing blight to the trees—I speak of my own kindly interference—nor the blast that robs the plants of their young buds, so that they extend not beyond their allotted space: let no dark disease come upon them to destroy the fruit, but may the earth supply food to the sheep thriving with double progeny at the appointed season of the year: and may the wealth produced from the womb of the earth ever pay returns for the lucky gift of the gods.*

ATHENA: *Hear ye these words, ye guardians of the land, what blessings she is bringing to pass? For great influence have the awful Erinyes both with the gods above and with those beneath the earth; and in their dealings with men it is plain that these bring all things to their end, to some giving songs, to others again a dull life of tears.*

CHORUS: *But I deprecate mishaps causing the untimely deaths of men. Grant that our lovely young maidens may have wedded lives, ye gods who have power over marriage, and ye Fates, our sisters by the mother's side, goddesses that direct aright the law, common to every family, at every time exercising due weight in their dealings with men, everywhere the most honored of the gods.*

ATHENA: *I am cheered by your solemnly ratifying these privileges in friendly spirit to my country; and I am grateful to the meek-eyed Persuasion for guiding aright my words and my eloquence in addressing these goddesses when they rudely refused. But Zeus the god of harangues hath prevailed, and our contest on the side of good for all time is crowned with success.*

CHORUS: *And that insatiable source of evils, Sedition, I pray may never make an uproar in this city; never may the dust drink the dark gore of the citizens, and in anger exact penalties for slaughter, to the bane of the state. And may they exchange kindnesses with sentiments of common interest, and hate with one mind; for unanimity is the remedy for many evils among mortals.*

ATHENA: *Are they not returning to the way of wisdom, and finding out the course of right language? From these formidable faces I perceive a great gain to my citizens here; for if you in kindly disposition greatly honor at all times these goddesses who are kindly disposed to you, you will exercise upright justice both in your land and your city, and be distinguished in whatever course of life you may pursue.*

CHORUS: *Farewell, farewell! May ye be possessed of all the blessings of wealth! Farewell, people of the city, seated near to Zeus, friends of your friend Pallas, becoming wise in time. For those who reside under the wings of his Pallas are revered by her father.*

ATHENA: *Farewell to you also! And now I must precede you to show you your abodes by the sacred light of these escorts. Go, speedily enter your caves below the earth; keep off all that is hurtful from the land, and send us all* that is gainful to the city and leading to victory. And do you, children of Cranaus, guardians of my citadel, show the way to these new residents among you; and may there remain a good feeling in the minds of the citizens for the good things they have received.

CHORUS: *Farewell, once more farewell—I repeat it—all you that reside in this city, whether gods or mortals, ruling the city of Pallas; hold in pious regard my residence among you, and you will not complain of the events of your life.*

ATHENA: I assent to the terms of these prayers, and I will escort you with the light of flashing torches to the cavernous recesses below the earth, with female attendants, and those who honestly guard my sacred image. For the best-born of all the land of Theseus shall come, a goodly company of girls and married women, and a train of ancient matrons in scarlet-dyed holiday vestments. Forward! let the light of torches also proceed, in order that these friendly dwellers in the land may become noted hereafter for the prosperous fortunes of the male inhabitants.

ESCORTS: *Enter now your abodes, ye powerful goddesses, jealous of your honors, childless children of Night, under this friendly escort—and do you raise songs of joy, ye people of the place—beneath the dark recesses of the earth, attended with the honors and sacrifices of fire-worship. Raise the song of joy, ye people of the place. And now proceed, propitiated and rightly-minded toward our country, this way, awful goddesses, rejoicing in being attended on your road with the fire-feeding torch. Shout, women, after our song. And let libations be made as you go, in the rear of the procession, to the light of blazing pine-wood. Thus hath Zeus the all-seeing and Fate together entered the lists in behalf of the citizens of Pallas. Shout, women, after our song.*

2

SOPHOCLES

Antigone

OEDIPUS' SONS Eteocles and
Polyneices had arranged to rule Thebes by turn, and when
Eteocles refused to yield Polyneices his turn, Polyneices, with
support from Argos, marched against his own city. Both brothers were killed in the battle, and the regent Creon ordained
that while Eteocles should receive honorable burial, Polyneices' body should be cast out unburied. *Antigone* tells how
Polyneices' sister contravened this order and suffered martyr-
dom in consequence. It is tempting to praise Antigone as a
saint and condemn Creon as a tyrant, but it must be noticed
that Antigone is not wholly right nor Creon wholly wrong.
How could a conscientious ruler honor the state's enemy,
and how could a girl disobey an authoritative order? Antigone is possessed, as the contrast with the normal Ismene
makes plain. We sympathize when she gives her brother
token burial by strewing dust on the corpse; but piety required no more, and her repetition of the merely ritual form
makes her sanity questionable. The great chorus which begins "Wonders are many, and none is more wonderful
than man" concludes by insisting that for all man's in-
genuity he must not ignore the laws of the state. Creon does
bluster, to cover his weakness, but his afflictions are almost
greater than Antigone's. He shows his devotion to duty, after
Teiresias' admonition, by *first* giving Polyneices proper burial
and *then* going to free Antigone. But the tragedy is properly
named for Antigone rather than Creon. Only a self-impelled

hero can extend the horizons of what is possible for man; for the rest of us, who must follow the discreetness of the chorus and the lesser characters, the spectacle of a young girl giving up life and love for the sake of an ideal must remain permanently edifying.

CHARACTERS

ANTIGONE $\Big\}$ *daughters of Oedipus*
ISMENE

CREON, *King of Thebes*

EURYDICE, *his wife*

HAEMON, *his son*

TEIRESIAS, *blind prophet*

GUARD

MESSENGERS

CHORUS OF THEBAN ELDERS

SCENE: Before the palace at Thebes

Translated by R. C. JEBB

(Enter ANTIGONE, *who motions* ISMENE *from palace.)*

ANTIGONE: Sister Ismene, my own dear sister, do you know
of any ill, of all those bequeathed by Oedipus, that Zeus
does not fulfill for us two while we live? There is nothing
painful, nothing fraught with ruin, no shame, no dishonor,
that I have not seen in your woes and mine.

And now what of this new edict of which men speak
that our Captain has just published to all Thebes? Have
you any knowledge of it? Have you heard? Or is it hidden
from you that our friends are threatened with the doom of
our foes?

ISMENE: No word of friends, Antigone, cheerful or painful
has come to me since we two sisters were bereft of our two
brothers, killed in one day by a twofold blow. Since the
Argive host fled, this past night, I know nothing more,
whether my fortune is brighter or more grievous.

ANTIGONE: I knew it well; that is why I sought to bring you
beyond the gates of the court, so that you could hear alone.

ISMENE: What is it? It is plain that you are brooding on
some dark tidings.

ANTIGONE: What? Has not Creon destined our brothers, the
one to honored burial, the other to unburied shame?
Eteocles, they say, with due observance of right and custom he has laid in the earth, for his honor among the
dead below. But the luckless corpse of Polyneices—accord-

ing to rumor it has been published to the town that none shall entomb him or mourn but leave him unwept, unsepulchered, a welcome object for the birds, when they spy him, to feast on at will.

Such, it is said, is the edict that the good Creon has set forth for you and for me—yes, for *me;* and he is coming here to proclaim it to those who do not know it. He does not count the matter light, but whoso disobeys in any way, his doom is death by stoning before all the people. You know now, and will soon show whether you are nobly bred or the base daughter of a noble line.

ISMENE: Poor sister—and if this is how things stand, what could I help to do or undo?

ANTIGONE: Consider whether you will share the toil and the deed.

ISMENE: In what venture? What can your meaning be?

ANTIGONE: Will you aid this hand of mine to lift the dead?

ISMENE: You would bury him when it is forbidden to Thebes?

ANTIGONE: I will do my part—and yours, if you will not—to a brother. False to him I will never be found.

ISMENE: Ah, overbold! When Creon has forbidden?

ANTIGONE: Nay, he has no right to keep me from my own.

ISMENE: Ah me! think, sister, how our father perished, amid hate and scorn, when sins bared by his own search had moved him to strike both eyes with self-blinding hand; then the mother and wife, two names in one, with twisted noose destroyed her own life; and last, our two brothers in one day—each shedding, luckless man, a kinsman's blood —wrought out with mutual hands their common doom. And now *we* in turn—we two left all alone—think how we shall perish, more miserably than all the rest if, in defiance of the law, we brave a king's decree or his powers. Nay, we must remember, first, that we were born women, who should not strive with men; next that we are ruled of the stronger, so that we must obey in these things, and in things still harder. Seeing that force is put upon me, therefore, I will ask the Spirits Infernal to pardon and will hearken to our ruler. It is foolish to meddle.

ANTIGONE: I will not urge you—no, even if you should yet have the mind would you be welcome as a worker with *me.* Be what you will, I will bury him; well for me to die

in doing so. I shall rest, a loved one with him whom I
have loved, sinless in my crime; for I owe a longer allegiance
to the dead than to the living, for in that world I shall
abide forever. If *you* will, be guilty of dishonoring laws
which the gods have established in honor.

ISMENE: I do them no dishonor. But to defy the State—I
have no strength for that.

ANTIGONE: So plead then; I will go to heap the earth above
the brother whom I love.

ISMENE: Unhappy you! How I fear for you!

ANTIGONE: Do not fear for me; guide your own fate aright.

ISMENE: At least, then, disclose this plan to none but hide it
closely—and so, too, will I.

ANTIGONE: Oh, denounce it! You will be far more hateful for
your silence if you do not proclaim these things to all.

ISMENE: You have a hot heart for chilling deeds.

ANTIGONE: I know that I please where I am most bound to
please.

ISMENE: Well enough if you can; but you would do what
you cannot.

ANTIGONE: Why then, when my strength fails I shall have
done.

ISMENE: A hopeless quest should not be made at all.

ANTIGONE: If this is how you speak you will have hatred
from me and will justly be subject to the lasting hatred of
the dead. But leave me, and the folly that is mine alone,
to suffer this dread thing; for I shall suffer nothing so dreadful as an ignoble death.

ISMENE: Go, then, if you must; and of this be sure: though
your errand is foolish to your dear ones you are truly dear.

(Exeunt.)

(*Enter* CHORUS.)

CHORUS: *Beam of the sun, fairest light that ever dawned on
Thebes of the seven gates, thou hast shone forth at last,
eye of golden day, arisen above Dirce's streams! The war-
rior of the white shield, who came from Argos in his
panoply, hath been stirred by thee to headlong flight, in
swifter career; who set forth against our land by reason of
the vexed claims of Polyneices; and, like a shrill-screaming
eagle, he flew over into our land, in snow-white pinion
sheathed, with an armed throng, and with plumage of
helms.*

He paused above our dwellings; he ravened around our

sevenfold portals with spears athirst for blood; but he went hence, or ever his jaws were glutted with our gore, or the Fire-god's pine-fed flame had seized our crown of towers. So fierce was the noise of battle raised behind him, a thing too hard for him to conquer, as he wrestled with his dragon foe.

For Zeus utterly abhors the boasts of a proud tongue; and when he beheld them coming on in a great stream, in the haughty pride of clanging gold, he smote with brandished fire one who was now hasting to shout victory at his goal upon our ramparts.

Swung down, he fell on the earth with a crash, torch in hand, he who so lately, in the frenzy of the mad onset, was raging against us with the blasts of his tempestuous hate. But those threats fared not as he hoped; and to other foes the mighty War-god dispensed their several dooms, dealing havoc around, a mighty helper at our need.

For seven captains at seven gates matched against seven, left the tribute of their panoplies to Zeus who turns the battle; save those two of cruel fate, who, born of one sire and one mother, set against each other their twain conquering spears, and are sharers in a common death.

But since Victory of glorious name hath come to us, with joy responsive to the joy of Thebes whose chariots are many, let us enjoy forgetfulness after the late wars, and visit all the temples of the gods with night-long dance and song; and may Bacchus be our leader, whose dancing shakes the land of Thebes.

But lo, the king of the land comes yonder, Creon, son of Menoeceus, our new ruler by the new fortunes that the gods have given; what counsel is he pondering, that he hath proposed this special conference of elders, summoned by his general mandate?

(*Enter* CREON.)

CREON: Sirs, the vessel of our State, after being tossed on wild waves, has once more been safely steadied by the gods; and you, out of all the folk, have been called apart by my summons, because I knew, first of all, how true and constant was your reverence for the royal power of Laius; how, again, when Oedipus was ruler of our land, and when he had perished, your steadfast loyalty still upheld their children. Since, then, his sons have fallen in one day by a twofold doom—each smitten by the other, each stained with a brother's blood—I now possess the throne and all its powers, by nearness of kinship to the dead.

No man can be fully known, in soul and spirit and mind, until he has been seen versed in rule and lawgiving. For if any, being supreme guide of the State, cleaves not to the best counsels, but, through some fear, keeps his lips locked, I hold, and have ever held, him most base; and if any makes a friend of more account than his fatherland, that man has no place in my regard. For I—be Zeus my witness, who sees all things always—would not be silent if I saw ruin, instead of safety, coming to the citizens; nor would I ever deem the country's foes a friend to myself; remembering this, that our country is the ship that bears us safe, and that only while she prospers in our voyage can we make true friends.

Such are the rules by which I guard this city's greatness. And in accord with them is the edict which I have now published to the folk touching the sons of Oedipus; that Eteocles, who has fallen fighting for our city, in all renown of arms shall be entombed and crowned with every rite that follows the noblest dead to their rest. But for his brother Polyneices, who came back from exile and sought to consume utterly with fire the city of his fathers and the shrines of his fathers' gods, sought to taste of kindred blood and to lead the remnant into slavery—touching this man it has been proclaimed to our people that none shall grace him with sepulture or lament, but leave him unburied, a corpse for birds and dogs to eat, a ghastly sight of shame.

Such the spirit of my dealing; and never, by deed of mine, shall the wicked stand in honor before the just; but whoso has good will to Thebes, he shall be honored of me, in his life and in his death.

CHORUS: Such is your pleasure, Creon son of Menoeceus, touching this city's foe and its friends; and you have power, I know, to enjoin what you will, both for the dead and for all us who live.

CREON: See to it, then, that you be guardians of the mandate.

CHORUS: Lay the burden of this task on some younger man.

CREON: Nay, watchers of the corpse have been found.

CHORUS: What then is this further charge that you would give?

CREON: That you do not side with the breakers of these commands.

CHORUS: No man is so foolish that he is enamored of death.

CREON: That is indeed the penalty; but lucre has often ruined men through their hopes.

(*Enter* GUARD.)

GUARD: My liege, I will not say that I come breathless from speed or that I have plied a nimble foot; for often did my thoughts make me pause and wheel round in my path to return. My mind was holding large discourse with me: "Fool, why are you going on to your certain doom?" "Wretch, tarrying again? And if Creon hears this from another, must you not smart for it?" So debating I went on my way with lagging steps, and thus a short road was made long. At last, however, it carried the day that I should come here to you; and though my tale is nothing yet I will tell it. I come with a good grip on one hope—that I can suffer nothing but what is my fate.

CREON: What is it that disquiets you so?

GUARD: I wish to tell you first about myself—I did not do the deed; I did not see the doer; it is not right that I should come to any harm.

CREON: You have a shrewd eye for your mark; you fence yourself round against blame very well. Clearly, you have some strange thing to tell.

GUARD: Yes, truly. Dread news makes a man pause long.

CREON: Then tell it, will you, and get gone.

GUARD: Well, this is it. The corpse—someone has just given it burial, and gone away, after sprinkling thirsty dust on the flesh, with such other rites as piety enjoins.

CREON: What are you saying? What man alive has dared this deed?

GUARD: I do not know. No stroke of pickax was seen there, no earth thrown up by mattock; the ground was hard and dry, unbroken, without track of wheels. The doer was one who left no trace. And when the first day-watchman showed it to us, troubled wonder fell upon us all. The dead man was veiled from us; not shut within a tomb, but lightly strewn with dust, as by the hand of one who shunned a curse. And no sign met the eye as though any beast of prey or any dog had come nigh to him or torn him.

Then evil words flew fast and loud among us, guard accusing guard; it would even have come to blows at last, nor was there any to hinder. Every man was the culprit and no one was convicted, but all disclaimed knowledge of the deed. And we were ready to take red-hot iron in our hands, to walk through fire, to make oath by the gods that we had not done the deed, that we were not privy to the planning or the doing.

At last, when all our searching was fruitless, a man spoke and made us all bend our faces on the earth in fear, for we did not see how we could gainsay him, or escape mischance if we obeyed. His counsel was that the deed must be reported to you and not hidden. This seemed best, and the lot doomed unlucky me to win this prize. So here I stand, as unwelcome as unwilling, I know well; for no man delights in the bearer of bad news.

CHORUS: O King, my thoughts have long been whispering: might this deed perhaps be the work of gods?

CREON: Cease before your words fill me utterly with wrath, lest you be found at once an old man and foolish. You say what is not to be borne when you say that the gods have care for this corpse. Was it for high reward of trusty service that they sought to hide the nakedness of a man who came to burn their pillared shrines and sacred treasures, to burn their land and scatter its laws to the winds? Or do you behold the gods honoring the wicked? It cannot be. No! From the first there were certain in the town that muttered against me, chafing at this edict, wagging their heads in secret; they did not keep their necks duly under the yoke, like men contented with my sway.

It is by them, well I know, that these have been beguiled and bribed to do this deed. Nothing so evil as money ever grew to be current among men. This lays cities low, this drives men from their homes, this trains and warps honest souls till they set themselves to works of shame; this still teaches folk to practice villainies and to know every godless deed.

But all the men who wrought this thing for hire have made it sure that, soon or late, they shall pay the price. Now as Zeus still has my reverence, know this—I tell it to you on my oath: If you do not find the very author of this burial and produce him before my eyes, death alone

shall not be enough for you till first, hung up alive, you
have revealed this outrage, so that henceforth you may
thieve with better knowledge whence lucre should be won
and learn that it is not well to love gain from every source.
You will find that ill-gotten pelf brings more men to ruin
than to prosperity.

GUARD: May I speak? Or shall I just turn and go?

CREON: Do you not know that even now your voice offends?

GUARD: Is your smart in the ears or in the soul?

CREON: And why would you define the seat of my pain?

GUARD: The doer vexes your mind, I your ears.

CREON: Ah, you are a born babbler, it's easy to see.

GUARD: Maybe, but never the doer of this deed.

CREON: More too, the seller of your life for silver.

GUARD: Alas, it's truly sad that he who judges should mis-
judge.

CREON: Let your fancy play with "judgment" as it will; but
if you do not show me the doers of these things you shall
avow that dastardly gains work sorrows.

GUARD: Well, may he be found! that would be best. But
whether he is caught or not—fortune must settle that—
you will surely not see me here again. Saved even now
beyond hope and thought, I owe the gods great thanks.

(Exeunt.)

CHORUS: *Wonders are many, and none is more wonderful
than man; the power that crosses the white sea, driven by
the stormy south-wind, making a path under surges that
threaten to engulf him; and Earth, the eldest of the gods,
the immortal, the unwearied, doth he wear, turning the
soil with the offspring of horses, as the plows go to and
fro from year to year.*

*And the lighthearted race of birds, and the tribes of
savage beasts, and the sea-brood of the deep, he snares in
the meshes of his woven toils, he leads captive, man excellent in wit. And he masters by his arts the beast whose
lair is in the wilds, who roams the hills; he tames the
horse of shaggy mane, he puts the yoke upon its neck, he
tames the tireless mountain bull.*

*And speech, and wind-swift thought, and all the moods
that mold a state, hath he taught himself; and how to
flee the arrows of the frost, when 'tis hard lodging under
the clear sky, and the arrows of the rushing rain; yea,
he hath resource for all; without resource he meets noth-*

*ing that must come: only against Death shall he call for
aid in vain; but from baffling maladies he hath devised
escapes.*

*Cunning beyond fancy's dream is the fertile skill which
brings him, now to evil, now to good. When he honors
the laws of the land, and that justice which he hath sworn
by the gods to uphold, proudly stands his city: no city
hath he who, for his rashness, dwells with sin. Never may
he share my hearth, never think my thoughts, who doth
these things!*

(*Enter* GUARD *leading* ANTIGONE.)

*What portent from the gods is this? My soul is amazed.
I know her—how can I deny that yonder maiden is Antigone?*

*O luckless, and child of luckless sire—of Oedipus! What
does this mean? Thou brought a prisoner?—thou, disloyal
to the king's laws, and taken in folly?*

GUARD: Here she is, the doer of the deed—we caught this
girl burying him—but where is Creon?

CHORUS: Look, he comes forth again from the house, at our
need.

(*Enter* CREON.)

CREON: What is it? What has happened that makes my coming timely?

GUARD: O King, against nothing should men pledge their
word; for the afterthought belies the first intent. I could
have vowed that I should not soon be here again, scared by
your threats with which I had just been lashed; but—since
the joy that surprises and transcends our hopes is like in
fullness to no other pleasure—I have come, though in
breach of my sworn oath, bringing this maid, who was
taken showing grace to the dead. This time there was no
casting of lots; no, this luck has fallen to me, and to none
else. And now, sire, take her yourself, question her, examine
her, as you will; but I have a right to free and final
quittance of this trouble.

CREON: And your prisoner here—how and where have you
taken her?

GUARD: She was burying the man; you know all.

CREON: Do you mean what you are saying? Do you speak
aright?

GUARD: I saw her burying the corpse that you had forbidden to bury. Is that plain and clear?

CREON: And how was she seen? How taken in the act?

GUARD: This is how it was. When we had come to the place, with those dread menaces of yours upon us, we swept away all the dust that covered the corpse, and bared the dank body well; and then sat us down on the brow of the hill, to windward, heedful that the smell from him should not strike us; every man was wide awake, and kept his neighbor alert with torrents of threats, if anyone should be careless of this task.

So it went, until the sun's bright orb stood in mid-heaven, and the heat began to burn. Then suddenly a whirlwind lifted from the earth a storm of dust, a trouble in the sky, and filled the plain, marring all the leafage of its woods, and the wide air was choked with it. We closed our eyes, and bore the plague from the gods.

And when, after a long while, this storm had passed, the maid was seen; and she cried aloud with the sharp cry of a bird in its bitterness, even as when within the empty nest it sees the bed stripped of its nestlings. So she also, when she saw the corpse bare, lifted up a voice of wailing, and called down curses on the doers of that deed. And straightway she brought thirsty dust in her hands, and from a shapely ewer of bronze, held high, with thrice-poured drink-offering she crowned the dead.

We rushed forward when we saw it, and at once closed upon our quarry, who was in no way dismayed. Then we taxed her with her past and present doings; and she denied nothing—at once to my joy and to my pain. To have escaped from ills oneself is a great joy; but it is painful to bring friends to ill. Nevertheless, all such things are of less account to me than my own safety.

CREON: You, you whose face is bent to earth, do you avow, or disavow, this deed?

ANTIGONE: I avow it; I make no denial.

CREON (*to* GUARD): You can go wherever you will, free and clear of a grave charge. (*Exit* GUARD.)

(*To* ANTIGONE.) Now, tell me, not in many words but briefly, did you know that an edict had forbidden this?

ANTIGONE: I knew it; could I help it? It was public.

CREON: Did you then dare transgress that law?

ANTIGONE: Yes, for it was not Zeus who had published that edict; not such are the laws set among men by the Justice who dwells with the gods below. Nor did I deem that your decrees were of such force that a mortal could override the unwritten and unfailing statutes of heaven. For their life is not of today or yesterday, but from all time; no man knows when they were first put forth.

Not through dread of any human pride could I answer to the gods for breaking *these*. Die I must; that I knew well (how should I not?) even without your edicts. But if I am to die before my time I count that a great gain. If anyone lives as I do compassed about with evils, could he find anything but gain in death?

So for me to meet this doom is trifling grief. But if I had suffered my mother's son to lie in death an unburied corpse, that would have grieved me; for this I am not grieved. And if my present deeds are foolish in your sight, it may be that a foolish judge arraigns my folly.

CHORUS: The girl shows herself passionate child of passionate sire; she does not know how to bend before troubles.

CREON: Yet I would have you know that overstubborn spirits are most often humbled. It is the stiffest iron, baked to hardness in the fire, that you will most often see snapped and shivered; and I have known horses that show temper brought to order by a little curb. There is no room for pride when you are your neighbor's slave. This girl was already versed in insolence when she transgressed the laws that had been set forth; that now done, look, a second insult, to boast of it and exult in her deed.

Now truly I am no man, she is the man, if this victory shall rest with her and bring no penalty. No! though she is my sister's child or nearer to me in blood than any that worships Zeus at the altar of our house, she and her kinsfolk shall not avoid a doom most dire; for I charge that other with a like share in the plotting of this burial.

Summon her; I saw her within just now, raving and not mistress of her wits. So often before the deed, when people plot mischief in the dark, the mind stands self-convicted in its treason. But this too is hateful, when one who has been caught in wickedness then seeks to make the crime a glory.

ANTIGONE: Would you do more than take and slay me?

CREON: No, no more; having that I have all.

ANTIGONE: Why then do you delay? In your discourse there is nothing that pleases me—may there never be—and so my words must needs be unpleasing to you. And yet for glory— how could I have won a nobler than by giving burial to my own brother. All here would own that they thought it well, if their lips were not sealed by fear. Royalty, blessed in so much besides, has the power to do and say what it will.

CREON: In that view you differ from all these Thebans.

ANTIGONE: They also share it, but they curb their tongues for you.

CREON: And are you not ashamed to act apart from them?

ANTIGONE: No; there is nothing shameful in piety to a brother.

CREON: Was it not a brother too that died in the opposite cause?

ANTIGONE: Brother by the same mother and the same sire.

CREON: Why then do you render a grace that is impious in his sight?

ANTIGONE: The dead man will not say that he so deems it.

CREON: Yes, if you make him but equal in honor with the wicked.

ANTIGONE: It was his brother, not his slave, that perished.

CREON: Wasting this land; while *he* fell as its champion.

ANTIGONE: Nevertheless Hades desires these rites.

CREON: But the good does not desire a like portion with the evil.

ANTIGONE: Who knows but this seems blameless in the world below?

CREON: A foe is never a friend—not even in death.

ANTIGONE: It is not my nature to join in hating, but in loving.

CREON: Pass then to the world of the dead, and if you must needs love, love them. While I live no woman shall rule me. (ISMENE *is led in.*)

CHORUS: Look, yonder Ismene comes forth, shedding such tears as fond sisters weep; a cloud upon her brow casts its shadow over her darkly flushing face and breaks in rain on her fair cheek.

CREON: You there who lurked like a viper in my house and were secretly draining my lifeblood while I did not know that I was nurturing two pests to rise against my throne— come tell me now, will you also confess your part in the burial or will you forswear all knowledge of it?

ISMENE: I have done the deed, if she allows my claim, and share the burden of the charge.

ANTIGONE: No, justice will not suffer you to do that; you did not consent to the deed, nor did I give you part in it.

ISMENE: But now that ills beset you I am not ashamed to sail the sea of trouble at your side.

ANTIGONE: Whose the deed was, Hades and the dead are witnesses; a friend in words is not the friend that I love.

ISMENE: Nay, sister, reject me not, but let me die with you and duly honor the dead.

ANTIGONE: Do not share my death nor claim deeds to which you have not put your hand; my death will suffice.

ISMENE: What life is dear to me bereft of you?

ANTIGONE: Ask Creon; all your care is for him.

ISMENE: Why vex me so when it does you no good?

ANTIGONE: If I am mocking it is with pain that I mock you.

ISMENE: Tell me, how can I serve you even now?

ANTIGONE: Save yourself; I do not grudge your escape.

ISMENE: Ah, misery! Shall I have no share in your fate?

ANTIGONE: Your choice was to live, mine to die.

ISMENE: At least your choice was not made without my protest.

ANTIGONE: One world approved your wisdom, another mine.

ISMENE: Nevertheless the offense is the same for both of us.

ANTIGONE: Be of good cheer: you live. My life has long been given to death, that so I might serve the dead.

CREON: Look, one of these girls has newly shown herself foolish, as the other has been since her life began.

ISMENE: So it is, O King; such reason as nature may have given does not abide with the unfortunate, but goes astray.

CREON: Yours did when you chose vile deeds with the vile.

ISMENE: How could I endure life without her presence?

CREON: Do not speak of her "presence"; she lives no more.

ISMENE: But will you slay the betrothed of your own son?

CREON: There are other fields for him to plow.

ISMENE: But there can never be such love as bound him to her.

CREON: I do not like an evil wife for my son.

ANTIGONE: Haemon, beloved! How your father wrongs you.

CREON: Enough, enough of you and of your marriage!

CHORUS: Will you indeed rob your son of this maiden?

CREON: It is Death that shall stay these bridals for me.

CHORUS: It is determined, it seems, that she shall die.

CREON: Determined, yes, for you and for me. (*To the* ATTENDANTS.) No more delay: servants, take them inside! Henceforth they must be women and not range at large;

even the bold seek to fly when they see Death now closing on their life.

(*Exeunt* ATTENDANTS, *guarding* ANTIGONE *and* ISMENE.)

CHORUS: *Blessed are they whose days have not tasted of evil. For when a house hath once been shaken from heaven, there the curse fails nevermore, passing from life to life of the race; even as, when the surge is driven over the darkness of the deep by the fierce breath of Thracian sea-winds, it rolls up the black sand from the depths, and there is a sullen roar from wind-vexed headlands that front the blows of the storm.*

I see that from olden time the sorrows in the house of the Labdacidae are heaped upon the sorrows of the dead; and generation is not freed by generation, but some god strikes them down, and the race hath no deliverance.

For now that hope of which the light had been spread above the last root of the house of Oedipus—that hope, in turn, is brought low—by the bloodstained dust due to the gods infernal, and by folly in speech, and frenzy at the heart.

Thy power, O Zeus, what human trespass can limit? That power which neither Sleep, the all-ensnaring, nor the untiring months of the gods can master; but thou, a ruler to whom time brings not old age, dwellest in the dazzling splendor of Olympus.

And through the future, near and far, as through the past, shall this law hold good: Nothing that is vast enters into the life of mortals without a curse.

For that hope whose wanderings are so wide is to many men a comfort, but to many a false lure of giddy desires; and the disappointment comes on one who knoweth nought till he burn his foot against the hot fire.

For with wisdom hath someone given forth the famous saying, that evil seems good, soon or late, to him whose mind the god draws to mischief; and but for the briefest space doth he fare free of woe.

But lo, Haemon, the last of thy sons; comes he grieving for the doom of his promised bride, Antigone, and bitter for the baffled hope of his marriage?

(*Enter* HAEMON.)

CREON: We shall soon know, better than seers could tell us. My son, have you come in rage against your father, when you heard the fixed doom of your betrothed? Or do I have your good will however I may act?

HAEMON: Father, I am yours, and in your wisdom you trace the rules which I shall follow. No marriage shall be deemed by me a greater gain than your good guidance.

CREON: Yes, this, my son, should be your heart's fixed law—in all things to obey your father's will. It is for this that men pray to see dutiful children grow up around them in their homes, to requite their father's foe with evil, and to honor his friend as he himself does. But the man who begets unprofitable children—what shall we say he has sown but troubles for himself and much triumph for his foes? Then do not you, my son, at pleasure's call dethrone your reason for a woman's sake, knowing that this is a joy that soon grows cold in clasping arms—an evil woman to share your bed and your home. What wound could strike deeper than a false friend? Nay, with loathing, and as if she were your enemy, let this girl go to find a husband in the house of Hades. For since I have taken her alone of all the city in open disobedience, I will not make myself a liar to my people: I will slay her.

So let her appeal as she will to the majesty of kindred blood. If I am to nurture my own kindred in naughtiness I shall have to bear with it in aliens. He who does his duty in his own household will be found righteous in the State also. But if any one transgresses and does violence to the laws or thinks to dictate to his rulers, such a man can win no praise from me. No, whomsoever the city may appoint, that man must be obeyed, in little things and great, in just things and unjust; and I should feel sure that a man who thus obeys would be a good ruler no less than a good subject, and in the storm of spears would stand his ground where he was set, loyal and dauntless at his comrade's side.

But disobedience is the worst of evils. This it is that ruins cities; this makes homes desolate; by this the ranks of allies are broken into headlong rout. But of the lives whose course is fair the greater part owes safety to obedience. Therefore we must support the cause of order and in no wise suffer a woman to worst us. Better to fall from power, if we must, by a man's hand; then we could not be called weaker than a woman.

CHORUS: To us, unless our years have stolen our wit, what you say you seem to say wisely.

HAEMON: Father, the gods implant reason in men, the highest of all things that we call our own. Not mine the skill, and may I never seek, to say wherein you speak not rightly; and yet another man too might have some useful thought. At least it is my natural office to watch, on your behalf, all that men say or do or find to blame. For the dread of your frown forbids the citizen to speak such words as would offend your ear; but I can hear these murmurs in the dark, these moanings of the city for this maiden. "No woman," they say, "ever merited her doom less, none ever was to die so shamefully for deeds so glorious as hers. When her own brother had fallen in bloody strife she would not leave him unburied to be devoured by carrion dogs or by any bird: does *she* not deserve the meed of golden honor?"

Such is the darkening rumor that spreads in secret. For me, my father, no treasure is so precious as your welfare. What indeed is a nobler ornament for children than a prospering sire's fair fame, or for sire than son's? Do not then persist in one mood alone for yourself; do not think that your word and yours alone must be right. For if any man thinks that he alone is wise, that in speech or in mind he has no peer, such a soul, when laid open, is always found empty.

No, though a man be wise, it is no shame for him to learn many things and to bend in season. Do you see, beside the wintry torrent's course, how the trees that yield to it save every twig while the stiffnecked perish root and branch? Even so he who keeps the sheet of his sail taut and never slackens it upsets his boat and finishes his voyage with keel uppermost.

Nay, forgo your wrath, permit yourself to change. If I, a younger man, may offer my thought, it would be far best, I suppose, that men should be all-wise by nature; but otherwise (and often the scale does not so incline) it is good also to learn from those who speak rightly.

CHORUS: It is meet that you should profit by his words, sire, if what he says is seasonable, and you, Haemon, by your father's. There has been wise speech on both parts.

CREON: Men of my age—are we to be schooled by men of his?

HAEMON: In nothing that is not right; if I am young you should look to my merits, not to my years.

CREON: Is it a merit to honor the unruly?

HAEMON: I could wish no one to show respect for evildoers.

CREON: Is not she tainted with that malady?

HAEMON: Our Theban folk with one voice deny it.

CREON: Shall Thebes prescribe to me how I must rule?

HAEMON: See, there you have spoken like a youth indeed.

CREON: Am I to rule this land by other judgment than my own?

HAEMON: That is no city which belongs to one man.

CREON: Is not the city held to be the ruler's?

HAEMON: You would make a good monarch of a desert.

CREON: This boy, it seems, is the woman's champion.

HAEMON: If you are a woman; my care is really for you.

CREON: Shameless, at open feud with your father!

HAEMON: No, I see you offending against justice.

CREON: Do I offend when I respect my own prerogatives?

HAEMON: You do not respect them when you trample on the gods' honors.

CREON: O dastard nature, yielding place to woman!

HAEMON: You will never find me yield to baseness.

CREON: All your words, at least, plead for that girl.

HAEMON: And for you, and for me, and for the gods below.

CREON: You can never marry her, on this side the grave.

HAEMON: Then she must die, and in death destroy another.

CREON: How! Does your boldness run to open threats?

HAEMON: What threat is it to combat vain resolves?

CREON: You shall rue your witless teaching of wisdom.

HAEMON: If you were not my father I would have called you unwise.

CREON: You woman's slave, use no wheedling speech with me.

HAEMON: You would speak and then hear no reply?

CREON: So? Now by the heaven above us, be sure of it, you shall smart for taunting me in this opprobrious strain. Bring forth that hated thing to die forthwith in his presence, before his eyes, at her bridegroom's side!

HAEMON: No, not at my side, never think it, shall she perish; nor shall you ever set eyes more upon my face. Rave, then, with such friends as can endure you.   (*Exit.*)

CHORUS: The man is gone, O King, in angry haste; a youthful mind when stung is fierce.

CREON: Let him do or dream more than man—good speed to him! But he shall not save these two girls from their doom.

CHORUS: Do you indeed purpose to slay both?

CREON: Not her whose hands are pure: you say well.

CHORUS: And by what doom do you mean to slay the other?

CREON: I will take her where the path is loneliest and hide her, living, in a rocky vault with so much food set forth as piety prescribes, that the city may avoid a public stain. And there, praying to Hades, the only god whom she worships, perhaps she will obtain release from death. Or else she will learn at last though late that it is lost labor to revere the dead. (*Exit.*)

CHORUS: *Love, unconquered in the fight, Love, who makest havoc of wealth, who keepest thy vigil on the soft cheek of a maiden; thou roamest over the sea, and among the homes of dwellers in the wilds; no immortal can escape thee, nor any among men whose life is for a day; and he to whom thou hast come is mad.*

The just themselves have their minds warped by thee to wrong, for their ruin: 'tis thou that has stirred up this present strife of kinsmen; victorious is the love-kindling light from the eyes of the fair bride; it is a power enthroned in sway beside the eternal laws; for there the goddess Aphrodite is working her unconquerable will.

(ANTIGONE *is led out to her execution.*)

But now I also am carried beyond the bounds of loyalty, and can no more keep back the streaming tears, when I see Antigone thus passing to the bridal chamber where all are laid to rest.

ANTIGONE: *See me, citizens of my fatherland, setting forth on my last way, looking my last on the sunlight that is for me no more. Hades who gives sleep to all is leading me living to Acheron's shore. I have had no portion in the chant that brings the bride, nor has any song been mine for the crowning of bridals. Me the lord of the Dark Lake shall wed.*

CHORUS: *Glorious, therefore, and with praise you depart to that deep place of the dead. Wasting sickness has not smitten you, you have not found the wages of the sword. No, mistress of your own fate and still alive you shall pass to Hades as no other of mortal kind has passed.*

ANTIGONE: *I have heard in other days how dread a doom*

befell our Phrygian guest, the daughter of Tantalus, on the Sipylian heights; how, like clinging ivy, the growth of stone subdued her; and the rains fail not, as men tell, from her wasting form, nor fails the snow, while beneath her weeping lids the tears bedew her bosom. Most like to hers is the fate that brings me to my rest.

CHORUS: *Yet she was a goddess, as you know, and born of gods; we are mortals and of mortal race. But it is great renown for a woman who has perished that she should have shared the doom of the godlike, in her life and afterward in death.*

ANTIGONE: *Ah, I am mocked! In the name of our fathers' gods, can you not wait till I am gone; must you taunt me to my face, O my city and you her wealthy sons? Ah, fount of Dirce, and thou holy ground of Thebes whose chariots are many; you, at least, will bear me witness, in what sort, unwept of friends, and by what laws I pass to the rock-closed prison of my strange tomb, ah me unhappy! who have no home on the earth or in the shades, no home with the living or with the dead.*

CHORUS: *You have rushed forward to the utmost verge of daring, and against that throne where Justice sits on high you have fallen, my daughter, with a grievous fall. But in this ordeal you are paying, perchance, for your father's sin.*

ANTIGONE: *You have touched on my bitterest thought, awaking the ever-new lament for my sire and for all the doom given to us, the famed house of Labdacus. Alas for the horrors of the mother's bed! Alas for the wretched mother's slumber at the side of her own son—and my sire! From what manner of parents did I take my miserable being! And to them I go in this wise, accursed, unwed, to share their home. Alas, my brother, ill-starred in your marriage, in your death you have undone my life!*

CHORUS: *Reverent action claims a certain praise for reverence; but an offense against power cannot be brooked by him who has power in his keeping. Your self-willed temper has wrought your ruin.*

ANTIGONE: *Unwept, unfriended, without marriage-song, I am led forth in my sorrow on this journey that can be delayed no more. No longer, luckless me, may I behold yonder day-star's sacred eye; but for my fate no tear is shed, no friend makes moan.*

(*Enter* CREON.)

CREON: Know you not that songs and wailings before death would never cease if it profited to utter them? Away with her, away! And when you have enclosed her, according to my word, in her vaulted grave leave her alone, forlorn, whether she wishes to die or live a buried life in such a home. Our hands are clean as touching this maiden. But this is certain: she shall be deprived of her sojourn in the light.

ANTIGONE: Tomb, bridal-chamber, eternal prison in the caverned rock whither I go to find my own, those many who have perished and whom Persephone has received among the dead! Last of all shall I pass thither and far most miserably of all, before the term of my life is spent. But I cherish good hope that my coming will be welcome to my father, and pleasant to you, my mother, and welcome, brother, to you. For when you died, with my own hands I washed and dressed you and poured drink-offerings at your graves; and now, Polyneices, it is for tending your corpse that I win such recompense as this.

And yet I honored you, as the wise will deem, rightly. Never, had I been a mother of children or if a husband had been moldering in death, would I have taken this task upon me in the city's despite. What law, you ask, is my warrant for that word? The husband lost, another might have been found, and child from another to replace the first-born; but father and mother hidden with Hades, no brother's life could ever bloom for me again. Such was the law by which I held you first in honor; but for it Creon deemed me guilty of error and of outrage, ah brother mine! And now he is leading me in this way, a captive in his hands. No bridal bed, no bridal song has been mine, no joy of marriage, no portion in the nurture of children; forlorn of friends, unhappy me, I go living to the vaults of death.

And what law of heaven have I transgressed? Why, unhappy me, should I look to the gods any more, what ally should I invoke, when by piety I have earned the name of impious? Nay, then, if these things are pleasing to the gods, when I have suffered my doom I shall come to know my sin; but if the sin is with my judges, I could wish them no fuller measure of evil than they, on their part, mete wrongfully to me.

CHORUS: Still the same tempest of the soul vexes this maiden with the same fierce gusts.

CREON: Then for this shall her guards have cause to rue their slowness.

ANTIGONE: Ah me! that word has come very near to death.

CREON: I can cheer you with no hope that this doom is not to be fulfilled.

ANTIGONE: O city of my fathers in the land of Thebes! O ye gods, eldest of our race! They are leading me hence, now, now, they tarry not! Behold me, princess of Thebes, the last daughter of the house of your kings, see what I suffer, and from whom, because I feared to cast away the fear of Heaven!

(ANTIGONE *is led away.*)

CHORUS: *Even thus endured Danae in her beauty to change the light of day for brass-bound walls; and in that chamber, secret as the grave, she was held close prisoner; yet was she of a proud lineage, O my daughter, and charged with the keeping of the seed of Zeus, that fell in the golden rain.*

But dreadful is the mysterious power of fate, there is no deliverance from it by wealth or by war, by fenced city, or dark, sea-beaten ships.

And bonds tamed the son of Dryas, swift to wrath, that king of the Edonians; so paid he for his frenzied taunts, when, by the will of Dionysus, he was pent in a rocky prison. There the fierce exuberance of his madness slowly passed away. That man learned to know the god, whom in his frenzy he had provoked with mockeries; for he had sought to quell the god-possessed women, and the Bacchanalian fire; and he angered the Muses that love the flute.

And by the waters of the Dark Rocks, the waters of the twofold sea, are the shores of Bosporus, and Thracian Salmydessus; where Ares, neighbor to the city, saw the accursed, blinding wound dealt to the two sons of Phineus by his fierce wife—the wound that brought darkness to those vengeance-craving orbs, smitten with her bloody hands, smitten with her shuttle for a dagger.

Pining in their misery, they bewailed their cruel doom, those sons of a mother hapless in her marriage; but she traced her descent from the ancient line of the Erech-

theidae; and in far-distant caves she was nursed amid her father's storms, that child of Boreas, swift as a steed over the steep hills, a daughter of gods; yet upon her also the gray Fates bore hard, my daughter.

(TEIRESIAS *is led in by a* BOY.)

TEIRESIAS: Prince of Thebes, we have come with linked steps, both served by the eyes of one; for so, by a guide's help, the blind must walk.

CREON: And what, aged Teiresias, are your tidings?

TEIRESIAS: I will tell you, and do you hearken to the seer.

CREON: Indeed, it has not been my wont to slight your counsel.

TEIRESIAS: And so you steered our city's course aright.

CREON: I have felt and can attest your benefits.

TEIRESIAS: Mark that now, once more, you are standing on fate's fine edge.

CREON: What does this mean? How I shudder at your message!

TEIRESIAS: You will learn when you hear the warnings of my art. As I took my place on my old seat of augury, where all birds have been wont to gather within my ken, I heard a strange voice among them. They were screaming with dire, feverish rage that drowned their language in a jargon, and I knew that they were rending each other with their talons, murderously; the whir of wings told no doubtful tale.

Forthwith, in fear, I essayed burnt-sacrifice on a duly kindled altar, but from my offerings the Fire-god showed no flame. A dank moisture oozing from the thigh-flesh trickled forth upon the embers and smoked and sputtered; the gall was scattered to the air; and the streaming thighs lay bared of the fat that had been wrapped round them.

Such was the failure of the rites by which I vainly asked a sign, as from this boy I learned; for he is my guide, as I am guide to others. And it is your counsel that has brought this sickness on our State. For the altars of our city and of our hearths have been tainted one and all by birds and dogs with carrion from the hapless corpse, the son of Oedipus. Therefore the gods no more accept prayer and sacrifice at our hands, or the flame of meat-offering; nor does any bird give a clear sign by its shrill cry, for they have tasted the fatness of a slain man's blood.

Think, then, on these things, my son. All men are liable to err; but when an error has been made, that man is no longer witless or unblessed who heals the ill into which he has fallen and does not remain stubborn.

Self-will, we know, incurs the charge of folly. Nay, allow the claim of the dead; do not stab the fallen. What prowess is it to slay the slain anew? I have sought your good, and for your good I speak. Never is it sweeter to learn from a good counsellor than when he counsels for your own gain.

CREON: Old man, you all shoot your shafts at me as archers at the butts. You must needs practice on me with seercraft also. Aye, the seer tribe has long trafficked in me and made me their merchandise. Gain your gains, drive your trade, if you like, in the silver-gold of Sardis and the gold of India; but you shall not hide that man in the grave—no, though the eagles of Zeus should bear the carrion morsels to their master's throne—no, not for dread of that defilement will I suffer his burial; for well I know that no mortal can defile the gods. But, aged Teiresias, the wisest fall with a shameful fall when they clothe shameful thoughts in fair words for lucre's sake.

TEIRESIAS: Alas! Does any man know, does any consider——

CREON: What? What general truth are you announcing?

TEIRESIAS: How precious, above all wealth, is good counsel.

CREON: As folly, I think, is the worst mischief.

TEIRESIAS: Yet you are tainted with that distemper.

CREON: I would not answer the seer with a taunt.

TEIRISIAS: But you do, in saying that I prophesy falsely.

CREON: Well, the prophet tribe was ever fond of money.

TEIRESIAS: And the race bred of tyrants loves base gain.

CREON: Do you know that your speech is spoken of your king?

TEIRESIAS: I do know it; for through me you have saved Thebes.

CREON: You are a wise seer, but you love evil deeds.

TEIRESIAS: You will rouse me to utter the dread secret in my soul.

CREON: Out with it! Only speak it not for gain.

TEIRESIAS: I am sure I shall not—as touching you.

CREON: Know that you shall not trade on my resolve.

TEIRESIAS: Then know you, and know it well, that you shall not live through many more courses of the sun's swift chariot before one begotten of your own loins shall have been given by you a corpse for corpses, because you have thrust children of the sunlight to the shades and ruthlessly lodged a living soul in the grave but keep in this world one who belongs to the gods infernal, a corpse unburied, unhonored, all unhallowed. In such you have no part, nor have the gods above, but this is a violence done to them by you. Therefore the avenging destroyers lie in wait for you, the Furies of Hades and of the gods, that you may be taken in these same ills.

And mark well if I speak these things as a hireling. A time not long to be delayed shall awaken the wailing of men and of women in your house. And a tumult of hatred against you stirs all the cities whose mangled sons had the burial rite from dogs or from wild beasts or from some winged bird that bore a polluting breath to each city that contains the hearths of the dead.

Such arrows for your heart, since you provoke me, have I launched at you, archerlike, in my anger, sure arrows of which you shall not escape the smart. Boy, lead me home, that he may spend his rage on younger men, and learn to keep a tongue more temperate, and to bear within his breast a better mind than now he bears.   (*Exeunt.*)

CHORUS: The man has gone, O King, with dread prophecies. And, since the hair on this head once black has been white, I know that he has never been a false prophet to our city.

CREON: I too know it well and am troubled in soul. It is dire to yield; but by resistance to smite my pride with ruin—this too is a dire choice.

CHORUS: Son of Menoeceus, it behooves you to take wise counsel.

CREON: What shall I do, then? Speak and I will obey.

CHORUS: Go and free the maiden from her rocky chamber, and make a tomb for the unburied dead.

CREON: Is this your counsel? Would you have me yield?

CHORUS: Yes, King, and with all speed; for swift harms from the gods cut short the folly of men.

CREON: Ah me, it is hard, but I resign my cherished resolve; I obey. We must not wage a vain war with destiny.

CHORUS: Do you go and do these things; do not leave them to others.

CREON: Even as I am I'll go. On, on, my servants, each and all of you, take axes in your hands and hasten to the

ground that you see yonder! Since our judgment has taken
this turn I will be present to unloose her, as I myself bound
her. My heart misgives me, it is best to keep the established laws, even to life's end.

CHORUS: *O thou of many names, glory of the Cadmeian
bride, offspring of loud-thundering Zeus! thou who watch-
est over famed Italia, and reignest, where all guests are
welcomed, in the sheltered plain of Eleusinian Deo! O
Bacchus, dweller in Thebes, mother-city of Bacchants,
by the softly-gliding stream of Ismenus, on the soil where
the fierce dragon's teeth were sown!*

*Thou hast been seen where torch-flames glare through
smoke, above the crests of the twin peaks, where move the
Corycian nymphs, thy votaries, hard by Castalia's stream.*

*Thou comest from the ivy-mantled slopes of Nysa's hills,
and from the shore green with many-clustered vines, while
thy name is lifted up on strains of more than mortal
power, as thou visitest the ways of Thebes:*

*Thebes, of all cities, thou holdest first in honor, thou,
and thy mother whom the lightning smote; and now, when
all our people is captive to a violent plague, come thou
with healing feet over the Parnassian height, or over the
moaning strait!*

*O thou with whom the stars rejoice as they move, the
stars whose breath is fire; O master of the voices of the
night; son begotten of Zeus; appear, O King, with thine
attendant Thyiads, who in nightlong frenzy dance before
thee, the giver of good gifts, Iacchus!*

(*Enter* MESSENGER.)

MESSENGER: Dwellers by the house of Cadmus and of
Amphion, there is no estate of mortal life that I would
ever praise or blame as settled. Fortune raises and Fortune
humbles the lucky or unlucky from day to day, and no one
can prophesy to men concerning those things which are
established. For Creon was blessed once, as I count bliss; he
had saved this land of Cadmus from its foes; he was
clothed with sole dominion in the land; he reigned, the
glorious sire of princely children. And now all has been
lost. For when a man has forfeited his pleasures, I count
him not as living—I hold him but a breathing corpse.
Heap up riches in your house, if you will; live in kingly
state; yet, if there be no gladness therewith, I would not

give the shadow of a vapor for all the rest, compared with joy.

CHORUS: And what is this new grief that you have to tell for our princes?

MESSENGER: Death; and the living are guilty for the dead.

CHORUS: Who is the slayer? Who the stricken? Speak.

MESSENGER: Haemon has perished; his blood has been shed by no stranger.

CHORUS: By his father's hand, or by his own?

MESSENGER: By his own, in wrath with his sire for the murder.

CHORUS: O prophet, how true have you proved your word!

MESSENGER: So these things stand; you must consider of the rest.

CHORUS: Look, I see unfortunate Eurydice, Creon's wife, approaching. She is coming from the house by chance, it may be, or because she knows the tidings of her son.

(*Enter* EURYDICE.)

EURYDICE: People of Thebes, I heard your words as I was going forth to salute the goddess Pallas with my prayers. Even as I was loosing the fastenings of the gate to open it, the message of a household woe smote my ear. I sank back, terror-stricken, into the arms of my handmaids and my senses fled. But say again what the tidings were; I shall hear them as one who is no stranger to sorrow.

MESSENGER: Dear lady, I will witness of what I saw and will leave no word of the truth untold. Why indeed should I soothe you with words in which I must presently be found false? Truth is ever best. I attended your lord as his guide to the furthest part of the plain, where the body of Polyneices, torn by dogs, still lay unpitied. We prayed the goddess of the roads, and Pluto, in mercy to restrain their wrath. We washed the dead with holy washing, and with freshly plucked boughs we solemnly burned such relics as there were. We raised a high mound of his native earth. And then we turned away to enter the maiden's nuptial chamber with rocky couch, the caverned mansion of the bride of Death. From afar one of us heard a voice of loud wailing at that bride's unhallowed bower, and came to tell our master Creon.

As the king drew nearer doubtful sounds of a bitter cry floated around him; he groaned and said in accents of

anguish, "Wretched that I am, can my foreboding be true?
Am I going on the woefullest way that ever I went? My
son's voice greets me. Go, my servants, quickly nearer, and
when you have reached the tomb pass through the gap
where the stones have been wrenched away, to the cell's
very mouth. Look and see if it is Haemon's voice that I
know, or if my ear is cheated by the gods."

This search, at our despairing master's word, we went
to make. In the furthest part of the tomb we descried
her hanging by the neck, slung by a thread-wrought halter
of fine linen; while *he* was embracing her with arms
thrown around her waist, bewailing the loss of his bride
who is with the dead, and his father's deeds, and his own
ill-starred love.

His father, when he saw him, cried aloud with a dread
cry and went in, and called to him with a voice of wailing: "Unhappy, what a deed you have done! What thought
has come to you? What manner of mischance has marred
your reason? Come forth, my child! I pray you, I implore!"
But the boy glared at him with fierce eyes, spat in his
face, and without a word of answer drew his cross-hilted
sword. As his father rushed forth in flight he missed his
aim; then, luckless man, angry with himself he straightway leaned with all his weight against his sword and
drove it, half its length, into his side. While sense lin-
gered he clasped the maiden to his faint embrace, and as
he gasped sent forth on her pale cheek the swift stream
of his oozing blood.

Corpse enfolding corpse he lies. He has won his nuptial
rites, poor youth, not here but in the halls of Death. And
he has witnessed to mankind that of all curses which
cleave to man ill counsel is the sovereign curse.

(*Exit* EURYDICE.)

CHORUS: What would you augur from this? The lady has
turned back and is gone without a word, good or evil.

MESSENGER: I too am startled. Yet I nourish the hope that at
these sad tidings of her son she cannot deign to give her
sorrow public vent, but in the privacy of the house will set
her handmaids to mourn the household grief. For she is not
untaught of discretion, that she should err.

CHORUS: I do not know. To me, at least, a strained silence
seems to portend evil, no less than vain abundance of lament.

MESSENGER: Well, I will enter the house and learn whether indeed she is not hiding some repressed purpose in the depths of a passionate heart. You say well: excess of silence, too, may have a perilous meaning.   (*Exit.*)

(*Enter* CREON *with* ATTENDANTS *bearing the body of* HAEMON.)

CHORUS: Look, yonder the king himself draws near, bearing that which tells too clear a tale—the work of no stranger's madness, if we may say it, but of his own misdeeds.

CREON: *Woe for the sins of a darkened soul, stubborn sins, fraught with death! Behold us, the sire who has slain, the son who has perished! Woe is me for the wretched blindness of my counsels! Alas, my son, you have died in your youth, by a timeless doom, woe is me! Your spirit has fled not by your folly but by my own!*

CHORUS: Ah me, how all too late you seem to see the right!

CREON: *Ah me, I have learned the bitter lesson! But then, methinks, oh then, some god smote me from above with crushing weight and hurled me into ways of cruelty, woe is me, overthrowing and trampling on my joy! Woe, woe, for the troublous toils of men!*

(*Enter* MESSENGER *from palace.*)

MESSENGER: Sire, you have come, it seems, as one whose hands are not empty but who has store laid up besides. You bear yonder burden with you, and you are soon to look upon the woes within your house.

CREON: And what worse ill is yet to follow upon ills?

MESSENGER: Your queen has died, true mother of yonder corpse—ah, unhappy lady—by blows newly dealt.

CREON: *Oh Hades, all-receiving, whom no sacrifice can appease. Have you no mercy for me? You herald of bitter evil tidings, what word are you uttering? Alas, I was already as dead, and you have smitten me anew! What are you saying, my son? What is this new message that you bring—woe, woe is me!—of a wife's doom, of slaughter heaped on slaughter?*

CHORUS: You can behold; it is no longer hidden within.

(*The corpse of* EURYDICE *is revealed.*)

CREON: *Ah me, yonder I behold a new, a second woe! What destiny, ah what, can yet await me? I have but now raised my son in my arms, and there again I see a corpse before me! Alas, alas, unhappy mother! Alas, my child!*

MESSENGER: There, at the altar, self-stabbed with a keen

knife, she suffered her darkening eyes to close, when she had wailed for the noble fate of Megareus who died before, and then for his fate who lies there, and when, with her last breath, she had invoked evil fortunes upon you, the slayer of her sons.

CREON: *Woe, woe! I thrill with dread. Is there none to strike me to the heart with two-edged sword? O miserable that I am, and steeped in miserable anguish!*

MESSENGER: Yes, both this son's doom, and that other's, were laid to your charge by her whose corpse you see.

CREON: And what was the manner of the violent deed by which she passed away?

MESSENGER: Her own hand struck her to the heart, when she had learned her son's sorely lamented fate.

CREON: *Ah me, this guilt can never be fixed on any other of mortal kind, for my acquittal! I, even I, was your slayer, wretched that I am—I own the truth. Lead me away, O my servants, lead me hence with all speed, whose life is but death!*

CHORUS: Your counsels are good, if there can be good with ills; briefest is best, when trouble is in our path.

CREON: *Oh, let it come, let it appear, that fairest of fates for me, that brings my last day—aye, best fate of all! Oh, let it come, that I may never look upon tomorrow's light.*

CHORUS: These things are in the future; present tasks claim our care: the ordering of the future rests where it should rest.

CREON: All my desires, at least, were summed in that prayer.

CHORUS: Pray no more; for mortals have no escape from destined woe.

CREON: *Lead me away, I pray you; a rash, foolish man; who have slain you, ah my son, unwittingly, and you too, my wife—unhappy that I am! I know not which way I should bend my gaze, or where I should seek support; for all is amiss with that which is in my hands—and yonder, again, a crushing fate has leapt upon my head.*

(*Exit.*)

CHORUS: *Wisdom is the supreme part of happiness, and reverence toward the gods must be inviolate. Great words of prideful men are ever punished with great blows, and, in old age, teach the chastened to be wise.*

Oedipus the King

FROM ARISTOTLE ONWARD critics have rated *Oedipus the King* the model tragedy. It is flawless in construction and over-powering in tragic force. The plot develops convincingly, each new revelation growing naturally after what has gone before, and the process of discovery maintains a steady cre-scendo. Only after Oedipus fears that he has killed Laius does he come to fear that he has killed his *father* Laius. Intrigue and suspense are masterly: when the shepherd who was sent for to say whether one or several robbers had attacked Laius arrives, the original question has been forgotten and he must answer a much weightier one—who gave him the infant to be exposed? Inherent improbabilities are made to seem nat-ural by skillful characterization. Only the impetuosity of Oedipus can make Teiresias speak, and only his quick temper can make him ignore Teiresias' revelation. Only the big-city glibness of the Corinthian messenger makes the reluctant shepherd speak out. Oedipus is hasty, arrogant, suspicious of the motives of his true friends; and his downfall is often ex-plained as retribution for these flaws of character. But to in-terpret Oedipus' fall as punishment is to assume an unjust moral order (he had committed his sins unwittingly and had done his best to avoid them) and to mistake the nature of tragedy. Oedipus is a true hero because he pursued the truth relentlessly, even after it had become manifestly dangerous to do so. Only a hasty and impatient man—one who would kill in a traffic dispute—could so conduct himself. No Greek hero was wholly perfect; there is regularly a prickly obverse which makes the heroism possible and which must be taken in the bargain. Oedipus has behaved well as a man and has merited heroism; he is the winner, despite the horrors that befall him, as Antigone is the winner in her play. If there is a villain in the piece it is Apollo; but Apollo cannot be blamed, for the calculations of the gods are in a different sphere from the calculations of men. When a man behaving admirably as man is nevertheless tripped up by forces beyond his understanding, we have tragedy. Oedipus then is a perfect example of the tragic hero.

CHARACTERS

OEDIPUS, *king of Thebes*
PRIEST
CREON, *brother of Jocasta*
TEIRESIAS, *blind prophet*
JOCASTA
MESSENGER, *from Corinth*
HERDSMAN, *formerly servant of Laius*
MESSENGER, *from the palace*
CHORUS OF THEBAN ELDERS
ANTIGONE *and* ISMENE (*mute characters*)
SUPPLIANTS, ATTENDANTS

SCENE: Before the palace at Thebes

Translated by R. C. JEBB

(*Enter* OEDIPUS, *to address band of* SUPPLIANTS *facing the doors.*)

OEDIPUS: My children, latest-born to Cadmus who was of old, why are you set before me thus with wreathed branches of suppliants, while the city reeks with incense, rings with prayers for health and cries of woe? I deemed it unfit, my children, to hear these things at the mouth of others, and have come here myself, I, Oedipus, renowned of all.

Tell me then, venerable man, since it is your natural part to speak for these others, in what mood are you placed here, with what dread or what desire? Be sure that I would gladly give all aid; I should be hard of heart if I did not pity such suppliants as these.

PRIEST: Nay, Oedipus, ruler of my land, you see of what years we are who beset your altars, some nestlings still too tender for far flights, some bowed with age, priests, as I of Zeus, and these, the chosen youth. The rest of the folk sit with wreathed branches in the marketplaces and before the two shrines of Pallas, and where Ismenus gives answer by fire.

For the city, as you yourself see, is now too sorely vexed

113

and can no more lift her head from beneath the angry waves of death. A blight is on her in the fruitful blossoms of the land, in the herds among the pastures, in the barren pangs of women. And that flaming god, the malign plague, has swooped on us and ravages the town; by him the house of Cadmus is made waste, but dark Hades rich in groans and tears.

It is not as deeming you ranked with gods that I and these children are suppliants at your hearth, but as deeming you first of men, both in life's common chances and when mortals have to do with more than man; for you came to the town of Cadmus and rid us of the tax we rendered to the hard songstress. This you did though you knew nothing from us that could help you and had not been instructed; no, by a god's aid, it is said and believed, did you uplift our life.

And now, Oedipus, king glorious in all eyes, we beseech you, all we suppliants, to find for us some succor, whether you know it by the whisper of a god, or perchance as in the power of man. When men have been proved in deeds past, the issues of their counsels too most often have effect.

On, best of mortals, again uplift our State! On, guard your fame, since now this land calls you savior for your former zeal. Never be it our memory of your reign that we were first restored and afterward cast down; nay, lift up this State in such wise that it fall no more!

With good omen did you give us that past happiness; now also show yourself the same. For if you are to rule this land, even as you are now its lord, it is better to be lord of men than of a waste; since neither walled town or ship is anything if it is void and no men dwell in it with you.

OEDIPUS: Oh my piteous children, known, well known to me are the desires wherewith you have come. I know well that you all suffer, yet sufferers as you are, there is not one of you whose suffering is as mine. Your pain comes on each one of you for himself alone and for no other; but my soul mourns at once for the city, and for myself, and for you.

You are not then rousing me as one sunk in sleep; no, be sure that I have wept full many tears, gone many ways in wanderings of thought. And the sole remedy which after much pondering I could find, this I have put into act. I have sent the son of Menoeceus, Creon, my own wife's brother, to the Pythian house of Phoebus, to learn by what deed or word I might deliver this town. Already, when the lapse of days is reckoned, I am troubled by his delay, for he tarries strangely, beyond the fitting space. But when he comes, then shall I be no true man if I do not all that the god shows.

PRIEST: You have spoken in season; at this moment these men show by their gestures that Creon is drawing near.

OEDIPUS: O King Apollo, may he come to us in the brightness of saving fortune, even as his face is bright!

PRIEST: To all seeming he brings comfort; else he would not be coming crowned so thickly with berry-laden bay.

OEDIPUS: We shall soon know; he is at range to hear. (*Enter* CREON.) Prince, my kinsman, son of Menoeceus, what news have you brought us from the god?

CREON: Good news. I tell you that even troubles hard to bear, if they find the right issue, will end in perfect peace.

OEDIPUS: But what is the oracle? So far your words make me neither bold nor yet afraid.

CREON: If you would hear while these people are near I am ready to speak; or else to go inside.

OEDIPUS: Speak before all. The sorrow which I bear is for these more than for my own life.

CREON: With your leave I will tell what I heard from the god. Phoebus our lord bids us plainly to drive out a defiling thing which, he says, has been harbored in this land, and not to harbor it so that it cannot be healed.

OEDIPUS: By what rite shall we cleanse us? What is the manner of the misfortune?

CREON: By banishing a man, or by bloodshed in quittance of bloodshed, since it is that blood which brings the tempest on our city.

OEDIPUS: And who is the man whose fate he thus reveals?

CREON: Laius, King, was lord of our land before you became pilot of this State.

OEDIPUS: I know it well—by hearsay, for I saw him never.

CREON: He was slain; and the god now bids us plainly to wreak vengeance on his murderers, whoever they may be.

OEDIPUS: And where on earth are they? Where shall the dim track of this old crime be found?

CREON: In this land, said the god. What is sought for can be caught; only that which is not watched escapes.

OEDIPUS: Was it in the house or in the field or on strange soil that Laius met this bloody end?

CREON: It was on a visit to Delphi, as he said, that he had left our land; and he came home no more after he had once set forth.

OEDIPUS: And was there none to tell? Was there no comrade of his journey who saw the deed from whom tidings might have been gained and used?

CREON: All perished, save one who fled in fear; and he could tell for certain but one thing of all that he saw.

OEDIPUS: And what was that? One thing might show the clue to many, could we get but a small beginning for hope.

CREON: He said that robbers met and fell on them, not in one man's might but with full many hands.

OEDIPUS: How then, unless there was some trafficking in bribes from here, should the robber have proved so daring?

CREON: Such things were surmised; but Laius once slain, amid our troubles no avenger arose.

OEDIPUS: But when royalty had thus fallen, what trouble in your path can have hindered a full search?

CREON: The riddling Sphinx had made us let dark things go and was inviting us to think of what lay at our doors.

OEDIPUS: Nay, I will start afresh and once more make dark things plain. Right worthily has Phoebus, and worthily have you, bestowed this care on the cause of the dead; and so, as is meet, you shall find me too leagued with you in seeking vengeance for this land, and for the god besides. On behalf of no far-off friend, no, but in my own cause shall I dispel this taint. For whoever was the slayer of Laius might wish to take vengeance on me also with a hand as fierce. Therefore in doing right to Laius I serve myself.

Come, my children, hasten, rise from the altar-steps and lift these suppliant boughs. Let someone summon the folk of Cadmus here, warned that I mean to leave nothing untried. Our health (with the god's help) shall be made certain—or our ruin.

PRIEST: My children, let us rise; we came at first to seek what this man promises of himself. And may Phoebus who sent these oracles come to us, our savior and deliverer from the pest.

(*Exeunt* OEDIPUS *and* PRIEST.)

(*Enter* CHORUS.)

CHORUS: *O sweetly-speaking message of Zeus, in what spirit hast thou come from golden Pytho unto glorious Thebes? I am on the rack, terror shakes my soul, O thou Delian healer to whom wild cries rise, in holy fear of thee, what thing thou wilt work for me, perchance unknown before, perchance renewed with the revolving years: tell me, thou immortal voice, born of Golden Hope!*

First call I on thee, daughter of Zeus, divine Athena, and on thy sister, guardian of our land, Artemis, who sits on her throne of fame, above the circle of our Agora, and on Phoebus the far-darter: O shine forth on me, my three-fold help against death! If ever aforetime, in arrest of ruin hurrying on the city, ye drove a fiery pest beyond our borders, come now, also!

Woe is me, countless are the sorrows that I bear; a plague is on all our host, and thought can find no weapon for defense. The fruits of the glorious earth grow not; by no birth of children do women surmount the pangs in which they shriek; and life on life mayest thou see sped, like bird on nimble wing, aye, swifter than resistless fire, to the shore of the western god.

By such deaths, past numbering, the city perishes: unpitied, her children lie on the ground, spreading pestilence, with none to mourn: and meanwhile young wives, and gray-haired mothers with them, uplift a wail at the steps of the altars, some here, some there, entreating for their weary woes. The prayer to the Healer rings clear, and, blended therewith, the voice of lamentation: for these things, golden daughter of Zeus, send us the bright face of comfort.

And grant that the fierce god of death, who now with no brazen shields, yet amid cries as of battle, wraps me in the flame on his onset, may turn his back in speedy flight from our land, borne by a fair wind to the great deep of Amphitrite, or to those waters in which none find haven, even to the Thracian wave; for if night leave aught undone, day follows to accomplish this. O thou who wieldest the powers of the fire-fraught lightning, O Zeus our father, slay him beneath thy thunderbolt!

Lycean King, fain were I that thy shafts also, from thy bent bow's string of woven gold, should go abroad in their might, our champions in the face of the foe; yea, and the flashing fires of Artemis wherewith she glances through the Lycian hills. And I call him whose locks are bound with gold, who is named with the name of this land, ruddy Bacchus to whom Bacchants cry, the comrade of the Maenads, to draw near with the blaze of his blithe torch, our ally against the god unhonored among gods.

OEDIPUS: You pray; in answer to your prayer—if you will give a loyal welcome to my words and minister to your own disease—you may hope to find succor and relief from woes. These words I will speak publicly, as one who has been a stranger to this report, a stranger to the deed; for I should not be far on the track if I were racing it alone, without a clue. But as it is, since it was only after the time of the deed that I was numbered a Theban among Thebans, to you, the Cadmeans all, I proclaim the following.

Whosoever of you knows by whom Laius son of Labdacus was slain, I bid him to declare all to me. And if he is afraid, I tell him to remove the danger of the charge by denouncing himself; he shall suffer nothing else unlovely but only leave the land, unhurt. Or if anyone knows an alien, from another land, as the assassin, let him not keep silence; for I will pay his reward, and my thanks shall rest with him besides.

But if you keep silence, if anyone through fear shall seek to screen friend or self from my behest, hear what I shall then do. I charge you that no one of this land, of which I hold dominion and throne, give shelter or speak word to that murderer whoever he may be, make him partner of his prayer or sacrifice, or serve him with the lustral rite; all must ban him their homes, knowing that *this* is our defiling thing, as the oracle of the Pythian god has newly shown me. In this way I am the ally of the god and of the slain man. And I pray solemnly that the slayer, whoever he be, whether his hidden guilt is lonely or has partners, may he wear his unblessed life out evilly, as he is evil. And for myself I pray that if, with my privity, he should become an inmate of my house, I may suffer the same things which I have just called down upon others. And on you I lay it to make all these words good, for my sake and for the sake of the god, and for our lands, so blasted with barrenness by angry heaven.

For even if the matter had not been urged on us by a god it was not meet that you should leave the guilt unpurged when one so noble, and he your king, had perished; you were bound to search it out. And now since it is I who hold the powers that once he held, who possess his bed and the wife who bore seed to him; and since, had his hope of issue not been frustrate, children born of one mother would have made ties between him and me—but as it was fate swooped upon his head; by reason of these things I will uphold this cause even as the cause of my own sire. I will leave nothing untried in seeking to find him whose hand shed that blood, for the honor of the son of Labdacus and of Polydorus and elder Cadmus and Agenor who was of old.

And for those who obey me not I pray that the god send them neither harvest of the earth nor fruit of the womb, but that they be wasted by their lot that now is or by one yet more dire. But for all you, the loyal folk of Cadmus to whom these things seem good, may Justice our ally and all the gods be with you graciously forever.

CHORUS: As you have put me on my oath, on my oath, O King, I will speak. I am not the slayer, nor can I point to him who slew. As for the question, it was for Phoebus who sent it to tell us this thing—who can have wrought the deed.

OEDIPUS: Justly said; but no man on the earth can force the gods to what they will not.

CHORUS: I would fain say what seems to me next best after this.

OEDIPUS: If there is yet a third course spare not to show it.

CHORUS: I know that our lord Teiresias is the seer most like to our lord Phoebus. From him, O King, a searcher of these things might learn them most clearly.

OEDIPUS: Not even this have I left out of my cares. On the hint of Creon I have twice sent a man to bring him; and this long while I marvel why he is not here.

CHORUS: Indeed, his skill apart, the rumors are but faint and old.

OEDIPUS: What rumors are they? I look to every story.

CHORUS: Certain wayfarers were said to have killed him.

OEDIPUS: I too have heard it, but none sees him who saw it.

CHORUS: Nay, if he knows what fear is he will not stay when he hears your curses, so dire as they are.

OEDIPUS: When a man shrinks not from a deed neither is he scared by a word.

CHORUS: But there is one to convict him. For here they bring at last the godlike prophet, in whom alone of men the truth lives.

(*Enter* TEIRESIAS, *led by a* BOY.)

OEDIPUS: Teiresias, whose soul grasps all things, the lore that may be told and the unspeakable, the secrets of heaven and the low things of earth, you feel, though you cannot see, what a plague is haunting our State, from which, great prophet, we find in you our protector and only savior. Now Phoebus—if indeed you do not know from the messengers— sent answer to our question that the only riddance from this pest which could come was if we should learn aright the slayers of Laius, and slay them or send them into exile from our land. Do you then grudge neither voice of birds nor any other way of seer lore you have, but rescue yourself and the State, rescue me, rescue all that is defiled by the dead. We are in your hand, and man's noblest task is to help others by his best means and powers.

TEIRESIAS: Alas, how dreadful to have wisdom where it profits not the wise! Aye, I knew this well but let it slip out of mind; else would I never have come here.

OEDIPUS: What now? How sad have you come in!

TEIRESIAS: Let me go home; most easily will you bear your own burden to the end and I mine if you will consent.

OEDIPUS: Your words are strange and not kindly to this State which nurtured you when you withhold this response.

TEIRESIAS: Nay, I see that you on your part do not open your lips in season; therefore do I not speak, that I may not have your mishap.

OEDIPUS: For the love of the gods, do not turn away if you have knowledge; all we suppliants implore you on our knees.

TEIRESIAS: Aye, for you are all without knowledge. But I will never reveal my griefs—that I say not yours.

OEDIPUS: How do you say? You know the secret and will not tell it, but are minded to betray us and to destroy the State?

TEIRESIAS: I will pain neither myself nor you. Why vainly ask these things? You will not learn them from me.

OEDIPUS: What, basest of the base—you would anger a very stone—will you never speak out? Can nothing touch you? Will you never make an end?

TEIRESIAS: You blame my temper but do not see that to which you yourself are wedded. No, you find fault with me.

OEDIPUS: And who would not be angry to hear the words with which you now slight this city?

TEIRESIAS: The future will come of itself though I shroud it in silence.

OEDIPUS: Then seeing that it must come, you on your part should tell me of it.

TEIRESIAS: I will speak no further. Rage, if you will, with the fiercest wrath your heart knows.

OEDIPUS: Aye, verily. I will not spare, so angry am I, to speak all my thought. Know that you seem to me even to have helped in plotting the deed, and to have done it, short of slaying with your hands. If you had eyesight I would have said that the doing of this thing also was yours alone.

TEIRESIAS: So? I charge you that you abide by the decree of your own mouth, and from this day speak neither to these nor to me. *You* are the accursed defiler of this land.

OEDIPUS: So brazen with your blustering taunt? And how do you trust to escape your due?

TEIRESIAS: I have escaped. In my truth is my strength.

OEDIPUS: Who taught you this? It was not, at least, your art.

TEIRESIAS: You, for you spurred me into speech against my will.

OEDIPUS: What speech? Speak again that I may learn it better.

TEIRESIAS: Did you not take my sense before? Or are you tempting me in talk?

OEDIPUS: No, I did not take it so that I can call it known; speak again.

TEIRESIAS: I say that you are the slayer of the man whose slayer you seek.

OEDIPUS: Now you shall rue that you have twice said words so dire.

TEIRESIAS: Would you have me say more, to make you angrier still?

OEDIPUS: What you will. It will be said in vain.

TEIRESIAS: I say that you have been living in unguessed

shame with your nearest kin, and do not see to what woe
you have come.

OEDIPUS: Do you indeed think that you shall always speak
thus without smarting?

TEIRESIAS: Yes, if there is any strength in truth.

OEDIPUS: Nay, there is, for all save you. For you there is
not that strength, since you are maimed in ear and in wit
and in eye.

TEIRESIAS: And you are a poor wretch to utter taunts which
every man here will soon hurl at you.

OEDIPUS: Night, endless night, holds you in her keeping, so
that you can never hurt me or any man who sees the sun.

TEIRESIAS: No, your doom is not to fall by *me*. Apollo
is enough; his care it is to work that out.

OEDIPUS: Are these Creon's devices or yours?

TEIRESIAS: Nay, Creon is no plague to you. You are your
own.

OEDIPUS: O wealth and empire and skill surpassing skill in
life's keen rivalries, how great is the envy that cleaves to
you if for the sake of this power which the city has put
into my hands, a gift unsought, Creon the trusty, Creon
my old friend, has crept on me by stealth, yearning to
thrust me out of it, and has suborned such a scheming
juggler as this, a tricky quack, who has eyes only for his
gains but in his art is blind!

   Come now, tell me, where have you proved yourself a
seer? Why, when the watcher was here who wove dark
song, did you say nothing that could free this folk? Yet
the riddle, at least, was not for the first comer to read.
There was need of a seer's skill, and none such were you
found to have, either by help of birds or as known from
any god. No, I came, I, Oedipus the ignorant, and made
her mute when I had seized the answer by my wit, untaught of birds. And it is I whom you are trying to oust,
thinking to stand close to Creon's throne. Methinks you
and the plotter of these things will rue your zeal to purge
the land. Nay, if you did not seem to be an old man you
would have learned to your cost how bold you are.

CHORUS: To our thinking, both this man's words and
yours, Oedipus, have been said in anger. Not for such
words is our need, but to seek how we shall best dis-
charge the mandates of the god.

TEIRESIAS: King though you are, the right of reply, at least, must be deemed the same for both; of that I too am lord. Not to you do I live servant but to Loxias; and so I shall not stand enrolled under Creon for my patron. And I tell you, since you have taunted me even with blindness, that you have sight but see not in what misery you are, nor where you live, nor with whom. Do you know of what stock you are? And you have been an unwitting foe to your own kin, in the shades and on the earth above. The double lash of your mother's and your father's curse shall one day drive you from this land in dreadful haste, with darkness then on the eyes that now see true.

What place shall not be harbor to your shriek, what of all Cithaeron shall not ring with it soon, when you have learnt the meaning of the nuptials in which, within that house, you found a fatal haven after a voyage so fair. And a throng of other ills you cannot guess will make you level with your true self and with your own brood.

Then heap you your scorns on Creon and on my message; no one among men shall ever be crushed more miserably than you.

OEDIPUS: Are these taunts to be indeed borne from *him?* Hence, ruin take you! Hence this instant! Back! Away, depart from these doors!

TEIRESIAS: I would never have come, not I, if you had not called me.

OEDIPUS: I did not know that you were about to speak folly; else it would have been long before I sent for you to my house.

TEIRESIAS: Such am I, as you think, a fool; but for the parents who begot you, sane.

OEDIPUS: What parents? Stay . . . and who of men is my sire?

TEIRESIAS: This day shall show your birth and shall bring your ruin.

OEDIPUS: What riddles, what dark words you always speak!

TEIRESIAS: Nay, are you not most skilled to unravel dark speech?

OEDIPUS: Make that my reproach in which you find me great.

TEIRESIAS: Yet it was just that fortune that undid you.

OEDIPUS: If I delivered this town, I care not.

TEIRESIAS: Then I will go. Boy, take me hence.

OEDIPUS: Yes, let him take you. While here you are a hindrance and a trouble; when you have vanished you will not vex me more.

TEIRESIAS: I will go when I have done my errand, fearless of your frown, for you can never destroy me. And I tell you, the man of whom you have this long while been in quest, uttering threats and proclaiming a search into the murder of Laius—that man is here, in seeming an alien sojourner, but soon he shall be found a native Theban, and shall not be glad of his fortune. A blind man, he who now has sight, a beggar who now is rich, he shall make his way to a strange land, feeling the ground before him with his staff. And he shall be found at once brother and father of the children with whom he consorts; son and husband of the woman who bore him; heir to his father's bed, shedder of his father's blood.

Go in now and think on that; and if you find that I have been at fault, say thenceforth that I have no wit in prophecy.   (*Exeunt.*)

CHORUS: *Who is he of whom the divine voice from the Delphian rock hath spoken, as having wrought with red hands horrors that no tongue can tell?*

It is time that he ply in flight a foot stronger than the feet of storm-swift steeds: for the son of Zeus is springing on him, all armed with fiery lightnings, and with him come the dread, unerring Fates.

Yea, newly given from snowy Parnassus, the message hath flashed forth to make all search for the unknown man. Into the wild wood's covert, among caves and rocks, he is roaming, fierce as a bull, wretched and forlorn on his joyless path, still seeking to put from him the doom spoken at Earth's central shrine: but that doom ever lives, ever flits around him.

Dreadly, in sooth, dreadly doth the wise augur move me, who approve not, nor am able to deny. How to speak, I know not; I am fluttered with forebodings; neither in the present have I clear vision, nor of the future. Never in past days, nor in these, have I heard how the house of Labdacus or the son of Polybus had, either against other, any grief that I could bring as proof in assailing the public fame of Oedipus, and seeking to avenge the line of Labdacus for the undiscovered murder.

Nay, Zeus indeed and Apollo are keen of thought, and

*know the things of earth; but that mortal seer wins knowl-
edge above mine, of this there can be no sure test; though
man may surpass man in lore. Yet, until I see the word
made good, never will I assent when men blame Oedipus.
Before all eyes, the winged maiden came against him of
old, and he was seen to be wise; he bore the test, in welcome service to our State; never, therefore, by the verdict
of my heart shall he be adjudged guilty of crime.*

(*Enter* CREON.)

CREON: Fellow citizens, having learned that Oedipus the
king lays dire charges against me, I am here, indignant.
If in the present troubles he thinks that he has suffered
from *me*, by word or deed, aught that tends to harm, in
truth I do not crave my full term of years, when I
must bear such blame as this. The wrong of this rumor
touches me not in one point alone, but has the largest
scope, if I am to be called a traitor in the city, a traitor
too by you and by my friends.

CHORUS: No, but this taunt came under stress, perhaps, of
anger, rather than from the purpose of the heart.

CREON: And the saying was uttered, that *my* counsels won
the seer to utter his falsehoods?

CHORUS: Such things were said—I do not know with what
meaning.

CREON: And was this charge laid against me with steady eyes
and steady mind?

CHORUS: I do not know; I see not what my masters do: but
here comes our lord forth from the house.

(*Enter* OEDIPUS.)

OEDIPUS: You there, how could you come here? Have you a
front so bold that you have come to my house when you
are the proved assassin of its master, the palpable robber
of my crown? Come, tell me in the name of the gods, was
it cowardice or folly you saw in me that you plotted to
do this thing? Did you think that I would not note this deed
of yours creeping on me by stealth or, aware of it, not
ward it off? Is your attempt not foolish, to seek, without
followers or friends, a throne, a prize which followers
and wealth must win?

CREON: Mark me now; in answer to your words hear a fair
reply, and then judge for yourself on knowledge.

OEDIPUS: You are apt in speech, but I have a poor wit for
your lessons, since I have found you my malignant foe.

CREON: Now hear first how I will explain this very thing——

OEDIPUS: One thing do not explain—that you are not false.

CREON: If you think that stubbornness without sense is a good gift you are not wise.

OEDIPUS: If you think you can wrong a kinsman and escape the penalty you are not sane.

CREON: Justly said, I grant you; but tell me what is the wrong you say you have suffered from me.

OEDIPUS: Did you advise or did you not that I should send for that reverend seer?

CREON: I am still of the same mind.

OEDIPUS: How long is it then since Laius—

CREON: Since Laius . . . ? I do not understand your drift. . . .

OEDIPUS: —was swept away from men's sight by a deadly violence?

CREON: The count of years would run far into the past.

OEDIPUS: Was the seer of the profession in those days?

CREON: Yes, skilled as now and in equal honor.

OEDIPUS: Did he make any mention of me at that time?

CREON: Never, certainly, when I was within hearing.

OEDIPUS: But did you hold no search touching the murder?

CREON: We held due search, of course, and learned nothing.

OEDIPUS: How was it that this sage did not tell his story *then?*

CREON: I do not know; where I lack light it is my wont to be silent.

OEDIPUS: So much, at least, you know and could declare with light enough.

CREON: What is that? If I know it I will not deny.

OEDIPUS: That if he had not conferred with you he would never have named *my* slaying of Laius.

CREON: If so he speaks you know best; but I claim to learn from you as much as you have now from me.

OEDIPUS: Learn your fill; I shall never be found guilty of the blood.

CREON: Say then: you are married to my sister?

OEDIPUS: The question does not allow of denial.

CREON: And you rule the land as she does, with like authority?

OEDIPUS: She obtains from me all her desire.

CREON: And do I not rank as a third peer of you two?

OEDIPUS: That is just where you are seen a false friend.

CREON: Not so, if you would reason with your own heart as I

with mine. First weigh this—whether you think that anyone would choose to rule amid terrors rather than in unruffled peace, granting that he is to have the same powers. Now I, for one, have no yearning in my nature to be a king rather than to do kingly deeds, no, nor has any man who knows how to keep a sober mind. Now I win all boons from you without fear; but if I were ruler myself I should be doing much even against my own desire. How then could royalty be sweeter for me to have than painless rule and influence? Not yet am I so misguided as to desire other honors than those which profit. Now, all wish me joy; now, every man has a greeting for me; now, those who have a suit to you crave speech with me, since that is all their hope of success. Then why should I resign these things and take those? No mind will become false while it is wise. Nay, I am no lover of such policy, and if another put it into deed I could never bear to act with him.

In proof of this first go to Pytho and ask if I brought you true word of the oracle. Next, if you find that I have planned anything in concert with the soothsayer take and slay me, by the sentence not of one mouth but of two— by my own no less than yours. But do not make me guilty in a corner, on unproved surmise. It is not right to adjudge bad men good at random, or good men bad. I count it a like thing for a man to cast off a true friend as to cast away the life in his own bosom, which he most loves. You will learn these things with sureness in time, for time alone shows a just man; but you could discern a knave even in one day.

CHORUS: Well has he spoken, O King, for one who gives heed not to fall; the quick in counsel are not sure.

OEDIPUS: When the stealthy plotter is moving on me in quick sort, I too must be quick with my counterplot. If I await him in repose his ends will have been gained and mine missed.

CREON: What would you do, then? Cast me out of the land?

OEDIPUS: No. I desire your death, not your banishment, that you may show forth what manner of thing is envy.

CREON: You speak as resolved not to yield or believe?

OEDIPUS: No, for you do not persuade me that you are worthy of belief.

CREON: No, for I do not find you sane.

OEDIPUS: Sane, at least, in my own interest.

CREON: You should be so in mine also.

OEDIPUS: Nay, you are false.

CREON: But if you understand nothing?

OEDIPUS: Yet must I rule.

CREON: Not if you rule ill.

OEDIPUS: Hear him, O Thebes!

CREON: Thebes is for me also, not for you alone.
(*Enter* JOCASTA.)

CHORUS: Cease, princes. In good time for you I see Jocasta coming yonder from the house; with her help you should compose your present feud.

JOCASTA: Misguided men, why have you raised such foolish strife of tongues? Are you not ashamed, while the land is thus sick, to stir up troubles of your own? Come, go you into the house, and you, Creon, to your house; forbear to make much of a petty grief.

CREON: Kinswoman, Oedipus your lord claims to do dread things to me, one or other of two ills—to thrust me from the land of my fathers or to take and slay me.

OEDIPUS: Yes; for I have caught him, lady, working evil, by ill arts, against my person.

CREON: Now may I see no good but perish accursed if I have done to you anything you charge me with.

JOCASTA: O, for the gods' love, believe it, Oedipus, first for the awful sake of this oath unto the gods, then for my sake and for theirs who stand before you.

CHORUS: *Consent, reflect, hearken, O my king, I pray you!*

OEDIPUS: *What grace, then, would you have me grant you?*

CHORUS: *Respect him who aforetime was not foolish and who now is strong in his oath.*

OEDIPUS: *Do you know what you are asking?*

CHORUS: *Yes.*

OEDIPUS: *Declare, then, what you mean.*

CHORUS: *That you should never use an unproved rumor to cast a dishonoring charge on the friend who has bound himself with a curse.*

OEDIPUS: *Then be very sure that, when you seek this, for me you are seeking destruction or exile from this land.*

CHORUS: *No, by him who stands in front of all the heavenly host, no, by the Sun! Unblessed, unfriended, may I die by the uttermost doom if I have that thought! But my unhappy soul is worn by the withering of the land, and again*

*by the thought that your old sorrows should be crowned
by sorrows springing from you two.*

OEDIPUS: Then let him go, though I am surely doomed to
death or to be thrust dishonored from the land. Your lips,
not his, move my compassion by their plaint; but he,
wherever he be, shall be hated.

CREON: Sullen in yielding you show yourself, even as you are
vehement in excesses of wrath. Such natures are justly
sorest for themselves to bear.

OEDIPUS: Then will you not leave me in peace and get you
gone?

CREON: I will go my way. I have found you undiscerning,
but in the sight of these I am just. (*Exit.*)

CHORUS: *Lady, why do you delay to take that man into the
house?*

JOCASTA: *I will do so when I have learned what has happened.*

CHORUS: *Blind suspicion, bred of talk, arose; and on the
other side wounds of injustice.*

JOCASTA: *It was on both sides?*

CHORUS: *Yes.*

JOCASTA: *What was the story?*

CHORUS: *Enough, surely enough, when our land is already
vexed, that the matter should rest where it ceased.*

OEDIPUS: *Do you see to what you have come, for all your
honest purpose, in seeking to slack and blunt my zeal?*

CHORUS: *King, I have said it not once alone: be sure that
I should have been shown a madman, bankrupt in sane
counsel, if I put you away, you who gave a true course
to my beloved country when distraught by troubles, you
who now also are likely to prove our prospering guide.*

JOCASTA: In the name of the gods, tell me also, O King, on
what account you have conceived this steadfast wrath.

OEDIPUS: That I will; for I honor you, lady, above yonder
men. The cause is Creon and the plots that he has laid
against me.

JOCASTA: Speak on, if you can tell clearly how the feud began.

OEDIPUS: He says that I stand guilty of the blood of Laius.

JOCASTA: As on his own knowledge? Or on hearsay from another?

OEDIPUS: He has made a rascal seer his mouthpiece; as for
himself, he keeps his lips wholly pure.

JOCASTA: Then absolve yourself of the things of which you speak. Hearken to me, and learn for your comfort that nothing of mortal birth is a sharer in the science of the seer. Of that I will give you pithy proof.

An oracle came to Laius once—I will not say from Phoebus himself, but from his ministers—that the doom should overtake him to die by the hand of his child, who should spring from him and me.

Now Laius—as, at least, rumor says—was murdered one day by foreign robbers at a place where three highways meet. And the child's birth was not three days past when Laius pinned its ankles together and had it thrown, by others' hands, on a trackless mountain.

So in that case Apollo did not bring it to pass that the babe should become the slayer of his sire, or that Laius should die—the dread thing which he feared—by his child's hand. Thus did the messages of seercraft map out the future. Do not you regard them, not at all. Whatever needful thing the god seeks he himself will easily bring to light.

OEDIPUS: What restlessness of soul, lady, what tumult of the mind has just come upon me since I heard you speak!

JOCASTA: What anxiety has startled you to make you say this?

OEDIPUS: I thought I heard this from you—that Laius was slain where three highways meet.

JOCASTA: Yes, that was the story; nor has it ceased yet.

OEDIPUS: And where is the place where this befell?

JOCASTA: The land is called Phocis. Branching roads lead to the same spot from Delphi and from Daulia.

OEDIPUS: And what is the time that has passed since these things happened?

JOCASTA: The news was published to the town shortly before you were first seen in power over this land.

OEDIPUS: O Zeus, what have you decreed to do to me?

JOCASTA: Why, Oedipus, does this thing weigh upon your soul?

OEDIPUS: Do not ask me yet. Tell me, what was the stature of Laius, and how ripe his manhood?

JOCASTA: He was tall, the silver just lightly strewn among his hair. His form was not greatly unlike yours.

OEDIPUS: Unhappy that I am! I think I have been laying myself even now under a dread curse without knowing it.

JOCASTA: What are you saying? I tremble when I look on you, my King.

OEDIPUS: I have dread misgivings that the seer can see. But you can show better if you will tell me one thing more.

JOCASTA: Indeed—though I tremble—I will answer all you ask when I hear it.

OEDIPUS: Did he go in small force, or with many armed followers, like a chieftain?

JOCASTA: There were five in all, one a herald; and there was one carriage, which bore Laius.

OEDIPUS: Alas! Now it is clear indeed. —Who was he who gave you these tidings, lady?

JOCASTA: A servant, the sole survivor who came home.

OEDIPUS: Is he perhaps in the house now?

JOCASTA: No, truly. As soon as he returned and found you reigning in the stead of Laius, he supplicated me, with hand laid on mine, that I would send him to the fields, to the pastures of the flocks, so that he might be far from the sight of this town. And I sent him; he was worthy, for a slave, to win even a larger boon than that.

OEDIPUS: Would, then, that he could return to us without delay!

JOCASTA: It is easy. But why do you enjoin this?

OEDIPUS: I fear, lady, that my own lips have been unguarded; that is why I am eager to behold him.

JOCASTA: He shall come. But I too, I think, have a claim to learn what lies heavy on your heart, my King.

OEDIPUS: Yes, and it shall not be kept from you, now that my forebodings have advanced so far. Who indeed is more to me than you, to whom I should speak in passing through such a fortune as this?

My father was Polybus of Corinth, my mother the Dorian Merope. I was held the first of all the folk in that town until a chance befell me, worthy indeed of wonder, but not worthy of my own heat concerning it. At a banquet a man full of wine cast it at me in his cups that I was not the true son of my sire. Though vexed I restrained myself for that day as best I might, but on the next I went to my mother and father and questioned them; and they were angry for the taunt with him who had let that word fly. So on their part I had comfort; but the thing was ever rankling in my heart, for it still crept abroad with strong rumor. Unknown to mother or father I went to

Delphi. Phoebus sent me forth disappointed of that knowledge for which I came, but in his response set forth other things, full of sorrow and terror and woe: that I was fated to defile my mother's bed, that I should show unto men a brood which they could not endure to behold, and that I should be the slayer of the sire who begot me.

And I, when I had listened to this, turned to flight from the land of Corinth, calculating its site by the stars alone, to some spot where I should never see fulfillment of the infamies foretold in my evil doom. On my way I came to the regions in which you say that this prince perished. Now, lady, I will tell you the truth. When in my journey I was near to the three roads there met me a herald and a man seated in a carriage drawn by colts, as you have described. He who was in front, and the old man himself, were for thrusting me rudely from the path. Then in anger I struck him who pushed me aside, the driver; and the old man, seeing it, watched the moment when I was passing, and from the carriage brought his goad with two teeth full down upon my head. But he was paid with interest; by one swift blow from the staff in this hand he was rolled right out of the carriage on his back. I slew every man of them.

But if this stranger had any tie of kinship with Laius, who is now more wretched than the man before you? What mortal could prove more hated of heaven? Whom no stranger, no citizen, is allowed to receive in his house; whom it is unlawful that anyone accost; whom all must repel from their homes! And this, this curse, was laid on me by no mouth but my own! I pollute the bed of the slain man with the hands by which he perished. Say, am I vile? Am I not utterly unclean? For I must be banished, and in banishment not see my own people nor set foot in my own land, or else be joined in wedlock to my mother and slay my sire, even Polybus, who begot and reared me.

Would not a man speak rightly of Oedipus if he judged these things sent by some cruel power above man? Forbid, forbid, you pure and awful gods, that I should see that day! No, may I be swept from among men before I behold myself visited with the brand of such a doom!

CHORUS: To us indeed, O King, these things are fraught with fear. Yet have hope, until at least you have gained full knowledge from him who saw the deed.

OEDIPUS: So far alone hope does rest with me: I can await the man summoned from the pastures.

JOCASTA: And when he has appeared what would you have of him?

OEDIPUS: I will tell you. If his story be found to tally with yours, I, at least, shall stand clear of disaster.

JOCASTA: And what of special note did you hear from me?

OEDIPUS: You were saying that he spoke of Laius as slain by robbers. If he speaks as before of several, I was not the slayer; a solitary man could not be held the same with that band. But if he names one lonely wayfarer, then beyond doubt this guilt leans to me.

JOCASTA: Nay, be assured that is how the tale was first told; that he cannot revoke, for the city heard it, not I alone. But even if he should diverge somewhat from his former story, never, King, can he show that the murder of Laius, at least, is truly square to prophecy; of him Loxias plainly said that he must die by the hand of my child. Yet that poor innocent never slew him, but perished first itself. So henceforth, for what touches divination, I would not look to my right hand or my left.

OEDIPUS: You judge well. Nevertheless, send someone to fetch the peasant; do not neglect this matter.

JOCASTA: I will send without delay. But let us come into the house. I will do nothing save at your good pleasure.
(*Exeunt.*)

CHORUS: *May destiny still find me winning the praise of reverent purity in all words and deeds sanctioned by those laws of range sublime, called into life throughout the high clear heaven, whose father is Olympus alone; their parent was no race of mortal men, no, nor shall oblivion ever lay them to sleep; the god is mighty in them, and he grows not old.*

Insolence breeds the tyrant; Insolence, once vainly surfeited on wealth that is not meet nor good for it, when it hath scaled the topmost ramparts, is hurled to a dire doom, wherein no service of the feet can serve. But I pray that the god never quell such rivalry as benefits the State; the god will I ever hold for our protector.

But if any man walks haughtily in deed or word, with no fear of Justice, no reverence for the images of gods, may an evil doom seize him for his ill-starred pride, if he will not win his vantage fairly, nor keep him from unholy deeds, but must lay profaning hands on sanctities.

Where such things are, what mortal shall boast any more that he can ward the arrows of the gods from his life? Nay, if such deeds are in honor, wherefore should we join in the sacred dance?

No more will I go reverently to earth's central and inviolate shrine, no more to Abae's temple or Olympia, if these oracles fit not the issue, so that all men shall point at them with the finger. Nay, King—if thou art rightly called—Zeus all-ruling, may it not escape thee and thine ever-deathless power!

The old prophecies concerning Laius are fading; already men are setting them at nought, and nowhere is Apollo glorified with honors; the worship of the gods is perishing.

(*Enter* Jocasta *with suppliant boughs.*)

JOCASTA: Princes of the land, the thought has come to me to visit the shrines of the gods with this wreathed branch in my hands and these gifts of incense. For Oedipus excites his soul overmuch with all manner of alarms. He does not, like a man of sense, judge the new things by the old, but is at the will of the speaker, if he speaks terrors.

Since I can do no good by counsel, I have come to you, Lycean Apollo, for you are nearest. I supplicate you with these symbols of prayer, that you may find us some riddance from uncleanness. For now we are all afraid seeing *him* affrighted, even as they who see fear in the helmsman of their ship.

(*Enter* MESSENGER.)

MESSENGER: Might I learn from you, strangers, where is the house of King Oedipus? Or better still, tell me where he himself is, if you know.

CHORUS: This is his dwelling, and he himself, stranger, is within. This lady is the mother of his children.

MESSENGER: Then may she be ever happy in a happy home, since she is his heaven-blessed queen.

JOCASTA: Happiness to you also, stranger! It is the due of your fair greeting. But say what you have come to seek or tell.

MESSENGER: Good tidings, lady, for your house and for your husband.

JOCASTA: What are they? From whom have you come?

MESSENGER: From Corinth. At the message which I will soon speak you will rejoice, doubtless, but perhaps grieve.

JOCASTA: What is it? How does it have this double potency?

MESSENGER: The people will make him king of the Isthmian land, as it was said there.

JOCASTA: How is that? Is the aged Polybus no more in power?

MESSENGER: No; death holds him in the tomb.

JOCASTA: What do you say? Is Polybus dead, old man?

MESSENGER: If I am not speaking the truth I am content to die.

JOCASTA: Handmaid, away with all speed and tell this to your master. O you oracles of the gods, where stand you now! This is the man whom Oedipus long feared and shunned, lest he should slay him; and now this man has died in the course of destiny, not by his hand.

(*Enter* OEDIPUS.)

OEDIPUS: Jocasta, dearest wife, why have you summoned me forth from these doors?

JOCASTA: Hear this man, and judge, as you listen, to what the awful oracles of the gods have come.

OEDIPUS: And he—who may he be, and what news does he have for me?

JOCASTA: He is from Corinth, to say that your father Polybus lives no longer but has perished.

OEDIPUS: How, stranger? Let me have it from your own mouth.

MESSENGER: If I must first make these tidings plain, know indeed that he is dead and gone.

OEDIPUS: By treachery, or by visit of disease?

MESSENGER: A light thing in the scale brings the aged to their rest.

OEDIPUS: Ah, he died, it seems, of sickness?

MESSENGER: Yes, and of the long years he had counted.

OEDIPUS: Alas, alas! Why indeed, my wife, should one look to the hearth of the Pythian seer, or to the birds that scream above our heads, on whose showing I was doomed to slay my sire? But he is dead and hid already beneath the earth; and here am I, who have not put hand to spear. Unless, perchance, he was killed by longing for me; so indeed I should be the cause of his death. But the oracles as they stand, at least, Polybus has swept with him to his rest in Hades; they are worth nothing.

JOCASTA: Nay, did I not so foretell you long since?

OEDIPUS: You did, but I was misled by my fear.

JOCASTA: No more lay any of those things to heart.

OEDIPUS: But surely I must needs fear my mother's bed?

JOCASTA: Nay, what should mortal fear for whom the decrees of fortune are supreme and who has clear foresight of nothing? It is best to live at random, as one may. But do not fear touching wedlock with your mother. Many men before now have so fared in dreams also; but he to whom these things are as nothing bears his life most easily.

OEDIPUS: All these bold words of yours would have been well if my mother were not living; but as it is, since she is alive, I must needs fear. But you say well.

JOCASTA: However, your father's death is a great sign to cheer us.

OEDIPUS: Great, I know. But my fear is of her who lives.

MESSENGER: And who is the woman about whom you fear?

OEDIPUS: Merope, old man, the consort of Polybus.

MESSENGER: And what is it in her that moves your fear?

OEDIPUS: A heaven-sent oracle of dread import, stranger.

MESSENGER: Lawful for another to know or unlawful?

OEDIPUS: Lawful, surely. Loxias once said that I was doomed to espouse my own mother and to shed with my own hands my father's blood. That is why my home in Corinth was long kept by me afar—with happy outcome, indeed, yet still it is sweet to see the face of parents.

MESSENGER: Was it indeed in fear of this that you were an exile from the city?

OEDIPUS: And because I did not wish, old man, to be the slayer of my sire.

MESSENGER: Then why have I not freed you, King, from this fear, seeing that I came with friendly purpose?

OEDIPUS: Indeed you would have due reward from me.

MESSENGER: Indeed it was chiefly for this that I came—that, on your return home, I might reap some good.

OEDIPUS: No, I will never go near my parents.

MESSENGER: Ah my son, it is plain enough that you do not know what you are doing.

OEDIPUS: How, old man? For the gods' love, tell me.

MESSENGER: If for these reasons you shrink from going home.

OEDIPUS: Aye, I dread least Phoebus prove himself true for me.

MESSENGER: You dread to be stained with guilt through your parents?

OEDIPUS: Just so, old man; this it is that always affrights me.

MESSENGER: Do you know then that your fears are wholly vain?

OEDIPUS: How so, if I was born of those parents?

MESSENGER: Because Polybus was nothing to you in blood.

OEDIPUS: What are you saying? Was Polybus not my sire?

MESSENGER: No more than he who speaks to you, but just so much.

OEDIPUS: And how can my sire be level with him who is nothing to me?

MESSENGER: He did not beget you any more than I.

OEDIPUS: Why then did he call me his son?

MESSENGER: Know that he had received you as a gift from my hands long ago.

OEDIPUS: And yet he loved me so dearly, when I came from another's hand?

MESSENGER: Yes, his former childlessness won him to do so.

OEDIPUS: And you—had you bought me or found me by chance when you gave me to him?

MESSENGER: Found you in Cithaeron's winding glens.

OEDIPUS: Why were you roaming in those regions?

MESSENGER: I was there in charge of mountain flocks.

OEDIPUS: What, you were a shepherd, a vagrant hireling?

MESSENGER: But your preserver, my son, in that hour.

OEDIPUS: And what pain was mine when you took me in your arms?

MESSENGER: The ankles of your feet might witness.

OEDIPUS: Ah me, why do you speak of that old trouble?

MESSENGER: I freed you when you had your ankles pinned together.

OEDIPUS: Aye, it was a dread brand of shame that I took from my cradle.

MESSENGER: Such, that from that fortune you were called by the name which is still yours.

OEDIPUS: Oh, for the gods' love, was the deed my mother's or father's? Speak!

MESSENGER: I do not know; he who gave you to me knows more of that than I.

OEDIPUS: What? You had me from another? You did not light on me yourself?

MESSENGER: No, another shepherd gave you up to me.

OEDIPUS: Who was he? Are you in position to tell clearly?

MESSENGER: I think he was called one of the household of Laius.

OEDIPUS: The king who ruled this country long ago?

MESSENGER: The same. It was in his service that the man was a herdsman.

OEDIPUS: Is he still alive for me to see?

MESSENGER: You folk of the country should know best.

OEDIPUS: Is there any of you here present that knows the herdsman of whom he speaks, any that has seen him in the pastures or the town? Answer! The hour has come that these things should be finally revealed.

CHORUS: He seems to mean no other than the peasant whom you were already eager to see; but our lady Jocasta might best tell that.

OEDIPUS: Lady, you remember the man we lately summoned? Is it of him that this man speaks?

JOCASTA: Why ask of whom he spoke? Do not regard it. . . . Do not waste a thought on what he said. . . . It is futile.

OEDIPUS: It must not be that with such clues in my grasp I should fail to bring my birth to light.

JOCASTA: For the gods' sake, if you have any care for your own life, forbear this search! My anguish is enough.

OEDIPUS: Be of good courage; though I be found the son of servile mother, yes, a slave by three descents, *you* will not be proved base-born.

JOCASTA: Yet hear me, I implore you: do not do this.

OEDIPUS: I must not hear of not discovering the whole truth.

JOCASTA: Yet I wish you well, I counsel you for the best.

OEDIPUS: These best counsels, then, vex my patience.

JOCASTA: Ill-fated one! May you never come to know who you are!

OEDIPUS: Go, someone, fetch me the herdsman here, and leave yonder woman to glory in her princely stock.

JOCASTA: Alas, alas, miserable!—that word alone can I say to you, and no other word henceforth forever.

(JOCASTA *rushes into the house.*)

CHORUS: Why has the lady gone, Oedipus, in a transport of wild grief? I misdoubt a storm of sorrow will break forth from this silence.

OEDIPUS: Break forth what will. Be my race never so lowly I must crave to learn it. That woman perhaps—for she is proud with more than a woman's pride—thinks shame of my base source. But I hold myself son of Fortune that gives good and will not be dishonored. She is the mother from whom I spring; and the months, my kinsmen, have marked me sometimes lowly, sometimes great. Such being my lineage, never more can I prove false to it, or spare to search out the secret of my birth.

CHORUS: *If I am a seer or wise of heart, O Cithaeron, you shall not fail, by yonder heaven you shall not, to know at tomorrow's full moon that Oedipus honors you as native to him, as his nurse, and his mother, and that you are celebrated in our dance and song, because you are well-pleasing to our prince. O Phoebus to whom we cry, may these things find favor in your sight!*

Who was it, my son, who of the race whose years are many that bore you in wedlock with Pan, the mountain-roaming father? Or was it a bride of Loxias that bore you? For dear to him are all the upland pastures. Or perchance it was Cyllene's lord, or the Bacchants' god, dweller on the hilltops, that received you, a newborn joy, from one of the nymphs of Helicon, with whom he most does sport.

OEDIPUS: Elders, if it is for me to guess, who have never met with him, I think I see the herdsman of whom we have long been in quest; for in his venerable age he tallies with yonder stranger's years, and furthermore I know those who bring him as servants of my own. But perhaps you may have the advantage of me in knowledge, if you have seen the herdsman before.

CHORUS: Yes, I know him, be sure. He was in the service of Laius, trusty as any man in his shepherd's place.

(*Enter* HERDSMAN.)

OEDIPUS: I ask you first, Corinthian stranger, is this the man you mean?

MESSENGER: This man whom you see.

OEDIPUS: Ho you, old man: I would have you look this way and answer all that I ask. You were once in the service of Laius?

HERDSMAN: I was, a slave not bought but reared in his house.

OEDIPUS: Employed in what labor or what way of life?

HERDSMAN: For the best part of my life I tended flocks.

OEDIPUS: And what the regions that you chiefly haunted?

HERDSMAN: Sometimes it was Cithaeron, sometimes the neighboring ground.

OEDIPUS: Do you recall having noted yonder man in these parts——

HERDSMAN: Doing what? . . . What man do you mean? . . .

OEDIPUS: This man here—or of having ever met him before?

HERDSMAN: Not so that I could speak at once from memory.

MESSENGER: And no wonder, master. But I will bring clear recollection to his ignorance. I am sure that he well remembers the time when we abode in the region of Cithaeron—he with two flocks, I, his comrade, with one—three full half-years, from spring to Arcturus; and then for the winter I used to drive my flock to my own fold and he took his to the fold of Laius. Did any of this happen as I tell or did it not?

HERDSMAN: You speak the truth, though it is long ago.

MESSENGER: Come, tell me now, do you recall having given me a boy in those days, to be reared as my own fosterson?

HERDSMAN: What now? Why do you ask the question?

MESSENGER: Yonder man, my friend, is he who was then young.

HERDSMAN: Plague seize you, be silent once for all!

OEDIPUS: Ha! Chide him not, old man; your words need chiding more than his.

HERDSMAN: Wherein, most noble master, do I offend?

OEDIPUS: In not telling of the boy concerning whom he asks.

HERDSMAN: He speaks without knowledge, he is busy to no purpose.

OEDIPUS: You will not speak with a good grace, but you shall on pain.

HERDSMAN: Nay, for the gods' love, misuse not an old man!

OEDIPUS: Ho, someone, pinion him this instant!

HERDSMAN: Alas, why? What more would you learn?

OEDIPUS: Did you give this man the child of whom he asks?

HERDSMAN: I did—and would I had perished that day!

OEDIPUS: You will come to that unless you tell the honest truth.

HERDSMAN: Much more am I lost if I speak.

OEDIPUS: The fellow is bent, it seems, on more delays.

HERDSMAN: No, no! I said before that I gave it to him.

OEDIPUS: Where had you got it? In your own house or from another?

HERDSMAN: My own it was not—I had received it from a man.

OEDIPUS: From whom of the citizens here? From what home?

HERDSMAN: Forbear, for the gods' love, master, forbear to ask more!

OEDIPUS: You are lost if I have to question you again.

HERDSMAN: It was a child, then, of the house of Laius.

OEDIPUS: A slave? Or one born of his own race?

HERDSMAN: Ah me—I am on the dreaded brink of speech.

OEDIPUS: And I of hearing; yet must I hear.

HERDSMAN: You must know, then, that it was said to be his own child—but your lady within could best say how these things are.

OEDIPUS: How? She gave it to you?

HERDSMAN: Yes, O King.

OEDIPUS: For what end?

HERDSMAN: That I should make away with it.

OEDIPUS: Her own child, the wretch?

HERDSMAN: Yes, from fear of evil prophecies.

OEDIPUS: What were they?

HERDSMAN: The tale ran that he must slay his sire.

OEDIPUS: Why then did you give him up to this old man?

HERDSMAN: Through pity, master, thinking that he would bear him away to another land, from which he himself came; but he saved him for the direst woe. For if you are what this man says, know that you were born to misery.

OEDIPUS: Oh, oh! All brought to pass, all true! You light, may I now look my last on you, I who have been found accursed in birth, accursed in wedlock, accursed in the shedding of blood!

(OEDIPUS *rushes into the palace.*)

CHORUS: *Alas, ye generations of men, how mere a shadow do I count your life! Where, where is the mortal who wins more of happiness than just the seeming, and, after the semblance, a falling away? Thine is a fate that warns me—thine, thine, unhappy Oedipus—to call no earthly creature blessed.*

For he, O Zeus, sped his shaft with peerless skill, and won the prize of an all-prosperous fortune; he slew the maiden with crooked talons who sang darkly; he arose for our land as a tower against death. And from that time,

Oedipus, thou hast been called our king, and hast been honored supremely, bearing sway in great Thebes.

But now whose story is more grievous in men's ears? Who is a more wretched captive to fierce plagues and troubles, with all his life reversed?

Alas, renowned Oedipus! The same bounteous place of rest sufficed thee, as child and as sire also, that thou shouldst make thereon thy nuptial couch. Oh, how can the soil wherein thy father sowed, unhappy one, have suffered thee in silence so long?

Time the all-seeing hath found thee out in thy despite: he judgeth the monstrous marriage wherein begetter and begotten have long been one.

Alas, thou child of Laius, would, would that I had never seen thee! I wail as one who pours a dirge from his lips; sooth to speak, 'twas thou that gavest me new life, and through thee darkness hath fallen upon mine eyes.

(*Enter* MESSENGER *from palace.*)

MESSENGER: You who are ever most honored in this land, what deeds you shall hear, what deeds behold, what burden of sorrow shall be yours, if true to your race, you still care for the house of Labdacus! Not Ister or Phasis, I declare, could wash this house clean, so many are the ills that it shrouds or will soon bring to light—ills wrought not unwittingly but of purpose. Those griefs smart most which are seen to be of our own choice.

CHORUS: Indeed those which we heard before do not fall short of claiming sore lamentation: besides them what do you announce?

MESSENGER: This is the shortest tale to tell and to hear: our royal lady Jocasta is dead.

CHORUS: Alas, luckless one! From what cause?

MESSENGER: By her own hand. The worst pain in what has chanced is not for you, for yours it is not to behold. Nevertheless, so far as my own memory serves, you shall learn that unhappy woman's fate.

When, frantic, she had passed within the vestibule, she rushed straight toward her nuptial couch, clutching her hair with the fingers of both hands. Once within the chamber she dashed the doors together at her back; then called on the name of Laius, long since a corpse, mindful of that son begotten long ago by whom the sire was slain, leaving the mother to breed accursed offspring with his own.

And she bewailed the wedlock whereby, wretched woman, she had borne a twofold brood, husband by husband, children by her child. How thereafter she perished is more than I know. For with a shriek Oedipus burst in, and suffered us not to watch her woe to the end; on him, as he rushed around, our eyes were set. To and fro he went, asking us to give him a sword, asking where he should find the wife who was no wife, but a mother whose womb had borne alike himself and his children. And in his frenzy a power above man was his guide, for it was none of us mortals who were nigh. With a dread shriek, as though someone beckoned him on, he sprang at the double doors, and from their sockets forced the bending bolts, and rushed into the room.

There we beheld the woman hanging by the neck in a twisted noose of swinging cords. But he, when he saw her, with a dread deep cry of misery loosed the halter by which she hung. When the hapless woman was stretched upon the ground, then was the sequel dread to see. He tore from her raiment the golden brooches with which she was decked, and lifted them, and smote full on his own eyeballs, uttering words like these: "No more shall you behold such horrors as I was suffering and working! Long enough have you looked on those whom you ought never to have seen, failed in knowledge of those whom I yearned to know: henceforth you shall be dark!"

To such dire refrain not once alone but oft he struck his eyes with lifted hand. At each blow the ensanguined eyeballs bedewed his beard; no sluggish drops of gore were sent forth, but all at once a dark shower of blood came down like hail.

From the deeds of both ills have broken forth not on one alone, but with mingled woe for man and wife. The old happiness of their ancestral fortune was aforetime happiness indeed; but today lamentation, ruin, death, shame, all earthly ills that can be named, all, all are theirs.

CHORUS: And has the sufferer now any respite from pain?

MESSENGER: He is crying for someone to unbar the gates and show to all the Cadmeans his father's slayer, his mother's —the unholy word must not pass my lips—as intending to cast himself out of the land and abide no more to make the house accursed under his own curse. But he lacks strength and one to guide his steps; for the anguish is

more than man may bear. And he will show this to you
also; for, look, the bars of the gates are withdrawn, and
soon you shall behold a sight which even he who abhors
it must pity.

(*Enter* OEDIPUS.)

CHORUS: O dread fate for men to see, O most dreadful
of all that have met my eyes! Unhappy man, what madness has come on you? Who is the unearthly foe that,
with a bound of more than mortal range, has made your
ill-starred life his prey?

  Alas, alas, you unfortunate! Nay, I cannot even look on
you, though there is much that I would like to ask, like
to learn, much that draws my wistful gaze—you fill me
with such shuddering!

OEDIPUS: Woe is me! Alas, alas, wretched that I am! Whither,
whither, am I borne in my misery? How is my voice swept
abroad on the wings of the air? O my Fate, how far have
you sprung!

CHORUS: To a dread place, dire in men's ears, dire in their
sight.

OEDIPUS: *O you horror of darkness that enfold me, visitant
unspeakable, resistless, sped by a wind too fair!*
  Ay me! And once again, ay me!
  *How is my soul pierced by the stab of these goads, and
too by the memory of sorrows!*

CHORUS: Yes, amid woes so many a twofold pain may well
be yours to mourn and to bear.

OEDIPUS: *Ah, friend, you still are steadfast in your attendance of me, you still have patience to care for the blind
man! Ah me! Your presence is not hid from me; no,
dark though I am yet I know your voice full well.*

CHORUS: Man of dread deeds, how could you so quench your
vision? What more than human power urged you?

OEDIPUS: *Apollo, friends, Apollo was he that brought these
woes of mine to pass, these sore, sore woes; but the hand
that struck the eyes was none save mine, wretched that I
am! Why was I to see when light could show me nothing
sweet?*

CHORUS: These things were just as you say.

OEDIPUS: *Say, friends, what more can I behold, what can I
love, what greeting can touch my ear with joy? Hasten,
lead me from the land, friends, lead me hence, the ut-*

*terly lost, the thrice accursed, yes, the mortal most ab-
horred of heaven!*

CHORUS: Wretched alike for your fortune and for your sense
of it, would that I had never so much as known you!

OEDIPUS: *Perish the man, whoever he was, that freed me
in the pastures from the cruel shackle on my feet, and
saved me from death, and gave me back to life—a thank-
less deed! Had I died then I would not have been so sore
a grief to my friends and to my own soul.*

CHORUS: I too would have preferred it so.

OEDIPUS: *I would not have come to shed my father's blood,
nor been called among men the spouse of her from whom
I sprang. But now I am forsaken of the gods, son of a defiled mother, successor to his bed who gave me my own
wretched being; and if there is yet a woe surpassing woes,
it has become the portion of Oedipus.*

CHORUS: I do not know how I can say that you have
counseled well, for you had better be dead than living and
blind.

OEDIPUS: Do not show me at length that these things had
better not be done so; give me no more counsel. If I had
sight I do not know with what eyes I could even have
looked on my father when I came to the place of the
dead, yes, or on my miserable mother, since I have sinned
against both such sins as strangling could not punish. Do
you suppose that the sight of children born as mine were
born was lovely for me to look upon? No, no, not lovely
to my eyes forever! No, nor was this town with its tow-
ered walls, nor the sacred statues of the gods, since I,
thrice wretched that I am, I, noblest of the sons of Thebes,
have doomed myself to know these no more by my own
command that all should thrust away the impious one,
even him whom the gods have shown to be unholy—
and of the race of Laius.

After bearing such a stain upon me, was I to look with
steady eyes on this folk? No, surely; no, if there were yet a
way to choke the fount of hearing I would not have spared
to make a fast prison of this wretched frame, that so I
should have known neither sight nor sound; for it is sweet
that our thought should dwell beyond the sphere of
griefs.

Alas, Cithaeron, why did you have a shelter for me?

When I was given to you why did you not slay me straight-way, that so I might never have revealed my source to men? Ah Polybus, ah Corinth, and you that were called the ancient house of my fathers, how seeming fair was I your nurseling, and what ills were festering beneath! For now I am found evil, and of evil birth. O you three roads, and you secret glen, you coppice, and narrow way where three paths met, you who drank from my hands that father's blood which was my own—do you remember what deeds I wrought for you to see, and then, when I came here, what fresh deeds I went on to do?

O marriage-rites, you gave me birth, and when you had brought me forth you bore children to your child, you created an incestuous kinship of fathers and brothers and sons, of brides and wives and mothers, yes, all the foulest shame that is wrought among men! Nay, but it is improper to name what it is improper to do. Hurry, for the gods' love, hide me somewhere beyond the land, or slay me, or cast me into the sea, where you shall never more behold me! Approach, deign to lay your hands on a wretched man; hearken, fear not—my plague can rest on no mortal beside.

(*Enter* CREON.)

CHORUS: Nay, here is Creon, in apt season for your requests, whether they require act or counsel; for he alone is left to guard the land in your stead.

OEDIPUS: Ah me, how indeed shall I accost him? What claim to credence can be shown on my part? For in the past I have been found wholly false to him.

CREON: I have not come in mockery, Oedipus, nor to reproach you with any bygone fault. (*To* ATTENDANTS.) But you, if you respect the children of men no more, revere at least the all-nurturing flame of our lord the Sun, spare to show thus nakedly a pollution such as this, one which neither earth can welcome, nor the holy rain, nor the light. Nay, take him into the house as quickly as you may, for it best accords with piety that kinsfolk alone should see and hear a kinsman's woes.

OEDIPUS: For the gods' love, since you have done a gentle violence to my presage when you come in a spirit so noble to me a man most vile, grant me a boon; for your good I will speak, not for my own.

CREON: What wish are you so eager to have of me?

OEDIPUS: Cast me out of this land with all speed, to a place where no mortal shall be found to greet me more.

CREON: This I would have done, be sure, but that I craved first to learn all my duty from the god.

OEDIPUS: Nay, his behest has been set forth in full—to let me perish, the parricide, the unholy one that I am.

CREON: Such was the purport; yet seeing to what a pass we have come it is better to learn clearly what should be done.

OEDIPUS: Will you then seek a response on behalf of such a wretch as I am?

CREON: Yes, for you yourself will now surely put faith in the god.

OEDIPUS: Yes; and on you I lay this charge, to you I will make this entreaty: give to her who is within such burial as you would yourself give, for you will render the last rites to your own properly. But for me, never let this city of my sire be condemned to have me dwelling in it, so long as I live. No, suffer me to abide on the hills, yonder where Cithaeron is, famed as mine, which my mother and father while they lived set for my appointed tomb, that so I may die by the decree of those who sought to slay me. Yet of this much I am sure, that neither sickness nor anything else can destroy me; for I would never have been snatched from death except to be reserved for some strange doom.

Let my fate go where it will; but as touching my children, I pray you, Creon, take no care upon yourself for my sons; they are men, so that wherever they may be they can never lack the means to live. But my two girls, poor unfortunates, who never knew my table spread apart or lacked their father's presence, but always in all things shared my daily bread—I pray you, care for *them*. If you can, suffer me to touch them with my hands and to indulge my grief. Grant it, Prince, grant it, you noble heart! Ah, could I but once touch them with my hands I should think that they were with me, even as when I had sight. . . .

(ANTIGONE *and* ISMENE *are led in.*)

Ha? Gods, can it be my loved ones that I hear sobbing, can Creon have taken pity on me and sent me my children, my darlings? Am I right?

CREON: Yes, it is of my contriving, for I knew your joy in them of old, the joy that now is yours.

OEDIPUS: Then blessed be you, and for reward of this errand may heaven prove a kinder guardian to you than it has to me. My children, where are you? Come here, here to the hands of him whose mother was your own, the hands whose doings have wrought that your sire's once bright eyes should be such orbs as these; seeing nothing, knowing nothing, he became your father by her from whom he sprang. For you too I weep—behold you I cannot—when I think of the bitter life in days to come which men will make you live. To what company of the citizens will you go, to what festival, from which you will not return home in tears, instead of sharing in the holiday? When you have come to years ripe for marriage, who shall he be, who shall be the man, my daughters, who will hazard taking unto him such reproaches as must be baneful alike to my offspring and to yours? What misery is wanting? Your sire slew his sire, he had seed of her who bore him, and begot you at the sources of his own being! Such are the taunts that will be cast at you; and who then will wed? The man does not live, no, it cannot be, my children, but you must wither in barren maidenhood.

Ah, son of Menoeceus, hear me—since you are the only father left to them, since their parents, both of us, are lost—do not allow them to wander poor and unwed, for they are your kinswomen, and do not abase them to the level of my woes. Pity them, when you see them at this tender age so utterly forlorn, except for you. Signify your promise, generous man, by the touch of your hand! To you, my children, I would have given much counsel if your minds were mature; but now I would have this to be your prayer, that you live where occasion suffers, and that the life which is your portion may be happier than your sire's.

CREON: Your grief has had large enough scope. Nay, pass into the house.

OEDIPUS: I must obey, though it is in no wise sweet.

CREON: Yes, for it is in season that all things are good.

OEDIPUS: Do you know on what conditions I will go?

CREON: You shall name them; I shall know them when I hear.

OEDIPUS: See that you send me to dwell beyond this land.

CREON: You are asking me for what the gods must give.

OEDIPUS: Nay, to the gods I have become most hateful.

CREON: Then you shall have your wish presently.

OEDIPUS: So you consent?

CREON: It is not my wont to speak idly what I do not mean.

OEDIPUS: Then it is time to lead me away.

CREON: Come then—but let your children go.

OEDIPUS: Do not take these from me!

CREON: Do not crave to be master in all things; the mastery which you won has not followed you through life.

CHORUS: *Dwellers in our native Thebes, behold, this is Oedipus, who knew the famed riddle and was a man most mighty; what citizen did not gaze with envy on his fortunes? Behold into what a stormy sea of dread trouble he has come.*

Therefore, while our eyes wait to see the destined final day, we must call no one happy who is of mortal race, until he has crossed life's border, free from pain.

SUMMARY OF
Oedipus at Colonus

AT THE END of his long life, when Athens was sinking to its fall, Sophocles returned to the Oedipus theme for his farewell to Athens and to the stage. The characters of *Oedipus at Colonus* are those with which Sophocles had won his greatest successes. Theseus is there to glorify Athenian traditions of justice and generosity, and the affectionately described locale is the parish of Sophocles' own boyhood. Oedipus, old and blind but still impetuous and impatient, is led in by his daughter Antigone. Theseus befriends Oedipus, who promises to defend Athens after his death. Ismene brings news of an oracle: in the imminent struggle between Eteocles and Polyneices the side that has possession of Oedipus' person will win. Oedipus curses them both. Creon enters to ask Oedipus' support, is bitterly reviled, seizes the two girls, and is about to seize Oedipus also; all are rescued by Theseus. Polyneices comes to beg his father's support, but is sent away with a curse. A peal of thunder announces that the moment of Oedipus' passing is at hand, and the blind man leads Theseus to the spot, known to no one else, destined for his transfiguration. Oedipus has at last been justified, and his spirit will be a blessing for Athens.

In *Oedipus the King,* crushed Oedipus readily agrees with the chorus that he is utterly vile; but when the elders of Colonus shrink back at hearing his name, Oedipus protests, "In *nature* how was I evil?" As a man he had behaved well, and his elevation to the status of hero, to be made manifest by his transfiguration, is a vindication of his total career. But the implied distinction between the measure of man, according to which Oedipus is innocent, and the conventional notion of sin, against which he was helpless, makes a transition to the thought of Euripides, for whom the disparate imperatives of nature and convention constituted a central element in tragedy.

Philoctetes

PHILOCTETES POSSESSED THE marvelous bow which Heracles on his pyre had given Philoctetes' father. He was a respected member of the Greek expedition that sailed against Troy, but while he was directing his fellow chieftains to a particular altar en route he was bitten by a snake, and his cries of anguish and the stench of his wound were so disconcerting that his shipmates, under Odysseus' direction, marooned him on the deserted island of Lemnos. For ten years the solitary cripple had eked out an existence with his bow, with growing hatred of the Greeks and particularly of Odysseus. In the tenth year of the Trojan War the Greeks received an oracle that Troy could be taken only with the help of Philoctetes and his bow, and Odysseus and Neoptolemus son of Achilles were sent to fetch them. *Philoctetes* begins with Odysseus (who dares not show himself to Philoctetes) persuading the ingenuous lad to inveigle Philoctetes to Troy. Neoptolemus is disillusioned; he had been nurtured on tales of his late father's chivalry, and now he finds that his first assignment is to cheat a helpless cripple of his only means of livelihood. Yielding to his mentor, he wins Philoctetes' confidence and falsely promises to carry him home. He gets possession of the bow when Philoctetes, helpless in a paroxysm of pain, entrusts it to him. Presently, and against Odysseus' vehement protest, conscience moves Neoptolemus to restore the bow. His pleas to Philoctetes to come of his free will are futile. When Odysseus comes to threaten force, Philoctetes is on the point of using the bow against him. Heracles (who had used the bow for the service of mankind) appears *ex machina* and persuades Philoctetes to go to Troy, where he will win both health and glory. In effect, Philoctetes had resigned from society and now consents to rejoin it. Neoptolemus, who had been isolated by a more amiable kind of self-centeredness, has learned to participate in adult life with

integrity. It is easy but unfair to condemn Odysseus as a
corrupter of youth. Another day, as he himself says, he will
be as honest as any other man; but the personal luxury of
honesty must give way when the needs of society as a whole
demand chicanery. That the theme of man and society is
central in this play (it is at least incidental in others of
Sophocles) is clear from the circumstance that Lemnos is
represented as uninhabited when it was in fact inhabited and
was accepted as such in (lost) plays of Aeschylus and Euripides on Philoctetes.

CHARACTERS

ODYSSEUS
NEOPTOLEMUS
PHILOCTETES
MERCHANT, *follower of Odysseus in disguise*
HERACLES
CHORUS, *sailors of Neoptolemus*

SCENE: Rocky cliff on Lemnos

Translated by **R. C. JEBB**

(Enter ODYSSEUS *and* NEOPTOLEMUS.)

ODYSSEUS: This is the shore of the sea-girt land of Lemnos,
untrodden of men and desolate. Neoptolemus, true-bred
son of Achilles, you whose sire was the noblest of the
Greeks, here long ago I put ashore the Malian, son of
Poeas (as I was bidden by my chiefs to do), his foot all
ulcerous with a gnawing sore, because we could attempt
neither drink-offering nor sacrifice in peace; with his fierce
ill-omened cries he filled the whole camp continually,
shrieking, moaning. But what need to speak of that? This
is no time for many words; if he learns that I am here
I shall waste the whole plan by which I expect to take
him soon.

Come, to work! It is for you to help in what remains.
Seek where in this region is a cave with twofold mouth,
such that in cold weather either front offers a sunny seat,
but in summer a breeze wafts sleep through the tunneled
grotto. And a little below, on the left hand, you might
see a spring if it has not failed.

Move toward the place silently, and signify to me
whether he is still living there or is to be sought elsewhere, so that our further course may be explained by me
and heard by you and sped by the joint work of both.

NEOPTOLEMUS: King Odysseus, the task that you set lies not
far off; I think I see such a cave as you have described.

ODYSSEUS: Above you or below? I do not see it.

NEOPTOLEMUS: Here, high up. Of footsteps not a sound.

ODYSSEUS: See whether he is not lodged there, asleep.

NEOPTOLEMUS: I see an empty chamber, no man in it.

ODYSSEUS: And no provision for man's abode?

NEOPTOLEMUS: Yes, a mattress of leaves, as if for someone who lives here.

ODYSSEUS: All else bare? Nothing else beneath the roof?

NEOPTOLEMUS: Just a rude cup of wood, the work of a sorry craftsman, and with it this tinder stuff.

ODYSSEUS: His is the household you describe.

NEOPTOLEMUS: Ha! Here are also some rags drying in the sun, stained with matter from some grievous sore.

ODYSSEUS: The man dwells in these regions, clearly, and is somewhere not far off; how could a man go far afield with foot maimed by that inveterate plague? No, he has gone forth in quest of food or perhaps of some soothing herb that he has noted somewhere. Send your attendant, therefore, to keep watch, lest the foe come on me unawares; for he would rather take me than all the Greeks beside.

NEOPTOLEMUS: Enough, the man is going and the path shall be watched. And now, if you would say more, proceed.

ODYSSEUS: Son of Achilles, you must be loyal to your mission, and not with your body alone. If you should hear some new thing, some plan unknown to you till now, you must help it; for to help is your part here.

NEOPTOLEMUS: What is your bidding?

ODYSSEUS: You must beguile the mind of Philoctetes by a story told in your conversation with him. When he asks you who and whence you are, say the son of Achilles—there must be no deception touching that. But say you are homeward bound: you have left the fleet of the Achaean warriors and have conceived a deadly hatred for them, because, when they had moved you by their prayers to come from home (since this was their only hope of taking Ilium), they deemed you not worthy of the arms of Achilles, did not deign to give them to you when you came and claimed them by right, but made them over to Odysseus. Of me say what you will, the vilest of vile reproaches; by that you will cost me no pang. But if you fail to do this deed you will bring sorrow on all our host. For if yonder man's bow is not to be taken, never can you sack the realm of Dardanus.

And mark why your intercourse with him may be free from mistrust or danger while mine cannot. *You* have come to Troy under no oath to any man and by no constraint, nor had you any part in the earlier voyage; but none of these things can I deny. And so if he shall perceive me while he is still master of his bow I am lost, and you as my comrade will share my doom. No, the thing that must be plotted is just this—how you may win the resistless arms by stealth. I well know, my son, that by nature you are not apt to utter or contrive such guile, yet seeing that victory is a sweet prize to gain bend your will to it; our honesty shall be shown forth another time. But now lend yourself to me for one little knavish day, and then, through all your days to come, be called the most righteous of mankind.

NEOPTOLEMUS: When counsels pain my ear, son of Laertes, then I abhor to aid them with my hand. It is not in my nature to compass anything by evil arts, nor was it, as men say, in my sire's. But I am ready to take the man by force, not by fraud; having the use of one foot only he cannot prevail in fight against us who are so many. And yet, having been sent to act with you, I am loth to be called traitor. But my wish, O King, is to do right and miss my aim rather than succeed by evil ways.

ODYSSEUS: Son of brave sire, time was when I too, in my youth, had a slow tongue and a ready hand; but now, when I come forth to the proof, I see that words, not deeds, are ever the masters among men.

NEOPTOLEMUS: What then is your command? What but that I should lie?

ODYSSEUS: I say that you are to take Philoctetes by guile.

NEOPTOLEMUS: And why by guile rather than by persuasion?

ODYSSEUS: He will never listen; and by force you cannot take him.

NEOPTOLEMUS: Has he such dread strength to make him bold?

ODYSSEUS: Shafts unavoidable and winged with death.

NEOPTOLEMUS: May none dare even to approach that foe?

ODYSSEUS: Not unless you take him by guile, as I say.

NEOPTOLEMUS: You think it no shame then to speak falsehoods?

ODYSSEUS: No, if the falsehood brings deliverance.

NEOPTOLEMUS: How have the face to speak those words?

ODYSSEUS: When your deed promises gain it is unmeet to shrink.

NEOPTOLEMUS: What gain is it for me that he should come to Troy?

ODYSSEUS: With these shafts alone can Troy be taken.

NEOPTOLEMUS: Then *I* am not to be the conqueror, as you said?

ODYSSEUS: Neither you apart from these, nor these from you.

NEOPTOLEMUS: It would seem that we must try to win them, if it stands thus.

ODYSSEUS: Know that if you do this thing two prizes are yours.

NEOPTOLEMUS: What are they? Tell me, and I will not refuse the deed.

ODYSSEUS: You will be called at once wise and valiant.

NEOPTOLEMUS: Come what may, I'll do it, and cast off all shame.

ODYSSEUS: Are you mindful, then, of the counsels that I gave?

NEOPTOLEMUS: Be sure of it, now that once I have consented.

ODYSSEUS: Stay here, then, in wait for him; I will go away, not to be seen with you, and will send our watcher back to the ship. If you seem to be tarrying at all beyond the due time I will send that same man here again, disguised as the captain of a merchant ship, so secrecy may help us. Then, my son, as he tells his artful story take such hints as may help you from the tenor of his words.

Now I will go to the ship, having left this charge with you. May speeding Hermes, the lord of stratagem, lead us on, and Victory, even Athena Polias, who saves me ever!
(*Exit.*)

(*Enter* CHORUS.)

CHORUS: *A stranger in a strange land, what am I to hide, what am I to speak, O Master, before a man who will be swift to think evil? You be my guide; his skill excels all other skill, his counsel has no peer, with whom is the sway of the godlike scepter given by Zeus. And to you, my son, that sovereign power has descended from of old; tell me, therefore, wherein I am to serve you.*

NEOPTOLEMUS: *For the present you may survey fearlessly the place where he lives at the ocean's edge; but when the dread wayfarer who has left this dwelling shall return, come forward at my beck from time to time and try to help as the moment may require.*

CHORUS: *Long have I been careful of that care, my prince, that my eye should be watchful for your good before all else. Now tell me, in what manner of shelter has he made his abode? In what region is he? It were not unseasonable for me to learn, lest he surprise me from some quarter. What is the place of his wandering, or of his rest? Where does he plant his steps, within his dwelling or abroad?*

NEOPTOLEMUS: *Here you see his home with its two portals, his rocky cell.*

CHORUS: *And its luckless inmate—where is he gone?*

NEOPTOLEMUS: *I doubt not but he is trailing his painful steps somewhere near this spot, in quest of food. Rumor says that in this fashion he lives, seeking prey with his winged shafts, all-wretched that he is. No healer of his woe comes near him.*

CHORUS: *I pity him, to think how, with no man to care for him, and seeing no companion's face, suffering, always lonely, he is vexed by fierce disease and bewildered by each want as it rises. How, how does he endure in his misery? Alas, the dark dealings of the gods! Alas, hapless races of men, whose destiny exceeds due measure!*

This man, noble, perchance, as any scion of the noblest house, reft of all life's gifts, lies lonely, apart from his fellows, with the dappled or shaggy beasts of the field, piteous alike in his torments and his hunger, bearing anguish that finds no cure; while the mountain nymph, babbling Echo, appearing afar, makes answer to his bitter cries.

NEOPTOLEMUS: *Nothing of this is a marvel to me. By heavenly ordinance, if such as I may judge, those first sufferings came on him from relentless Chryse. The woes that now he bears, with none to tend him, surely he bears by the providence of some god, that so he might not bend against Troy the resistless shafts divine till the time be fulfilled when, as men say, Troy is fated by those shafts to fall.*

CHORUS: *Hush, peace, my son!*

NEOPTOLEMUS: *What now?*

CHORUS: *A sound rose on the air such as might haunt the*

*life of a man in weary pain. From this point it came I
think—or this. It smites, it smites indeed upon my ear—
the voice of one who creeps painfully on his way. I cannot mistake that grievous cry of human anguish from afar
—its accents are too clear.*

Then turn, my son—

NEOPTOLEMUS: *Say where?*

CHORUS: *—to new counsels; the man is not far off but near.
Not with music of the reed does he come, like a shepherd
in the pastures, no, but with far-sounding moan as he stum-
bles, perhaps from stress of pain, or as he gazes on the
haven that has no ship for guest. Loud is his cry and dread.*

(*Enter* PHILOCTETES.)

PHILOCTETES: O strangers!

Who may you be and from what country have you put
into this land that is harborless and desolate? What should
I deem to be your city or your race?

The fashion of your garb is Greek, most welcome to my
sight, but I would like to hear your speech. Do not shrink
from me in fear or be scared by my wild looks; nay, in
pity for one so wretched and so lonely, for a sufferer so
desolate and so friendless, speak to me, if indeed you have
come as friends. Oh, answer! It is not meet that I should
fail of this, at least, from you, or you from me.

NEOPTOLEMUS: Then know this first, good sir, that we are
Greeks, since you are eager to learn that.

PHILOCTETES: O well-loved sound! Ah, that I should indeed
be greeted by such a man, after so long a time! What
quest, my son, has drawn you toward these shores and
to this spot? What enterprise? What kindliest of winds?
Speak, tell me all, so I may know who you are.

NEOPTOLEMUS: My birthplace is the sea-girt Scyros; I am
sailing homeward; Achilles was my sire; my name is Neoptolemus. You know all.

PHILOCTETES: O son of well-loved father and dear land,
foster child of aged Lycomedes, on what errand have you
touched this coast? Whence are you sailing?

NEOPTOLEMUS: It is from Ilium that I hold my present
course.

PHILOCTETES: What? You were not, certainly, our shipmate
at the beginning of the voyage to Ilium?

NEOPTOLEMUS: Had you indeed a part in that emprise?

PHILOCTETES: O my son, then you do not know who is before you?

NEOPTOLEMUS: How should I know one whom I had never seen before?

PHILOCTETES: Then you have not even heard my name or any rumor of those miseries by which I was perishing?

NEOPTOLEMUS: Be assured that I know nothing of what you ask.

PHILOCTETES: O wretched indeed that I am, O abhorred of heaven, that no word of this my plight should have won its way to my home or to any home of Greeks! No, the men who wickedly cast me out keep their secret and laugh, while my plague still rejoices in its strength and grows to more!

O my son, O boy whose father was Achilles, behold, I am he of whom you may have heard as lord of the bow of Heracles. I am the son of Poeas, Philoctetes, whom the two chieftains and the Cephallenian king foully cast upon this solitude when I was wasting with a fierce disease, stricken down by the furious bite of the destroying serpent. With that plague for sole companion, O my son, those men put me out here and were gone, when from sea-girt Chryse they touched at this coast with their fleet. They were glad when they saw me asleep, after much tossing on the waves; they abandoned me in the shelter of a cave upon the shore, first putting out a few rags, good enough for such a wretch, and also a scanty dole of food: may heaven give them the like!

Think now, my son, think what a waking was mine when they had gone and I rose from sleep that day! What bitter tears started from my eyes, what miseries were those that I bewailed when I saw that the ships with which I had sailed were all gone, and that there was no man in the place, not one to help, not one to ease the burden of the sickness that vexed me, when, looking all around, I could find no provision, save for anguish—but of that a plenteous store, my son!

So time went on for me, season by season; and alone in this narrow house I was content to meet each want by my own service. For hunger's needs this bow provided, bringing down the winged doves; and whatever my string-sped shaft might strike I would crawl to it myself, luckless me, trailing my wretched foot just so far. Or if, again, water had to be fetched, or if, when the frost was out, as happens often in winter, a bit of firewood had to be broken, I would creep forth, poor wretch, and manage it. Then fire would be lacking; but by rubbing stone on stone I would at last draw forth the hidden spark; and this it is that keeps life in me from day to day. Indeed, a roof over my head, and with it fire, gives all that I want—save release from my disease.

Come now, my son, you must learn what manner of isle this is. No mariner approaches it by choice; there is no anchorage; there is no seaport where he can find a gainful market or a kindly welcome. This is not a place to which prudent men make voyages. Well, suppose that someone has put in against his will; such things may often happen in the long course of a man's life. These visitors when they come have compassionate words for me, and perhaps they are moved by pity to give me a little food or some raiment; but there is one thing that no one will do when I speak of it—take me safe home. No, this is now the tenth year that I am wearing out my wretched days, in hunger and in misery, feeding the plague that is never sated with my flesh.

Thus have the Atreidae and the proud Odysseus dealt with me, my son: may the Olympian gods some day give them the like sufferings in requital for mine!

CHORUS: I too pity you, son of Poeas, in like measure with your former visitors.

NEOPTOLEMUS: And I am myself a witness to your words; I know that they are true, for I have felt the villainy of the Atreidae and the proud Odysseus.

PHILOCTETES: What, have you too a grief against the accursed sons of Atreus, a cause to resent ill-usage?

NEOPTOLEMUS: O that it might be mine one day to wreak my hatred with my hand, that so Mycenae might learn, and Sparta, that Scyros also is a mother of brave men.

PHILOCTETES: Well said, my son! Now why have you come in this fierce wrath which you denounce against them?

NEOPTOLEMUS: Son of Poeas, I will speak out—and yet it is hard to speak—concerning the outrage that I suffered from them at my coming. When fate decreed that Achilles should die——

PHILOCTETES: Ah me! Tell me no more until I first know this: are you saying that the son of Peleus is dead?

NEOPTOLEMUS: Dead—by no mortal hand, but by a god's; laid low, as men say, by the arrow of Phoebus.

PHILOCTETES: Well, noble alike are the slayer and the slain! I scarcely know, my son, which I should do first, inquire into your wrong or mourn the dead.

NEOPTOLEMUS: Your own sorrows, I think, are enough for you, without mourning for the woes of your neighbor.

PHILOCTETES: You speak the truth. Resume your story, then, and tell me in what way they wronged you.

NEOPTOLEMUS: They came for me in a ship with gaily decked prow—princely Odysseus and he who watched over my father's youth—saying (whether truly or falsely I do not know) that since my father had perished fate now forbade that the towers of Troy should be taken by any hand but mine.

Saying that these things were so, my friend, they made me pause not long before I set forth in haste, chiefly through my yearning toward the dead, that I might see him before burial—for I had never seen him. Besides, there was a charm in their promise if, when I went, I should sack the towers of Troy.

It was now the second day of my voyage when, sped by breeze and oar, I drew nigh to cruel Sigeum. And when I landed straightway all the host thronged about me with greetings, vowing that they saw their lost Achilles once more alive.

He then lay dead; and I, unlucky me, when I had wept for him, presently went to the Atreidae—to friends, as I might well suppose—and claimed my father's arms with all else that had been his. O, it was a shameless answer that they made! "Seed of Achilles, you can take all else that was your sire's; but of the arms another man is now lord, the son of Laertes." The tears came into my eyes, I sprang up in passionate anger, and I said in my bitterness, "Wretch! What, have you dared to give my arms to another man, without my leave?" Then said Odysseus, for he chanced to be near, "Yes, boy, this award of theirs is just; I saved the arms and their master at his need." Then straightway in my fury I began to hurl all manner of taunts at him and spared not one, if I was indeed to be robbed of my arms by *him*. At this point, stung by the abuse though not prone to wrath, he answered, "You were not here with us but absent from your duty. And since you must talk so saucily, you shall never carry those arms back to Scyros."

Thus upbraided, thus insulted, I am sailing for home, despoiled of my own by that worst offspring of an evil breed, Odysseus. And yet he, I think, is less to blame than the rulers. For an army, like a city, hangs wholly on its leaders, and when men do lawless deeds it is the counsel of their teachers that corrupts them. My tale is told; and may the foe of the Atreidae have the favor of heaven as he has mine!

CHORUS: *Goddess of the hills, all-fostering Earth mother of Zeus most high, thou through whose realm the great Pactolus rolls golden sands—there also, dread Mother, I called upon thy name when all the insults of the Atreidae were being heaped upon this man—when they were giving his sire's armor, that peerless marvel, to the son of Lartius —hear it, thou immortal one, who ridest on bull-slaughtering lions!*

PHILOCTETES: It seems that you have come to me, friends, well commended by a common grief; your story is of a like strain with mine, so that I can recognize the work of the Atreidae and of Odysseus. Well I know that he would lend his tongue to any base pretext, to any villainy, if thereby he could hope to compass some dishonest end. No, it is not at this that I wonder, but rather that the elder Ajax, if he was there, could endure to see it.

NEOPTOLEMUS: Ah, friend, he was no more; I should never have been thus plundered while he lived.

PHILOCTETES: How do you say? Is he too dead and gone?

NEOPTOLEMUS: Think of him as one who sees the light no more.

PHILOCTETES: Woe is me! But the son of Tydeus and the offspring of Sisyphus that was bought by Laertes—they will not die, for they ought not to live.

NEOPTOLEMUS: Not they, be sure of it. No, they are now prospering full greatly in the Argive host.

PHILOCTETES: And what of my brave old friend Nestor of Pylos—is he not alive? *Their* mischiefs were often baffled by his wise counsels.

ght, if I should not be unworthy, shall live in my grate-
thoughts. But tell me just what it is of which you have
ken, that I may learn what strange design on the part
the Greeks you are announcing to me.

CHANT: Pursuers have started in quest of you with ships,
e aged Phoenix and the sons of Theseus.

PTOLEMUS: To bring me back by force or by fair words?

RCHANT: I do not know, but I have come to tell you what
have heard.

OPTOLEMUS: Can Phoenix and his comrades be showing
such zeal on such an errand to please the Atreidae?

ERCHANT: The errand is being done, I assure you, and without delay.

EOPTOLEMUS: Why then was not Odysseus ready to sail for
this purpose and to bring the message himself? Or did some
fear restrain him?

MERCHANT: Oh, he and the son of Tydeus were setting
forth in pursuit of another man as I was leaving port.

NEOPTOLEMUS: Who was this other in quest of whom
Odysseus himself was sailing?

MERCHANT: There was a man . . . But tell me first who
that is yonder—and whatever you say do not speak loud.

NEOPTOLEMUS: Sir, you see the renowned Philoctetes.

MERCHANT: Ask me no more, then, but convey yourself with
all speed out of this land.

PHILOCTETES: What is he saying, my son? Why is the sailor
trafficking with you about me in these dark whispers?

NEOPTOLEMUS: I do not know his meaning yet, but whatever
he would say he must say openly to you and me and these
men.

MERCHANT: Seed of Achilles, do not accuse me to the army
of saying what I should not. I receive many benefits from
them for my services, as a poor man may.

NEOPTOLEMUS: I am the foe of the Atreidae, and this man
is my best friend because he hates them. Since then you
have come with a kindly purpose toward me you must
not keep from us any part of the tidings that you have
heard.

MERCHANT: Watch what you are doing, my son.

NEOPTOLEMUS: I am well aware.

MERCHANT: I will hold you accountable.

NEOPTOLEMUS: Do so, but speak.

NEOPTOLEMUS: He has trouble now; death has taken An-
tilochus, the son that was at his side.

PHILOCTETES: Ah me! These two again whom you have
named are men of whose death I had least wished to hear.
Alas! What are we to look for when these have died
and here again Odysseus lives—when he should have been
numbered with the dead in their place?

NEOPTOLEMUS: A clever wrestler he; but even clever
schemes, Philoctetes, are often tripped up.

PHILOCTETES: Now tell me, pray, where was Patroclus in
your need, he whom your father loved so well?

NEOPTOLEMUS: He too was dead. To be brief I would tell
you this: war takes no evil man by choice but good men always.

PHILOCTETES: I bear you witness. For that same reason I
will ask you how fares a man of little worth but shrewd
of tongue and clever——

NEOPTOLEMUS: Surely this will be no one but Odysseus?

PHILOCTETES: I did not mean him; there was one Thersites,
who could never be content with brief speech though all
men chafed. Do you know if he is alive?

NEOPTOLEMUS: I did not see him, but heard that he still
lives.

PHILOCTETES: It was his due. No evil thing has been known
to perish; no, the gods take a tender care of such and have
a strange joy in turning back from Hades all things villainous and knavish, while they are ever sending the just
and the good out of life. How am I to imagine these
things or wherein shall I praise them when, praising
the ways of the gods, I find that the gods are evil?

NEOPTOLEMUS: Son of Oetean sire, I at least shall be on my
guard henceforth against Ilium and the Atreidae, nor look
on them save from afar. Where the worse man is stronger
than the good, where honesty fails and the dastard bears
sway—among such men I will never make my friends. No,
rocky Scyros shall suffice for me henceforth, nor shall I
ask a better home.

Now to my ship! And you, son of Poeas, farewell, heartily
farewell; may the gods deliver you from your sickness,
even as you would! But we must be going, so that we may
set forth whenever the god permits our voyage.

PHILOCTETES: Are you starting now, my son?

NEOPTOLEMUS: Aye, prudence bids us watch the weather near our ship rather than from afar.

PHILOCTETES: Now by your father and by your mother, my son, by all that is dear to you in your home solemnly I implore you, leave me not thus forlorn, helpless amid these miseries in which I live, such as you see and many that you have heard! Nay, spare a passing thought to me. Great is the discomfort, I well know, of such a freight, yet bear with it. To noble minds baseness is hateful and a good deed is glorious. Forsake this task and your fair name is sullied; perform it, my son, and a rich meed of glory will be yours if I return alive to Oeta's land. Come, the trouble does not last one whole day; make the effort, take and thrust me where you will, in hold, in prow, in stern, wherever I shall least annoy my shipmates.

O consent, by the great Zeus of suppliants, my son, be persuaded! I supplicate you on my knees, infirm as I am, poor wretch and maimed! Do not leave me thus desolate, far from the steps of men! Bring me safely to your own home, or to Euboea, Chalcodon's seat; from there it will be no long journey for me to Oeta and the Trachinian heights and the fair-flowing Spercheius, that you may show me to my beloved sire. I have long feared that he may have gone from me. Often have I summoned him by those who came, with imploring prayers that he would himself send a ship and fetch me home. But either he is dead, or else, I suppose, my messengers—as was likely—made small account of my concerns and hastened on their homeward voyage.

Now, however, since in you I have found one who can carry at once my message and myself, do you save me, do you show me mercy, seeing how all human destiny is full of the fear and the peril that good fortune may be followed by evil. He who stands clear of trouble should beware of dangers; and when a man lives at ease, then it is that he should look most closely to his life, lest ruin come on it by stealth.

CHORUS: *Have pity, O King; he has told of a struggle with sufferings manifold and grievous; may the like befall no friend of mine! And if, my Prince, you hate the hateful Atreidae, then turning their misdeeds to this man's gain I would waft him in your good swift ship to the home*

for which he yearns, that so you flee   166 *Heaven.*

NEOPTOLEMUS: Beware lest, though now as ⟨⟩ are pliant, yet when wearied of his malad⟨⟩ with it you be found no longer constant to ⟨⟩

CHORUS: No indeed; never will you have cause ⟨⟩ reproach against me!

NEOPTOLEMUS: Nay then, it would be shameful fo⟨⟩ ger to find me less prompt than you are to ser⟨⟩ his need. Come, if it please you, let us sail. Let ⟨⟩ set forth at once; our ship for her part will carry ⟨⟩ will not refuse. Only may the gods convey us sa⟨⟩ of this land, and hence to our haven, wherever it ⟨⟩

PHILOCTETES: O most joyful day! O kindest friend, a⟨⟩ good sailors, would that I could prove to you in ⟨⟩ what love you have won from me! Let us be going, ⟨⟩ when you and I have made a solemn farewell to the ⟨⟩ less home within, so that you may learn by what me⟨⟩ sustained life and how stout a heart has been mine. ⟨⟩ lieve that the bare sight would have deterred any ⟨⟩ man from enduring such a lot; but I have been scho⟨⟩ by necessity to patience.

(NEOPTOLEMUS *is about to follow* PHILOCTETES *into* ⟨⟩ *cave.*)

CHORUS: Stay, let us give heed. Two men are coming, one ⟨⟩ seaman of your ship, the other a stranger. You should he⟨⟩ their tidings before you go in.

(*Enter* MERCHANT.)

MERCHANT: Son of Achilles, I asked my companion here— who with two others was guarding your ship—to tell me where you might be, since I have fallen in with you, when I did not expect it, by the chance of coming to anchor off the same coast. Sailing in trader's wise with no great company, homeward bound from Ilium to Peparethus with its cluster-laden vines, when I heard that the sailors were all of your crew, I resolved not to go on my voyage in silence without first giving you my news and reaping due reward. You know nothing, I suspect, of your own affairs, the new designs that the Greeks have concerning you, nay, not designs merely but deeds in progress and no longer tarrying.

NEOPTOLEMUS: Truly sir, the grace shown me by your fore-

MERCHANT: I obey. It is in quest of this man that those two are sailing that I named to you, the son of Tydeus and mighty Odysseus, sworn to bring him, either by winning words or by constraining force. All the Achaeans heard this plainly from Odysseus, for his confidence of success was higher than his comrade's.

NEOPTOLEMUS: Why, after so long a time, did the Atreidae turn their thoughts toward this man, whom they had long since cast forth? What was the yearning that came to them, what compulsion, or what vengeance from gods who requite evil deeds?

MERCHANT: I can expound all that to you, since it seems that you have not heard it. There was a seer of noble birth, a son of Priam, Helenus by name, whom this guileful Odysseus, of whom all shameful and dishonoring words are spoken, made his prisoner. Leading him in bonds, he showed him publicly to the Achaeans, a goodly prize. Helenus then prophesied to them whatever else they asked and also that they would never sack the towers of Troy unless by winning words they should bring this man from the island upon which he now dwells.

And the son of Laertes, when he heard the seer say this, straightway promised that he would bring this man and show him to the Achaeans—most likely, he thought, as a willing captive, but if reluctant, then by force; adding that should he fail whoso wished might have his head. You have heard all, my son, and I commend speed to you and to any man for whom you care.

PHILOCTETES: Luckless that I am! Has he, that utter pest, sworn to bring me by persuasion to the Achaeans? As soon shall I be persuaded, when I am dead, to come up from Hades to the light, as his father came!

MERCHANT: I know nothing about that. But I must go to ship, and may Heaven be with you both for all good.

(*Exit.*)

PHILOCTETES: Now is not this wonderful, my son, that the offspring of Laertes should have hoped by means of soft words to lead me forth from his ship and show me amidst the Greeks? No! Sooner would I hearken to that deadliest of my foes, the viper which made me the cripple that I am! But there is nothing that *he* would not say or dare; and now I know that he will be here. Come, my son, let us

be moving, that a wide sea may part us from the ship of
Odysseus. Let us go: good speed in good season brings
sleep and rest when toil is over.

NEOPTOLEMUS: We will sail, then, as soon as the head wind
falls; at present it is adverse.

PHILOCTETES: It is ever fair sailing when you flee from evil.

NEOPTOLEMUS: Nay, but this weather is against them also.

PHILOCTETES: No wind comes amiss to pirates when there is
a chance to steal or rob by force.

NEOPTOLEMUS: Well, let us be going if you will, when you
have taken from within whatever you need or desire most.

PHILOCTETES: Yes, there are some things that I need, though
the choice is not large.

NEOPTOLEMUS: What is there that will not be found aboard
my ship?

PHILOCTETES: I keep by me a certain herb with which I can
always best assuage this wound, till it is wholly soothed.

NEOPTOLEMUS: Fetch it then. Now what else would you
take?

PHILOCTETES: Any of these arrows that may have been forgotten and may have slipped away from me, lest I leave
it to be another's prize.

NEOPTOLEMUS: Is that indeed the famous bow which you
are holding?

PHILOCTETES: This and no other, that I carry in my hand.

NEOPTOLEMUS: Is it lawful for me to have a nearer view of
it, to handle it and salute it as a god?

PHILOCTETES: To you, my son, this shall be granted, and
anything else in my power that is for your good.

NEOPTOLEMUS: I certainly long to touch it, but my longing
is on this wise: if it be lawful, I should be glad; if not,
think no more of it.

PHILOCTETES: Your words are reverent and your wish, my
son, is lawful. You alone have given to my eyes the light
of life, the hope to see the Oetean land, to see my aged
father and my friends; when I lay beneath the feet of my
foes, you have lifted me beyond their reach. Be of good
cheer; the bow shall be yours, to handle and to return to
the hand that gave it. You shall be able to vaunt that in
reward of your kindness you alone of mortals have touched
it; for it was by a good deed that I myself won it.

NEOPTOLEMUS: I rejoice to have found you and to have
gained your friendship; a man who knows how to render

benefit for benefit must prove a friend above price. Go in, I pray you.

PHILOCTETES: Yes, and I will lead you in, for my sick estate craves the comfort of your presence. (*Exeunt.*)

Chorus: *I have heard in story, but seen not with mine eyes, how he who once came near the bed of Zeus was bound upon a swift wheel by the almighty son of Cronus; but of no other mortal know I, by hearsay or by sight, that hath encountered a doom so dreadful as this man's; who, though he had wronged none by force or fraud, but lived at peace with his fellow-men, was left to perish thus cruelly.*

Verily I marvel how, as he listened in his solitude to the surges that beat around him, he kept his hold upon a life so full of woe; where he was neighbor to himself alone—powerless to walk—with no one in the land to be near him while he suffered, in whose ear he could pour forth the lament, awaking response, for the plague that gnawed his flesh and drained his blood; no one to assuage the burning flux, oozing from the ulcers of his envenomed foot, with healing herbs gathered from the bounteous earth, so often as the torment came upon him.

Then would he creep this way or that, with painful steps, like a child without kindly nurse, to any place whence his need might be supplied, whenever the devouring anguish abated; gathering not for food the fruit of holy Earth, nor aught else that we mortals gain by toil; save when haply he found wherewith to stay his hunger by winged shafts from his swift-smiting bow. Ah, joyless was his life, who for ten years never knew the gladness of the wine-cup, but still bent his way toward any stagnant pool that he could descry as he gazed around him.

But now, after these troubles, he shall be happy and mighty at the last; for he hath met with the son of a noble race, who in the fullness of many months bears him on sea-cleaving ship to his home, haunt of Malian nymphs, and to the banks of the Spercheius; where, above Oeta's heights, the lord of the brazen shield drew near to the gods, amid the splendor of the lightnings of his sire.

(*Enter* NEOPTOLEMUS *and* PHILOCTETES.)

NEOPTOLEMUS: I pray you, come on. Why are you so silent? Why do you halt, as if dismayed, without a cause?

PHILOCTETES: Alas, alas!

NEOPTOLEMUS: What is the matter?

PHILOCTETES: Nothing serious. Go on, my son.

NEOPTOLEMUS: Are you in pain from the disease that vexes you?

PHILOCTETES: No indeed. No, I think I am better just now. Ye gods!

NEOPTOLEMUS: Why are you groaning so and calling on the gods?

PHILOCTETES: That they may come to us with power to save and soothe. Ah me! ah me!

NEOPTOLEMUS: What ails you? Speak; do not persist in this silence. It is plain that something is amiss with you.

PHILOCTETES: I am lost, my son. I can never hide my trouble from you. Ah, it pierces me, it pierces! O misery, O wretched that I am! I am undone, my son, it devours me. O, for the gods' love, if you have a sword ready to your hand, strike at my heel, shear it off straightway, do not heed my life! Quick, quick, my son!

NEOPTOLEMUS: What new thing has come on you so suddenly that you are bewailing yourself with such loud laments?

PHILOCTETES: You know, my son.

NEOPTOLEMUS: What is it?

PHILOCTETES: You know, boy.

NEOPTOLEMUS: What is the matter with you? I do not know.

PHILOCTETES: How can you help knowing? Oh, oh!

NEOPTOLEMUS: Dread indeed is the burden of the malady.

PHILOCTETES: Yes, dread beyond telling. Oh, pity me!

NEOPTOLEMUS: What shall I do?

PHILOCTETES: Do not forsake me in fear. This visitant comes but now and then, when she has been sated, perchance, with her roamings.

NEOPTOLEMUS: Ah, luckless man! Luckless indeed are you found in all manner of woe! Shall I take hold of you, or lend you a helping hand?

PHILOCTETES: No, no. But take this bow of mine, I pray you, as you asked of me just now, and keep it safe until this present access of my disease is past. For indeed sleep falls on me when this plague is passing away, nor can the pain cease sooner; but you must allow me to slumber in peace. And if meanwhile those men come, I charge you by Heaven that in no wise, willingly or unwillingly, you give up this bow to them, lest you bring destruction at once on yourself and on me who am your suppliant.

NEOPTOLEMUS: Have no fears as to my caution. The bow shall pass into no hands but yours and mine. Give it to me, and may good luck come with it!

PHILOCTETES: There it is, my son. Pray the jealous gods that it may not bring you troubles such as it brought to me and to him who was its lord before me.

NEOPTOLEMUS: Ye gods, grant this to us two! Grant us a voyage prosperous and swift, withersoever the god approves and our purpose tends!

PHILOCTETES: Nay, my son, I fear that your prayers are vain. Once more the dark blood oozes drop by drop from the depths, and I look for worse to come. Ah me, oh, oh! You wretched foot, what torment will you work for me! It creeps on me, it is drawing near! Woe, woe is me! You know it now; do not flee, I pray you!

O Cephallenian friend, would that this anguish might cleave to you and transfix your breast! Ah me! Ah me! O you chieftains both, Agamemnon, Menelaus, would that you instead of me might have this malady upon you and for as long! Ah me! Ah me! O Death, Death, when I am thus ever calling you, day by day, why can you never come? O my son, generous youth, come, seize me, burn me up, truehearted friend, in yonder fire famed as Lemnian; I too once deemed it lawful to do the same to the son of Zeus, for the meed of these same arms which are now in your keeping. What do you say, boy, what do you say? Why are you silent? Where are your thoughts, my son?

NEOPTOLEMUS: I have long been grieving in my heart for your load of pain.

PHILOCTETES: Nay, my son, have good hope nevertheless. This visitor comes sharply but goes quickly. Only, I beseech you, do not leave me alone.

NEOPTOLEMUS: Fear not, we will remain.

PHILOCTETES: You will remain?

NEOPTOLEMUS: Be sure of it.

PHILOCTETES: Well, I do not ask to put you on your oath, my son.

NEOPTOLEMUS: Rest satisfied. It is not lawful for me to go without you.

PHILOCTETES: Your hand for pledge!

NEOPTOLEMUS: I give it, to stay.

PHILOCTETES: Now take me yonder, yonder——

NEOPTOLEMUS: Where do you mean?

PHILOCTETES: Up yonder——

NEOPTOLEMUS: What is this new frenzy? Why are you gazing on the vault above us?

PHILOCTETES: Let me go, let me go!

NEOPTOLEMUS: Where?

PHILOCTETES: Let me go, I say!

NEOPTOLEMUS: I will not.

PHILOCTETES: You will kill me if you touch me.

NEOPTOLEMUS: There, then; I release you, since you are calmer.

PHILOCTETES: O Earth, receive me as I die, here and now! The pain no longer suffers me to stand upright.

NEOPTOLEMUS: Sleep is likely to come to him before long. See, his head sinks backward; yes, a sweat is bathing his whole body, and a thin stream of dark blood has broken forth from his heel.

Come, friends, let us leave him in quietness, that he may fall on slumber.

CHORUS: *Sleep, stranger to anguish, painless Sleep, come at our prayer, with gentle breath, come with benison, O King, and keep before his eyes such light as is spread before them now. Come, I pray you, come with power to heal!*

O son, bethink you where you will stand and to what counsels you will next turn our course. You see how it is now! Why should we delay to act? Opportunity, arbiter of all action, often wins a great victory by one swift stroke.

NEOPTOLEMUS: Nay, though he hears nothing, I see that in vain we have made this bow our prize if we sail without him. He must be the crown. It would be a foul shame for us to boast of deeds in which failure has waited on fraud.

CHORUS: *Nay, my son, the god will look to that. But when you answer me again, softly, softly, whisper your words, my son. Sick men's restless sleep is ever quick of vision.*

But I pray you, use your utmost care to win that prize, that great prize, by stealth. For if you maintain your present purpose toward this man—you know of what purpose I speak—a prudent mind can foresee troubles most grievous.

Now, my son, now the wind is fair for you. Sightless and helpless the man lies stretched in darkness—sleep in the heat is sound—with no command of hand or foot, but reft of all his powers, like one who rests with Hades.

Take heed, look if your counsels be seasonable. So far as my thoughts can seize the truth, my son, the best strategy is that which gives no alarm.

NEOPTOLEMUS: Hush, I say, and let not your wits forsake you. Yonder man opens his eyes and lifts his head.

PHILOCTETES: Ah, sunlight following on sleep, ah, you friendly watchers, undreamed of by my hopes! Never, my son, could I have dared to look for this, that you should have patience to wait so tenderly upon my sufferings, staying beside me and helping to relieve me. The Atreidae certainly, those valiant chieftains, had no heart to bear this burden so lightly. But your nature, my son, is noble and of noble breed; and so you have made little of all this, though loud cries and noisome odors vexed your senses.

And now, since the plague seems to allow me a space of forgetfulness and peace at last, raise me yourself, my son, set me on my feet, so that when the faintness shall at length release me we may set forth to the ship and not delay to sail.

NEOPTOLEMUS: Right glad am I to see you, beyond my hope, living and breathing, free from pain; judged by the sufferings that afflict you, your symptoms seemed to speak of death. But now lift yourself, or if you prefer it these men will carry you; the trouble would not be grudged, since you and I are of one mind.

PHILOCTETES: Thanks, my son, and help me to rise, as you say. But do not trouble these men, so that they may not suffer from the noisome smell before the time. It will be trial enough for them to live on board with me.

NEOPTOLEMUS: So be it. Now stand up, and take hold of me yourself.

PHILOCTETES: Do not fear; the old habit will help me to my feet.

NEOPTOLEMUS: Alack! What am I to do next!

PHILOCTETES: What is the matter, my son? Where is your speech straying?

NEOPTOLEMUS: I do not know how I should turn my faltering words.

PHILOCTETES: Faltering? Do not say so, my son.

NEOPTOLEMUS: Indeed, perplexity has now brought me to that pass.

PHILOCTETES: It cannot be that the offense of my disease has changed your purpose of receiving me in your ship?

NEOPTOLEMUS: All is offense when a man has forsaken his true nature and is doing what does not befit him.

PHILOCTETES: Nay, you, at least, are not departing from your sire's example in word or deed by helping one who deserves it.

NEOPTOLEMUS: I shall be found base; this is the thought that torments me.

PHILOCTETES: Not in your present deeds. But the presage of your words disquiets me.

NEOPTOLEMUS: O Zeus, what shall I do? Must I be found twice a villain, by disloyal silence as well as by shameful speech?

PHILOCTETES: If my judgment is not mistaken, that man means to betray me and forsake me and go his way!

NEOPTOLEMUS: Forsake you, no; but take you, perhaps, on a bitter voyage. That is the pain that haunts me.

PHILOCTETES: What do you mean, my son? I do not understand.

NEOPTOLEMUS: I will tell you all. You must sail to Troy, to the Achaeans and the host of the Atreidae.

PHILOCTETES: Oh, what have you said?

NEOPTOLEMUS: Do not lament until you learn——

PHILOCTETES: Learn what? What would you do to me?

NEOPTOLEMUS: Save you, first, from this misery, then go and ravage Troy's plains with you.

PHILOCTETES: And this is indeed your purpose?

NEOPTOLEMUS: A stern necessity ordains it; do not be angry to hear it.

PHILOCTETES: I am lost, luckless one, betrayed! What have you done to me, stranger? Restore my bow at once!

NEOPTOLEMUS: I cannot; duty and policy alike constrain me to obey my chiefs.

PHILOCTETES: You fire, you utter monster, you hateful masterpiece of subtle villainy—how have you dealt with me, how have you deceived me! And you are not ashamed to look upon me, you wretch, the suppliant who turned to you for pity? In taking my bow you have despoiled me of my life. Restore it, I beseech you, restore it, I implore you, my son! By the gods of your fathers, do not rob me of my life! Ah me! No, he speaks to me no more; he looks away. He will not give it up!

O you creeks and headlands, O you wild creatures of the hills with whom I dwell, O you steep cliffs! To you—for to whom else can I speak?—to you, my wonted listeners I bewail my treatment by the son of Achilles. He swore to convey me home—to Troy he carries me; he clinched his word with the pledge of his right hand—yet has he taken my bow, the sacred bow once borne by Heracles son of Zeus, and keeps it, and is eager to show it to the Argives as his own.

He drags me away, as if he had captured a strong man, and does not see that he is slaying a corpse, the shadow of a vapor, a mere phantom. In my strength he would not have taken me, no, nor as I am, save by guile. But now I have been tricked, unhappy that I am. What shall I do? Nay, give it back, return, even now, to your true self! What do you say? Silent? Woe is me, I am lost!

Ah, you cave with twofold entrance, familiar to my eyes, once more I must return to you—but disarmed and without the means to live. Yes, in yonder chamber my lonely life shall fade away. No winged bird, no beast that roams the hills shall I slay with yonder bow. Rather I myself, wretched one, shall make a feast for those who fed me and become a prey to those on whom I preyed. Alas, I shall render my lifeblood for the blood which I have shed, the victim of a man who seemed innocent of evil! Perish! No, not yet, till I see if you will still change your purpose; if you will not may you die accursed!

CHORUS: What shall we do? It now rests with you, O prince, whether we sail or hearken to that man's prayer.

NEOPTOLEMUS: A strange pity for him has smitten my heart— and not now for the first time but long ago.

PHILOCTETES: Show mercy, my son, for the love of the gods; do not give men cause to reproach you for having ensnared me.

NEOPTOLEMUS: Ah me, what shall I do? Would I had never left Scyros! so grievous is my plight.

PHILOCTETES: You are no villain, but you seem to have come here as one schooled by villains to a base part. Now leave that part to others whom it befits, and sail away—when you have given me back my arms.

NEOPTOLEMUS: What shall we do, friends?

(ODYSSEUS *appears suddenly.*)

ODYSSEUS: Wretch, what are you doing? Back with you, and give that bow to me!

PHILOCTETES: Ah, who is this? Do I hear Odysseus?

ODYSSEUS: Odysseus, be sure of it, me whom you see.

PHILOCTETES: Ah me, I am betrayed, lost! He it was, then, that entrapped me and robbed me of my arms.

ODYSSEUS: I, surely, and no other; I avow it.

PHILOCTETES: Give back my bow, give it up, my son.

ODYSSEUS: That he shall never do, even if he would. Moreover you must come along with it or they will bring you by force.

PHILOCTETES: What, you basest and boldest of villains, are these men to take *me* by force?

ODYSSEUS: Unless you come of your free will.

PHILOCTETES: O Lemnian land, and you all-conquering flame whose kindler is Hephaestus, is this indeed to be borne, that yonder man should take me from your realm by force?

ODYSSEUS: It is Zeus, let me tell you, Zeus who rules this land, Zeus whose pleasure this is; and I am his servant.

PHILOCTETES: Hateful wretch, what pleas you can invent! Sheltering yourself behind gods, you make those gods liars.

ODYSSEUS: No, true prophets. Our march must begin.

PHILOCTETES: Never!

ODYSSEUS: But I say Yes. There is no help for it.

PHILOCTETES: Woe is me! Plainly, then, my father begot me to be a slave and no free man.

ODYSSEUS: No, but to be the peer of the bravest, with whom you are destined to take Troy by storm and raze it to the dust.

PHILOCTETES: No, never—though I must suffer the worst— while I have this isle's steep crags beneath me!

ODYSSEUS: What would you do?

PHILOCTETES: Throw myself straightway from the rock and shatter this head upon the rock below!

ODYSSEUS: Seize him, both of you! Put it out of his power!

PHILOCTETES: Ah, hands, how ill you fare for lack of the bow that you loved to draw, yonder man's close prisoners! O you who cannot think one honest or one generous thought, how have you once more stolen upon me, how have you snared me, taking this boy for your screen, a stranger to me, too good for your company but meet for mine, who had no thought but to perform your bidding, and who already shows remorse for his own errors and for my wrongs. But your base soul, ever peering from some ambush, had well trained him, all unapt and unwilling as he was, to be cunning in evil.

And now, wretch, you purpose to bind me hand and foot and take me from this shore where you flung me forth, friendless, helpless, homeless, dead among the living!

Alas!

Perdition seize you! So have I often prayed for you. But since the gods grant nothing sweet to me you live and are glad, while life itself is pain to me, steeped in misery as I am, mocked by you and by the sons of Atreus, the two chieftains for whom you are doing this errand. Yet you sailed with them only when brought under their yoke by stratagem and constraint; but I, thrice wretched that I am, joined the fleet of my own accord, with seven ships, and then was spurned and cast out—by *them* as you say, or as they say, by you.

And now, why would you take me? why carry me with you? for what purpose? I am nothing; for you I have long been dead. Wretch abhorred of heaven, how is it that you no longer find me lame and noisome? How, if I sail with you, can you burn sacrifices to the gods or make drink-offerings any more? That was your pretext for casting me forth.

Miserably may you perish! And perish you shall, for the wrong that you have wrought against me, if the gods regard justice. But I know that they regard it, for you would never have come on this voyage in quest of one so wretched unless some heaven-sent yearning for me had goaded you on.

O my fatherland and you watchful gods, bring your vengeance, bring your vengeance on them all, at last though late, if you see anything to pity in my lot! Yes, a piteous life is mine; but if I saw those men overthrown I could dream that I was delivered from my plague.

CHORUS: Bitter with his soul's bitterness are the stranger's words, Odysseus; he does not bend before his woes.

ODYSSEUS: I could answer him at length if leisure served, but now I can say one thing only. Such as the time needs, such am I. Where the question is of just men and good, you will find no man more scrupulous. Victory, however, is my aim in every field—save in regard to you—to you, in this case, I will gladly give way.

Yes, release him, lay no finger upon him more, let him stay here. Indeed we have no further need of you, now that these arms are ours. Teucer is there to serve us, well-skilled in this craft, and I, who can wield this bow no worse than you, I think, and point it with as true a hand. What need then of you? Pace your Lemnos and joy be with you! We must be going. Perhaps your treasure will bring to me the honor which ought to have been your own.

PHILOCTETES: Ah, unhappy that I am, what shall I do? Shall *you* be seen among the Argives graced with the arms that are mine?

ODYSSEUS: Bandy no more speech with me; I am going.

PHILOCTETES: Son of Achilles, will you too speak no more to me but depart without a word?

ODYSSEUS (*to* NEOPTOLEMUS): Come on. Do not look at him, generous though you are, lest you mar our fortune.

PHILOCTETES (*to* CHORUS): Will you also, friends, indeed leave me thus desolate and show no pity?

CHORUS: This youth is our commander; whatever he says to you, that answer is ours also.

NEOPTOLEMUS (*to* CHORUS): I shall be told by my chief that I am too softhearted. Yet tarry here, if yonder man will have it so, until the sailors have made all ready on board and we have offered our prayers to the gods. Meanwhile, perhaps, he may come to a better mind concerning us. So we two will be going; when we call you, you are to set forth with speed.

(*Exeunt* ODYSSEUS *and* NEOPTOLEMUS.)

PHILOCTETES: *You hollow of the caverned rock, now hot now icy-cold—so then it was my unlucky destiny never to leave you! No, you are witness to my death also. Woe, woe is me! Ah, you sad dwelling, so long haunted by the pain of my presence, what shall be my daily portion henceforth? Where and whence, wretched that I am, shall I find a hope of sustenance? Above my head the timorous doves will go their way through the shrill breeze, for I can arrest their flight no more.*

CHORUS: *It is you, it is you yourself, ill-fated man, that have so decreed. This fortune to which you are captive comes not from without or from a stronger hand, for when it was in your power to show wisdom your choice was to reject the better fate and accept the worse.*

PHILOCTETES: *Ah, luckless, luckless then that I am and broken by suffering! Henceforth I must dwell here in my misery, with no man for companion in days to come, and waste away—woe, woe is me—no longer bringing food to my home, no longer gaining it with the winged weapons held in my strong hands.*

But the unsuspected deceits of a treacherous soul beguiled me. Would that I might see him, the contriver of this plot, doomed to my pangs, and for as long a time!

CHORUS: *Fate, heaven-appointed fate, has come upon you in this, not any treachery to which my hand was lent. Do not point your dread and baneful curse at me! I am eager that you should not reject my friendship.*

PHILOCTETES: *Ah me, ah me! Sitting on the margin of the white waves he mocks me, I suppose, brandishing the weapon that sustained my luckless life, the weapon which no other living man had borne! Ah, you well-loved bow, ah, you that have been torn from loving hands, surely if you can feel you see with pity that the comrade of Heracles is never to use you again! You have found a new and wily master; by him are you wielded. Foul deceits you see, and the face of that abhorred foe by whom countless mischiefs springing from vile arts have been contrived against me— be you, O Zeus, my witness!*

CHORUS: *It is the part of a man ever to assert the right; but when he has done so, to refrain from stinging with rancorous taunts. Odysseus was only the agent of the host, and at their mandate achieved a public benefit for his friends.*

PHILOCTETES: *Ah, my winged prey and you tribes of bright-eyed beasts that this place holds in its upland pastures, start no more in flight from your lairs, for I do not bear in my hands those shafts which were my strength of old— ah, wretched that I now am! Nay, roam at large—the place now has no more terrors for you, no more! Now is the moment to take blood for blood, to glut yourselves at will on my discolored flesh! Soon I shall pass out of life, for where shall I find the means to live? Who can feed on the winds when he no longer commands anything that life-giving earth supplies?*

CHORUS: *For the love of the gods, if you have any regard for a friend who draws near to you in all kindness, approach him. Consider, consider well—it is in your own power to escape from this plague. Cruel is it to him on whom it feeds, and time cannot teach patience under the countless woes that dwell with it.*

PHILOCTETES: *Again, again, you have recalled the old pain to my thoughts, kindest though you are of all who have visited this shore. Why have you afflicted me? What have you done to me?*

CHORUS: *How do you mean?*

PHILOCTETES: *It was your hope to take me to that Trojan land which I abhor.*

CHORUS: *So I deemed it best.*

PHILOCTETES: *Leave me, then, begone!*

CHORUS: *Welcome is your word, right welcome. I am not loath to obey. Come, let us be going, each to his place in the ship!*

PHILOCTETES: *By the Zeus who hears men's curses, do not depart, I implore you!*

CHORUS: *Be calm.*

PHILOCTETES: *Friends, in the god's name, stay!*

CHORUS: *Why do you call?*

PHILOCTETES: *Alas, alas! My doom, my doom! Luckless, I am undone! O foot, foot, what shall I do with you, wretched that I am, in the days to come? O friends, return!*

CHORUS: *What would you have us do different from the purport of your former bidding?*

PHILOCTETES: *It is no just cause for anger if one who is distraught with stormy pain speaks frantic words.*

CHORUS: *Come then, unhappy man, as we exhort you.*

PHILOCTETES: *Never, never—of that be assured—no, though the lord of the fiery lightning threaten to wrap me in the blaze of his thunderbolts! Perish Ilium and the men before its walls who had the heart to spurn me from them, thus crippled! But oh, my friends, grant me one boon!*

CHORUS: *What would you ask?*

PHILOCTETES: *A sword, if you can find one, or an ax, or any weapon—oh, bring it to me!*

CHORUS: *What rash deed would you do?*

PHILOCTETES: *Mangle this body utterly, hew limb from limb with my own hand! Death, death is my thought now——*

CHORUS: *What does this mean?*

PHILOCTETES: *I would seek my sire——*

CHORUS: *In what land?*

PHILOCTETES: *In the realm of the dead; he is in the sunlight no more. Ah, my home, city of my fathers! Would I might behold you! Misguided indeed I was when I left your sacred stream and went forth to help the Danae, my enemies. Undone, undone!*

CHORUS: Long since I should have left you, and should now have been near my ship, had I not seen Odysseus approaching, and the son of Achilles too, coming here to us.

(*Enter* NEOPTOLEMUS *followed by* ODYSSEUS.)

ODYSSEUS: Will you not tell me on what errand you are returning in such hot haste?

NEOPTOLEMUS: To undo the fault that I committed before.

ODYSSEUS: A strange saying. And what was the fault?

NEOPTOLEMUS: When, obeying you and all the host——

ODYSSEUS: What deed did you do that did not become you?

NEOPTOLEMUS: When I ensnared a man with base fraud and guile.

ODYSSEUS: Whom? Alas!—can you be planning some rash act?

NEOPTOLEMUS: Rash, no; but to the son of Poeas—

ODYSSEUS: What will you do? A strange fear comes over me.

NEOPTOLEMUS: —from whom I took this bow, to him again——

ODYSSEUS: Zeus! What would you say? You will not give it back?

NEOPTOLEMUS: Yes, I have gotten it basely and without right.

ODYSSEUS: In the name of the gods, are you saying this to mock me?

NEOPTOLEMUS: If it be mockery to speak the truth.

ODYSSEUS: What do you mean, son of Achilles? What have you said?

NEOPTOLEMUS: Must I repeat the same words twice and thrice?

ODYSSEUS: I should have wished not to hear them at all.

NEOPTOLEMUS: Rest assured that I have nothing more to say.

ODYSSEUS: There is a power, I tell you, that shall prevent your deed.

NEOPTOLEMUS: What do you mean? Who is to hinder me in this?

ODYSSEUS: The whole host of the Achaeans—and I for one.

NEOPTOLEMUS: Wise though you be, your words are void of wisdom.

ODYSSEUS: Your speech is not wise, nor yet your purpose.

NEOPTOLEMUS: But if just, that is better than wise.

ODYSSEUS: How is it just to give up what you have won by my counsels?

NEOPTOLEMUS: My fault has been shameful, and I must seek to retrieve it.

ODYSSEUS: Have you no fear of the Achaean host in doing this?

NEOPTOLEMUS: With justice on my side, I do not fear your terrors.

ODYSSEUS: But I will compel you.

NEOPTOLEMUS: Nay, not even to your force do I yield obedience.

ODYSSEUS: Then we shall fight, not with the Trojans but with you.

NEOPTOLEMUS: Come then what must.

ODYSSEUS: Do you see my right hand on my sword-hilt?

NEOPTOLEMUS: You shall see me doing the same, and that promptly.

ODYSSEUS: Well, I will take no more heed of you; I will go and tell this to all the host, and by them you shall be punished.

NEOPTOLEMUS: You have come to your senses, and if you are thus prudent henceforth perhaps you may keep clear of trouble.

(*Exit* ODYSSEUS.)

But you, O son of Poeas, Philoctetes, come forth, leave the shelter of your rocky home!

PHILOCTETES (*within*): What means this noise of voices rising once more beside my cave? Why do you call me forth? What would you have of me, sirs? (PHILOCTETES *appears at the mouth of the cave and sees* NEOPTOLEMUS.) Ah me! this bodes no good. Can you have come as heralds of new woe for me to crown the old?

NEOPTOLEMUS: Fear not, but hearken to the words that I bring.

PHILOCTETES: I am afraid. Fair words brought me evil fortune once before, when I believed your promises.

NEOPTOLEMUS: Is there no room, then, for repentance?

PHILOCTETES: Just such were you in speech when seeking to steal my bow, a trusty friend with treason in his heart.

NEOPTOLEMUS: But not so now. I wish to learn whether your resolve is to abide here and endure or to sail with us.

PHILOCTETES: Stop, speak no more! All that you can say will be said in vain.

NEOPTOLEMUS: You are resolved?

PHILOCTETES: More firmly, believe me, than speech can tell.

NEOPTOLEMUS: Well, I could have wished that you had listened to my words. But if I am not speaking in season I have done.

PHILOCTETES: Yes, all you will say is in vain. Never can you win the amity of my soul, you who have taken the stay of my life by fraud and robbed me of it, and have then come here to give me counsel, you most hateful offspring of a noble sire! Perdition seize you all, the Atreidae first, and next the son of Laertes, and you!

NEOPTOLEMUS: Utter no more curses, but receive these weapons from my hand.

PHILOCTETES: What are you saying? Am I being tricked a second time?

NEOPTOLEMUS: No, I swear it by the pure majesty of Zeus most high!

PHILOCTETES: O welcome words—if your words are true!

NEOPTOLEMUS: The deed shall soon prove the word. Come, stretch forth your right hand and be master of your bow!

(ODYSSEUS *appears.*)

ODYSSEUS: But I forbid it—be the gods my witnesses—in the name of the Atreidae and all the host!

PHILOCTETES: My son, whose voice was that? Did I hear Odysseus?

ODYSSEUS: Be sure of it, and you see him at your side. I will carry you to the plains of Troy perforce, whether the son of Achilles will or no.

PHILOCTETES: But to your cost if this arrow fly straight.

NEOPTOLEMUS (*seizing* PHILOCTETES' *arm*): Ah, for the gods' love, forbear, do not launch your shaft.

PHILOCTETES: Unhand me, in Heaven's name, dear youth!

NEOPTOLEMUS: I will not.

PHILOCTETES: Alas! why have you disappointed me of slaying my hated enemy with my bow!

NEOPTOLEMUS: It suits not with my honor, nor with yours.

(*Exit* ODYSSEUS.)

PHILOCTETES: Well, you may be sure of one thing. The chiefs of the host, the lying heralds of the Greeks, though brave with words are cowards in fight.

NEOPTOLEMUS: Good. The bow is yours and you have no cause of anger or complaint against me.

PHILOCTETES: I grant it. You have shown the race, my son,

from which you spring; no child, you, of Sisyphus but of Achilles, whose fame was fairest when he was with the living, as it is now among the dead.

NEOPTOLEMUS: Sweet to me is your praise of my sire, and of myself. But hear the boon I wish to win from you. Men must needs bear the fortunes given by the gods; but when they cling to self-inflicted miseries as you do, no one can justly excuse or pity them. You have become intractable. You can tolerate no counselor. If anyone advises you, speaking with good will, you hate him, deeming him a foe who wishes you ill. Yet I will speak, calling Zeus to witness, who hears men's oaths, and do you mark these words and write them in your heart.

You suffer this sore plague by a heaven-sent doom, because you drew near Chryse's watcher, the serpent, secret warder of her home, that guards her roofless sanctuary. Know that relief from this grievous sickness can never be your portion, so long as the sun still rises in the east and sets in the west, until you come of your own free will to the plains of Troy, where you shall meet with the sons of Asclepius, our comrades, and shall be eased of this malady; and, with this bow's aid and mine, shall achieve the capture of the Ilian towers.

I will tell you how I know that these things are so ordained. We have a Trojan prisoner, Helenus, foremost among seers; he says plainly that all this must come to pass. He says further that this present summer must see the utter overthrow of Troy, or else he is willing that his life be forfeit if this word of his prove false.

Now that you know this, therefore, yield with a good grace. It is a glorious heightening of your gain to be singled out as bravest of the Greeks—first to come into healing hands, then to take Troy of many tears, and so to win a matchless renown.

PHILOCTETES: O hateful life, why do you keep me in the light of day instead of suffering me to seek the world of the dead? Ah me, what shall I do? How can I be deaf to this man's words, who has counseled me with kindly purpose? But shall I yield, then? How, after doing so, shall I come into men's sight, wretched that I am? Who will speak to me? You eyes that have beheld all my wrongs, how could you endure to see me consorting with the sons of

Atreus, who wrought my ruin, or with the accursed son of Laertes?

It is not the resentment for the past that stings me: I seem to foresee what I am doomed to suffer from these men in the future; for when the mind once becomes a parent of evil it teaches men to be evil thenceforth. And in you too this conduct moves my wonder. It behooved you never to revisit Troy yourself and to hinder me from going there. Those men have done you outrage by wresting from you the honors of your sire, when, in their award of your father's arms, they adjudged unlucky Ajax inferior to Odysseus. After that, will you go to fight at their side, and would you constrain me to do likewise?

Nay, do not do so, my son; but rather, as you have sworn to me, convey me home; and yourself abiding in Scyros, leave those evil men to their evil doom. So shall you win double thanks from me, as from my sire, and you shall not seem, through helping bad men, to be like them in nature.

NEOPTOLEMUS: There is reason in what you say; nevertheless I would have you put your trust in the gods and in my words, and sail forth from this land with me, my friend.

PHILOCTETES: What! to the plains of Troy, and to the abhorred sons of Atreus—with this wretched foot?

NEOPTOLEMUS: Nay, but to those who will free you and your ulcered limb from pain and will heal your sickness.

PHILOCTETES: You giver of dire counsel, what can you mean?

NEOPTOLEMUS: What I see is fraught with the best issue for us both.

PHILOCTETES: Have you no shame that the gods should hear these words?

NEOPTOLEMUS: Why should a man be ashamed of benefiting his friends?

PHILOCTETES: Is this benefit to the Atreidae, or for me?

NEOPTOLEMUS: For you, I believe; I am your friend and speak in friendship.

PHILOCTETES: How so, when you would give me up to my foes?

NEOPTOLEMUS: I pray you, learn to be less defiant in misfortune.

PHILOCTETES: You will ruin me, I know you will, with these words.

NEOPTOLEMUS: *I* will not; but I say that you do not understand.

PHILOCTETES: Do I not know that the Atreidae cast me out?

NEOPTOLEMUS: They cast you out, but look if they will not restore you to welfare.

PHILOCTETES: Never—if I must first consent to visit Troy.

NEOPTOLEMUS: What am I to do, then, if my pleading cannot win you to anything I urge? The easiest course for me is that I should cease from speech and that you should live, as you do now, without deliverance.

PHILOCTETES: Let me bear the sufferings that are my portion, but the promise which you made me, with hand laid in mine—to bring me home—that promise fulfill, my son. Do not tarry, and do not speak any more of Troy, for the measure of my lamentation is full.

NEOPTOLEMUS: If you will, let us be going.

PHILOCTETES: O generous word!

NEOPTOLEMUS: Now plant your steps firmly.

PHILOCTETES: To the utmost of my strength.

NEOPTOLEMUS: But how shall I escape blame from the Achaeans?

PHILOCTETES: Do not heed it.

NEOPTOLEMUS: What if they ravage my country?

PHILOCTETES: I will be there——

NEOPTOLEMUS: And what help will you render?

PHILOCTETES: With the shafts of Heracles——

NEOPTOLEMUS: What is your meaning?

PHILOCTETES: I will keep them afar.

NEOPTOLEMUS: Take your farewell of this land and set forth.

(HERACLES *appears.*)

HERACLES: *Nay, not yet, till you have hearkened to my words, son of Poeas. Know that the voice of Heracles sounds in your ears and you look upon his face.*

For your sake I have come from the heavenly seats, to show you the purpose of Zeus, and to stay the journey upon which you are departing. Give heed to my counsel.

First I would tell you of my own fortunes, how, after enduring many labors to the end, I have won deathless glory, as you see. And for you, be sure, the destiny is ordained that through these sufferings of yours you should glorify your life.

You shall go with yonder man to the Trojan city, where, first, you shall be healed of your sore malady. Then, chosen out as foremost in prowess of the host, with my bow you shall slay Paris, the author of these ills. You shall sack Troy; the prize of valor shall be given to you by our warriors; and you shall carry the spoils to your home, for the joy of Poeas your sire, even to your own Oetaean heights. And whatever spoils you receive from the host, take from them a thank-offering for my bow to my pyre.

These my counsels are for you too, son of Achilles, for you cannot subdue the Trojan realm without his help, nor he without yours. You are like two lions that roam together; each of you guards the other's life.

For the healing of your sickness I will send Asclepius to Troy, since it is doomed to fall a second time before my arrows. But of this be mindful when you lay waste the land: show reverence toward the gods. All things else are of less account in the sight of our father Zeus. Piety dies not with men; in their life and in their death it is immortal.

PHILOCTETES: Ah, you whose accents I had yearned to hear, you whose form is seen after many days, I will not disobey your words!

NEOPTOLEMUS: I too consent.

HERACLES: Tarry not long, then, before you act. Occasion urges, and the fair wind yonder at the stern.　　　(*Exit.*)

PHILOCTETES: Come, then, let me greet this land as I depart. Farewell, chamber that have shared my watches, farewell, nymphs of stream and meadow, and you, deep voice of the sea-lashed cape—where, in the cavern's inmost recess, my head was often wetted by the south wind's blasts, and where often the Hermaean mount sent an echo to my mournful cries, in the tempest of my sorrow!

But now, you springs and you Lycian fount, I am leaving you, leaving you at last, I who had never attained to such a hope!

Farewell, you sea-girt Lemnos. Speed me with fair course, for my contentment, to that haven whither I am borne by mighty fate, and by the counsel of friends, and by the all-subduing god who has brought these things to fulfillment.

CHORUS: Now let us all set forth together, when we have made our prayer to the Nymphs of the sea, that they come to us for the prospering of our return.

3

EURIPIDES

Medea

IF MEDEA HAD not fallen in love with Jason and helped him when he was in quest of the Golden Fleece in far-off Colchis, Jason would never have survived. To enable him to escape she forsook her royal heritage and murdered her brother, and again when the pair returned to Greece she committed murder for his sake. Now after years of marriage and after she has borne him two children whom he loved dearly, Jason is casting her off in order to marry the princess of Corinth. We should surely condemn Jason's conduct, and so would Euripides' audience also—after they had seen his play, but hardly before. In Athens children of an alien mother did not enjoy the protection of citizenship and Jason was doubtless sincere in declaring that he wished to ensure his children's future by giving them royal half-brothers. When Medea taxes him with ingratitude Jason says that if he owes any gratitude it is to Aphrodite, for Medea only did what is expected of women in love. Furthermore, he adds, he gave more than he received, for Medea was only an alien and he had brought her to the civilization of Greece. What Euripides is attacking, then, is Athenian smugness in their conventional superiority to foreigners and to women. But in nature foreigners and women are as human as Greeks and deserve the same consideration. When they are denied it, the results may be as tragic as they prove to be in the *Medea*. It is not that Euripides approves Medea's behavior or thinks she should escape punishment:

the god out of the machine who saves her in the end is intended to be as incredible as it is improbable. It is rather that Euripides condemns the conventional attitudes which make such conduct on the part of a passionate woman inevitable.

CHARACTERS

NURSE
CREON, *king of Corinth*
CHILDREN *of Medea*
MEDEA
TUTOR
JASON
CHORUS, *Corinthian women*
AEGEUS, *king of Athens*
MESSENGER

SCENE: The home of Medea at Corinth

Translated by M. HADAS *and* J. McLEAN

(*Enter* NURSE.)

NURSE: How I wish that the ship *Argo* had never winged its way through the gray Clashing Rocks to the land of the Colchians! How I wish the pines had never been hewn down in the glens of Pelion, to put oars into the hands of the Heroes who went to fetch for Pelias the Golden Fleece! Then Medea my mistress would not have sailed to the towers of Iolcus, her heart pierced through and through with love for Jason, would not have prevailed on the daughters of Pelias to murder their father, would not now be dwelling here in Corinth with her husband and children. When she fled here she found favor with the citizens to whose land she had come and was herself a perfect partner in all things for Jason. (And therein lies a woman's best security, to avoid conflict with her husband.) But now there is nothing but enmity, a blight has come over their great love.

Jason has betrayed his own children and my mistress to sleep beside a royal bride, the daughter of Creon who rules this land, while Medea, luckless Medea, in her desolation invokes the promises he made, appeals to the pledges in which she put her deepest trust, and calls Heaven to witness the sorry recompense she has from Jason. Ever since she realized her husband's perfidy, she has been lying there prostrated, eating no food, her whole frame subdued to sorrow, wasting away with incessant weeping. She has not lifted an eye nor ever turned her face from the floor. The admonitions of her friends she receives with unhearing ears, like a rock or a wave of the sea. Only now and then she turns her white neck and talks to herself, in sorrow, of her dear father and her country and the home which she betrayed to come here with a husband who now holds her in contempt. Now she knows, from bitter experience, how sad a thing it is to lose one's fatherland. She hates her own children and has no pleasure at the sight of them. I fear she may form some new and horrible resolve. For hers is a dangerous mind, and she will not lie down to injury. I know her and she frightens me lest she make her way stealthily into the palace where his couch is spread and drive a sharp sword into his vitals or even kill both the king and the bridegroom and then incur some greater misfortune. She is cunning. Whoever crosses swords with her will not find victory easy, I tell you.

But here come the children, their playtime over. Little thought have they of their mother's troubles. Children do not like sad thoughts.

(*Enter* TUTOR, *with* BOYS.)

TUTOR: Ancient household chattel of my mistress, why are you standing here all alone at the gates, muttering darkly to yourself? What makes Medea want you to leave her alone?

NURSE: Aged escort of Jason's children, when their master's affairs go ill, good slaves find not only their misfortune but also their heart's grief. My sorrow has now become so great that a longing came over me to come out here and tell to earth and sky the story of my mistress' woes.

TUTOR: What? Is the poor lady not yet through with weeping?

NURSE: I wish I had your optimism. Why, her sorrow is only beginning, it's not yet at the turning point.

TUTOR: Poor foolish woman!—if one may speak thus of one's masters. Little she knows of the latest ills!

NURSE: What's that, old man? Don't grudge me your news.

TUTOR: It's nothing at all. I'm sorry I even said what I said.

NURSE: Please, I beg of you, don't keep it from a fellow slave. I'll keep it dark, if need be.

TUTOR: I had drawn near the checkerboards where the old

men sit, beside the sacred water of Pirene, and there, when nobody thought I was listening, I heard somebody say that Creon the ruler of this land was planning to expel these children *and* their mother from Corinth. Whether the tale is true or not I do not know. I would wish it were not so.

NURSE: But will Jason ever allow his children to be so treated, even if he *is* at variance with their mother?

TUTOR: Old loves are weaker than new loves, and that man is no friend to this household.

NURSE: That's the end of us then, if we are to ship a second wave of trouble before we are rid of the first.

TUTOR: Meanwhile you keep quiet and don't say a word. This is no time for the mistress to be told.

NURSE: O children, do you hear what love your father bears you? Since he is my master, I do not wish him dead, but he is certainly proving the enemy of those he should love.

TUTOR: Like the rest of the world. Are you only now learning that every man loves himself more than his neighbor? Some justly, others for profit, as now for a new bride their father hates these children.

NURSE: Inside, children, inside. It will be all right. (*To the* TUTOR.) And you keep them alone as much as you can, and don't let them near their mother when she's melancholy. I have already noticed her casting a baleful eye at them as if she would gladly do them mischief. She'll not recover from her rage, I know well, till the lightning of her fury has struck somebody to the ground. May it be enemies, not loved ones, that suffer!

MEDEA (*within*): *Oh! My grief! The misery of it all! Why can I not die?*

NURSE: *What did I tell you, dear children? Your mother's heart is troubled, her anger is roused. Hurry indoors, quick. Keep out of her sight, don't go near her. Beware of her fierce manner, her implacable temper. Hers is a self-willed nature. Go now, get you inside, be quick. Soon, it is clear, her sorrow like a gathering cloud will burst in a tempest of fury. What deed will she do then, that impetuous, indomitable heart, poisoned by injustice?*

(*Exeunt* CHILDREN *with* TUTOR.)

MEDEA (*within*): *O misery! the things I have suffered, cause enough for deep lamentations! O you cursed sons of a hateful mother, a plague on you! And on your father! Ruin seize the whole household!*

NURSE: *Ah me, unhappy me! Why will you have your sons partake of their father's guilt? Why hate them? Ah children, your danger overwhelms me with anxiety. The souls of royalty are vindictive; they do not easily forget their resentment, possibly because being used to command they are seldom checked. It is better to be used to living among equals. For myself, at any rate, I ask not greatness but a safe old age. Moderation! Firstly, the very name of it is excellent; to practice it is easily the best thing for mortals. Excess avails to no good purpose for men, and if the gods are provoked, brings greater ruin on a house.*

(Enter CHORUS.*)*

CHORUS: *I heard a voice, I heard a cry. It was the unhappy Colchian woman's. She is not yet calm. Pray tell us, old woman. From the court outside I heard her cries within. I do not rejoice, woman, in the griefs of this house. Dear, dear it is to me.*

NURSE: *It is a home no more; the life has gone out of it. Its master a princess' bed enthralls, while the mistress in her chamber is pining to death, and her friends have no words to comfort her heart.*

MEDEA *(within)*: *Oh! Would that a flaming bolt from Heaven might pierce my brain! What is the good of living any longer? O Misery! Let me give up this life I find so hateful. Let me seek lodging in the house of death.*

CHORUS: *O Zeus, O Earth, O Light, hear what a sad lament the hapless wife intones. What is this yearning, rash woman, after that fearful bed? Will you hasten to the end that is Death? Pray not for that. If your husband worships a new bride, it is a common event; be not exasperated. Zeus will support your cause. Do not let grief for a lost husband waste away your life.*

MEDEA *(within)*: *Great Zeus and Lady Themis, see you how I am treated, for all the strong oaths with which I bound my cursed husband? May I live to see him and his bride, palace and all, in one common destruction, for the wrongs that they inflict, unprovoked, on me! O father, O country, that I forsook so shamefully, killing my brother, my own!*

NURSE: *Hear what she says, how she cries out to Themis of Prayers and to Zeus whom mortals regard as the steward of oaths. With no small revenge will my mistress bate her rage.*

CHORUS: *I wish she would come into our presence and hear*

*the sound of the words we would speak. Then she might
forget the resentment in her heart and change her purpose.
May my zeal be ever at the service of my friends. But
bring her here, make her come forth from the palace. Tell
her that here too are friends. Make haste before she does
any harm to those within. Furious is the surge of such a
sorrow.*

NURSE: *I shall do so, though I am not hopeful of persuading
the mistress. But I freely present you with the gift of my
labor. Yet she throws a baleful glare, like a lioness with
cubs, at any servant who approaches her as if to speak.
Blunderers and fools! that is the only proper name for the
men of old who invented songs to bring the joy of life to
feasts and banquets and festive boards, but never discovered a music of song or sounding lyre to dispel the
weary sorrows of humanity, that bring death and fell havoc
and destruction of homes. Yet what a boon to man, could
these ills be cured by some! At sumptuous banquets why
raise a useless strain? The food that is served and the
satisfaction that comes to full men, that in itself is pleasure
enough.*   (*Exit.*)

CHORUS: *I hear a cry of grief and deep sorrow. In piercing
accents of misery she proclaims her woes, her ill-starred
marriage and her love betrayed. The victim of grievous
wrongs, she calls on the daughter of Zeus, even Themis,
Lady of Vows, who led her through the night by difficult
straits across the briny sea to Hellas.*

(*Enter* MEDEA.)

MEDEA: Women of Corinth, do not criticize me, I come forth
from the palace. Well I know that snobbery is a common
charge, that may be leveled against recluse and busy man
alike. And the former, by their choice of a quiet life, ac-
quire an extra stigma: they are deficient in energy and
spirit. There is no justice in the eyes of men; a man who
has never harmed them they may hate at sight, without
ever knowing anything about his essential nature. An alien,
to be sure, should adapt himself to the citizens with whom
he lives. Even the citizen is to be condemned if he is too
self-willed or too uncouth to avoid offending his fellows.
So I . . . but this unexpected blow which has befallen me
has broken my heart.

It's all over, my friends; I would gladly die. Life has lost
its savor. The man who was everything to me, well he

knows it, has turned out to be the basest of men. Of all creatures that feel and think, we women are the unhappiest species. In the first place, we must pay a great dowry to a husband who will be the tyrant of our bodies (that's a further aggravation of the evil); and there is another fearful hazard: whether we shall get a good man or a bad. For separations bring disgrace on the woman and it is not possible to renounce one's husband. Then, landed among strange habits and regulations unheard of in her own home, a woman needs second sight to know how best to handle her bedmate. And if we manage this well and have a husband who does not find the yoke of intercourse too galling, ours is a life to be envied. Otherwise, one is better dead. When the man wearies of the company of his wife, he goes outdoors and relieves the disgust of his heart having recourse to some friend or the companions of his own age, but we women have only one person to turn to.

They say that we have a safe life at home, whereas men must go to war. Nonsense! I had rather fight three battles than bear one child. But be that as it may, you and I are not in the same case. You have your city here, your paternal homes; you know the delights of life and association with your loved ones. But I, homeless and forsaken, carried off from a foreign land, am being wronged by a husband, with neither mother nor brother nor kinsman with whom I might find refuge from the storms of misfortune. One little boon I crave of you, if I discover any ways and means of punishing my husband for these wrongs: your silence. Woman in most respects is a timid creature, with no heart for strife and aghast at the sight of steel; but wronged in love, there is no heart more murderous than hers.

LEADER: Do as you say, Medea, for just will be your vengeance. I do not wonder that you bemoan your fate. But I see Creon coming, the ruler of this land, bringing tidings of new plans.

(*Enter* CREON.)

CREON: You there, Medea, looking black with rage against your husband; I have proclaimed that you are to be driven forth in exile from this land, you and your two sons. Immediately. I am the absolute judge of the case, and I shall not go back to my palace till I have cast you over the frontier of the land.

MEDEA: Ah! Destruction, double destruction is my unhappy

lot. My enemies are letting out every sail and there is no
harbor into which I may flee from the menace of their attack. But ill-treated and all, Creon, still I shall put the
question to you: Why are you sending me out of the
country?

CREON: I am afraid of you—there's no need to hide behind
a cloak of words—afraid you will do my child some irrepa-
rable injury. There's plenty of logic in that fear. You are a
wizard possessed of evil knowledge. You are stung by the
loss of your husband's love. And I have heard of your
threats—they told me of them—to injure bridegroom and
bride and father of the bride. Therefore before anything
happens to me, I shall take precautions. Better for me now
to be hateful in your eyes than to relent and rue it greatly
later.

MEDEA: Alas! Alas! Often ere now—this is not the first time
—my reputation has hurt me and done me grievous wrong.
If a man's really shrewd, he ought never to have his children taught too much. For over and above a name for use-
lessness that it will earn them, they incur the hostility and
envy of their fellow men. Offer clever reforms to dullards,
and you will be thought a useless fool yourself. And the
reported wiseacres, feeling your superiority, will dislike you
intensely. I myself have met this fate. Because I have skill,
some are jealous of me, others think me unsociable. But
my wisdom does not go very far. However, you are afraid
you may suffer something unpleasant at my hands, aren't
you? Fear not, Creon; it is not my way to commit my
crimes against kings. What wrong have you done me? You
have only bestowed your daughter on the suitor of your
choice. No, it is my husband I hate. You, I dare say, knew
what you were doing in the matter. And now I don't grudge
success to your scheme. Make your match, and good luck
to you. But allow me to stay in this country. Though foully
used, I shall keep my peace, submitting to my masters.

CREON: Your words are comforting to hear, but inside my
heart there is a horrible fear that you are plotting some
mischief, which makes me trust you even less than before.
The hot-tempered woman, like the hot-tempered man, is
easier to guard against than the cunning and silent. But
off with you at once, make no speeches. My resolve is
fixed; for all your skill you will not stay amongst us to
hate me.

MEDEA: Please no, I beseech you, by your knees, by the young bride . . .

CREON: You are wasting your words; you will never convince me.

MEDEA: Will you drive me out and have no respect for my prayers?

CREON: Yes, for I love you less than I love my own family.

MEDEA: O fatherland, how strongly do I now remember you!

CREON: Yes, apart from my children, that is *my* dearest love.

MEDEA: Alas! the loves of men are a mighty evil.

CREON: In my opinion, that depends on the circumstances.

MEDEA: O Zeus, do not forget the author of this wickedness.

CREON: On your way, vain woman, and end my troubles.

MEDEA: The troubles are mine, I have no lack of troubles.

CREON: In a moment you will be thrust out by the hands of servants.

MEDEA: No, no, not that. But Creon, I entreat you. . . .

CREON: You seem to be bent on causing trouble, woman.

MEDEA: I shall go into exile. It is not *that* I beg you to grant me.

CREON: Why then are you clinging so violently to my hand?

MEDEA: Allow me to stay for this one day to complete my plans for departure and get together provision for my children, since their father prefers not to bother about his own sons. Have pity on them. You too are the father of children. It is natural that you should feel kindly. Stay or go, I care nothing for myself. It's them I weep for in their misfortune.

CREON: My mind is not tyrannical enough; mercy has often been my undoing. So now, though I know that it is a mistake, woman, you will have your request. But I give you warning: if tomorrow's divine sun sees you and your children inside the borders of this country, you die. True is the word I have spoken. Stay, if you must, this one day. You'll not have time to do what I dread.   (*Exit.*)

CHORUS: *Hapless woman! overwhelmed by sorrow! Where will you turn? What stranger will afford you hospitality? God has steered you, Medea, into an unmanageable surge of troubles.*

MEDEA: Ill fortune's everywhere, who can gainsay it? But it is not yet as bad as that, never think so. There is still heavy weather ahead for the new bride and groom, and no little trouble for the maker of the match. Do you think I would ever have wheedled the king just now except to further my own plans? I would not even have spoken to him, nor touched him either. But he is such a fool that though he might have thwarted my plans by expelling me from the country he has allowed me to stay over for this one day, in which I shall make corpses of three of my enemies, father and daughter and my own husband.

My friends, I know several ways of causing their death, and I cannot decide which I should turn my hand to first. Shall I set fire to the bridal chamber or make my way in stealthily to where their bed is laid and drive a sword through their vitals? But there is one little difficulty. If I am caught entering the palace or devising my bonfire I shall be slain and my enemies shall laugh. Better take the direct way and the one for which I have the natural gift. Poison. Destroy them with poison. So be it.

But suppose them slain. What city will receive me? Whose hospitality will rescue me and afford me a land where I shall be safe from punishment, a home where I can live in security? It cannot be. I shall wait, therefore, a little longer and if any tower of safety shows up I shall carry out the murders in stealth and secrecy. However, if circumstances drive me to my wits' end, I shall take a sword in my own hands and face certain death to slay them. I shall not shirk the difficult adventure. No! by Queen Hecate who has her abode in the recesses of my hearth—her I revere above all gods and have chosen to assist me—never shall any one of them torture my heart with impunity. I shall make their marriage a torment and grief to them. Bitterly shall they rue the match they have made and the exile they inflict on me.

But enough! Medea, use all your wiles; plot and devise. Onward to the dreadful moment. Now is the test of courage. Do you see how you are being treated? It is not right that the seed of Sisyphus and Aeson should gloat over you, the daughter of a noble sire and descendant of the Sun. But you realize that. Moreover, by our mere nature we women are helpless for good, but adept at contriving all manner of wickedness.

CHORUS: *Back to their sources flow the sacred rivers. The world and morality are turned upside-down. The hearts of*

men are treacherous; the sanctions of Heaven are under-
mined. The voice of time will change, and our glory will
ring down the ages. Womankind will be honored. No
longer will ill-sounding report attach to our sex.

The strains of ancient minstrelsy will cease, that hymned
our faithlessness. Would that Phoebus, Lord of Song, had
put into woman's heart the inspired song of the lyre. Then
I would have sung a song in answer to the tribe of males.
History has much to tell of the relations of men with
women.

You, Medea, in the mad passion of your heart sailed
away from your father's home, threading your way through
the twin rocks of the Euxine, to settle in a foreign land.
Now, your bed empty, your lover lost, unhappy woman,
you are being driven forth in dishonor into exile.

Gone is respect for oaths. Nowhere in all the breadth of
Hellas is honor any more to be found; it has vanished into
the clouds. Hapless one, you have no father's house to
which you might fly for shelter from the gales of misfortune; and another woman, a princess, has charmed your
husband away and stepped into your place.

(*Enter* JASON.)

JASON: Often and often ere now I have observed that an intractable nature is a curse almost impossible to deal with.
So with you. When you might have stayed on in this land
and in this house by submitting quietly to the wishes of your
superiors, your forward tongue has got you expelled from
the country. Not that your abuse troubles *me* at all. Keep
on saying that Jason is a villain of the deepest dye. But for
your insolence to royalty consider yourself more than fortunate that you are only being punished by exile. I was
constantly mollifying the angry monarch and expressing the
wish that you be allowed to stay. But in unabated folly
you keep on reviling the king. That is why you are to be
expelled.

But still, despite everything, I come here now with unwearied goodwill, to contrive on your behalf, madam, that
you and the children will not leave this country lacking
money or anything else. Exile brings many hardships in its
wake. And even if you do hate me, I could never think
cruelly of you.

MEDEA: Rotten, heart-rotten, that is the word for you.
Words, words, magnificent words. In reality a craven. You

come to me, you come, my worst enemy! This isn't bravery, you know, this isn't valor, to come and face your victims. No! it's the ugliest sore on the face of humanity, shamelessness. But I thank you for coming. It will lighten the weight on my heart to tell your wickedness, and it will hurt you to hear it. I shall begin my tale at the very beginning.

I saved your life, as all know who embarked with you on the *Argo*, when you were sent to master with the yoke the fire-breathing bulls and to sow with dragon's teeth that acre of death. The dragon, too, with wreathed coils, that kept safe watch over the Golden Fleece and never slept—I slew it and raised for you the light of life again. Then, forsaking my father and my own dear ones, I came to Iolcus where Pelias reigned, came with you, more than fond and less than wise. On Pelias too I brought death, the most painful death there is, at the hands of his own children. Thus I have removed every danger from your path.

And after all those benefits at my hands, you basest of men, you have betrayed me and made a new marriage, though I have borne you children. If you were still childless, I could have understood this love of yours for a new wife. Gone now is all reliance on pledges. You puzzle me. Do you believe that the gods of the old days are no longer in office? Do you think that men are now living under a new dispensation? For surely you know that you have broken all your oaths to me. Ah my hand, which you so often grasped, and oh my knees, how all for nothing have we been defiled by this false man, who has disappointed all our hopes.

But come, I shall confide in you as though you were my friend, not that I expect to receive any benefit from you. But let that go. My questions will serve to underline your infamy. As things are now, where am I to turn? Home to my father? But when I came here with you, I betrayed my home and my country. To the wretched daughters of Pelias? They would surely give me a royal welcome to their home; I only murdered their father. For it is how it is. My loved ones at home have learned to hate me; the others, whom I need not have harmed, I have made my enemies to oblige you. And so in return for these services you have made me envied among the women of Hellas! A wonderful, faithful husband I have in you, if I must be expelled from the country into exile, deserted by my friends, alone with my friendless children! A fine story to tell of the new bridegroom, that his children and the woman who saved his life are wandering about in aimless beggary! O Zeus, why O why have you given to mortals sure means of knowing gold from tinsel, yet men's exteriors show no mark by which to descry the rotten heart?

LEADER: Horrible and hard to heal is the anger of friend at strife with friend.

JASON: It looks as if I need no small skill in speech if, like a skillful steersman riding the storm with close-reefed sheets, I am to escape the howling gale of your verbosity, woman. Well, since you are making a mountain out of the favors you have done me, I'll tell *you* what *I* think. It was the goddess of Love and none other, mortal or immortal, who delivered me from the dangers of my quest. You have indeed much subtlety of wit, but it would be an invidious story to go into, how the inescapable shafts of Love compelled you to save my life. Still, I shall not put too fine a point on it. If you helped me in some way or other, good and well. But as I shall demonstrate, in the matter of my rescue you got more than you gave.

In the first place, you have your home in Greece, instead of in a barbarian land. You have learned the blessings of Law and Justice, instead of the caprice of the strong. And all the Greeks have realized your wisdom, and you have won great fame. If you had been living on the edges of the earth, nobody would ever have heard of you. May I have neither gold in my house nor skill to sing a sweeter song than Orpheus if my fortune is to be hid from the eyes of men. That, then, is my position in the matter of the fetching of the Fleece. (It was you who proposed the debate.)

There remains my wedding with the princess, which you have cast in my teeth. In this connection I shall demonstrate, one, my wisdom; two, my rightness; three, my great service of love to you and my children. (Be quiet, please.) When I emigrated here from the land of Iolcus, dragging behind me an unmanageable chain of troubles, what greater windfall could I have hit upon, I an exile, than a marriage with the king's daughter? Not that I was weary of your charms (that's the thought that galls you) or that I was smitten with longing for a fresh bride; still less that I wanted to outdo my neighbors in begetting numerous children. Those I have are enough, there I have no criticism to make. No! what I wanted, first and foremost, was a good home where we would lack for nothing (well I knew that the poor man is shunned and avoided by all his friends); and secondly, I wanted to bring up the children in a style worthy of my house, and, begetting other children to be brothers to the children born of you, to bring them all together and unite the families. Then my happiness would be complete. What do *you* want with more children? As for me, it will pay me to advance the children I have by means of those I intend to beget. Surely that is no bad plan? You yourself would admit it, if jealousy were not pricking you.

You women have actually come to believe that, lucky in love, you are lucky in all things, but let some mischance befall that love, and you will think the best of all possible worlds a most loathsome place. There ought to have been some other way for men to beget their children, dispensing with the assistance of women. Then there would be no trouble in the world.

LEADER: Jason, you arrange your arguments very skillfully. And yet in my opinion, like it or not, you have acted unjustly in betraying your wife.

MEDEA: Yes! I do hold many opinions that are not shared by the majority of people. In my opinion, for example, the plausible scoundrel is the worst type of scoundrel. Confident in his ability to trick out his wickedness with fair phrases he shrinks from no depth of villainy. But there is a limit to his cleverness. As there is also to yours. You may as well drop that fine front with me, and all that rhetoric. One word will floor you. If you had been an honorable man, you would have sought my consent to the new match and not kept your plans secret from your own family.

JASON: And if I had announced to you my intention to marry, I am sure I would have found you a most enthusiastic accomplice. Why! even now you cannot bring yourself to master your heart's deep resentment.

MEDEA: That's not what griped you. No! your foreign wife was passing into an old age that did you little credit.

JASON: Accept my assurance, it was not for the sake of a woman that I made the match I have made. As I told you once already, I wanted to save you and to beget princes to be brothers to my own sons, thereby establishing our family.

MEDEA: May it never be mine . . . a happiness that hurts, a blessedness that frets my soul.

JASON: Do you know how to change your prayer to show better sense? "May I regard nothing useful as grievous, no good fortune as ill."

MEDEA: Insult me. *You* have a refuge, but I am helpless, faced with exile.

JASON: It was your own choice. Don't blame anyone else.

MEDEA: What did I do? Did I betray you and marry somebody else?

JASON: You heaped foul curses on the king.

MEDEA: And to your house also I shall prove a curse.

JASON: Look here, I do not intend to continue this discussion any further. If you want anything of mine to assist you or the children in your exile, just tell me. I am ready to give it with an ungrudging hand and to send letters of introduction to my foreign friends who will treat you well. If you reject this offer, woman, you will be a great fool. Forget your anger, and you will find it greatly to your advantage.

MEDEA: I would not use your friends on any terms or accept anything of yours. Do not offer it. The gifts of the wicked bring no profit.

JASON: At any rate, heaven be my witness that I am willing to render every assistance to you and the children. But you do not like what is good for you. Your obstinacy repulses your friends; it will only aggravate your suffering.

MEDEA: Be off with you. As you loiter outside here, you are burning with longing for the girl who has just been made your wife. Make the most of the union. Perhaps, god willing, you are making the kind of marriage you will some day wish unmade.

(Exit JASON.)

CHORUS: *Love may go too far and involve men in dishonor and disgrace. But if the goddess comes in just measure, there is none so rich in blessing. May you never launch at me, O Lady of Cyprus, your golden bow's passion-poisoned arrows, which no man can avoid.*

May Moderation content me, the fairest gift of Heaven. Never may the Cyprian pierce my heart with longing for another's love and bring on me angry quarrelings and never-ending recriminations. May she have respect for har-

monious unions and with discernment assort the matings of women.

O Home and Fatherland, never, never, I pray, may I be cityless. It is an intolerable existence, hopeless, piteous, grievous. Let me die first, die and bring this life to a close. There is no sorrow that surpasses the loss of country.

My eyes have seen it; not from hearsay do I speak. You have neither city nor friend to pity you in your most terrible trials. Perish, abhorred, the man who never brings himself to unbolt his heart in frankness to some honored friends! Never shall such a man be a friend of mine.

(*Enter* AEGEUS, *in traveler's dress.*)

AEGEUS: Medea, good health to you. A better prelude than that in addressing one's friends, no man knows.

MEDEA: Good health be yours also, wise Pandion's son, Aegeus. Where do you come from to visit this land?

AEGEUS: I have just left the ancient oracle of Phoebus.

MEDEA: What sent you to the earth's oracular hub?

AEGEUS: I was enquiring how I might get children.

MEDEA: In the name of Heaven, have you come thus far in life still childless?

AEGEUS: By some supernatural influence I am still without children.

MEDEA: Have you a wife or are you still unmarried?

AEGEUS: I have a wedded wife to share my bed.

MEDEA: Tell me, what did Phoebus tell you about offspring?

AEGEUS: His words were too cunning for a mere man to interpret.

MEDEA: Is it lawful to tell me the answer of the god?

AEGEUS: Surely. For, believe me, it requires a cunning mind to understand.

MEDEA: What then was the oracle? Tell me, if I may hear it.

AEGEUS: I am not to open the cock that projects from the skin. . . .

MEDEA: Till you do what? Till you reach what land?

AEGEUS: Till I return to my ancestral hearth.

MEDEA: Then what errand brings your ship to this land?

AEGEUS: There is one Pittheus, king of Troezen . . .

MEDEA: The child of Pelops, as they say, and a most pious man.

AEGEUS: To him I will communicate the oracle of the god.

MEDEA: Yes, he is a cunning man and well-versed in such matters.

AEGEUS: Yes, and of all my comrades in arms the one I love most.

MEDEA: Well, good luck to you, and may you win your heart's desire.

AEGEUS: Why, what's the reason for those sad eyes, that wasted complexion?

MEDEA: Aegeus, I've got the basest husband in all the world.

AEGEUS: What do you mean? Tell me the reason of your despondency, tell me plainly.

MEDEA: Jason is wronging me; I never did him wrong.

AEGEUS: What has he done? Speak more bluntly.

MEDEA: He has another wife, to lord it over me in our home.

AEGEUS: You don't mean that he has done so callous, so shameful a deed!

MEDEA: Indeed he did. Me that used to be his darling he now despises.

AEGEUS: Has he fallen in love? Does he hate your embraces?

MEDEA: Yes, it's a grand passion! He was born to betray his loved ones.

AEGEUS: Let him go, then, since he is so base, as you say.

MEDEA: He became enamored of getting a king for a father-in-law.

AEGEUS: Who gave him the bride? Please finish your story.

MEDEA: Creon, the ruler of this Corinth.

AEGEUS: In that case, madam, I can sympathize with your resentment.

MEDEA: My life is ruined. What is more, I am being expelled from the land.

AEGEUS: By whom? This new trouble is hard.

MEDEA: Creon is driving me out of Corinth into exile.

AEGEUS: And does Jason allow this? I don't like that either.

MEDEA: He says he does not, but he'll stand it. Oh! I beseech you by this beard, by these knees, a suppliant I entreat you, show pity, show pity for my misery. Do not stand by and see me driven forth to a lonely exile. Receive me into your land, into your home and the shelter of your hearth. So may the gods grant you the children you desire, to throw joy round your deathbed. You do not know what a lucky path you have taken to me. I shall put an end to your childlessness. I shall make you beget heirs of your blood. I know the magic potions that will do it.

AEGEUS: Many things make me eager to do this favor for you, madam. Firstly, the gods, and secondly, the children that you promise will be born to me. In that matter I am quite at my wits' end. But here is how I stand. If you yourself come to Athens, I shall try to be your champion, as in duty bound. This warning, however, I must give you! I shall not consent to take you with me out of Corinth. If you yourself come to my palace, you will find a home and a sanctuary. Never will I surrender you to anybody. But your own efforts must get you away from this place. I wish to be free from blame in the eyes of my hosts also.

MEDEA: And so you shall. But just let me have a pledge for these services, and I shall have all I could desire of you.

AEGEUS: Do you not trust me? What is your difficulty?

MEDEA: I do trust you. But both the house of Pelias and Creon are my enemies. Bound by oaths, you would never hand me over to them if they tried to extradite me. But with an agreement of mere words, unfettered by any sacred pledge, you might be won over by their diplomatic advances to become *their* friend. For I have no influence or power, whereas they have the wealth of a royal palace.

AEGEUS: You take great precautions, madam. Still, if you wish, I will not refuse to do your bidding. For me too it will be safer that way, if I have some excuse to offer to your enemies, and *you* will have more security. Dictate the oath.

MEDEA: Swear by the Floor of Earth, by the Sun my father's father, by the whole family of the gods, one and all——

AEGEUS: To do or not do what? Say on.

MEDEA: Never yourself to cast me out of your country and never, willingly, during your lifetime, to surrender me to any of my foes that desire to seize me.

AEGEUS: I swear by the Earth, by the holy majesty of the Sun, and by all the gods, to abide by the terms you propose.

MEDEA: Enough! And if you abide not by your oath, what punishment do you pray to receive?

AEGEUS: The doom of sacrilegious mortals.

MEDEA: Go and fare well. All is well. I shall arrive at your city as soon as possible, when I have done what I intend to do, and obtained my desire.

LEADER (*as* AEGEUS *departs*): May Maia's son, the Lord of Journeys, bring you safe to Athens, and may you achieve the desire that hurries you homeward; for you are a generous man in my esteem.

MEDEA: O Zeus and his Justice, O Light of the Sun! The time has come, my friends, when I shall sing songs of triumph over my enemies. I am on my way. Now I can hope that my foes will pay the penalty. Just as my plans were most storm-tossed at sea, this man has appeared, a veritable harbor, where I shall fix my moorings, when I get to the town and citadel of Pallas.

Now I shall tell you all my plans; what you hear will not be said in fun. I shall send one of my servants to ask Jason to come and see me. When he comes, I shall make my language submissive, tell him I approve of everything else and am quite contented with his royal marriage and his betrayal of me, that I agree it is all for the best; I shall only ask him to allow my children to remain. Not that I wish to leave them in a hostile land for my enemies to insult. No! I have a cunning plan to kill the princess. I shall send them with gifts to offer to the bride, to allow them to stay in the land—a dainty robe and a headdress of beaten gold. If she takes the finery and puts it on her, she will die in agony. She and anyone who touches her. So deadly are the poisons in which I shall steep my gifts.

But now I change my tone. It grieves me sorely, the horrible deed I must do next. I shall murder my children, these children of mine. No man shall take them away from me. Then when I have accomplished the utter overthrow of the house of Jason, I shall flee from the land, to escape the consequences of my own dear children's murder and my other accursed crimes. My friends, I cannot bear being laughed at by my enemies.

So be it. Tell me, what has life to offer them. They have no father, no home, no refuge from danger.

My mistake was in leaving my father's house, won over by the words of a Greek. But, as god is my ally, he shall pay for his crime. Never, if I can help it, shall he behold his sons again in this life. Never shall he beget children by his new bride. She must die by my poisons, die the death she deserves. Nobody shall despise *me* or think me weak or passive. Quite the contrary. I am a good friend, but a dangerous enemy. For that is the type the world delights to honor.

LEADER: You have confided your plan in me, and I should like to help you, but since I also would support the laws of mankind, I entreat you not to do this deed.

MEDEA: It is the only way. But I can sympathize with your sentiments. You have not been wronged like me.

LEADER: Surely you will not have the heart to destroy your own flesh and blood?

MEDEA: I shall. It will hurt my husband most that way.

LEADER: But it will make you the unhappiest woman in the world.

MEDEA: Let it. From now on all words are superfluous. (*To the* NURSE.) Go now, please, and fetch Jason. Whenever loyalty is wanted, I turn to you. Tell him nothing of my intentions, as you are a woman and a loyal servant of your mistress.

(*Exit* NURSE.)

CHORUS: *The people of Erechtheus have been favored of Heaven from the beginning. Children of the blessed gods are they, sprung from a hallowed land that no foeman's foot has trodden. Their food is glorious Wisdom. There the skies are always clear, and lightly do they walk in that land where once on a time blond Harmony bore nine chaste daughters, the Muses of Pieria.*

Such is the tale, which tells also how Aphrodite sprinkled the land with water from the fair streams of Cephissus and breathed over it breezes soft and fragrant. Ever on her hair she wears a garland of sweet-smelling roses, and ever she sends the Loves to assist in the court of Wisdom. No good thing is wrought without their help.

How then shall that land of sacred rivers, that hospitable land receive you the slayer of your children? It would be sacrilege for you to live with them. Think. You are stabbing your children. Think. You are earning the name of murderess. By your knees we entreat you, by all the world holds sacred, do not murder your children.

Whence got you the hardihood to conceive such a plan? And in the horrible act, as you bring death on your own children, how will you steel your heart and hand? When you cast your eyes on them, your own children, will you not weep that you should be their murderess? When your own children fall at your feet and beg for mercy, you will never be able to dye your hands with their blood. Your heart will not stand it.

(*Enter* JASON, *followed by the* NURSE.)

JASON: I come at your bidding. Though you hate me, I shall not refuse you an audience. What new favor have you to ask of me, woman?

MEDEA: Jason, please forgive me for all I said. After all the services of love you have rendered me before, I can count on you to put up with my fits of temper. I have been arguing the matter out with myself. Wretched woman (thus I scolded myself), why am I so mad as to hate those that mean me well, to treat as enemies the rulers of this land and my husband who, in marrying a princess and getting brothers for my children, is only doing what is best for us all? What is the matter with me? Why am I still furious, when the gods are showering their blessings on me? Have I not children of my own? Am I forgetting that I am an exile from my native land, in sore need of friends? These reflections let me see how very foolish I have been and how groundless is my resentment. Now, I want to thank you. I think you are only doing the right thing in making this new match. I have been the fool. I ought to have entered into your designs, helped you to accomplish them, even stood by your nuptial couch and been glad to be of service to the new bride. But I am what I am . . . to say no worse, a woman. You ought not therefore to imitate me in my error or to compete with me in childishness. I beg your pardon, and confess that I was wrong then. But now I have taken better counsel, as you see.

Children, children, come here, leave the house, come out and greet your father as I do. Speak to him. Join your mother in making friends with him, forgetting our former hate. It's a truce; the quarrel is over. Take his right hand. Alas! my imagination sickens strangely. My children, will you stretch out loving arms like that in the long hereafter? My grief! How quick my tears are! My fears brim over. It is that long quarrel with your father, now done with, that fills my tender eyes with tears.

LEADER: From my eyes, too, the burning tears gush forth. May Sorrow's advance proceed no further.

JASON: That is the talk I like to hear, woman. The past I can forgive. It is only natural for your sex to show resentment when their husbands contract another marriage. But your heart has now changed for the better. It took time, to be sure, but you have now seen the light of reason. That's

the action of a wise woman. As for you, my children, your
father has not forgotten you. God willing, he has secured
your perfect safety. I feel sure that you will yet occupy
the first place here in Corinth, with your brothers. Merely
grow up. Your father, and any friends he has in heaven,
will see to the rest. May I see you, sturdy and strong, in
the flower of your youth, triumphant over my enemies.

You there, why wet your eyes with hot tears, and avert
your pale cheek? Why are you not happy to hear me speak
thus?

MEDEA: It's nothing. Just a thought about the children here.

JASON: Why all this weeping over the children? It's too
much.

MEDEA: I am their mother. Just now when you were wish-
ing them long life, a pang of sorrow came over me, in
case things would not work out that way.

JASON: Cheer up, then. I shall see that they are all right.

MEDEA: Very well, I shall not doubt your word. Women are
frail things and naturally apt to cry.

But to return to the object of this conference, something has been said, something remains to be mentioned.
Since it is their royal pleasure to expel me from the country—oh yes! it's the best thing for me too, I know well,
not to stay on here in the way of you and the king; I am
supposed to be their bitter enemy—*I* then shall go off into
exile. But see that the children are reared by your own
hand, ask Creon to let *them* stay.

JASON: I don't know if he will listen to me, but I shall try,
as I ought.

MEDEA: At least you can get your wife to intercede with her
father on their behalf.

JASON: Certainly, and I imagine I shall persuade her.

MEDEA: If she is a woman like the rest of us. In this task,
I too shall play my part. I shall send the children with
gifts for her, gifts far surpassing the things men make today, a fine robe, and a headdress of beaten gold. Be quick
there. Let one of my maids bring the finery here. What
joy will be hers, joys rather, joys innumerable, getting not
only a hero like you for a husband, but also raiment which
the Sun, my father's father, gave to his children. (MEDEA
*takes the casket from a maid who has brought it, and
hands it to the* CHILDREN.) Here, my children, take

these wedding gifts in your hands. Carry them to the
princess, the happy bride, and give them to her. They are
not the kind of gifts she will despise.

JASON: Impetuous woman! Why leave yourself thus empty-
handed? Do you think a royal palace lacks for raiment
and gold? Keep these things for yourself, don't give them
away. If my wife has any regard for me at all, she will
prefer me to wealth, I'm sure.

MEDEA: Please let me. They say that gifts persuade even the
gods, and gold is stronger than ten thousand words. Hers
is the fortune of the hour; her now is god exalting. She
has youth, and a king for a father. And to save my children from exile, I would give my very life, let alone gold.

Away, my children, enter the rich palace and entreat
your father's young wife, my mistress, to let you stay in
Corinth. Give her the finery. That is most important. She
must take these gifts in her hands. Go as fast as you can.
Success attend your mission, and may you bring back to
your mother the tidings she longs to hear.

(*Exeunt* CHILDREN *with* TUTOR, *and* JASON.)

CHORUS: *Now are my hopes dead. The children are doomed.
Already they are on the road to death. She will take it,
the bride will take the golden diadem, and with it will
take her ruin, luckless girl. With her own hands she will
put the precious circlet of death on her blond hair.*

*The beauty of it, the heavenly sheen, will pesuade her
to put on the robe and the golden crown. It is in the halls
of death that she will put on her bridal dress forthwith.
Into that fearful trap she will fall. Death will be her
portion, hapless girl. She cannot overleap her doom.*

*And you, poor man. Little luck your royal father-in-law
is bringing you. Unwittingly, you are bringing death on
your children, and on your wife an awful end. Ill-starred
man, what a way you are from happiness.*

*And now I weep for your sorrow, hapless mother of these
children. You will slaughter them to avenge the dishonor
of your bed betrayed, criminally betrayed by your husband who now sleeps beside another bride.*

(*Enter* CHILDREN *with their* TUTOR.)

TUTOR: Mistress, here are your children, reprieved from
exile. Your gifts the royal bride took gladly in her hands.
The children have made their peace with *her*. What's the

matter? Why stand in such confusion, when fortune is smiling? Why do you turn away your cheek? Why are you not glad to hear my message?

MEDEA: Misery!

TUTOR: That note does not harmonize with the news I have brought.

MEDEA: Misery, and again Misery!

TUTOR: Have I unwittingly brought you bad news? I thought it was good. Was I mistaken?

MEDEA: Your message was . . . your message. It is not you I blame.

TUTOR: Why then are your eyes downcast and your tears flowing?

MEDEA: Of necessity, old man, of strong necessity. This is the gods' doing, and mine, in my folly.

TUTOR: Have courage. Some day your children will bring you too back home.

MEDEA: Ah me! Before that day I shall bring others to another home.

TUTOR: You are not the first woman to be separated from her children. We are mortals and must endure calamity with patience.

MEDEA: That I shall do. Now go inside and prepare their usual food for the children.

(*Exit* TUTOR.)

O my children, my children. For you indeed a city is assured, and a home in which, leaving me to my misery, you will dwell forever, motherless. But I must go forth to exile in a strange land, before I have ever tasted the joy of seeing *your* happiness, before I have got you brides and bedecked your marriage beds and held aloft the bridal torches. Alas! my own self-will has brought me to misery. Was it all for nothing, my children, the rearing of you, and all the agonizing labor, all the fierce pangs I endured at your birth? Ah me, there was a time when I had strong hopes, fool as I was, that you would tend my old age and with your own hands dress my body for the grave, a fate that the world might envy. Now the sweet dream is gone. Deprived of you, I shall live a life of pain and sorrow. And you, in another world altogether will never again see your mother with your dear, dear eyes.

O the pain of it! Why do your eyes look at me, my children? Why smile at me that last smile? Ah! What can

*they are a blessing or a curse, and so he does not miss a
joy he has never had and he escapes a multitude of sorrows. But them that have in their home young, growing
children that they love, I see them consumed with anxiety,
day in day out, how they are to rear them properly, how
they are to get a livelihood to leave to them. And, after
all that, whether the children for whom they toil are worth
it or not, who can tell?*

*And now I shall tell you the last and crowning sorrow for
all mortals. Suppose they have found livelihood enough,
their children have grown up, and turned out honest. Then,
if it is fated that way, death carries their bodies away
beneath the earth. What then is the use, when the love of
children brings from the gods this crowning sorrow to top
the rest?*

MEDEA: My friends, all this time I have been wait[
something to happen, watching to see what they wil
the royal palace. Now I see one of Jason's attendants
this way. His excited breathing shows that he has a
strange evils to tell.

(*Enter* MESSENGER.)

MESSENGER: What a horrible deed of crime you have done,
Medea. Flee, flee. Take anything you can find, sea vessel or
land carriage.

MEDEA: Tell me, what has happened that I should flee.

MESSENGER: The princess has just died. Her father Creon,
too, killed by your poisons.

MEDEA: Best of news! From this moment and forever you
are one of my friends and benefactors.

MESSENGER: What's that? Are you sane and of sound mind,
woman? You have inflicted a foul outrage on a king's home,
yet you rejoice at the word of it and are not afraid.

MEDEA: I too have a reply that I might make to you. But
take your time, my friend. Speak on. How did they die?
You would double my delight, if they died in agony.

MESSENGER: When your children, both your offspring, arrived with their father and entered the bride's house, we rejoiced, we servants who had been grieved by your troubles.
Immediately a whisper ran from ear to ear that you and
your husband had patched up your earlier quarrel. And one
kisses your children's hands, another their yellow hair. I myself, in my delight, accompanied the children to the wom-
en's rooms. The mistress, whom we now respect in your

I do? My heart is water, women, at the sight of my children's bright faces. I could never do it. Good-bye to my
former plans. I shall take my children away with me. Why
should I hurt their father by *their* misfortunes, only to reap
a double harvest of sorrow myself? No! I cannot do it.
Good-bye to my plans.

And yet . . . what is the matter with me? Do I want to
make myself a laughingstock by letting my enemies off
scot-free? I must go through with it. What a coward heart
is mine, to admit those soft pleas. Come, my children,
into the palace. Those that may not attend my sacrifices can
see to it that they are absent. I shall not let my hand be
unnerved.

Ah! Ah! Stop, my heart. Do not you commit this crime.
Leave them alone, unhappy one, spare the children. Even
they live far from us, they will bring you joy. No! by
the unforgetting dead in hell, it cannot be! I shall not
leave my children for my enemies to insult. In any case
they must die. And if die they must, *I* shall slay them, who
gave them birth. My schemes are crowned with success
She shall not escape. Already the diadem is on her head
wrapped in the robe the royal bride is dying, I know
well. And now I am setting out on a most sorrowful roa
and shall send these on one still more sorrowful. I wish
speak to my children. Give your mother your hands,
children, give her your hands to kiss.

O dear, dear hand. O dear, dear mouth, dear shap
dear noble faces, happiness be yours, but not here. Y
father has stolen this world from you. How sweet to to
The softness of their skin, the sweetness of their breath
babies! Away, away, I cannot bear to see you any lo
(CHILDREN *retire within.*) My misery overwhelms m
I *do* realize how terrible is the crime I am about
passion overrules my resolutions, passion that causes
of the misery in the world.

CHORUS: *Often ere now I have grappled with subtle s*
and sounded depths of argument deeper than womo
plumb. But, you see, we also have a Muse who tea
philosophy. It is a small class—perhaps you might
in a thousand—the women that love the Muse.

And I declare that in this world those who have
experience of paternity are happier than the fo
children. Without children a man does not know

place, did not see the two boys at first, but cast a longing look at Jason. Then, however, resenting the entrance of the children, she covered her eyes with a veil and averted her white cheek.

Your husband tried to allay the maiden's angry resentment, saying, "You must not hate your friends. Won't you calm your temper, and turn your head this way? You must consider your husband's friends your own. Won't you accept the gifts and ask your father to recall their sentence of exile, for my sake?" Well, when she saw the finery, she could not refrain, but promised her husband everything, and before Jason and your children were far away from the house she took the elaborate robes and put them on her. She placed the golden diadem on her clustering locks and began to arrange her coiffure before a shining mirror, smiling at her body's lifeless reflection. Then she arose from her seat and walked through the rooms, stepping delicately with her fair white feet, overjoyed with the gifts. Time and time again, standing erect, she gazed with all her eyes at her ankles.

But then ensued a fearful sight to see. Her color changed, she staggered, and ran back, her limbs all atremble, and only escaped falling by sinking upon her chair. An old attendant, thinking, I suppose, it was a panic fit, or something else of divine sending, raised a cry of prayer, until she saw a white froth drooling from her mouth, saw her rolling up the pupils of her eyes, and all the blood leaving her skin. Then, instead of a cry of prayer, she let out a scream of lamentation. Immediately one maid rushed to Creon's palace, another to the new bridegroom, to tell of the bride's misfortune. From end to end, the house echoed to hurrying steps. A quick walker, stepping out well, would have reached the end of the two-hundred-yard track, when the poor girl, lying there quiet, with closed eyes, gave a fearful groan and began to come to. A double plague assailed her. The golden diadem on her head emitted a strange flow of devouring fire, while the fine robes, the gifts of your children, were eating up the poor girl's white flesh. All aflame, she jumped from her seat and fled, shaking her head and hair this way and that, trying to throw off the crown. But the golden band held firmly, and after she had shaken her hair more violently, the fire began to blaze twice as fiercely. Overcome by the agony she fell on the ground, and none but her father could have recognized her. The position of her eyes could not be distinguished, nor the beauty of her face. The blood, clotted with fire, dripped from the crown of her head, and the flesh melted from her bones, like resin from a pine tree, as the poisons ate their unseen way. It was a fearful sight. All were afraid to touch the corpse, taught by what had happened to her.

But her father, unlucky man, rushed suddenly into the room, not knowing what had happened, and threw himself on the body. At once he groaned, and embracing his daughter's form he kissed it and cried, "My poor, poor child, what god has destroyed you so shamefully? Who is it deprives this aged tomb of his only child? Ah! let me join you in death, my child." Then, when he ceased his weeping and lamentation and sought to lift his aged frame upright, he stuck to the fine robes, like ivy to a laurel bush. His struggles were horrible. He would try to free a leg, but the girl's body stuck to his. And if he pulled violently, he tore his shrunken flesh off his bones. At last his life went out; doomed, he gave up the ghost. Side by side lie the two bodies, daughter and old father. Who would not weep at such a calamity?

It seems to me . . . I need not speak of what's in store for you; you yourself will see how well the punishment fits the crime . . . it's not the first time the thought has come, that the life of man is a shadow. I might assert with confidence that the mortals who pass for philosophers and subtle reasoners are most to be condemned. No mortal man has lasting happiness. When the tide of fortune flows his way, one man may have more prosperity than another, but happiness never.   (*Exit.*)

LEADER: It seems that this day Fate is visiting his sins on Jason. Unfortunate daughter of Creon, we pity your calamity. The love of Jason has carried you through the gates of death.

MEDEA: My friends, I am resolved to act, and act quickly to slay the children and depart from the land. I can delay no longer, or my children will fall into the murderous hands of those that love them less than I do. In any case they must die. And if they must, I shall slay them, who gave them birth. Now, my heart, steel yourself. Why do we still hold back? The deed is terrible, but necessary.

Come, my unhappy hand, seize the sword, seize it. Before
you is a course of misery, lifelong misery; on now to the
starting post. No flinching now, no thinking of the children, the darling children, that call you mother. This day,
this one short day, forget your children. You have all the
future to mourn for them. Aye, to mourn. Though you
mean to kill them, at least you loved them. Oh! I am a most
unhappy woman.   (*Exit.*)

CHORUS: *O Earth, O glorious radiance of the Sun, look and*
behold the accursed woman. Stop her before she lays her
bloody, murderous hands on her children. Sprung are they
from your golden race, O Sun, and it is a fearful thing
that the blood of a god should be spilt by mortals. Nay,
stop her, skyborn light, prevent her. Deliver the house from
the misery of slaughter, and the curse of the unforgetting
dead.

Gone, gone for nothing, are your maternal pangs. For
nothing did you bear these lovely boys, O woman, who
made the inhospitable passage through the gray Clashing
Rocks! Why let your spleen poison your heart? Why this
murderlust, where love was? On the man that spills the
blood of kinsmen the curse of heaven descends. Go where
he may, it rings ever in his ears, bringing sorrows and
tribulations on his house.

(*The* CHILDREN *are heard within.*)

Listen, listen. It is the cry of the children. O cruel, ill-
starred woman.

ONE OF THE CHILDREN (*within*): Ah me! What am I to do?
Where can I escape my mother's murderous hands?

THE OTHER (*within*): I know not, my dear, dear brother.
She is killing us.

CHORUS: *Should we break in? Yes! I will save them from*
death.

ONE OF THE CHILDREN (*within*): Do, for god's sake. Save
us. We need your help.

THE OTHER (*within*): Yes, we are already in the toils of
the sword.

CHORUS: *Heartless woman! Are you made of stone or steel?*
Will you slaughter the children, your own seed, slaughter
them with your own hands?

Only one woman, only one in the history of the world,
laid murderous hands on her children, Ino whom the gods
made mad, driven from home to a life of wandering by the

wife of Zeus. Hapless girl, bent on that foul slaughter, she
stepped over a precipice by the shore and fell headlong
into the sea, killing herself and her two children together.
What crime, more horrible still, may yet come to pass? O
the loves of women, fraught with sorrow, how many ills
ere now have you brought on mortals!

(*Enter* JASON, *attended.*)

JASON: You women there, standing in front of this house,
is Medea still within, who wrought these dreadful deeds?
Or has she made her escape? I tell you, she had better
hide under the earth or take herself off on wings to the
recesses of the sky, unless she wishes to give satisfaction
to the family of the king. Does she think she can slay the
rulers of the land and get safely away from this house?
But I am not so anxious about her as I am about the children. The victims of her crimes will attend to her. It's my
own children I am here to save, in case the relatives of
the king do them some injury, in revenge for the foul
murders their mother has committed.

LEADER: Jason, poor Jason, you do not know the sum of
your sorrows, or you would not have said these words.

JASON: What is it? She does not want to kill me too, does
she?

LEADER: Your children are dead, slain by their mother's
hand.

JASON: For pity's sake, what do you mean? You have slain
me, woman.

LEADER: Your children are dead, make no mistake.

JASON: Why, where did she slay them? Indoors or out here?

LEADER: Open the doors and you will see their bodies.

JASON: Quick, servants, loosen the bolts, undo the fastenings.
Let me see the double horror, the dead bodies of my children, and the woman who ... oh! let me punish her.

(MEDEA *appears aloft in a chariot drawn by winged*
dragons. She has the bodies of the CHILDREN.)

MEDEA: What's all this talk of battering and unbarring?
Are you searching for the bodies and me who did the
deed? Spare yourself the trouble. If you have anything
to ask of me, speak if you will, but never shall you lay a
hand on me. I have a magic chariot, given me by the Sun,
my father's father, to protect me against my enemies.

JASON: You abominable thing! You most loathsomest woman, to the gods and me and all mankind. You had the heart

to take the sword to your children, you their mother, leaving me childless. And you still behold the earth and the sun, you who have done this deed, you who have perpetrated this abominable outrage. My curses on you! At last I have come to my senses, the senses I lost when I brought you from your barbarian home and country to a home in Greece, an evil plague, treacherous alike to your father and the land that reared you. There is a fiend in you, whom the gods have launched against me. In your own home you had already slain your brother when you came aboard the *Argo*, that lovely ship. Such was your beginning. Then you married me and bore me children, whom you have now destroyed because I left your bed. No Greek woman would ever have done such a deed. Yet I saw fit to marry you, rather than any woman of Greece, a wife to hate me and destroy me, not a woman at all, but a tigress, with a disposition more savage than Tuscan Scylla. But why all this? Ten thousand reproaches could not sting you; your impudence is too engrained. The devil take you, shameless, abominable murderess of your children. I must bemoan my fate; no joy shall I have of my new marriage, and I shall never see alive the children I begot and reared and lost.

MEDEA: I might have made an elaborate rebuttal of the speech you have made, but Zeus the Father knows what you received at my hands and what you have done. You could not hope, nor your princess either, to scorn my love, make a fool of me, and live happily ever after. Nor was Creon, the matchmaker, to drive me out of the country with impunity. Go ahead, then. Call me tigress if you like, or Scylla that haunts the Tuscan coast. I don't mind, now I have got properly under your skin.

JASON: You too are suffering. You have your share of the sorrow.

MEDEA: True, but it's worth the grief, since you cannot scoff.

JASON: O children, what a wicked mother you got!

MEDEA: O children, your father's sins have caused your death.

JASON: Yet it was not *my* hand that slew them.

MEDEA: No, it was your lust, and your new marriage.

JASON: Because your love was scorned you actually thought it right to murder.

MEDEA: Do you think a woman considers that a small injury?

JASON: Good women do. But you are wholly vicious.

MEDEA: The children here are dead. That will sting you.

JASON: No! they live to bring fierce curses on your head.

MEDEA: The gods know who began it all.

JASON: They know, indeed, they know the abominable wickedness of your heart.

MEDEA: Hate me then. I despise your bitter words.

JASON: And I yours. But it is easy for us to be quit of each other.

MEDEA: How, pray? Certainly I am willing.

JASON: Allow me to bury these bodies and lament them.

MEDEA: Certainly not. I shall bury them with my own hands, taking them to the sanctuary of Hera of the Cape, where no enemy may violate their tombs and do them insult. Here in the land of Sisyphus we shall establish a solemn festival, and appoint rites for the future to expiate their impious murder. I myself shall go to the land of Erechtheus, to live with Aegeus, the son of Pandion. You, as is proper, will die the death you deserve, struck on the head by a fragment of the *Argo,* now you have seen the bitter fruits of your new marriage.

JASON: May you be slain by the curse of your children, and Justice that avenges murder!

MEDEA: What god or power above will listen to you, the breaker of oaths, the treacherous guest?

JASON: Oh! abominable slayer of children.

MEDEA: Get along to the palace and bury your wife.

JASON: I go, bereft of my two sons.

MEDEA: You have nothing yet to bemoan. Wait till you are old.

JASON: My dear, dear children!

MEDEA: Yes, dear to their mother, not to you.

JASON: And yet you slew them.

MEDEA: I did, to hurt you.

JASON: Alas! my grief! I long to kiss their dear mouths.

MEDEA: Now you speak to them, now you greet them, but in the past you spurned them.

JASON: For god's sake, let me touch my children's soft skin.

MEDEA: No! You have gambled and lost.

JASON: O Zeus, do you hear how I am repelled, how I am wronged by this foul tigress, that slew her own children?

But such lament as I may and can make, I hereby make. I call upon the gods. I invoke the powers above to bear me witness that you slew my children and now prevent me from embracing their bodies and giving them burial. Would that I had never begotten them, to live to see them slain at your hands.

CHORUS: *Zeus on Olympus hath a wide stewardship. Many things beyond expectation do the gods fulfill. That which was expected has not been accomplished; for that which was unexpected has god found the way. Such was the end of this story.* (*Exeunt.*)

Hippolytus

APHRODITE OPENS *Hippolytus* with an assertion of her power over all mankind and declares that she will ruin Hippolytus, son of Theseus and an Amazon, because he alone scorns love and devotes himself to the chaste huntress Artemis. Her instrument will be Hippolytus' stepmother Phaedra, who has fallen in love with him.

Phaedra is resolved to starve herself to death rather than reveal her infatuation; her secret is elicited from her, in a state of semidelirium, by the coaxing of her solicitous nurse, who promises to obtain some remedy. When Hippolytus discovers that the nurse is attempting to procure incest he is horrified; Phaedra hangs herself, when she finds her secret is known, and in order to spare the reputation of her children she leaves a note accusing Hippolytus of having made an attempt upon her virtue. Theseus returns from a long absence, believes the accusation, upbraids Hippolytus, and pronounces a powerful curse upon him, in consequence of which he is fatally mangled by his horses as he rides into exile. Artemis appears *ex machina* to vindicate Hippolytus, and promises that she will one day ruin some devotee of Aphrodite's.

It is tempting but wrong to look upon Hippolytus as a martyr to the ideal of chastity and Phaedra as a lascivious woman who merits her fate. Phaedra resists the affliction before which she is helpless to the utmost of her power; she did not know that the officious nurse would appeal to Hippolytus directly. Hippolytus is an appealing young man, but objectionable in his priggishness. To abdicate an essential element of life was not, in the Greek view, praiseworthy. What moved Hippolytus to eschew the goddess who is "marvelous after dark"? He himself labored under the stigma of illegitimacy, which, in Athens of Euripides' day, imposed certain disabilities upon a man. Hippolytus hated Aphrodite because it was Aphrodite who was responsible for his embarrassment. In nature the bastard, like the foreigner or the woman, is no different from other human beings; it was convention that warped the character of Hippolytus, as it did Medea's, and so was the ultimate cause of tragedy. But no more than *Medea* is *Hippolytus* merely a pamphlet; it is a beautiful and poignant and compassionate poem.

CHARACTERS

APHRODITE
HIPPOLYTUS
CHORUS, *of Huntsmen*
ATTENDANT, *of Hippolytus*
CHORUS, *of Troezenian Women*
NURSE
PHAEDRA
THESEUS
MESSENGER
ARTEMIS

SCENE: The palace of Theseus at Troezen. At either side are the statues of Aphrodite and Artemis

Translated by M. HADAS *and* J. McLEAN

(*Enter* APHRODITE *upon the speaking platform reserved for gods.*)

APHRODITE: Great is my power and wide my fame among mortals and also in heaven; I am the Goddess Cypris. All men that look upon the light of the sun, all that dwell between the Euxine Sea and the boundaries of Atlas are under my sway: I bless those that respect my power, and disappoint those who are not humble toward me. Yes, even the family of gods have this trait: they are pleased when people respect them. I shall demonstrate the truth of this forthwith. Theseus' son Hippolytus, born of the Amazon and brought up by temperate Pittheus, is the only inhabitant of this land of Troezen who declares that I am the very vilest of divinities. He spurns love and will have nothing to do with sex. *He* honors Phoebus' sister Artemis, Zeus' maiden, and thinks her the greatest of goddesses. He consorts with her continually in the green forests, clearing away the beasts of the earth with his swift dogs, pursuing a more than mortal companionship. Of course I don't grudge them that: why should I? It is his sinful neglect for *me* for which I shall punish Hippolytus this very day. The ground was prepared long ago: there is not much left for me to do. Once when he was going from Pittheus' house to the land of Pandion to see the Mysteries and be initiated, his father's noble wife Phaedra saw him, and her heart was smitten with a fearful love—all by my scheming. Even before she came to this land of Troezen she built a shrine of Cypris there on the rock of Pallas, commanding a view of this land, because she loved an absent love; and the place she established she called Hippolytus' Belvedere in his honor forevermore. Then Theseus left the land of Cecrops and sailed to this land with his wife. To expiate his guilt in the murder of Pallas' sons, he has consented to a year's banishment from home. And here the wretched woman, moaning and distraught with the pricks of love, love undeclared, is dying. None of her maids understands her trouble. But this passion must not end so simply. I will reveal the thing to Theseus, to everybody. The young man who is hostile to me will be killed by his father's curses. Poseidon, the master of the sea, has granted a boon to Theseus: thrice shall he have fulfillment for his prayers to him. Phaedra dies though she saves her good name. Yes, she must die; I shall not let the thought of her suffering stop me from punishing my enemies to my heart's content.

But I see Hippolytus striding on after his work at the chase, so I will leave this place. Behind him there comes a great crowd of henchmen, doing honor to Goddess Artemis with ringing hymns. Little he knows that the gates of Hades are wide open, and that he is looking at this light for the last time. *(Disappears.)*

(From the left there enters HIPPOLYTUS *with javelin and garland, attended by a crowd of* HUNTSMEN; *they pay no notice to the statue of* APHRODITE.*)*

HIPPOLYTUS: *Follow, follow, sing heavenly Artemis, Zeus' child, whose charge we are.*

HUNTSMEN: *Revered, revered, hallowed daughter of Zeus, hail Artemis, hail maiden of Leto and Zeus, most beautiful of maidens by far. You dwell in heaven in your noble sire's hall, in the house of Zeus bedecked with gold. Hail most beautiful, most beautiful of maidens in Olympus, hail Artemis!*

*(*HIPPOLYTUS *advances, bows to the statue of* ARTEMIS, *and places his garland upon her altar.)*

HIPPOLYTUS: For you, dear Lady, I bring this garland, this lovely chain of flowers, from a virgin meadow, where no shepherd presumes to pasture his flock, nor has iron ever come there. Virgin it is, and in summer the bees frequent it, while Purity waters it like a garden. He whose fortune it is to be in all things wholly virtuous, not by teaching of men but by nature, may cull flowers in that meadow; for others it is not lawful. From a reverent hand, then, dear Lady, accept this diadem for your golden tresses. To me alone of mortals does this grace belong—to live with you and converse in words; I hear your voice though I do not see your face. May I round the goal of life even as I have begun.

(*An* ATTENDANT *who has come out of the house and watched* HIPPOLYTUS *steps forward.*)

ATTENDANT: Prince—for only gods may be addressed as Lords—would you accept a word of sound advice from me?

HIPPOLYTUS: To be sure: it would seem foolish not to.

ATTENDANT: You know, of course, the general tendency of men——

HIPPOLYTUS: I do not. What are you getting at?

ATTENDANT: To hate haughtiness and reserve.

HIPPOLYTUS: And rightly; are not all haughty people hateful?

ATTENDANT: Affable people have a certain charm?

HIPPOLYTUS: A great deal; and what's more, they get on in the world with little effort.

ATTENDANT: Don't you expect the same thing is true with the gods?

HIPPOLYTUS: Yes; for men act on the same principles as gods.

ATTENDANT: Why then are you so haughty, in not worshiping a deity that——

HIPPOLYTUS: What deity? Mind your mouth doesn't stumble.

ATTENDANT: This goddess here, this Cypris that stands at your gates.

HIPPOLYTUS: I keep at a respectful distance; *I* am chaste.

ATTENDANT (*soothingly*): Yes, yes; and reverend, and famous among men.

HIPPOLYTUS: With gods and men tastes vary.

ATTENDANT: Good luck to you; you have your share of wisdom.

HIPPOLYTUS: I don't like deities who are marvelous after dark.

ATTENDANT (*half aside*): You should have respect for religion, my boy.

HIPPOLYTUS: Forward, comrades, enter the house and see about some food. A full table is a delight after hunting. And the horses must be groomed, so that I may harness them to my car and give them a proper workout when I have had my fill. As for this Cypris of yours—I bid her a long farewell.   (*Exeunt.*)

(*Enter* CHORUS OF TROEZENIAN WOMEN, *right and left.*)

CHORUS: *There is a certain rock (from Ocean, they say, its waters distill), which sends forth from its crannies a flowing stream in which pitchers can be dipped. There a friend of mine was washing her bright colored clothes in the running water, and putting them to dry in the sun on the face of a warm rock. From her I heard the first rumor that my mistress was keeping to her house, wasting away on a bed of sickness, her blond head veiled in dainty fabrics. I hear that for three days now her lovely lips have not been profaned by Demeter's grain. Some secret trouble makes her yearn to put into the sad haven of death.*

SOME WOMEN: *You must be possessed, young woman, whether it is Pan or Hecate, or the dread Corybants, or the mountain Mother, that haunts you.*

OTHERS: *Or perhaps you are pining away for sins against the huntress Dictynna, who afflicts you for offerings withheld. For she can go in pursuit over the land and also across the sea, through the eddies of the briny surge.*

OTHERS: *Or has someone in the house beguiled your husband, the first chief of the Erechtheids, the nobly born, to steal away to another woman's love?*

OTHERS: *Or has some sailor man outward bound from Crete voyaged to this harbor so friendly to sailors, and brought a rumor to the queen prostrating her on a bed of grief, Sorrow's prisoner?*

OTHERS: *This agony of grief, this feeling of desperation, is a common symptom of the delirium which attends travail, in women whose constitution is highstrung. I experienced this thrill, this chill, in my own womb, but I cried to the heavenly archer, Goddess Artemis, who presides over childbirth. And always, much wanted, by god's grace, she comes.*

THE LEADER: *But here she is, being carried outside the doors by her old nurse. The cloud on her brow lowers dark. My spirit is most eager to know what it is that has thus ravaged my queen's face and driven away her color.*

(*Enter, from the house,* NURSE, *followed by* PHAEDRA, *supported by female* ATTENDANTS.)

NURSE: *Oh, the troubles and hateful sicknesses of mortals! What shall I do with you, what not do? Here you have the clear light, here is the fresh air. The bedding of your sick couch is now outdoors. You could speak of nothing but coming out here; soon enough you will be eager to go to your room again. You are easily put out, nothing pleases you. You are not satisfied with what you have; it takes absence to make your heart grow fonder.*

Rather be sick than be nurse. The one is simple, but the other combines mental worry with manual labor. But all man's life is grievous; there is no rest for the weary. If there is anything dearer than life, darkness swathes it and clouds it over. So we find ourselves hopelessly in love with the thing we see, this world of brightness, because we have no experience of any other mode of living, and no proof of the other world; myths merely lead us astray.

PHAEDRA (*to* ATTENDANTS): *Raise my body, hold my head up. The joints of my limbs are paralyzed. Take hold of my pretty arms and hands. My tiara is too heavy on my head. Take it off and spread my curls out on my shoulders.*

NURSE: *Cheer up, child. Don't toss about; it hurts. You will bear your troubles more easily if you are quiet and brave. Man is made to mourn.*

PHAEDRA: *Ah, ah! Oh to drink a cup of pure water from a dewy spring! Oh to lie down and rest under the poplars in a leafy meadow!*

NURSE: *Child, what are you shrieking? Don't talk that way before people, blurting out mad, nightmarish words.*

PHAEDRA: *Take me to the mountain! I go to the forest, to the pines, where the hounds chase their prey to the death, and leap upon the dappled hinds. Gods, I yearn to urge on the dogs, to poise the Thessalian dart beside my yellow hair and fling it, to hold a barbed lance in my hand!*

NURSE: *What in the world are you raving about now, child? What concern have you with hunting? What is this hankering for mountain streams? Right here next door to the castle is a well of water from which you could get a drink.*

PHAEDRA (*paying no attention to* NURSE): *Artemis, Queen of Limna by the sea, queen of the tracks that echo with the hooves of horses, would I were there now, breaking colts of Enetia.*

NURSE: *What new raving is this you are uttering? A moment ago you were heading for the mountain and yearning for wild animals. Now you hanker for colts on the level sands. It would take a deal of prophesy to discover which of the gods is wrenching your reins and upsetting your mind, girl.*

PHAEDRA (*falls back and clasps her head*): *Wretched me! What in the world have I done? How far have I wandered from good sense? I was mad, I have been overthrown by some god's spite. Dear, dear, what misery! Nanna, hide my head again. I'm ashamed of what I've said. Hide it. From my eyes tears are trickling. My eyes are fascinated by my shame. To come to one's senses brings pain. To be mad is an evil, but it is better to remain mad and perish.*

NURSE: *I am covering you. But when will death cover my body? Long life teaches me many things. Friendship between mortals should be taken in moderation. Don't let it get down into the marrow of the soul. Bonds of affection ought to be elastic, for letting apart or drawing together. It's a heavy load for one soul to be in pain for two, as I am now in anguish for her. Too strict regimentation brings more breakdowns than triumphs, I am told, and is bad for the health. So I have less praise for extremes than for "nothing in excess"; and you will find that the sages agree with me.*

LEADER: Old woman, loyal nurse to the queen, we perceive the sad misfortune of Phaedra, but the nature of her disease is not clear. We should like to inquire and learn from you.

NURSE: I do not know, though I keep questioning her. She does not choose to tell.

LEADER: Not even what the beginning of her pains was?

NURSE: It amounts to the same thing. She keeps quiet about it all.

LEADER: How feeble she is, how wasted her figure!

NURSE: How could it be otherwise when she hasn't eaten for three days?

LEADER: Is it madness, or is she trying to die?

NURSE: She is; she is starving herself to death.

LEADER: It's a wonder that her husband is content with such behavior.

NURSE: She hides her troubles and doesn't say she is ill.

LEADER: Does he not surmise it from the look of her face?

NURSE: He happens to be out of the country.

LEADER: But you—haven't you tried to *force* her to tell you what this illness, this madness, is?

NURSE: I have tried everything, but have had no success. But I'll not abate my zeal even now, so that you can appear and testify to my loyalty toward my mistress in her affliction. (*She turns back to* PHAEDRA.) Come now, precious child, let us both forget our earlier talk. You be more amiable. Smooth out your gloomy brow; change the direction of your thoughts. I too took the wrong road with you, but I'll leave it and turn to a better course. If your trouble is one of the unmentionable passions, here are women to help you out. If your affliction can be communicated to men, speak and your case can be referred to physicians.

Ah, why are you silent? You ought not to stay silent, child. Disprove me if I am saying anything out of place, or give in to my reasonable pleas.

Say something! Look at me! —Women, we are giving ourselves all this trouble for nothing. We are as far off as ever. She was not touched by our words before, and she pays no attention now.

But mark this. You may be stubborner than the sea, if you like, but if you die you will betray your children and deprive them of their father's house, as sure as the horse-loving Amazon queen bore a master for your own children, a bastard, but with no bastard heart—you know well whom I mean, Hippolytus——

PHAEDRA: Ah me!

NURSE: It touches you, does it?

PHAEDRA: You have undone me, Nanna. I beseech you, 'fore the gods, do not mention that man again.

NURSE: You see. You are sane enough; but for all your sanity, you are unwilling to benefit your children and save your own life.

PHAEDRA: I do love my children. I am storm-tossed by another misfortune.

NURSE: Surely your hands are pure of blood?

PHAEDRA: My hands are pure, but my heart is defiled.

NURSE: Is it a spell brought on by some enemy?

PHAEDRA: It is a friend that destroys me; but it is not his choice any more than mine.

NURSE: Has Theseus wronged you in any way?

PHAEDRA: May it turn out that I do not wrong him!

NURSE: What then is this terrible thing which compels you to die?

PHAEDRA: O let me sin! It's not against you I sin!

NURSE: I will not, but it is your fault if I fail.

PHAEDRA: What are you doing? Will you force me, clinging to my hand?

NURSE: Yes, and to your knees, and shall never let go!

PHAEDRA: These woes will be yours too when you learn them, poor woman.

NURSE: What can be a greater woe than to be rebuffed by you?

PHAEDRA: You will be my death. But the thing does me credit.

NURSE: Then will you hide your good deeds when I implore you to tell me?

PHAEDRA: Yes, for it is out of evil that I am contriving good.

NURSE: Speak then, and make your goodness known.

PHAEDRA: Go away, 'fore the gods, and let go my hand.

NURSE: I will not, for you do not give me the gift you should.

PHAEDRA: I will; I must respect the sanctity of your suppliant hand.

NURSE: I am silent at once. From now on *you* speak.

PHAEDRA: My poor mother, how strange was your love——

NURSE: For the bull, you mean? Or what?

PHAEDRA: And you, poor sister, bride of Dionysus——

NURSE: What ails you, child? You are maligning your relatives!

PHAEDRA: And I am the third—how sadly I perish!

NURSE: I am dumfounded. What is coming next?

PHAEDRA: There, not here, my misery began.

NURSE: I am no nearer knowing the things I want to hear.

PHAEDRA: Ah, would you could say for me what I must say!

NURSE: I am not a prophet, to have sure knowledge of the unseen.

PHAEDRA: What sort of a thing do they mean when they say that people . . . love?

NURSE: A sweet thing, girl; yes, and painful too.

PHAEDRA: I have known only the pain.

NURSE: What are you saying? You are in love, child? With a *man?*

PHAEDRA: If he is a man, that Amazon's——

NURSE: Hippolytus are you saying?

PHAEDRA: From your lips it came, not mine.

NURSE: Oh, what *will* you say, child? Ah, but you have ruined me. It is intolerable, women. I will not endure it and live. Hateful is the day, hateful is the light I see. I shall fling, I shall hurl this body, I shall quit this life and die. Farewell, I no longer live. Good people fall in love with evil—despite all their good intentions. It's not a goddess that Cypris is, it seems, but whatever there is more powerful than a goddess; she has ruined this woman, and me, and the house.

SOME WOMEN OF THE CHORUS: *You have heard, O you have heard the queen confessing her unspeakable, miserable woe.*

OTHERS: *May I perish before I reach your state of mind, dear to me as you are. Woe is me! Alas! Alack!*

OTHERS: *Poor woman! Such agony!*

OTHERS: *O Misery, man's daily bread!*

OTHERS: *You are ruined. You have shown your evils forth to the light.*

OTHERS: *How will this long day end for you?*

OTHERS: *Some strange evil is coming to a head in this household.*

OTHERS: *It is no longer doubtful how far the luck of love has waned, poor child of Crete.*

PHAEDRA: Women of Troezen, who live in this outpost of the land of Pelops, I have often meditated in the long hours of the night how the life of man is wrecked. It seems to me that it is not by any natural defect in judgment that men fare ill; for many have good sense. But this is how we must look at it. We understand and know what is right, but we do not carry it out in practice, some of us through indolence, others from preferring some other kind of pleasure to duty. And there are many pleasures of life, long talks, and leisure, that delightful evil. And there is shame. This is of two sorts, one not bad, the other the bane of houses. But if the distinction were clear, there would not have been the same word for both meanings.

So in this case. Once I saw how my trouble was developing, I knew there was no medicine with which I could combat it; there was no changing my mind. Now I will tell you the way I reasoned it out. When love had wounded me I looked about how I might best put up with it. I began with the resolve to keep quiet and hide my disease. You cannot trust the tongue, which knows well enough how to rebuke the willfulness of other people but is its own worst enemy. Next, I intended to overcome my folly by my self-control, and so endure it.

And thirdly, when I could not master Cypris by these means I thought it the best plan—none will gainsay me—to die. As I would not wish my good deeds to pass unnoticed, so I did not want a crowd of witnesses to my sin. To own the passion, I knew, would be no less disgraceful than if I gratified it. Besides, I realized full well that I was that object of universal detestation, a Woman. A foul curse on the woman who first committed adultery with strange men! It was from noble families that this evil first started, and when shameful things seem to be approved by the fashionable, then the common people will surely think them correct. Those women who talk chastity, but secretly have their disreputable affairs, I hate. Sea-Goddess Cypris! How in the world can they look their husbands in the face, without quaking for fear lest the darkness, the partner in their crimes, some day take voice; or the walls of their chamber?

There you have my reason for killing myself: the desire to spare my husband and children that shame. Free in fact and free in speech may they live and flourish in illustrious Athens, glorious in their mother! It makes a man cringe, however stouthearted he may be, when he knows his mother's or his father's baseness. This only, they say, stands the stress of life: a good and just spirit in a man. Time, like a young girl, has a mirror, wherein, in his own good time, he shows the base their baseness. Among such may *I* never be seen!

LEADER: Ah, how fair is chastity everywhere, what fruit of noble reputation does it produce!

NURSE: Mistress, that trouble of yours just now gave me a terrible fright at the moment. Now on reflection, I see I was stupid. People's second thoughts are somehow saner. It's nothing odd or inexplicable that has happened to you. Love's passions have swooped down over you. You are in love. What is remarkable in that? Many people are in the same state. Will you throw your life away because of love? Little will it profit those who are or ever will be in love with others if they have to die for it. You cannot withstand Cypris if she rushes upon you full tilt. When she finds a person yielding she comes on gently, but when she finds a person too high and mighty she takes him and—what do you think?—knocks the pride out of him. She roves through the air. She is in the waves of the sea; from her do all things spring. It is she that sows love and bestows it, and all we who are upon earth are born of love.

Those who possess the writings of the ancients and spend all their time with the Muses know that Zeus was once madly in love with Semele, they know that Dawn of the lovely light carried Cephalus off to the gods for the sake of love. Still they live in Heaven and do not shun the presence of the gods. They acquiesce, I imagine, in the fate that has mastered them.

Will *you* not yield? Your father ought to have begotten you by special arrangement, or with different gods for masters, if you will not acquiesce in the present dispensation. How many men, and very sensible men too, do you think, look the other way when their wives are unfaithful? How many fathers, do you think, play pander to their own amorous sons? The wise men of this world hold this principle: Don't notice what you don't like. People ought not to work out their lives too precisely. Why, they cannot even make a roof with rafters that would stand precise measuring! When you have got in as deep as you have, how can you expect to swim out unscathed? No! If you have more good than evil in your character, being only human, you will be doing well enough.

Now, dear girl, don't be wrongheaded, don't be presumptuous. Yes, that is just what it is, pure presumption, wanting to be better than the gods. Have the courage to love: a god has willed it. You are sick; find some way to cure your sickness. There are charms and soothing spells. Some remedy for this affliction will turn up. Believe me, men would be slow in making discoveries if we women did not contrive devices.

LEADER: Phaedra, this woman is the more practical, things being as they are; but it's you I approve. But this approval may be less welcome to you than her talk, and more painful to hear.

PHAEDRA: This it is which ruins well-ordered cities and houses of men: words too plausible. One ought not to speak to tickle the ear; eloquence should promote virtue.

NURSE: Why this unctuous talk? This is no time to mince words. It's time to use plain talk about you. With all speed we must determine the *man's* feelings. He must be told the blunt truth about you. If you had not got your affairs into this tangle, if you had been a really good woman, I should never have urged you to this course, merely to gratify your lust. But now the struggle is to save your life, and there's no disgrace in that.

PHAEDRA: Horrible things you say! —Will you not shut your mouth? Don't start that wicked, wicked talk again.

NURSE: Wicked, perhaps, but better for you than your fine principles. Better the deed if it can save you than an empty name in the pride of which you perish.

PHAEDRA: Please don't, by the gods—you speak so well, your words are so shameful—do not go further. Already my heart is prepared to receive love, and if you put so fair a face on what is shameful, my reserves of resistance will be exhausted.

NURSE: If that is your mind you ought not to have sinned. But things being as they are, hear me. This is the next best thing I can do for you. I have at home a philter, a soothing charm for love—I just now thought of it—which will put an end to this malady neither on disgraceful terms nor to the injury of your mind, if only you do not turn coward. We must get hold of some token from the man you crave, some of his hair or some scrap from his clothing, to conjoin one willing love out of two.

PHAEDRA: Is this medicine a salve, or is it to be swallowed?

NURSE: I do not know; try to be helped, not educated, child.

PHAEDRA: I am afraid you may turn out too much a sophist for me.

NURSE: You would be afraid of anything, you know. What is your worry?

PHAEDRA: That you may hint something of my state to Theseus' son.

NURSE: Let be, girl. I shall fix that up. (*Turns to statue of* APHRODITE.) Be my fellow-worker, Lady Cypris, Sea-Goddess! The other things I am minded to do it will be enough to tell our friends within. (*Exit.*)

CHORUS: *Eros, Eros, you make the eye misty with longing; you import a sweet delight into the hearts of those against whom you march: may you never show yourself to me to my hurt, may you never come inordinately. Neither the flash of fire nor the bolt of the stars is more deadly than the shafts of Aphrodite which Eros, Zeus' boy, hurls from his hands.*

In vain, in vain, has Hellas multiplied the slaughter of cattle on the banks of the Alpheus and at the Pythian shrine of Phoebus; all in vain if we revere not Eros, tyrant over men, chamberlain of the dearest bowers of Aphrodite, the destroyer that brings all manner of calamities on mortals when he attacks.

There was a maiden in Oechalia, a filly unbroken, loverless. But Cypris drove her far from the house of Eurytus, like a flying Naiad or a Bacchant, and bestowed her on Alcmena's son, with blood and flame and gory bridals: O woeful wedlock!

O sacred wall of Thebes, O mouth of Dirce, you might well tell how Cypris creeps on. The mother of divine Bacchus she gave as a bride to the forked thunderbolt and brought her to bed with murderous Death. Fearfully does Cypris breathe upon all the world, like some bee ever hovering.

PHAEDRA (*who has approached the door and there listened during the last lines of the* CHORUS): Be still, women. I am ruined.

LEADER: What is it, Phaedra? What is so fearful in the house?

PHAEDRA: Silence! Let me hear what they are saying inside.

LEADER: I am silent. But I do not like this prelude.

PHAEDRA: Alas! Alas! Oh! Oh! O wretched me! What sufferings are mine!

LEADER: *What means this cry? What are you shrieking? Tell us what you've heard that frightens you, that startles your senses?*

PHAEDRA: I am ruined. Stand at the door here and listen to the brawl going on indoors.

LEADER: *You are nearest the door: attend to the sound coming from within. Tell me, O tell me, what evil has come to pass?*

PHAEDRA: The horse-loving Amazon's son, Hippolytus, is shouting. He is saying dreadful things to my maid.

LEADER: *The sound I hear, but I do not catch the words distinctly. You must have heard what came through the door.*

PHAEDRA: Only too well. He is calling her a pander of sin, a betrayer of her master's bed.

LEADER: *O Misery! You are betrayed, my dear. How can I counsel you? Your secret is out; you are utterly ruined.*

PHAEDRA: Oh! Oh! Ah! Ah!

LEADER: *Betrayed by your friends.*

PHAEDRA: She has ruined me; she has divulged my trouble. She meant well but she has made a sorry cure of my disease.

LEADER: What now? What will you do? Your case is desperate.

PHAEDRA: One thing I know: to die as soon as possible is the only cure for my present troubles.

(*Enter from the house* HIPPOLYTUS *followed by the* NURSE.)

HIPPOLYTUS: O mother earth! O eye of the sun! What unspeakable words I have heard!

NURSE: Quiet, boy, before anyone hears your noise!

HIPPOLYTUS: I cannot be silent when I have heard such horror.

NURSE: Do, by your lovely right hand!

HIPPOLYTUS: Don't lay your hand on me! Don't touch my clothes!

NURSE: Oh, by your knees, do not ruin me!

HIPPOLYTUS: How ruin, if, as you say, you have spoken no wrong?

NURSE: This story, boy, is not for every ear.

HIPPOLYTUS: Fair deeds become fairer when spoken in public.

NURSE: Child, do not disregard your oath.

HIPPOLYTUS: My tongue swore, my mind is unsworn.

NURSE: Boy, what are you about? Will you kill your own?

HIPPOLYTUS: I spit the word out! No unjust person can be "my own."

NURSE: Be charitable. To err is human, child.

HIPPOLYTUS: Zeus! Why did you let women settle in this world of light, a curse and a snare to men? If you wished to propagate the human race you should have arranged it without women. Men might have deposited in your temples gold or iron or a weight of copper to purchase offspring, each to the value of the price he paid, and so lived in free houses, relieved of womankind. Here is a proof that woman is a great nuisance. The father who begot her and brought her up pays a great dowry to get her out of his house and be rid of the plague. The man who receives the poisonous weed into his home rejoices and adds beautiful decorations to the useless ornament and tricks her out in gowns—poor fool, frittering away the family property. He is under constraint: if his in-laws are good people he must keep his cheerless bed; if his spouse is agreeable but her relatives useless, the evil he must accept oppresses the good. Happiest is he who has a cipher for a wife, a useless simpleton to sit at home. A clever woman I hate; may there never be in my house a woman more intellectual than a woman ought to be. Mischief is hatched by Cypris in clever women; the helpless kind is kept from misconduct by the shortness of her wit. No maids should be allowed near a wife; beasts that can bite but cannot talk should be their only company in the house, so that they could neither address anyone or receive speech in return. As it is, the vile women weave their vile schemes within, and the maids carry word outdoors.

So you, sorry wretch, come to me to procure incest in my father's bed. But I will scour it away, sluicing fresh running water into my ears. How could I be base, who feel polluted by the mere hearing? Know well, woman, it's only my piety that saves you. If I had not been taken unaware by sacred oaths I should never have kept from telling my father this. Now I will stay away from the house as long as Theseus is out of the country, and I shall keep my mouth shut. But I shall watch, when I come back with my father, how you will look at him, you and that mistress of yours. Then I shall know fully the brazenness of which I have had the taste.

Curse you! *Let* people say I am always harping on the same theme. Still I shall never tire of hating women. For that matter, *they* never tire of wickedness. Either teach them to be chaste or leave me to assail them always.

(Exit.)

PHAEDRA: *Miserable, unhappy doom of women! What skill have we, what words, when we have fallen, to break the hold of scandal? I have got my deserts. O earth! O light! How can I avoid my doom? How shall I hide my calamity, friends? What god will be my helper, what mortal will appear as my advocate and ally in this unfair procedure? This suffering that comes upon my life is inescapable. Most unhappy of women am I.*

LEADER: Alas, alas, it is over and done. Your maid's devices have not succeeded, lady; things have gone awry.

PHAEDRA: Vilest of vile women, ruin of your friends, what have you done to me! May father Zeus uproot and blast and shatter you with fire! Did I not bid you—did I not foresee your purpose?—to keep silent about the thing which is now my dishonor? But you could not refrain, and now I can no longer die with honor.

But I need some new scheme. That man's heart is whetted with rage: he will blame *me* to Theseus for *your* mistakes. He will relate these happenings to the old man Pittheus. He will fill the whole land with the worst sort of scandal. Curse you and whoever else is overzealous to render dishonorable service to friends who don't wish it!

NURSE: Mistress, of course you can blame me and miscall me—the sting of grief warps your judgment—but I too have an answer to make, if you will listen. I raised you and am devoted to you. I sought a drug for your malady, and I lost. If it had worked, I would now be among the wise ones, no doubt. According to success do we gain a reputation for judgment.

PHAEDRA: Is this fair, will this suffice me, to wound me first and then calmly admit it?

NURSE: We talk too long. I was not wise. But there is an escape even from this, child.

PHAEDRA: Stop your talk. Your first advice was not good; your first attempt was fatal. Get out of my way and look out for yourself. I will set my own affairs to rights.

(Exit NURSE.)

And do you, noble daughters of Troezen, grant me this petition: enfold in silence what you have here heard.

LEADER: I swear by revered Artemis, Zeus' maiden, never to reveal your sins to the light.

PHAEDRA: Thank you. I have thought it over; there is only one solution to my problem, if I am to bequeath an honorable life to my children and turn this disaster to my own credit. Never will I disgrace my Cretan home, nor will I face Theseus on so vile a charge—not for the sake of one little life.

LEADER: Are you about to do some irretrievable evil?

PHAEDRA: Die. But I must plan how.

LEADER: Don't say such a thing!

PHAEDRA: You too lecture me! I shall pleasure Aphrodite (it is she who has destroyed me) by departing from life this day. I am worsted by bitter love. But I shall become a bane to another when I am dead. He may learn not to be superior about my troubles; when he has shared this trouble with me he shall learn to be reasonable.

(*Exit.*)

CHORUS: *Sink me beneath earth's deepest abysses! Or make me a winged bird, O god, among the feathered flocks! Let me fly over the waves to the Adriatic shore, to the waters of Eridanus, where the sad daughters of the Sun, mourning for Phaethon, distill amber splendors of tears into the dark flood.*

To that orchard on the shore, where the Hesperides sing, would I take me; where the Sea Lord of the darkling deep no longer vouchsafes a path for mariners, fixing there the holy boundary of heaven which Atlas holds; where ambrosial fountains gush by the couches of the halls of Zeus; where divine earth, the good giver, multiplies blessings for the gods.

Cretan bark white-winged, through the resounding wave of the briny surge you carried my lady from her happy home to the joy of a joyless marriage. Verily, ill luck attended the departure, as the bark flew from the Cretan land to glorious Athens; and ill luck was there, on the shores of Munychus, as they knotted the ends of their cables, and set foot on the mainland.

True were the omens; she has been smitten to the heart by Aphrodite's dread plague, the plague of incestuous love. And now, overwhelmed in the surge of calamity, to the beams of her bridal chamber she will fix a hanging noose and fit it to her white neck, from shame and loathing of life, choosing rather the glory of a fair name and seeking to rid her heart of the pains of love.

NURSE (*within*): Help! To the rescue, all that are near the house! In the noose is our mistress, Theseus' wife.

SOME WOMEN OF THE CHORUS: Alas, alas, it is done. The royal lady no longer lives. She is caught in the swinging noose.

NURSE (*within*): Will you not hurry? Will nobody bring a sharp knife to loosen the knot from her neck?

OTHERS OF THE CHORUS: Friends, what shall we do? Do you think we should enter the house and loosen the queen from the suicide's noose?

OTHERS: Why? Aren't there young serving women? Meddling is not a safe way of life.

NURSE (*within*): Straighten her limbs, arrange the poor body. A bitter housewifery is this for my masters.

CHORUS: She is dead, poor woman, if I hear right. They are already arranging her corpse.

(*Enter* THESEUS, *garlanded as one returning from an oracle.*)

THESEUS: Women, do you know the meaning of the commotion in the house? A grievous sound from the maidservants reached me. Nor does the house deign to open its doors and welcome me with joy, as coming from the oracle. Has any ill befallen old Pittheus? He is well on in life, yet I should be sorry if he left us.

LEADER: This misfortune, I tell you, pertains not to the old, Theseus; the death of the young will grieve you.

THESEUS: Ah me! The life of my children is not taken from me?

LEADER: They are alive, but their mother is dead: how sad for you!

THESEUS: What are you saying? My wife dead? How?

LEADER: She fastened a suicide's noose about her neck.

THESEUS: Was she chilled with grief? Or what was the trouble?

LEADER: That is all we know. I have but just come to your house, Theseus, to mourn for your sorrow.

THESEUS (*flinging away his garland*): Ah! why is my head crowned with these twisted leaves, sorry pilgrim that I am! Loosen, servants, the bars of the gates, undo the bolts, that I may see the bitter spectacle of my wife, who by her death has ruined me.

(*The palace doors are thrown open, and the body of* PHAEDRA, *surrounded by wailing* DOMESTICS, *is revealed.*)

SOME WOMEN OF THE CHORUS: *Alas, poor woman, for your bitter woes! Victim of your own deed, a deed to confound this house!*

OTHERS: *Woe, woe, for your boldness! Ruthlessly slain by an unholy chance, a sorry triumph over your own self!*

OTHERS: *What is it, poor woman, that darkened your life?*

THESEUS: *Alas for my woes! I have suffered, O my city, the greatest sorrow I ever suffered. How heavily have you trampled upon me and my house, O fortune, mysterious blight of some avenging fiend, nay, very annihilation of life! A sea of evils do I behold, unhappy, so wide that I shall never see the shore again, never rise above the flood of this calamity. Unhappy me! What words can rightly describe your heavy fortune, my wife? Like some bird have you vanished out of my hands, launching yourself with a sheer leap to Hades, woe is me! Oh, oh! Oh, oh! Pitiable, pitiable, is my affliction. From some far-off time, from the sins of someone long ago, the gods bring disaster home to me.*

LEADER: Not upon you alone has this disaster fallen, O King; many beside you have lost excellent wives.

THESEUS: *Below earth, in the shades below earth, I would abide in darkness, wretchedly dying; for I am bereft of your dearest companionship. Your death has destroyed much more than yourself.*

Who will tell me? Whence came this deadly doom to your heart, poor wife? Will someone tell me what has happened? Is it to no purpose that my lordly house shelters a crowd of domestics? Alas for you, woe is me! Such a grief have I seen for my house, unendurable, unspeakable! I am ruined. Desolate is my house and my children are orphaned. You have forsaken me, forsaken me, O dearest and best of women whom the light of the sun and the starry radiance of night behold!

CHORUS: *Alas! Unhappy, unhappy man! What sorrow reigns in your house! My eyes are wet with blinding tears for your loss. But for the woe to follow I have been trembling long.*

THESEUS: Ah! Ah! What is this tablet clutched in that dear hand? Will it tell some new sorrow? Has the poor woman written her desires, her requests, about remarriage, about the children? Reassure yourself, hapless one, the woman does not live who will enter the bed of Theseus or his home. Look! the imprint of the golden seal of her who is no more smiles up at me. Come, let me unroll the string of the seal and see what this tablet would say to me.

SOME WOMEN OF THE CHORUS: *Woe, woe, here is another, a new evil sent by a god to succeed the former. For me life has become unlivable in the face of what has happened.*

OTHERS: *Ruined, utterly overthrown, alas, alas, do I call the house of my lords.*

OTHERS: *O god, if it is in any wise possible, do not confound this house; hear my petition. I see, like a prophet, an omen of further evil.*

THESEUS: Ah, a new evil is this added to the old—unendurable, intolerable! Ah, poor devil that I am!

LEADER: What is it? Tell me if I may hear.

THESEUS: *The tablet cries aloud, it cries aloud of horrors. Whither can I flee this weight of woe? I am undone, utterly ruined. Such an elegy I have read, ah me! It has a tongue, this writing.*

LEADER: Alas, your words are harbingers of evil.

THESEUS: No longer will I keep it behind the gates of my reluctant lips. This abominable, abominable crime! O my city, my city, Hippolytus has laid violent hands on my wife, brazenly despising the awful eye of Zeus! Father Poseidon, with one of those three curses which once you promised me destroy my son; let him not escape this day, if the curses you granted me are genuine.

LEADER: For the gods' sake, King, recall that prayer! You will come to realize the mistake you have made; believe me!

THESEUS: It cannot be. Further, I drive him forth from this land. By one of two fates will he be smitten. Either Poseidon will honor my curses and send him dead to the house of Hades, or exiled from here, wandering from land to land, a homeless stranger, he will drain the cup of life's bitterness to the dregs.

LEADER: Here he comes himself, most opportunely—your son, Hippolytus. Bate your fierce rage, Lord Theseus. Consider what is best for your house.

(*Enter* HIPPOLYTUS *from the right.*)

HIPPOLYTUS: I heard your cries, father, and have come in haste. What thing is making you groan I do not know, but I should like to hear it from you. Ha! What's this? Your wife, father. Dead. This is a terrible shock. Just a little while ago I left her; no long time ago she was looking on the light.

What happened to her? How did she die? Father, I want to learn about it from you. You keep silent. But there's no use of silence in trouble. The heart which yearns to be told all inquires as eagerly in time of trouble too. It is not right to hide your grief from friends, indeed more than friends.

THESEUS: Mankind, vain and misguided, why do you teach ten thousand arts and contrive and invent all manner of devices, yet do not understand and have not investigated the one thing—how to teach sense to people who have no mind?

HIPPOLYTUS: You posit a wise sage indeed, to be able to compel those who have no sense to have good sense. But you are spinning fancies, father, at an unfitting time; I fear your tongue is running wild from grief.

THESEUS: Ah, men ought to have a true yardstick of friendship, deposited somewhere, some means of discerning the heart, to know who is the true friend and who is not. And all men should have two separate voices, one a just voice and the other so-so. Then the one which was dishonest would be convicted by the just one, and we should not be liable to error, as we are.

HIPPOLYTUS: Has some friend got your ear for slander against me? Am I infected though altogether innocent? I am astonished. Yes, your words astound me: they wander far from the seat of reason.

THESEUS: Ah, the heart of man—how far can it go? What limit is there to brazenness and effrontery? If it is to expand generation by generation, and the new transcend the old in rascality, the gods will have to add some new land to the earth to make room for the rogues that are born.

Look at this man. My own son, yet he tried to seduce my wife. He is manifestly proven most base by the hand of her who is dead. (HIPPOLYTUS *covers his face in horror.*) Show your face here to your father: your company has already polluted me. *You* are that superior creature that associates with gods? *You* are temperate and uncontaminated by evil? Your high claims will never convince me; I won't be such a fool as to attribute to the gods such a lack of discernment. Go then and brag, cry up your vegetarian diet like a quack. Hold Orpheus your master, rant away, revere the vaporings of your many screeds. But you are

caught. I charge you all, shun such men as this. They en-
snare with pious words, but their aims are evil. She is
dead: do you think that will save you? You are only the
more caught, you utter villain. What oaths, what arguments could outweigh this tablet to deliver you from the
charge?

You will say that she hated you: you will plead the natural antipathy of bastard and true born. You are making
her a bad bargainer in the business of lives, if for hatred
of you she sacrificed the dearest thing she had. Well, will
you say that folly resides not in men but is innate in
women? I have known young men no more proof against
temptation than women when Cypris troubled their adoles-
cent spirits. But the epithet "masculine" is their excuse.

But why do I stand here arguing with you when this
corpse lies here, a most irrefragable witness? Go to your
ruin, an exile from this land, and go at once. Go not to
divinely built Athens nor to the bounds of any land where
my spear holds sway. If I lie down to the wrongs you have
done me, Sinis of the Isthmus will swear that I never slew
him, that I have been making an empty boast; and the
rocks of Sciron, beside the sea, will deny that I am dangerous to evildoers.

LEADER: I know not how I can call any mortal happy. They
that were exalted are debased.

HIPPOLYTUS: Father, this passion, this emotional intensity,
is dreadful. That sort of thing makes for a plausible ha-
rangue, but when you get to the bottom of it, it is not a
good thing. I have no skill in speaking before the crowd; I
am cleverer, on the other hand, with my friends, and
those few. That too is quite natural; those who are accounted of no consequence among the wise are eloquent
before the mob. But the predicament which has come
upon me forces me to loosen my tongue. I shall begin my
speech at the point where you first assailed me, thinking
to crush me beyond reply.

You see this light, this earth: within their range there
lives not a man of chaster heart than mine, deny it as you
will. I have learnt, first, to reverence the gods, and next, to
have as friends not those who would attempt iniquity but
those who would blush to suggest evil to their friends, or
to act on a base suggestion. I am not a mocker of my
companions, father; I am always the same to my friends,

whether present or absent. And if there is one thing of which I am without spot it is the thing in which you think you have caught me. Of sexual intercourse I am to this day pure. I know nothing of the deed except what I have heard people say or seen in pictures. And I am not keen to look at such things, for I have a virgin soul.

Suppose my chastity fails to convince you. Then it is for you to demonstrate how I was corrupted. Was it because this woman excelled all other women in beauty of person? Or did I expect to rule your house, attaching myself to a woman that was an heiress? I must then have been a fool, quite out of my wits. But "it is delightful to be king"? Not at all, at least not for the temperate man, unless dominion has corrupted the minds of mortals that take pleasure in it. While I might like to be first in the Games, in the city I should prefer to take a back seat, living a contented life with the help of my friends among the best people. In that way there is freedom of conduct, and the absence of danger provides a greater joy than kingship.

Of my arguments one is yet unspoken; you have the rest. If I had a witness to my innocence, if this woman were alive to be present at my trial, then an examination of the facts would reveal the guilty. As things are, I can but swear by Zeus, guardian of oaths, by this land's level plain, that I have never touched the wife of your bed, never would have desired it, never even have thought of it. Yea, may I perish unhonored, unknown, without a city, without a house, an exile wandering over the earth; may neither sea nor land receive the flesh of me when I am dead, if I am a guilty man.

Whether it was through fear that she destroyed her life, I know not; for me it is not lawful to say more. Right has she done when she could not do right; right I had, and it has done me wrong.

LEADER: The oaths you have offered by the gods, no mean pledge, are a sufficient rebuttal of the charge against you.

THESEUS: Is not this fellow a wizard and a mountebank to believe that nonchalance will help him to prevail over me, after making a cuckold of his father?

HIPPOLYTUS: And I am equally surprised at you, father. If you were my son and I your father I should have killed you on the spot, and would not now be punishing you with exile if you had presumed to touch my wife.

THESEUS: A characteristic suggestion! But not so shall you die. A quick death is easiest for a poor wretch. But an exile wandering far from your native soil, as you pronounced the terms for yourself——

HIPPOLYTUS: What will you do? Will you not await time's testimony about me? Will you drive me out of the land?

THESEUS: Ay, beyond the sea and the Atlantic limits, if I could: so utterly do I hate you.

HIPPOLYTUS: Will you cast me out of the land untried, without examination of oath or pledge or prophet's oracle?

THESEUS: This tablet here, though it has no oracular cachet, authenticates the charge against you. For the birds of omen which fly overhead—I bid them a long farewell.

HIPPOLYTUS: Ye gods! Why do I not open my mouth, when I am being destroyed by you whom I worship? But I cannot. In any case, I should not persuade the one I must, and I should be violating to no purpose the oaths that I swore.

THESEUS: Your cant is killing me. Out from your country's soil, and at once!

HIPPOLYTUS: Whither shall I turn my unhappy steps? What host will receive me in his house, exiled on such a charge?

THESEUS: One who is pleased to entertain ravishers of wives and partners of evil.

HIPPOLYTUS: Ah me! This strikes me to the heart and brings me nigh to tears, that I should appear unrighteous and that *you* should believe me so.

THESEUS: Then was the time to groan and to realize what you were about, when you shamelessly and brutally defiled your father's wife.

HIPPOLYTUS: O halls, would that you could utter forth a clear voice, and bear witness whether I am a base man!

THESEUS: You take refuge in speechless witnesses—quite clever. This deed, though it speak not, testifies to your villainy.

HIPPOLYTUS: Alas! If only I could stand apart and look myself in the face, that I might weep at the evils I have suffered!

THESEUS: You've had much more practice at regarding yourself than doing your duty by your parents as you ought.

HIPPOLYTUS: Unhappy mother! Bitter hour of birth! May none of my friends ever be a bastard!

THESEUS: Drag him away, slaves, won't you? Did you not hear me long since decreeing banishment for this man?

HIPPOLYTUS: At his peril shall any of them touch me. Do you yourself thrust me out of the land, if you have the moral courage.

THESEUS: I will so, if you do not heed my words. No pity at all for your exile moves me.

(HIPPOLYTUS *moves off; exit* THESEUS.)
(HIPPOLYTUS *pauses at the statue of* ARTEMIS.)

HIPPOLYTUS: It is settled, it seems, and I am ruined. I know these things, but I know not how to say them. O dearest of deities, maiden daughter of Leto, companion at home, companion in the woods, I am banished from glorious Athens. Farewell, city and land of Erechtheus. O plain of Troezen, what a delightful land for lads to grow up in! Farewell. For the last time I see you, address you.

Come, lads, my age-fellows in this land, bid me good speed, escort me forth from the land. Never will you see a man more chaste, even if my father thinks otherwise.

(*Exit* HIPPOLYTUS *with his following.*)

CHORUS OF HUNTSMEN: *Verily, it is a great thing, to believe in gods that care; it soothes the griefs of the believer. Though my secret heart hopes in an intelligent Providence, yet when I look at the fortunes of men and their actions, the hope fails me. One thing comes, another goes, and life for man is ever shifting, ever wandering.*

CHORUS OF WOMEN: *Heaven hear my prayer and Fate grant me this boon: good fortune and wealth, and a mind ungrieved, unanxious! May my opinions be neither uncompromising nor (on the other hand) mere glosses. May my disposition be easy, adjusting itself to every new morrow, in lifelong happiness.*

CHORUS OF HUNTSMEN: *My temper is no longer orthodox, when I behold the frustration of my hopes. We have seen the star of Athens, the most brilliant of Hellas, we have seen him sent forth to a strange land by his father's fury.*

O sands of my country's shore, O mountain thickets, where with swift hounds he used to slay the wild beasts, in the company of revered Dictynna!

CHORUS OF WOMEN: *No more shall you mount the car of Enetian coursers, holding the hooves of your trained steed to the chariot course at Limna! The Muse that was ever wakeful within the frame of the lyre will be heard no more*

*in your father's house. The retreats of Leto's maiden in the
green forest depths will stand ungarlanded. Your exile has
killed the competition of the maidens for the prize of your
love.*

A MATRON OF THE CHORUS: *But I—with tears for your
calamity I shall endure a life that is no life. You had no
joy of your son, poor mother. Alas! I am angry with the
gods. Woe! Triad of Graces, why do you let him go forth
from his fatherland, from these halls, the poor sufferer?
He was not the cause of the calamity.*

LEADER: Look! I see a henchman of Hippolytus, gloomy-
visaged, striding toward the house in haste.

(*Enter* MESSENGER.)

MESSENGER: Where might I go to find Theseus, ruler of this
land, women? Tell me, if you know. Is he within the
house?

LEADER: Here is himself, coming out of it.

(*Enter* THESEUS.)

MESSENGER: Theseus, I bring a story which should cause
concern to you and to the citizens that live in the city of
Athens or at the ends of the land of Troezen.

THESEUS: What is it? No sudden calamity has befallen the
two neighboring cities?

MESSENGER: Hippolytus is dead, or practically so. He yet
looks upon the light, but it is touch and go.

THESEUS: By whose hand? In a feud with someone whose
wife he had defiled, like his father's?

MESSENGER: His own chariot team destroyed him, and the
curses of your mouth, with which you cursed your son to
your father who is lord of the sea.

THESEUS: Ye gods! Poseidon! So you *are* my father right
enough. For you have heeded my prayers.

How did he die? Tell me. How did Justice bring her
cudgel down upon him that wronged me?

MESSENGER: Hard by the wave-beaten shore we were comb-
ing the horses' manes with currycombs, all in tears; for a
messenger had come saying that Hippolytus might no
longer set foot in this land because you had doomed him
to miserable exile. Then he came, bringing the same sad
song to us on the shore. A countless following of his
friends, a throng of his age-fellows, came with him. After
a time, when he had ceased from his groans he spoke:
"Why am I so distracted? My father's behests must be

obeyed. Harness the yoke-bearing steeds to my car. This city is no longer mine."

Then did every man bestir himself, and quicker than you could say the word we set the mares all harnessed before their master. He grasped the reins in his hand from the rim of the car and fitted his feet neatly into the sockets, but first he spread out his hands in prayer to the gods: "Zeus, may I live no longer if I am a man that is base. Let my father realize how he has abused me, either after I am dead or while I still see the light." With that he took the goad in his hand and whipped up the horses. We servants followed our master close to the car, near the horses' heads, out the road which leads directly to Argos and Epidauria. When we had come to a deserted stretch, there is a beach beyond this land, sloping toward the Saronic Sea. From there came a noise, like an earthquake, a deep roar, horrible to hear. The horses held their heads erect and pointed their ears toward heaven. Upon us broke a mighty dread, whence that sound could be. When we looked toward the sea-beaten shores we saw an unearthly wave reaching to the sky in a pillar, preventing me from seeing the headland of Sciron beyond; it hid all the Isthmus and the Rock of Asclepius. And then swelling up and splashing quantities of foam with a snorting of the sea it proceeded toward the shore, where the four-horse chariot was. Together with the breaker and its triple surge the wave set forth a bull, a prodigious monster. With its bellowing the whole land was filled, and it reechoed horribly; to the onlookers it was a sight more than eyes could bear.

Straightway a dreadful fright fell upon the mares. Their master, who was quite at home with the ways of horses, seized the reins in his hands and strained at them as a seafaring man pulls at his oar, and he planted his body to lean backward with the reins. But the mares bit down on the fire-begotten bits in their jaws and bore on violently, paying no heed either to the steersman's hand nor to the traces nor to the jointed chariot. When he steered the course with his reins to the soft ground the bull appeared in front to head him off, throwing a frenzy into the four-horse team. And when they careened madly toward the rocks it kept close to the rail in silence, and kept up until it fouled the chariot and overturned it, striking its wheel-rim against a rock. Then everything was in confusion. The hubs of the wheels flew up, and the linch-pins of the axles. Himself, poor man, tangled in the traces, was caught in an inextricable bond and dragged along, dashing his dear head against the rocks, lacerating his flesh; and he cried out in a voice dreadful to hear: "Stand, you that were fattened at my stalls; do not crush me out! O my father's unhappy curses! Who here wills to save a good man?"

Many of us willed to, but we were left far behind. Meanwhile he was freed from his bonds, the traces neatly cut, I know not how, and he fell, breathing yet some little life. The horses vanished, and that ill-starred monster of a bull, I know not where in the rocky ground.

I am a slave of your house, sire, but so much I can never do—be persuaded that your son is base; nay, not even if the whole race of womankind hang themselves or if someone fill all the pines of Ida with accusations; for I know that he is a good man.

LEADER: Alas, the disaster of new evils is consummated. There is no refuge from destiny and the inevitable.

THESEUS: Hatred of the man who suffered these things gave me pleasure in the account. But now I respect the gods and him too, because he is of my body, and so I am neither rejoiced nor grieved by these evils.

MESSENGER: Well then? Shall we bring the sufferer here, or what shall we do with him to please you? Think it over. If you take my advice, you will not be cruel to your boy in his misfortune.

THESEUS: Bring him to me, so that I may look with my own eyes upon him who denies he defiled my bed, and may confute him with words and with the dispensations of the gods.

(*Exit* MESSENGER.)

CHORUS: *Thou, Cypris, dost ply the stubborn hearts of gods and mortals, and with thee is he of varied plume that circles round on swiftest wing. He darts over the earth and the tuneful briny deep, Eros the winged, gleaming with gold. He enchants with a heart-frenzy all whom he assails; he charms the natures of the young beasts on the mountains, and those of the sea, as many as earth sustains and the gleaming sun beholds, and men also. Over these all, Cypris, dost thou alone hold queenly sway.*

(ARTEMIS *appears aloft.*)

ARTEMIS: *You, the nobly born child of Aegeus, do I bid hearken: Leto's maiden Artemis addresses you.*

Theseus, why, miserable man, do you take pleasure in these circumstances, when you have slain your son unrighteously, crediting for things secret the lying tales of your wife? But not secret is the retribution that has overtaken you. Why do you not hide your body in shame in Tartarus beneath the earth, or change your being to a bird of the sky, to fly far from this woe? You can have no portion in the life of good men.

Hear, Theseus, the state of your sorrows; I shall not make it easy for you, but cause you pain. For this purpose have I come, to reveal to you the righteous heart of your son that he may die with honor, and also the frenzy of your wife and, in a sense, her nobleness.

Stung by the pricks of that goddess most hateful to us who delight in virginity, your wife became enamored of your son. With her will she tried to overcome Cypris, but was ruined, unwittingly, by the devices of her nurse, who revealed her passion to your son, under pledge of secrecy. As became a righteous man, he yielded not to her proposals. But neither did he repudiate the oath he had sworn, though vilely treated by you; for a pious man he was. But she feared an investigation, and wrote lying writings, and destroyed your son by guile. Yet you believed her.

THESEUS: Woe is me!

ARTEMIS: Does the tale sting you, Theseus? But stay quiet and hear what happened thereafter, that you may groan the more. You know that you had three true curses from your father? Of these you have misused one, against your own son, base villain, when you could have used it against some enemy. Your father of the sea, though kindly disposed, granted as much as he was bound to; for he had promised. But to him and to me alike do you appear base; for you awaited neither pledge nor sign of oracles, you neither made examination nor left proof to length of time; but quicker than became you, you hurled curses upon your son and slew him.

THESEUS: Lady, let me perish!

ARTEMIS: Dreadful was your act. Nevertheless, even for you it is possible to attain forgiveness. It was Aphrodite, sating her wrath, who willed these things to happen. The gods have this rule: none will cross the course of another's humor; we stand aside always. Yet, if I did not fear Zeus, I would never have stooped to this dishonor—to let die the man I loved most of all mortals. As for your sin, in the first place your ignorance acquits you of malice; secondly, your wife's death beggared argument and forced your judgment.

Upon you in chief have these woes burst forth, but the sorrow is mine too. The gods have little joy in the death of the pious; but the wicked we destroy with their children and their houses.

(*Enter* HIPPOLYTUS *supported by* ATTENDANTS.)

CHORUS: *Lo! Hither comes the pitiable man: mangled are his youthful flesh and his fair head. O the misery of this house! What a double grief, launched from Heaven, has been fulfilled for these halls!*

HIPPOLYTUS: *Ah! Ah! Oh! Oh! An unfortunate am I. By the unjust imprecations of an unjust father am I mangled, ah, miserably. Woe is me, woe! Pains shoot through my head, a spasm darts through my brain. Hold, I will rest my failing body.*

O hateful chariot team, fed by my own hand, you have utterly destroyed me, you have utterly slain me. Alas, alas! 'Fore the gods, gently, slaves, take hold of my wounded body with your hands. Who stands at my side to the right? Carefully raise me, carry me evenly, the ill-starred, accursed by my father's errors. Zeus, Zeus, do you see this? Here am I, the pious, the reverent, here am I, who excelled all in temperance—to Hades manifest I go; I have lost my life utterly. In vain have I toiled at the labors of piety toward men.

Ah, ah! Ah, ah! The pain, now the pain is come: let me go, ah me! Let Death the Healer come upon me. Come, come and destroy the unhappy wretch. For a two-edged sword I yearn, to cut myself in pieces and lay my life to rest. O ill-starred curse of my father! The evil of bloodguilty kinsmen, ancestors of old, finds its issue in me and tarries not; it comes upon me—why, when I am in no way guilty of evil? Woe is me, woe! How can I free my life from these unfeeling sufferings? Masterful Death, lay my miseries to rest in the blackness of thy night!

ARTEMIS (*who has remained upon her platform unobserved*): *Ah, unhappy man! To what a calamity are you yoked! Your own nobility of heart has destroyed you.*

HIPPOLYTUS: Ah, breath of divine fragrance! Even in the midst of evils I perceive thee, and my body is alleviated. Artemis the goddess is in this place.

ARTEMIS: She is, hapless man; and of the gods most friendly to you.

HIPPOLYTUS: You see how it is with me, Lady—how pitiful——

ARTEMIS: I see. But gods may not weep.

HIPPOLYTUS: Your huntsman, your henchman, is no more——

ARTEMIS: Ah, no. Very dear to me you are, even in your death.

HIPPOLYTUS: The keeper of your horses, the guardian of your images.

ARTEMIS: Pernicious Cypris has devised it so.

HIPPOLYTUS: Ah me! I recognize the deity that ruined me.

ARTEMIS: She was aggrieved for the worship she missed; she hated you for your chastity.

HIPPOLYTUS: The three of us has Cypris destroyed; I perceive it.

ARTEMIS: Your father and you and the third, his wife.

HIPPOLYTUS: I mourn too for my father's catastrophe.

ARTEMIS: He was deceived by a deity's scheming.

HIPPOLYTUS: Ah, unhappy father! What a calamity is yours.

THESEUS: I am ruined, child; life has no pleasure for me.

HIPPOLYTUS: For your sake rather than for mine do I groan for this mistake.

THESEUS: Would that *I* were a corpse, child, instead of you.

HIPPOLYTUS: Ah, bitter gifts of your father Poseidon!

THESEUS: O that the prayer had never come to my mouth!

HIPPOLYTUS: Why? You would have killed me in any case; you were so infuriated.

THESEUS: Yes; my wits were confused by the gods.

HIPPOLYTUS: Ah! Would that the human race might bring a curse on the gods!

ARTEMIS: Let be. Though you are buried in the darkness of earth, I shall not forget Goddess Cypris. It was she who willed the wrath that has fallen on you, because you were pious and pure of heart. With these arrows of mine from which there is no escape I will wreak vengeance with my own hand upon another mortal—whoever is most dear to her. To you, sore sufferer, I shall vouchsafe in return for these evils the highest of honors in the city of Troezen. Maidens unwed shall shear their tresses for you before their bridal night, and you shall reap as your reward through the long ages to come the bountiful sorrow of tears. Ever shall virgins cherish you, singing songs in your honor, and Phaedra's love for you shall not fall into silent oblivion.

And you, son of ancient Aegeus, take your child into your arms and clasp him close. Unwittingly did you destroy him. It is but natural for humans to err when gods put it in their way. And you I bid, Hippolytus, not to hate your father. You understand the doom by which you were ruined.

Farewell! For me it is not lawful to look on death or to pollute my eyes with the gasps of the dying. I see that you are now near that sad case.   (*Vanishes*.)

HIPPOLYTUS: Farewell, blessed maiden, in thy going! Right easily do you forsake our long companionship. My father I absolve from all blame, as you request; for in the past also I obeyed your counsels.

Ah! Ah! Already the darkness is shrouding my eyes. Take me, father, raise me up.

THESEUS: Ah me, child, what are you doing to wretched me?

HIPPOLYTUS: I am gone. Already I see the gates of the dead.

THESEUS: Will you leave me with my hands defiled?

HIPPOLYTUS: Nay, I free you from guilt for this death.

THESEUS: What do you say? Do you set me free of this bloodshed?

HIPPOLYTUS: I call to witness Artemis, mistress of the bow.

THESEUS: Best beloved, how noble do you show yourself to your father!

HIPPOLYTUS: Pray to obtain such sons—true-born.

THESEUS: Woe for your good and pious heart!

HIPPOLYTUS: Farewell, a long farewell, to you, my father.

THESEUS: Forsake me not, child; bear up!

HIPPOLYTUS: My bearing up is done. Father, I have died. Quickly hide my face with garments.

THESEUS: O glorious Athens, realm of Pallas, what a man you are losing! My grief! Long will I remember the evil you have done, O Cypris!

CHORUS: *Upon all the citizens has this common grief come unexpected: there shall be a downpouring of many a tear. The fame of the great endures, commanding sorrow.*

                                        (*Exeunt*.)

Trojan Women

ABOUT 416 B.C. Athens demanded that the island of Melos, which was kindred to Sparta in blood and wished to remain neutral, should cooperate in the war against Sparta, and when Melos refused the Athenians slaughtered its men and enslaved its women and children. Such an atrocity against a *Greek* city was unexampled; war was not only ruinous to its victims but demoralizing even to its victors. Soon after the Melian episode Athens was preparing its ambitious overseas expedition against Syracuse. In the midst of the war fever Euripides (whose earlier *Andromache* had demonstrated his Athenian patriotism) wrote the pacifist *Trojan Women*, which prophesies that a Greek force about to embark on a long voyage after trampling its victims' sanctities would meet with disaster—as the Syracusan expedition eventually did. It is an index of Athenian liberalism that such a play could be presented, under state auspices, at such a time.

In the prologue Athena herself, the patroness of the Greeks and in particular of Athens, is shown conspiring with Poseidon, who had favored the Trojans, to exact vengeance from the Greeks. After this initial shock we see one wave after another of wanton cruelty sweeping over a broken old woman, once queen of Troy, who is moaning in the dust. The victors themselves are uneasy and dehumanized, to the point of sacrificing a young girl to a ghost and dashing an innocent infant to its death. Even the tough Talthybius can no longer stomach the heartlessness of which he must be the herald. What high objective could have been worth so frightful a price? The final stroke is the appearance of self-assured and bedizened Helen among the havoc she had caused. It was for such a trifling wanton as this that a great city had been crushed, its men butchered, and its women enslaved, and for such a cause as this that doom hung over the executioners also.

CHARACTERS

POSEIDON
ATHENA
HECUBA
CHORUS, *of Trojan Women*
TALTHYBIUS, *Herald of the
    Greeks*
CASSANDRA, *daughter of Hecuba, and Priestess
    of Apollo*
ANDROMACHE, *widow of Hector*
ASTYANAX, *son of Hector*
MENELAUS, *husband of Helen*
HELEN

SCENE: The camp of the Greeks before
Troy; in the background, the smoking ruins
of the city. At the entrance of one of the
tents Hecuba is stretched on the ground

Translated by M. HADAS and J. McLEAN

(POSEIDON *enters, unseen by* HECUBA.)

POSEIDON: I am Poseidon, come from the salt depths of
the Aegean sea, where the bands of Nereids ply their lovely
feet in the intricacies of the dance. Ever since Phoebus and
I threw the stone circle of towers, true and plumb, round
this Troy, my goodwill toward the city of my Phrygians
has not failed. Now the city is a smoking ruin, sacked by
the Argive spear. That man of Parnassus, Epeius the
Phocian, aided by the devices of Pallas, constructed a horse
teeming with armed men, and sent the fatal monster inside
the towers. Therefore men of after time will call it the
Horse of Spears.

The sacred groves are abandoned. The shrines of the gods
run with human blood. On the steps of the altar of Zeus
the Protector, Priam lies dead. All the gold, all the spoils
of Phrygia are being transported to the Achaean ships.
They are now waiting for a following wind: after ten

winters and summers they yearn to see their wives and
children, those Greeks that came in war against this city.
I too, vanquished by Hera the Argive goddess and Athena,
who united to destroy the Phrygians, now leave famous
Ilium and my altars. When the evil of desolation overtakes a city, a blight falls on the cult of the gods; they
delight no more in their worship. Scamander echoes to
the loud wailings of multitudes of captured women being
allotted their masters. Some have fallen to the Arcadians,
others to the Thessalians, others to the two sons of Theseus,
princes of Athens. All the Trojan women that are not to
be assigned by lot are within these tents, specially picked
for the first men of the army. With them is the daughter
of Tyndareus, Helen the Laconian, rightly regarded as a
captive woman.

If anyone wants to see an unhappy woman, here is
Hecuba prostrate before the entrance, weeping many tears
for many miseries. Her daughter Polyxena has been slain
at the tomb of Achilles, bravely dying, hapless girl. Priam
is gone and the children, all but the virgin Cassandra,
whom Lord Apollo has given over to prophetic frenzy.
And now Agamemnon, religion and reverence forgot, forces
her to be his concubine.

O city that once was fortunate, O shining battlements,
farewell! If Pallas, daughter of Zeus, had not willed your
ruin, you would still be standing on firm foundations.

(*Enter* ATHENA.)

ATHENA: You who are nearest in lineage to my father,
god powerful and respected in heaven, may I end our ancient feud and address you?

POSEIDON: You may, Queen Athena. The company of kinsfolk is a great charm to the heart.

ATHENA: I thank you for your courtesy. My lord, I have a
plan for you and me to discuss.

POSEIDON: Do you bring some news from heaven? Is it from
Zeus or some other god?

ATHENA: No, it is for Troy's sake, whose soil we tread. I
have come to enlist your might in a common cause.

POSEIDON: Have you renounced your former hatred and taken
compassion on the city, now it is in flames and ashes?

ATHENA: First get back to where we were. Will you share
my plan and help me to work out my will?

POSEIDON: I will. But I wish to learn your purpose in coming here. Does it concern the Achaeans, or the Phrygians?

ATHENA: I wish to bring gladness to my former enemies, the Trojans, and to inflict on the host of the Achaeans a sorrowful homecoming.

POSEIDON: Why do you jump like this from mood to mood and rush to excesses of hate and love?

ATHENA: Have you not heard of the insult to me and my temples?

POSEIDON: I have: Ajax dragged Cassandra off with violence.

ATHENA: Yes, and nothing was done to him by the Achaeans, nothing even said to him.

POSEIDON: And yet it was thanks to your might that they captured Ilium.

ATHENA: That is why, with your help, I will do them an injury.

POSEIDON: Anything you want from me is at your disposal. But what do you mean to do?

ATHENA: I mean to give them a homecoming they will not recognize.

POSEIDON: While they are still on land, or when they are on the salt sea?

ATHENA: Whenever they sail off home from Ilium. Zeus will send torrents of rain and hail and hurricanes that will black out the sky. He says he will lend me the fire of his thunderbolts to smite the Achaeans and set their ships ablaze. You, on the other hand, must do your part. Make the crossing of the Aegean a din of monstrous waves, a maelstrom of waters. Fill the sheltered straits of Euboea with drowned bodies. The Achaeans must learn in future to stand in proper awe of my shrines and to respect the other gods.

POSEIDON: So shall it be. You need make no long speech to get this favor. I shall stir up the waters of the Aegean Sea. The shores of Myconus, the reefs of Delos, Scyros, Lemnos, and the promontories of Caphareium will receive innumerable bodies of drowned men. But go to Olympus, get the Father's thunderbolts in your hands and be on watch when the Argive fleet loosens its cables.

(Exit ATHENA.)

The mortal is mad who sacks cities and desolates temples and tombs, the holy places of the dead; his own doom is only delayed. *(Exit.)*

(HECUBA *begins to rise, slowly.*)

HECUBA: *Up, poor soul, lift your head, your neck, from the ground. This is no longer Troy nor we Troy's royal family. Fortune veers; be brave. Sail with the stream, sail with the wind of fate. Do not run your ship of life head-on into the billows of disaster. Alas! I weep. And why may I not weep in my misery? My country is lost, my children, my husband. O ancestry, with your spread of pride lowered, you come to nothing after all.*

What should I tell of, what leave untold? What a sorry bed on which I lay my heavy, weary limbs, lying stretched on my back, in a hard, hard couch! Oh my head, my temples, my sides! Oh how lovely, to shift my bony back, to let my body keel over to this side and that, to the rhythm of my complaints, my unceasing tears. This is the music of the sorrowful—to chant the jarring dirges of their doom.

O prows of ships, to the horrid call of the trumpet and the loud scream of fifes you came on swift oars over the purple brine, across the safe seas of Hellas to sacred Ilium, and in the bay of Troy (alas!) you dropped your cable ropes, produce of Egypt. You came to fetch Menelaus' loathsome wife, that affront to Castor, that scandal of the Eurotas. It is she who has murdered the father of fifty sons and grounded me on these sorry shoals of disaster.

Ah me! Here I sit, a sorry seat, beside the tents of Agamemnon. They carry me off to slavery, an old woman like me, my poor head laid bare by sorrow's cutting edge. Enough! Woeful widows of Troy's warriors, and you virgin brides of violence, Troy is in smoke, let us weep for Troy. Like a mother hen clucking over her fluttering chicks, I shall lead your song, ah how unlike those songs I used to lead in honor of the gods, leaning on Priam's scepter as my foot gave the loud stamp, and the dance started to the Phrygian strains.

(*Enter* CHORUS *in two halves, one consisting of the older women, the other of the younger.*)

LEADER: *Hecuba, why those shouts, why those cries? Has word come for one of us? I heard your piteous lamentations ringing through the tents. And shuddering fear grips the hearts of the Trojan women within, who are bemoaning their slavery.*

HECUBA: *My child, the crews of rowers are stirring down by the Argive ships.*

LEADER: *Ah me! What does that mean? The time has come, I suppose, when the ships will carry me away from my native land.*

HECUBA: *I do not know, but I suspect the worst.*

LEADER: *Ho! woeful women of Troy, come and hear your doom, out of the tents with you, the Argives are setting sail for home.*

HECUBA: *Ah! do not bring frenzied, fey Cassandra out here, for the Argives to insult. Spare me grief on grief. O Troy, hapless Troy, this is your end. Hapless are they that have lost you, the living and the dead.*

CHORUS: *Ah me! In fear and trembling I quit these tents of Agamemnon to hear your words. O Queen. Have the Argives made their decision? Is it death for hapless me? Or are the sailors already preparing to push off and ply their oars?*

HECUBA: *My child, I have been here since daybreak, my heart in a swoon of dread.*

CHORUS: *Has some herald of the Greeks been here already?*

HECUBA: *The hour of allotment must be near.*

CHORUS: *Oh! Oh! Will it be to Argos or Phthia or one of the islands that they will take me, unhappy me, far from Troy?*

HECUBA: *Alas! Alas! Whose wretched slave shall I be? Where, where on earth shall this old woman toil, useless as a drone, poor counterpart of a corpse, a feeble, ghastly ornament? To be posted to watch at the door, to become a children's nurse—I who in Troy was paid the honors of a queen!*

CHORUS (*individually*): *Alas! Alas! How piteous are the lamentations with which you bemoan your indignities!*

No more shall I ply my flying shuttle in Trojan looms.

For the last time I see the graves of my parents, for the very last time.

I shall have worse sorrows, forced to lie in the bed of Greeks——

My curse on the night when that is my fate.

Or kept as a slave woman to draw water from holy Pirene.

May I come to Theseus' land, the glorious, the blessed.

Never, never, I pray, to the swirling Eurotas, the cursed abode of Helen, there to look upon Menelaus as my master, the sacker of Troy.

I have heard tales of the loads of wealth, the profusion

of fine fruitfulness, in the grand land of Peneus, the beauti-
ful pedestal of Olympus. There let me come; that is my
second choice, after Theseus' land, holy, august.

Then there is the land of Etna and Hephaestus, Sicily,
mother of mountains, looking across to Phoenicia; I have
heard of its fame, of its crowns of valor. Likewise its
neighbor, as you sail over the Ionian sea, the land watered
by the loveliest of rivers, Crathis, whose mysterious waters
(waters that put yellow fire in your hair) bring prosperity
to the land and a breed of valiant men.

And now here comes a herald from the army of the
Danaans; he comes, quickening his steps at his journey's
end, to dispense his budget of news. What does he bring?
What has he to tell? What matter? We are already slaves
of the Dorian land.

(*Enter* TALTHYBIUS.)

TALTHYBIUS: Hecuba, you know I made many trips to Troy
as messenger from the Greek army. That makes me an ac-
quaintance of yours, of long standing. I am Talthybius,
here to announce the latest news.

HECUBA: *Here it comes, my Trojan friends. This is what I*
have long been dreading.

TALTHYBIUS: The assignments have already been made, if
that was your dread.

HECUBA: *Ah! Where do we go? Some city in Thessaly or in*
Phthia or in the land of Cadmus?

TALTHYBIUS: You were each assigned individually to separate
masters.

HECUBA: *Then who got whom? Is there good luck ahead*
for any of Troy's daughters?

TALTHYBIUS: I can tell you, but you must particularize your
questions, one at a time.

HECUBA: *Then tell me, who got my daughter, poor Cassan-*
dra?

TALTHYBIUS: King Agamemnon took her, as a special prize.

HECUBA: *What? To be the slave of his Lacedaemonian wife?*
Ah me!

TALTHYBIUS: No, she is to be his concubine.

HECUBA: *His concubine? The virgin of Phoebus, the girl on*
whom the golden-haired god bestowed virginity, as a pe-
culiar favor?

TALTHYBIUS: Love's shafts pierced him for the prophetic
maiden.

HECUBA: *O my daughter, throw away the holy branches, throw off the sacred livery of chaplets that deck your person.*

TALTHYBIUS: Why? Isn't it a great thing to get a king for a lover?

HECUBA: *And what of the daughter you lately took away from me? Where is she?*

TALTHYBIUS: You mean Polyxena? Or whom do you speak of?

HECUBA: *Just her. To whom did the lot yoke her?*

TALTHYBIUS: She has been appointed to serve at the tomb of Achilles.

HECUBA: *Ah me! My daughter? To serve at a tomb? But what new usage or ordinance is this that the Greeks have?*

TALTHYBIUS: God bless your child. She rests well.

HECUBA: *What words are these? Tell me, does she see the sun?*

TALTHYBIUS: She is in the hands of fate; her troubles are over.

HECUBA: *And what of fire-eating Hector's wife, unhappy Andromache? What luck had she?*

TALTHYBIUS: Achilles' son took her also, as a special gift.

HECUBA: *And whose servant am I, this ancient body who needs a staff in her hand to help her two legs to walk?*

TALTHYBIUS: The king of Ithaca, Odysseus, got you for his slave.

HECUBA: *Ah! Hecuba, smash your shaven head, tear your two cheeks with your nails. Ah me! An abominable, treacherous scoundrel I have got for master, an enemy of justice, a lawless beast, whose double tongue twists all things up and down and down and up, who turns every friendship to hate, who—O women of Troy, wail for me. I go to my doom, ruin and misery are mine. The unluckiest lot has fallen to me.*

LEADER: Mistress, you know *your* fate, but which of the Peloponnesians, which of the Thessalians, is the master of my life?

TALTHYBIUS: On, servants, you must fetch Cassandra out here at once. I will put her into my general's hands and then come for the others.

Ha! What is that torch flame blazing inside? What are these Trojan women up to? Now that they are about to be carried abroad to Argos, are they starting a fire in the heart of the tents? Are they deliberately burning themselves to death? Truly, in people like these the love of freedom does not offer an easy neck to misery. Open up! Open up! Their death may be all very fine for them, but the Achaeans won't like it, and I don't want to get me into any trouble.

HECUBA: It is not that. It is no fire. It is my child, frantic Cassandra; here she comes hurrying out.

(*Enter* CASSANDRA, *dressed as* APOLLO's *priestess, and waving a nuptial torch. She fancies she is about to be married in* APOLLO's *temple, while the god himself leads the choir.*)

CASSANDRA: *Lift up the torch, bring it to me. I bear the flame, I do reverence, and look! look! I light up this temple with the blaze. O King hymeneal, blessed is the bridegroom, blessed too am I; in Argos I am to marry a royal lover. Hymen, O King hymeneal! Poor mother, your time is all taken with mourning for my dead father and our dear country, with tears and lamentations. Therefore I now must hold aloft the blazing torch myself, for my own wedding. See its radiance, see its brilliance, giving light to thee, Hymenaeus, and thee, Hecate, as custom prescribes for the weddings of maidens.*

Lift high the light foot. On, on with the dance. Evan! Evoe! Let it be as in the proudest days of my father's prosperity. The choir is sacred; lead it, Phoebus, in honor of thy priestess, in thy temple among the laurels. Hymen, O Hymen hymeneal! Sing, mother, sing and dance, whirling mazily in and out, trip it with me, as you love me. Shout the marriage greeting to the bride, wish her joy with songs and shouts. Come, daughters of Phrygia, in your loveliest robes, sing my wedding, sing the husband that Fate brings to my bed.

LEADER: Queen, will you not seize your frantic daughter before she trips lightly off to the Argive host?

HECUBA: Hephaestus, you carry the torches at the weddings of mortals, but this was cruel of you to fan this flame. How unlike the high hopes I had!

Ah me! my child, never, never did I think your nuptials would be held amidst the spears and lances of Argives. Give me that light. In your frantic haste you do not hold the torch straight. Our disasters have not made you sober; you are still the same.

Women of Troy, take the torches; let your tears answer her wedding songs.

CASSANDRA: Mother, crown my conquering head; rejoice in the royal match I make. Escort me; if you do not find me eager, push me by force. As Loxias exists, Agamemnon, the Achaeans' noble king, will find me a more fatal bride than Helen ever was. For I shall kill him; *I* shall ruin *his* house. I shall take vengeance for my brothers and my father——

But these things can wait: I shall not sing of the ax which will fall on my neck and another's, or of the matricidal tournament which my wedding will start, or of the utter overthrow of Atreus' house.

But I will show that our city is more fortunate than the Achaeans. Possessed though I am, I shall for once emerge from my frenzy. For the sake of one woman and one woman's passion, the Greeks went chasing after Helen and perished in their thousands. Their general, their clever general, to help those he should hate most, sacrificed the dearest thing he owned; his own child, the joy of his house, he gave up for his brother; and that for a woman, who had not been carried off by force, but had left home willingly. Then after they had come to the banks of Scamander, they met their deaths, not resisting any encroachments on their border lands nor in defence of their towering cities. Those that Ares took never saw their children; no wives' hands wrapped them in their cerements; they lie in a foreign land. And back home the misery was no less: widows dying lonely, old men left childless in their halls, the sons they reared serving others, none to visit their graves and make them blood offerings. This is the praise the expedition has earned. . . . Of their crimes it is better to say nothing; may my muse never lend her voice to sing of evil things.

As for the Trojans, in the first place, what fame could be more glorious than theirs? They died for their country. When any fell in battle, their bodies were brought home by their comrades; they were dressed for the grave by the proper hands, and the soil of their native land wrapped them about. All that did not fall in battle spent their every day with their wives and children in their own homes. The Achaeans were denied those pleasures. Hector's fate brought you grief, but hear the truth of it; he is gone, but he lived long enough to win a hero's fame.

And it was the coming of the Achaeans that brought this
to pass. If they had stayed at home, his virtues would
have remained unknown. Paris, too, married the daughter
of Zeus. If he had not done so, nobody would have heard
of him or the bride in his house.

It comes to this: if a man is wise he will shun war.
But if war must come, it is a crown of honor for a city to
perish in a good cause; in an evil cause there is infamy.
Therefore, mother, you must not feel sorry for our country
or my concubinage. This wedlock of mine is the means by
which I shall destroy our worst enemies, mine and yours.

LEADER: It is fine to be able to laugh at your own miseries
and sing riddling songs. Perhaps some day you will show
your meaning.

TALTHYBIUS (*who has been listening, at first in amazement,
then with impatience*): It's as well Apollo gave you crazy
wits. Otherwise it would have cost you dear to be speeding
my commanders from the land with such maledictions.

Right enough, the grand folks in the world, the folks
everybody thinks so clever, are no better than the nobodies.
Witness Atreus' precious son, the all powerful king of
united Greece, saddled with a peculiar passion for this daft
creature. I'm a poor man, to be sure, but I would never
have taken a woman like this to *my* bed.

(*To* CASSANDRA.) Here you, since you are not quite
right in the head, I'll let your words go down the wind,
this reviling of the Argives and praising of the Phrygians.
Come with me to the ships, a fine bride for the general.

(*To* HECUBA.) And you, be ready to come when Laertes'
son wants you brought. It's a virtuous woman whose servant
you will be, judging by the reports that have come to Ilium.

CASSANDRA: What a rogue of a servant. Why do heralds
have such an honorable name, that profession which the
whole world unites in detesting, these go-betweens of kings
and states?

So you say my mother will go to the halls of Odysseus?
Where then are the declarations of Apollo, made plain to
me, which say she will die here? —The insulting de-
tails I omit. Hapless Odysseus, he does not know the
dreadful trials in store for him. The day will come when
my woes and my city's will seem to him like golden joys.
Ten weary years must roll by, in addition to the years spent
here, before he gets back to his native land, companionless.

He must see dread Charybdis, whose dwelling is in the ebb and flow of that rockbound strait, and that cannibal of the mountains the Cyclops, and Ligurian Circe who changes fine men into swine; he must endure shipwreck on the salt sea, and the temptations of the lotus, and the holy cows of the Sun, whose flesh will take voice and utter a tale of agony for Odysseus. To cut a long story short, he will descend alive to Hades, and when he finally escapes from the clutches of the sea he will come home to a multitude of sorrows in his house.

But why launch forth all the sorrows of Odysseus? (*To* TALTHYBIUS.) March; let me lose no time, let me fly to my bridegroom's bed—of death. Great general of the Greeks, miserable will be your interment, in the night, not by day. O you whose fortune seems so grand! I too, of course, must die; my body will be thrown naked down a ravine, into a torrent of winter floods, near the grave of my bridegroom; I shall be given to the wild beasts to devour, I Apollo's servant. O chaplets of the god whom I love most of any, O raiment of exaltation, farewell; I leave the feasts in which once I gloried. Go, I wrench you from my skin. While my body is still undefiled I give them to the rushing winds, to carry them to you, O Lord of Prophecy.

Where is the general's ship? Where must I embark? There is no time to lose, be on the lookout for a breeze to fill your sails, to carry me off, one of three Furies. Farewell, mother, do not weep. O dear country, O my brothers under the earth and my father that begot me, you will not have long to wait for me. But I shall descend to the dead a conquering hero, having destroyed the house of Atreus, by whom our house was destroyed.

(*Exeunt* CASSANDRA *and* TALTHYBIUS.)

(HECUBA *collapses.*)

LEADER: Nurses of old Hecuba, don't you see that your mistress has fallen, prostrate and speechless? Take hold of her. Will you leave the old woman lying? O cruel! Lift her upright.

HECUBA: Leave me, my daughters; an unwanted service is no service. Let me lie where I have fallen. I have full cause for falling, the things I have to endure and have endured and shall endure. O ye gods! It's poor helpers indeed I am now invoking; but still it's the fashion to call upon the gods when trouble overtakes us. This is my swan-song; first I will sing of my blessings and thus accentuate the pity of my woes.

I was a queen, I married into a king's house, and there I bore my excellent children, no mere figures but the best of the Phrygians, of whose like no mother can boast, Trojan or Greek or barbarian. These children I saw fall in battle with the Greeks, and I cut my hair over their tombs. And Priam their father—his loss was not reported to me by others; with my very own eyes I saw him slaughtered at his own hearth, the hearth of Zeus Protector. I saw my city taken. The virgin daughters whom I reared to bestow on bridegrooms of the highest rank, have been snatched out of my hands; another type of bridegroom had the fruits of my care. No hope have I that they will ever see me again or I them. And finally, the crown of wretched misery, I go to Greece to an old age of slavery. They will put me to all the tasks that are most intolerable to the aged. I shall be a door servant, looking after the keys, I the mother of Hector! Or I shall have to bake bread, and lay to rest on the hard ground the wrinkled back that slept in palace beds. This poor battered body of mine will be dressed in rags and tatters, an insult to my former prosperity. Unhappy woman that I am, what a present, what a future, and all because of one woman's marriage.

O my child, O Cassandra and your divine ecstasies, how horrible the circumstances that have destroyed your sacred purity! And O Polyxena, poor girl, where, where are you? Of all my many children neither son nor daughter is here to help their poor mother. Why then do you lift me up? What is there to hope for? Lead me, me that once walked delicately in Troy and am now a slave, lead me to some groveling lair, where the stones will be my pillow. Let me fling myself on the ground there and waste out my cursed life in weeping. Never hold any man happy, even the favorites of fortune, this side of death.

CHORUS: *Sing me, O Muse, of Ilium. Sing a new strain, a strain of weeping, a funeral dirge. The song I shall now utter I dedicate to Troy. It was that four-footed wagon of the Greeks that was our sad undoing, that made us prisoners of war, from that moment when the Achaeans left at our gates that horse, accoutered in gold and rattling to heaven with the armor within. The population of Troy, standing on rocks around, cried out, "Come, men, your troubles are over, lead in this idol, consecrate it to the Maiden of Ilium, daughter of Zeus." All the young women left their homes, and all the old men. With singing and rejoicing they took possession of the deadly trap.*

Every son and daughter of Phrygia rushed to the gates to do honor to the Immortal Virgin, to give to the goddess the cunning fabrication of mountain pine, wherein lurked the Argive ambush and Troy's destruction. They threw hempen ropes around it, as if it were some black ship they were launching, and brought it to the stone abode of Goddess Pallas and set it on the floor, the floor that was to cost our land its lifeblood. On this labor of joy the darkness of night descended. Then the Libyan flute shrilled forth and the ringing songs of Phrygia. The air was filled with the patter of dancing feet, with the gladsome choruses of maidens. Everywhere was the glare of torch fire; even within the houses the rooms of the sleepers glowed darkly.

I myself that night was singing in the choirs before the temple of the Virgin of the Mountains, the daughter of Zeus, when suddenly the castle and all the city rang with cries of havoc. Darling infants clung in terror to their mothers' skirts. Ares issued from his ambush; the will of Pallas was accomplished. Phrygian blood ran on every altar. In their lonely beds the young women shore off their tresses, crowns of triumph for the Grecian breed, offerings of sorrow for the land of the Phrygians.

(*A wagon enters. In it are* ANDROMACHE *and her young son* ASTYANAX, *also Trojan spoils, among them Hector's armor.*)

Hecuba, look. Here comes Andromache in an enemy wagon, bound for a foreign land. Clutched to her heaving breast is her darling Astyanax, Hector's son. Hapless woman, where are they taking you on this wagon's top, seated amid Hector's bronze armor and the spoils of sacked Ilium, with which Achilles' son will adorn the temples of Phthia, far, far from Troy?

ANDROMACHE: *Our masters, the Greeks, are haling me off.*

HECUBA: *Ah me!*

ANDROMACHE: *Why do you lament? Lamentation is mine—*

HECUBA: *Ah! Ah!*

ANDROMACHE: *—for grief is mine—*

HECUBA: *O Zeus!*

ANDROMACHE:—*and misery is mine.*

HECUBA: *My children*—

ANDROMACHE: —*now no longer.*

HECUBA: *Gone is the glory, gone is Troy*—

ANDROMACHE: *O grief!*

HECUBA: —*and gone my children, my noble children.*

ANDROMACHE: *Alas! Alas!*

HECUBA: *Alas indeed, and again alas for what was mine*——

ANDROMACHE: *Ah me!*

HECUBA: *The splendor, the fortune*—

ANDROMACHE: —*of the city*—

HECUBA: —*in smoke.*

ANDROMACHE: *O come, my husband, I beseech you*—

HECUBA: *You cry on one that lies with Hades, a son of mine, unhappy me!*

ANDROMACHE: —*come and save your wife.*

HECUBA: *And you, O you, whose foul murder dishonored Greece*—

ANDROMACHE: —*father of my Hector, Priam old and venerable*—

HECUBA: —*lull me asleep, the sleep of death.*

ANDROMACHE: *Deep are our yearnings*—

HECUBA: *Deep also (O cruel!) are the griefs we bear*—

ANDROMACHE: —*for the city that is gone*—

HECUBA: *Grief on grief accumulates.*

ANDROMACHE: —*destroyed by the illwill of the gods, from that hour when your infant son escaped death; the son who for a wicked woman destroyed the towers of Troy. Before the temple of Pallas the bloody bodies of our dead are exposed, for the vultures to harry. The end has come and the yoke of slavery for Troy.*

HECUBA: *O my country, my poor country*—

ANDROMACHE: *I weep at leaving you*—

HECUBA: —*now you see the bitter end.*

ANDROMACHE: —*and my own home, where my baby was born.*

HECUBA: *O my children, you have gone and left your mother in a deserted city—to the bitterness of dirges and lamentations and tears, fountains of tears, in our home. The dead shed no tears; they have forgotten their griefs.*

LEADER: What a sweet thing tears are to the miserable, dirges and lamentations and songs burdened with pain.

ANDROMACHE: O mother of Hector, of the hero whose spear destroyed so many Argives, do you see this sight?

HECUBA: I see the hand of the gods; some men they raise from nothingness to towering heights, others they humiliate and destroy.

ANDROMACHE: Away we are led like stolen cattle, I and my son. Nobility enslaved! O the heavy change!

HECUBA: Strange are the ways of Necessity. They have just now torn Cassandra away from me with violence.

ANDROMACHE: Alas! A second Ajax, I suppose, another ravisher, awaits your daughter. And you have other sorrows.

HECUBA: Ay, I have, beyond measure, beyond my counting. Sorrow outsorrows sorrow.

ANDROMACHE: Your child Polyxena is dead, slain at the tomb of Achilles, an offering to the lifeless dead.

HECUBA: Unhappy me! It becomes clear; this is what Talthybius meant just now with his dark riddle.

ANDROMACHE: I saw her myself. I got off this carriage and covered her with her robes and beat my breast for the dead.

HECUBA: Ah, my child! Brutally butchered! Ah and again ah! How shameful a death!

ANDROMACHE: She died as she died. —And yet in death she was luckier than I who live.

HECUBA: Death and life are not the same, my child. Death is nothingness; in life there is hope.

ANDROMACHE: Lady, mother of Polyxena, listen to my words of comfort; let me breathe gladness into your heart. The dead, I say, are as if they had not been born. It is better to die than to live in pain; the dead have no sorrows to hurt them, but when a man passes from happiness to misery his heart hankers restlessly after the joys he once knew. Polyxena is as dead as if she had never seen this life; she knows nothing of her sorrows. I aimed at fame, and the more I won the more I had to lose. In Hector's house I toiled to master all the accomplishments of a virtuous wife. In the first place I kept to the house and had no longing for those places where her mere presence is enough to earn a woman who does not stay at home an evil name, whether she is that sort of woman or not. I did not admit inside my doors the smart talk of women. I had my native wit to teach me virtue; I needed no more. My tongue was still and my countenance serene in my husband's presence. I knew when to insist with my husband and when to allow him to overrule me.

This was the reputation that reached the Achaean host and ruined me. For when I was captured, the son of Achilles wanted to make me his wife. I shall slave in the house of my husband's murderers. And if I forget dear Hector and open my heart to my present lord, I shall seem a traitor to the dead. On the other hand if I cherish Hector's love, I shall get myself hated by my lord and master. However, they say that a single night abates a woman's aversion for a man's bed. But I abominate the woman who marries again and forgets her first husband in the arms of the second. Why, even the draft-horse, separated from his old partner in the yoke, will pull reluctantly. And yet brutes have neither speech nor use of reason and are lower than man.

In you, dear Hector, I had all the husband I wanted: wise, noble, wealthy, brave, a great man. You got me virgin from my father's house; you were the first to enter my innocent bed. And now you are dead, and I am being shipped captive to the yoke of slavery in Greece. (*To* HECUBA.) Do you not think that the death of Polyxena, whom you weep for, is a lesser evil for her than my evils? Even hope, that remains to all the living, stays not with me; I nurse no delusion that things will ever be all right for me—it would be pleasant if I could even think so.

LEADER: Your misery is mine. As you bewail *your* lot, you teach me the depth of my own sorrows.

HECUBA: Never in my life have I set foot on a ship myself, but the pictures I have seen and the stories I have heard have taught me. If sailors have to face a storm that is not too great, they rally eagerly to the task of saving themselves from peril; one man takes the helm, another looks to the sails, another keeps out the sea water. But if the waves are too high, the storm too fierce, they give in to fate and submit to the mercy of the running seas. So I who have sorrows aplenty am dumb; I submit, I have no use for words. The waves of misery, heaven-sent, overpower me.

My dear child, think no more of Hector's fate. Your tears will not save him. Respect your present master; ply your husband with the allurements of your ways. If you do that, you will have a happiness in which all your friends will share, and you will bring up this grandson of mine to be a mighty aid to Troy; some day descendants of his may return and settle here, and Troy be again a city.

But what is this? One thing after another. Here I see the servant of the Achaeans, with word of new decisions. What brings him back?

(*Enter* TALTHYBIUS *and armed* ESCORT.)

TALTHYBIUS: Wife of Hector who was the bravest of the Phrygians in days gone by, do not hate me. It is not of my choice that I bring you word of the common purpose of the Danaans and the sons of Pelops——

ANDROMACHE: What is it? I feel you are beginning a song of sorrows.

TALTHYBIUS: They have decided that the boy here ... How can I speak the word?

ANDROMACHE: What? Is he not to have the same master as I?

TALTHYBIUS: None of the Achaeans will ever be this boy's master.

ANDROMACHE: Are they leaving him here, sole survivor of the Phrygians?

TALTHYBIUS: I don't know how to break the sorrowful news gently.

ANDROMACHE: I thank you for your consideration. But I will not thank you for a tale of sorrows.

TALTHYBIUS: They are going to kill your child. Now you know the extent of your sorrow.

ANDROMACHE: Ah me! This word you bring me is a greater sorrow than my new marriage.

TALTHYBIUS: Odysseus prevailed in the general council with his advice——

ANDROMACHE: Alas and alas! My sorrows are too much.

TALTHYBIUS: He advised them not to allow the son of a heroic father to grow up——

ANDROMACHE: May his advice be applied to his own children.

TALTHYBIUS: But to hurl him from the battlements of Troy.

Come now, let things take their course, and you will show wisdom. Don't hold on to the boy. Bear the agony of sorrow gallantly. You are powerless; don't think you are strong. There is no help for you anywhere. Just look around. Your city is destroyed, your husband dead, yourself overpowered. We are quite able to contend with a solitary woman. Therefore, do not invite a struggle; don't do anything that will humiliate you and just make things more objectionable. And another thing: I don't want you to utter imprecations against the Achaeans. If you say anything to provoke the army, this boy may get no burial, no service of tears. Say nothing; make the best of the situation, and you will not leave this boy's body unburied, and you yourself may find the Achaeans kindlier to you.

ANDROMACHE: My dearest child, my special care, you will leave your hapless mother, you will be slain by our enemies. Your father's gallantry, that brought salvation to others, has brought death to you. Your father's virtues flowered unseasonably for you.

Ah my luckless bridals, the luckless wedding that brought me long ago to Hector's hall, not to bear a son to be slaughtered by Greeks, but one to rule over the broad acres of Asia. My child, are you crying? Do you realize your evil fate? Why do your hands clutch me, why do you hang on to my skirts, like a little bird cowering under my wings? Hector cannot come to you, snatching up his famous spear; he cannot leave his grave to succor you. Your father's kinsmen cannot help you, nor the strength of Phrygia. A dolorous leap you must make; mercilessly hurled head first from the heights, your broken body will give up the ghost. O young thing, your mother's lovely armful! How sweet the fragrance of your body! So it was in vain that this breast suckled you, as you lay in your baby clothes. In vain I labored, in vain I wore myself out with toil. Greet your mother, now, it is your last chance. Embrace her that gave you birth. Wrap your arms around me, right around me. Press your lips to mine.

O you Greeks, un-Greek are the tortures you devise. Why are you killing this innocent child? O scion of Tyndareus, Zeus was never your father. I declare you are the daughter of many fathers, first the Spirit of Evil, then Hate, and Murder, and Death, and every monster that earth rears. Never shall I affirm that Zeus begot you, to be the death of Greeks and barbarians innumerable. Be damned! The loveliness of your eyes has brought hideous ruin on the famous fields of Phrygia. (*She hands* ASTYANAX *to* TALTHYBIUS.) There! take him, take him away, hurl him to his death, if that is your will. Feast on his flesh.

It is the gods who are destroying us and I shall never be able to save my child from death. Cover my poor body, hurry me to the ships. I go to a fine wedding, having lost my child.

LEADER: Hapless Troy, you have lost thousands of your sons, thanks to one woman and her hateful bed.

TALTHYBIUS: Come, child. Leave your poor mother's loving embraces. Come to the highest parapet of your ancestral towers. There you must relinquish life, as the decree demands. Seize him. You want another sort of herald for jobs like this, one who is merciless, one whose heart has more taste for brutality than mine has.

(*Exit* TALTHYBIUS *with party.*)

HECUBA: O my child, son of my poor son, we are robbed of you, unjustly robbed, your mother and I. What has come over me? What can I do for you, luckless one? Here is my offering to you; I smite my head, I rend my breasts. This is all I am mistress of. I grieve for my city, I grieve for you. What sorrow is not ours? What more is wanting to complete our utter ruin? (*She collapses.*)

CHORUS: *O Telamon, king of Salamis, haunt of the bees, you established your abode on the sea-girt isle that nestles under the sacred hills where Athena revealed the first green shoots of olive, shining Athens' heavenly crown of glory. Then you went away, away to the field of valor, with Alcmena's archer son, to sack Ilium, our city of Ilium —yes, ours even in that far-off time when you came from Greece.*

In his fury at the loss of the mares, he brought with him the flower of Greece's chivalry. Over the sea came his ships and in the lovely estuary of Simois he hove to and made fast his cables to the sterns. Then he took from his ship his sure arrows, that meant death for Laomedon. The walls that the chisel of Phoebus had made square and plumb he destroyed with the red breath of fire and he pillaged the land of Troy. Thus twice has the blow fallen; twice has the bloody spear overthrown the defenses round Dardania.

Then it is of no avail, it seems, O son of Laomedon, that you walk delicately with goblets of gold and have the filling of Zeus's cups, a most honorable service. And the land that gave you birth is devastated by fire. On the shore by the sea there is wailing, like the scream of a bird

*over her brood; wailing for husbands, for children, for
aged mothers. Gone are the baths that refreshed you, gone
are the gymnasiums and the race tracks. Yet you, beside
the throne of Zeus, compose your lovely young face in un-
troubled serenity, while the Greek spear destroys the land
of Priam.*

*Love, Love, you came of old to the halls of Dardanus,
troubling the hearts of the Heavenly Ones. How greatly
you exalted Troy in those days when she made connections
in heaven. Of Zeus and his shame I shall say no more.
But this very day Dawn with her white wings, the light
that mortals love, saw the havoc of our land, saw the destruction of our towers. Yet in this land she got the husband of her bridal bower, the father of her children,
Tithonus, carried off to Heaven on a golden car drawn by
four stars. High ran the hopes in his native land. But
Troy has lost the charm that held the gods.*

(*Enter* MENELAUS, *with* SOLDIERS.)

MENELAUS: How beautiful is the brilliance of the sun today, this day in which I shall get possession of my wife
Helen. I am Menelaus and I have labored much for her, I
and the Achaean army. I came to Troy not so much to get
my wife (that's what men are thinking) but rather to meet
the man who deceived his host and carried off my wife
from my house. That man, thanks to heaven, has paid the
penalty; the Greek spear has destroyed him and his country. Now I am come to take away the Woman of Sparta—
I hate to say the name of my wife, my wife that was.
She is within these prisoners' tents, reckoned amongst the
other Trojan women. They that fought this weary war to
get her have given her to me to kill—or, if I do not choose
to kill her, to have her taken back to the land of Argos.
For my part I have decided to postpone her fate while I
am in Troy and to take her back on my ship to the land
of Greece and *then* hand her over to the vengeance of
those whose friends have died at Ilium; they will kill her.

Well then, my men, enter the tents and fetch her here.
Drag her by her cursed hair. Whenever favorable breezes
come, we shall escort her to Greece.

HECUBA (*rising*): O you who are the support of the earth
and are by earth supported, whatever you are, you who
defy the guess of our knowledge, O Zeus, whether you are
the Law of Necessity in nature, or the Law of Reason in

man, hear my prayers. You are everywhere, pursuing your
noiseless path, ordering the affairs of mortals according
to justice.

MENELAUS: What's this? You are starting a new fashion in
prayer.

HECUBA: I commend you, Menelaus, for your intention to
kill your wife. But flee the sight of her, lest she captivate
you with longing. She captivates the eyes of men, she destroys cities, she sets homes aflame. Such are her witcheries.
I know her; so do you and all her victims.

(*Enter* HELEN, *beautifully dressed, and her* GUARDS.)

HELEN: Menelaus, this is a prelude well calculated to terrify
me; your servants lay rude hands on me and hustle me
out of these tents. I can well imagine, of course, that
you may hate me, but still I want to ask: what is the
mind of the Greeks and you concerning my life?

MENELAUS: Your case was not specifically discussed, but
the whole host has given you to me, whom you wronged, to
be put to death.

HELEN: Have I permission to reply, to prove that my death,
if I am killed, will be unjust?

MENELAUS: I did not come here to argue; I came to kill
you.

HECUBA: Give her a hearing, Menelaus; you don't want to
kill her without a hearing. But allow me to handle the
prosecution's case against her. You do not know the evils
she did in Troy; the indictment, compact and comprehen-
sive, will justify her death and leave her no loophole of
escape.

MENELAUS: I must have little to do to grant this favor. But
if she wants to speak, she may. But I hope she realizes
that I am making this concession on *your* urging, not as a
favor to her.

HELEN (*to* MENELAUS): Since you regard me as your enemy,
I don't suppose you will try to meet my points, however
sound or unsound you may think them. But I think I know
what charges you would make against me if it came to a
debate, and I shall arrange my answers correspondingly,
your charges against mine, mine against yours.

In the first place, it was this woman here who gave birth
to the whole bad business when she gave birth to Paris.
Secondly, it was old Priam who ruined both Troy and me,
when he did not kill the infant, the dream of the firebrand

come true, too true, the future Alexander. That was the
start of it; hear now the sequel. This Alexander was made
the judge of the three goddesses. The offer of Pallas was
the leadership of a Phrygian army that would overthrow
Greece. Hera promised him empire over Asia and the
furthest limits of Europe, if he would decide in her favor.
Cypris told of my marvelous beauty and promised it to
him, if she surpassed the other goddesses in beauty. Consider what follows logically from that. Cypris prevails,
and see what a boon my nuptials conferred on Greece:
she was not conquered by the barbarians, you had neither
to meet them in battle nor submit to their empire.
Greece's good fortune was my ruin. I was bought and sold
for my beauty. And now I am reproached for what ought
to have earned me a crown of honor for my head. You
will say that I have not yet come to the point at issue,
the explanation of my secret flight from your house. The
evil genius that was this woman's son, whether you wish
to call him Alexander or Paris, brought an ally along with
him, a most powerful goddess. Yet you, my unworthy husband, left him in your halls and sailed off to Crete on a
Spartan ship. So be it. The next question I shall put to
myself, not to you. Was I in my right mind when I ran
away from home with a stranger and left my country and
my house? Chastise the goddess, be stronger than Zeus who
bears rule over the other divinities but is the slave of
Love. I am not to blame.

There is another point which might afford you a specious
argument against me. When Alexander was dead and gone
below the earth, that ended divine interference in my love
affairs; I ought then to have left my home and returned to
the ships of the Argives. That is the very thing I sought
to do. My witnesses are the guards of the towers, the sentinels on the walls, who time and again discovered me
stealthily letting myself down by ropes from the battlements. Moreover it was by force that that new husband of
mine, Deiphobus, took me and kept me as his wife, in
defiance of the Trojans. What justification then would you
have, my husband, if you put me to an undeserved death?
On the one hand I was married against my will. On the
other hand my services to my own people have earned
me bitter servitude, instead of a victor's prize. So be

stronger than the gods if you want to, but it's a silly thing to want.

LEADER: O Queen, defend your children and your country. Destroy the cogency of her pleadings. Eloquence allied to wickedness, it is a fearful combination.

HECUBA: First of all I shall come to the defense of the goddesses and show that her charges against them are unjust. For my part I do not believe that Hera and virgin Pallas were ever so silly that the one was ready to barter away Argos to the barbarian, and the other to make her Athens the slave of Phrygia, and all for a childish whim that took them to Ida to quarrel about their beauty. For why should goddess Hera have conceived such a passion for beauty? Did she hope to get a better husband than Zeus? Was Athena laying her lines for a match with one of the gods, Athena who shuns wedlock and begged the Father to let her remain virgin? Don't make the gods silly to cover up your own wickedness. You'll find you cannot convince the wise. And Cypris—this is very funny—you say she came with my son to the home of Menelaus. Could she not have stayed quietly in heaven and brought you, Amyclae and all, to Ilium?

My son was of surpassing beauty; at the sight of him your heart transformed itself into Cypris. Every lewd impulse in man passes for Aphrodite. Rightly does her name begin like the word Aphrosyne—lewdness. So when you saw my son in the splendor of gold and barbaric raiment, mad desire took possession of your heart. In Argos you were used to a small retinue; having got rid of the Spartan city, you looked forward to a deluge of extravagance in Phrygia with its rivers of gold. The halls of Menelaus weren't large enough for your luxury to wanton in.

And so to your next point. You say you were *forced* to go with my son. Did anybody in Sparta hear anything? What sort of outcry did you make? Yet Castor was there, a strong young man, and his brother, not yet translated to the stars. Then when you had come to Troy with the Argives at your heels and the deadly jousting of spears had started, whenever a success of Menelaus was announced to you, you would praise him, just to torment my son with the reminder that he had a formidable rival in the lists of love. But if ever the Trojans were successful, Menelaus here was nobody. You kept an eye on Fortune and made it your practice to stick to her side. You had no taste for Virtue's side. Furthermore, you speak of trying to escape by stealth, of letting ropes down from the towers, as if you were there against your will. When, tell me, were you ever caught fixing a noose for your neck or whetting a sword? Yet that's what a noble woman would do who yearned for her former husband. In any case, I was constantly at you, remonstrating with you. "Go away, my daughter. My sons will find other brides, and I will have you conveyed out secretly to the Achaean ships. Stop this fighting between the Greeks and us." But you didn't like that. Why? Because you gloried and reveled in the palace of Alexander, because it gave you pleasure to receive the adoration of barbarians. That, to you, was greatness. And after all this you titivate yourself and come out here and brave the light of day beside your husband. O you abomination! You should have come crawling out in rags and tatters, in fear and trembling, your hair cropped to the scalp; modesty would become your guilty past better than impudence.

Menelaus, here is the culmination of my argument: crown Greece with honor, and do yourself justice, by killing this woman. And make this law for all other women: the woman who betrays her husband dies.

LEADER: Menelaus, be worthy of your ancestors and your house. Punish your wife. You have proved your quality to the Trojans; save yourself from the tongues of Greece, from the reproach of uxoriousness.

MENELAUS: You have come to the same conclusion as I, that she willingly left my home for a foreign bed; Cypris has been injected into her argument to make it sound well. (To HELEN). March, to the stoning party; die, and in an instant atone for the Achaeans' years of labor. You will learn not to dishonor me.

HELEN: Do not kill me, by your knees I ask you, do not blame me for the trouble that came from heaven. Forgive me.

HECUBA: There are also your allies whom she slew; do not betray them. On behalf of them and their children I entreat you.

MENELAUS: Say no more, old woman; I do not give her a thought. I command my servants to lead her away to the ships on which she is to sail.

HECUBA: Do not let her on board the same ship with you.

MENELAUS: What do you mean? Is she heavier than she was?

HECUBA: No lover ever loses all his liking.

MENELAUS: That depends on what comes of the disposition of the loved one. But your wish will be granted. She will not embark on the same ship as I. And when she comes to Argos she will get her deserts, a vile death for a vile woman, and she will teach all women to be chaste. No easy task, to be sure, but her death will put a godly fear in their lewd hearts, even if they are more detestable than she is.

(*Exit* MENELAUS *with* HELEN.)

(HECUBA *lies down.*)

CHORUS: *So you have betrayed us to the Achaeans, O Zeus, you have deserted the temple in Ilium with its altars and incense, the burning wafers and the air filled with the fumes of burnt myrrh; you have forsaken holy Pergamum and the ivy-clad glens of Ida, where the torrents run swollen with snow, Ida where the sky ends, the holy ground that catches the radiance of the first shafts of the sun.*

Gone are the sacrifices and the cheerful songs of the dancers; gone are the festivals of the gods in the darkness of night, gone are the graven images of gold. The moons of Phrygia look down no more on the Feasts of the Twelve Cakes. I wonder, O Lord, I wonder if you take thought of these things, mounted on your ethereal throne in heaven, while my city perishes, destroyed by the blazing rush of fire.

O my beloved, O husband mine, in the world of the dead you wander, unburied, unpurified, while I must cross the seas on the wings of a swift ship to Argos, land of horses, where men inhabit the soaring walls of stone that the Cyclopes built. At the gates a multitude of children cling to their mothers' skirts, weeping and wailing. A young girl cries: "Mother, ah me! The Achaeans are taking me away from you, away to the dark ship; over the sea the oars will carry me, either to sacred Salamis or to the peak at the Isthmus looking down on the two seas, the gates to the stronghold of Pelops."

When the ship of Menelaus is halfway over the sea, may a blazing Aegean thunderbolt, hurled by Jove's holy hands, come crashing down into the midst of his fleet; for he is

carrying me away from Ilium's land to exile and tearful
servitude in Greece, while the daughter of Zeus takes up
in her hands her golden mirrors that maidens love. May he
never reach the Laconian land and the hearth and home
of his fathers; may he never see the city of Pitana or the
temple of the Bronze Gates; for he has taken his evil wife
who brought shame on great Hellas and sorrow and suffer-
ing to the streams of Simois.

(TALTHYBIUS *and his men arrive with the body of*
ASTYANAX.)

Oh! Oh! Here are fresh sorrows, succeeding sorrows still
fresh, for our land. Hapless wives of the Trojans, you see
here the body of Astyanax, whom the Danaans have slain,
hurling him (O cruel throw!) from the battlements.

TALTHYBIUS: Hecuba, one ship is left; its oars are about to
take the rest of the booty of Neoptolemus to the shores of
Phthia. He has already put to sea on hearing of fresh disasters that have befallen Peleus. They say that Acastus, son
of Pelias, has driven him out of his land. This moved
Neoptolemus more than any pleasure in staying here. So he
is gone, and Andromache with him. When she left she
brought tears aplenty to my eyes, as she wept for her native land and bade farewell to Hector's tomb. She asked
Neoptolemus to grant burial to this body, your Hector's
child, who lost his life when he was thrown from the walls.
She begged him also not to take with him to Phthia this
brazen shield, the terror of the Achaeans, with which the
boy's father used to cover his sides, not to install it (a sorry
sight to see) in the same chamber in which she herself,
this dead child's mother, would receive her new bridegroom; but to let it serve as a cedar or stone coffin for her
son's burial. The body was to be put into your arms, to be
wrapped in its cerements and crowned with flowers, and
everything done for it that your strength and your circumstances would allow. For she has gone and her master's
urgency has prevented her from burying her own boy. So
whenever you have dressed the corpse, we will cover it
with earth and set sail.

You must lose no time in fulfilling your appointed task.
There is one labor I have spared you. When I came across
the streams of Scamander here I took the body and washed
out the wounds. Well, I'll be off to break up the ground for
his grave. You and I, sharing the work together, will save

time and get our ship launched for home all the sooner.
HECUBA: Lay Hector's shield on the ground. Its trim lines
are a sorry sight, and a dear one, for my eyes.

O you Achaeans, with whom prowess in war bulks larger
than wisdom, why did you fear this child and add slaughter
to slaughter? Were you afraid he might some day raise
fallen Troy? Then you are cowards after all. Our city is
taken, Phrygia is destroyed, yet you were afraid of a child,
a little child, though even Hector's victories and thousands
of brave men besides could not prevent our doom. I do not
admire a fear that has no basis of reason.

O dearest child, what a sorry death has overtaken you!
If you had died in your city's defense, if you had enjoyed
youth and wedlock and the royal power that makes men
gods, then you would have been happy, if there is any happiness in these. As it was, my child, your life did know
these joys, but knew them only by sight; you got no use of
the kingship which was your heritage. Poor boy, what a
tragic death! Your own ancestral walls, the battlements of
Loxias, have shorn off the curls on which your mother lav-
ished her care and her kisses. From the crushed skull (forgive me!) Death grins forth. O arms so sweet, to me so
like your father's, you hang now loose and lifeless from the
sockets. O dear mouth, you are gone, with all your pretty
prattle. It was not true, what you used to say to me, climb-
ing on to my bed: "Mother, I'll cut off from my hair a
great big curl for you and I'll bring crowds of my friends
to your grave and give you fond farewells." But it was the
other way round; it is I, the old crone, landless, childless,
who bury your poor young corpse. Ah me! All my kisses,
all my care, all our nights asleep together, all have been
wasted. What will be the verse inscribed on your tomb?
"Within this grave a little child is laid, slain by the Greeks
because they were afraid." An inscription to make Greece
blush. At any rate though you have lost your patrimony
you will still have your father's bronze shield to be buried
in.

O shield that kept safe my Hector's strong arms, you
have lost the hero that kept you safe. How sweet it is to
see in your loop the mark of Hector's arm, and on the
skillful fashioning of the rim the sweat which dripped from
Hector's face as, chin on shield, he bore the brunt of many
a fight. Come, let such stores as we have afford a decent

burial to this poor corpse. As god has shaped our circumstances, we cannot aim at splendor. But all I have is yours to take.

The mortal is mad who rests his happiness on the expectation of lasting welfare. Fortune is a whirling dervish that twists and turns and leaps now this way, now that. Success is not of a man's own making.

LEADER: Look, here are your women bringing in their arms from the spoils of Troy, adornments to wrap the corpse in.

HECUBA: O my child, not for a triumph won over your fellows with chariot or bow in the honored exercises of Phrygia does your father's mother bring you these poor adornments; better she cannot hope for, from the wealth that was once yours. Now accursed Helen has robbed you of it, robbed you and destroyed your life, and ruined utterly your whole house.

CHORUS: *Ah! you move me. Ah! you touch my heart. O the mighty one I have lost, the prince of my land no more!*

HECUBA: The robes, the pride of Phrygia, which you were to wear on your wedding day, when you would wed the proudest princess in Asia, I now put on your body. And you, dear shield of Hector, mother of triumphs innumerable, for the glory of victories past receive this garland. Immortal shield, you will die with the dead. Yet you are much more to be honored than the armor of Odysseus, wise only in wickedness.

FIRST PART OF CHORUS: *Alas! What a bitter sorrow—*

SECOND PART OF CHORUS: *O child, the earth will receive you.*

FIRST PART: *—for you to bewail, mother.*

HECUBA: *Alas!*

SECOND PART: *'Tis the Song of the Dead.*

HECUBA: *My grief!*

FIRST PART: *Ah grief indeed! Ghastly are your afflictions.*

HECUBA: With bandages I shall play the doctor to your wounds, a sorry doctor, doctor in name with no skill to heal. For the rest, your father will take care of you, amongst the dead.

CHORUS: *Strike, strike your head. Sound the measured beat of hands. Ah me! Ah me!*

HECUBA (*gazing fixedly at the sky*): Oh dearest women—— (*She breaks off, rapt, intense.*)

CHORUS (*alarmed*): *Hecuba, we are with you, tell us, what means that cry?*

HECUBA (*as if coming out of a trance*): In Heaven—there is nothing there for us—only my miseries—only hate for Troy, most hated of cities. We have been slaughtering our hecatombs for nothing. If only god had taken us—sunk beneath the earth—disappeared—unknown to fame. . . .

Go then, bury the body in its wretched grave. It has received such tendance as Hell requires. I imagine it makes little difference to the dead to honor them with rich ritual. It is the living who attach importance to such vanities.

(*Cortege departs.*)

CHORUS: *Oh! Oh! Your unhappy mother! Your death has torn to shreds and tatters her high hopes for the future. Greatly envied you were for your noble birth, but horrible was the death by which you perished.*

Ah! Ah! What do I see yonder on the heights of Ilium, arms waving wildly in the blaze of firebrands? Some fresh sorrow threatens to fall on Troy.

(*Enter* TALTHYBIUS *and* SOLDIERS.)

TALTHYBIUS: You captains who have been assigned to set fire to this city of Priam, I give you the word. No longer keep the torches idle in your hands; apply the fire. Let us demolish the city of Ilium and then sail away happy to our homes.

As for you, daughters of Troy, I have two commands in one. The rest of you, march to the ships of the Achaeans whenever the commanders of the army sound the shrill note of the echoing trumpet, and you, old Hecuba, unhappiest of women, go with these men whom Odysseus has sent to fetch you. The lot made you his slave; he will take you away from Troy.

HECUBA: Ah wretched me! It has come at last, the culmination and crown of all my sorrows. I leave my country; the torch is put to my city. Old legs, press on, try hard; let me bid farewell to my hapless city. O Troy, that once held your head so high amongst barbarians, soon you will be robbed of your name and fame. They are burning you and leading us out of the land to slavery. O ye gods! Yet why should I call upon the gods? In the past they did not hear when they were called. Come, let us rush to the pyre; our greatest glory will be to perish in the flames in which our country perishes.

TALTHYBIUS: Poor thing, your sorrows are driving you frantic. (*To the* SOLDIERS.) Come there, lead her away. Don't stand on ceremony. We must take Odysseus his prize and put her into his hands.

HECUBA: *Alas! Alas! Alas! Son of Cronus, Lord of Phrygia, Father of our folk, do you see how they treat us, how they outrage the seed of Dardanus?*

CHORUS: *He sees, but the city, the great city, is a city no longer, it is fallen. Troy is dead.*

HECUBA: *Alas! Alas! Alas! Ilium is ablaze; the fire consumes the citadel, the roofs of the city, the tops of the walls!*

CHORUS: *Like smoke blown to heaven on the wings of the wind, our country, our conquered country, perishes. Its palaces are overrun by the fierce flames and the murderous spear.*

HECUBA: *O land that reared my children!*

CHORUS: *Ah! Ah!*

HECUBA: *Hear me, my children, listen to the voice of your mother.*

CHORUS: *You call on the dead with lamentation.*

HECUBA: *Yes, I call on them, as I lay my old limbs on the ground and knock on the earth with my two hands.*

CHORUS: *We too in turn kneel on the earth and call on our husbands in the world of the dead.*

HECUBA: *We are driven off, we are haled away—*

CHORUS: *Grievous, grievous is your cry.*

HECUBA: *—to the halls where we must slave.*

CHORUS: *Ay, far from our fatherland.*

HECUBA: *Oh! Priam, Priam, dead, unburied, unbefriended, yet you are unconscious of my doom.*

CHORUS: *Yes, for darkness has enveloped his eyes, the darkness of blessed death, though cursed be his murderers.*

HECUBA: *O temples of the gods, O city of my love—*

CHORUS: *Ah! Ah!*

HECUBA: *—the deadly flames got you, and the spear of battle.*

CHORUS: *Soon you will fall, our dear land will cover you, and your name will be no more.*

HECUBA: *And the dust, like smoke, with wing outspread to heaven, will rob me of the sight of my home.*

CHORUS: *The name of the land will pass into oblivion. One thing after another, everything disappears. Hapless Troy is finished.*

(*The citadel collapses.*)

HECUBA: *Did you notice, did you hear?*

CHORUS: *The crash of the falling citadel.*

HECUBA: *Ruin, everywhere ruin——*

CHORUS: *It will engulf the city.*

(*Trumpets sound.*)

HECUBA: *Ah! My trembling limbs, lead me on my path.
On with you, poor limbs, to lifelong slavery.*

CHORUS: *Ah hapless city! But still—forward, feet, to the
waiting ships of the Achaeans.* (*Exeunt.*)

4

ARISTOPHANES

Frogs

IF THERE ARE no more good poets on earth the sensible solution, according to the fantastic logic of Aristophanic comedy, is to fetch a dead one out of Hell. *Frogs* depicts the amusing adventures of Dionysus, the patron deity of the theater, and his slave Xanthias on their way to Pluto's court in Hades, the elaborate trial there to determine whether Euripides or Aeschylus deserved the master's chair in tragic poetry, and the final decision to bring Aeschylus back to earth. The comparative criticism of the diction, syntax, imagery, meters, themes, and doctrines of the two poets is of a high level of professional expertness. As might be expected, Euripides is condemned for bringing tragedy down from the high level of Aeschylus by his prosy simplicity and his vulgarity, yet even so there are sharp hits at Aeschylus' turgidity and obscurity; incidentally, Aristophanes pays Euripides the compliment of imitating him. Not only is a huge audience in a mood of merrymaking expected to recognize allusions to numerous particular plays, but it is expected to be amused by technical literary criticism; there can be no better testimony to the high intellectual level of the Athenian citizenry. It is an index too to the high civic responsibility expected of poets that the final decision is reached not on the basis of literary merit alone but on a question of political import: What should be done about Alcibiades?

CHARACTERS

XANTHIAS, *servant of Dionysus*
DIONYSUS
HERACLES
A CORPSE
CHARON
AEACUS
A HOUSEMAID, *of Persephone*
LANDLADY, *keeper of cookshop*
PLATHANE, *her partner*
EURIPIDES
AESCHYLUS
PLUTO
CHORUS, *of Frogs*
CHORUS, *of Blessed Mystics*

SCENE: On the way to and at
Pluto's court in Hades

Translated by R. H. WEBB

(DIONYSUS *with the lionskin of* HERACLES *over his saffron robe, and his slave* XANTHIAS *on a donkey, carrying the luggage on a pole, appear as travelers. The house of* HERACLES *is in the background.*)

XANTHIAS: Boss, would you mind it if I started off
With a good old gag that always gets a laugh?

DIONYSUS: Any you like—except *I got the pip!*
My stomach just can't take it any more.

XANTHIAS: Some other pearl?

DIONYSUS: Except *I'm fit to pop!*

XANTHIAS: What about one that really is a *scream?*

DIONYSUS: Go right ahead—but don't you dare . . .

XANTHIAS: Dare what?

DIONYSUS: To shift your load and say that you are *pooped!*

XANTHIAS: Or, that if nobody will relieve the strain,
I'm going to "relieve *myself*"?

DIONYSUS: No, please—
Unless you see that I am sick already!

XANTHIAS: Why do I have to pack this stuff around
And not have fun like all the other boys—
Phrynichus, Lycis, and Ameipsias?

DIONYSUS: Because you can't! . . . I never miss a play;
And every time I hear that sort of wit
I go home twelve months older than I was!

XANTHIAS: Pity a poor old neck that's *fit to pop,*
And isn't allowed to crack a single joke!

DIONYSUS: Dear me, what airs! What pampered insolence—
When Dionysus, Earl of Brandywine,
Struggles along on foot, and gives his slave
An ass to bear his burden and himself.

XANTHIAS: Do *I* not bear it?

DIONYSUS: How, when you are *borne*?

XANTHIAS: By carrying *this*.

DIONYSUS: But how . . . ?

XANTHIAS: With pain, *that's* how!

DIONYSUS: Doesn't the donkey bear the weight *you* bear?

XANTHIAS: This load I'm toting on my back? No *sir!*

DIONYSUS: How *can* you tote it when *he's* toting *you*?

XANTHIAS: All I know is, my shoulder's *got the pip!*

DIONYSUS: Well, since the donkey isn't helping you,
Suppose you take *your* turn and carry *him*?

XANTHIAS: I wish to God I'd signed up with the fleet.
Then I could say to *you,* Oh go to hell!

DIONYSUS: Get down, you rascal. Here is where we stop—
First stop upon the way to journey's end.
My legs have made it!—Hi there! Open up!

HERACLES: Who's hammering my door? Might be a centaur,
Throwing his weight around! —Say, what on earth . . . ?

DIONYSUS (*aside to* XANTHIAS): Psst!

XANTHIAS: Well?

DIONYSUS: Didn't you notice?

XANTHIAS: Notice what?

DIONYSUS: How scared he was of me.

XANTHIAS: Scared you were *crazy!*

HERACLES: Honest to God, I can't control myself—
Biting my lips in two, but all the same . . .

DIONYSUS: Hey, listen, can't you? I've a request to make.

HERACLES: Ha ha! Shiver me timbers, what a sight—
A lionskin on top of yellow silk!
What's the idea? Club and buskins *both*? . . .
Where go you?

DIONYSUS: Shipping aboard the *Cleisthenes* ...

HERACLES: Get in the fight?

DIONYSUS: *And,* incidentally,
We sank some twelve or thirteen Spartan ships ...

HERACLES: The *two* of you?

DIONYSUS: Quite so.

XANTHIAS (*aside*): Then *I* woke *up!*

DIONYSUS: And, bless you, sitting on the deck one day,
Reading once more that dear *Andromeda,*
My heart was smitten by desire so strong ...

HERACLES: *How* strong?

DIONYSUS: A "Tiny" Molon of desire!

HERACLES: For whom? A woman?

DIONYSUS: No!

HERACLES: A boy?

DIONYSUS: No, no!

HERACLES: A man?

DIONYSUS: Oh gee!

HERACLES: Have you and Cleisthenes ...?

DIONYSUS: Don't tease me, brother. Truly, I am ill.
This love is making havoc of my life!

HERACLES: Tell me about it, son.

DIONYSUS: Impossible!
I can't describe it ... only illustrate.
You've felt a sudden passion for pea soup?

HERACLES: Thousands of times!

DIONYSUS: Do I reveal my thought, then?
Or shall I tell thee in another way?

HERACLES: About pea soup? No, *that* I understand!

DIONYSUS: Such is the longing that devours my soul
For sweet ... Euripides.

HERACLES: A *dead* man?

DIONYSUS: Yes!
And no one can dissuade me on this earth
From going for him!

HERACLES: Down to *Hades?*

DIONYSUS: Yes,
And lower still, if such a place there be.

HERACLES: But why?

DIONYSUS: I want a poet who can *write!*
Some are no more, and they that live are base.

HERACLES: Iophon's living, isn't he?

DIONYSUS: That's true—

The only blessing that remains to us . . .
If it's a blessing. I am not quite sure.
HERACLES: Why resurrect, if resurrect you must,
Euripides, instead of Sophocles?
DIONYSUS: Because I want to test young Iophon,
And see what he can do all by himself.
Besides, Euripides, the clever rogue,
Would aid my kidnap scheme; while Sophocles,
Gentleman always, is a gentleman still.
HERACLES: And what of Agathon?
DIONYSUS: Too bad, he's gone.
Good poet, sadly missed.
HERACLES: Poor chap! Gone where?
DIONYSUS: To the Elysian Feasts of Macedon.
HERACLES: How about Xenocles?
DIONYSUS: Bad cess to *him!*
HERACLES: Pythangelus?
XANTHIAS: Nobody thinks of *me*—
My shoulder rubbed until it's raw!
HERACLES: But surely myriads of little men
Still scribble for the Tragic Boards up there,
Out prattling your Euripides a mile.
DIONYSUS: Mere nubbins, with a silly gift of gab;
Shrill swallow choirs, murderers of Art!
One single play produced, and they are spent—
Small piss-ants, fouling the bed of Tragedy!
What potent poet can you find today,
To father one full-bodied, ringing phrase?
HERACLES: Potent? You mean . . . ?
DIONYSUS: A poet who will risk
A bold, a reckless utterance, such as
Aether, the Inglenook of Zeus; Time's tread;
The mind refused its solemn oath to plight,
The tongue was perjured, in the mind's despite!
HERACLES: You like that stuff?
DIONYSUS: I'm mad about it!
HERACLES: Pshaw!
Cheap hocus-pocus, and you know it is!
DIONYSUS: *My mind, sir, is my castle.* Mind your own!
HERACLES: Well anyway, it's pure humbuggery.
DIONYSUS: I'll *listen,* when you lecture me on *food!*
XANTHIAS: Nobody thinks of *me!*
DIONYSUS: Now look, here's why

I came here in this toggery of yours—
To learn what hospitality you found,
That time you went down after Cerberus:
Who put you up, the highways, harbors, springs,
Bakeries, bawdyhouses, restrooms, towns,
Madams and lodgings, inns with fewest bugs . . .
I want them all.

XANTHIAS: Nobody thinks of *me*!

HERACLES: Poor kid! You dare attempt this journey? *You?*

DIONYSUS: No more of that, now! Tell me first the roads—
The quickest way to get from here to Hell—
Neither too hot, however, nor too cold.

HERACLES: Well, let me see, what shall I recommend?
The Lynch-Gate Road is one of the easiest—
You hang yourself!

DIONYSUS: Too hot—a *stifling* way!

HERACLES: A slippery cutoff, known as Evergreen Lane,
Mid the murmuring pine and the . . .

DIONYSUS: *Hemlock?*

HERACLES: Right you are!

DIONYSUS: Br-r-r! Makes me shiver just to think of it!
You're frozen stiff—numb from the ankles up!

HERACLES: A shorter route, then, but precipitate . . .

DIONYSUS: Shorter the better. Walking's not my forte!

HERACLES: Stroll to the Ceramicus . . .

DIONYSUS: Well, what next?

HERACLES: And climb the tower—that high one——

DIONYSUS: And do what?

HERACLES: Watch till the torch race is about to start;
And when the crowd is shouting *Let 'em go!*
You let *yourself* go.

                    Where?

                              Headforemost . . . *down!*

DIONYSUS: I'd ruin two potential brain croquettes!
That road I'll *never* take!

HERACLES: Which *will* you take?

DIONYSUS: The one *you* took.

HERACLES: But that's a lengthy *cruise*.
First you will come to an enormous lake,
Bottomless, huge.

DIONYSUS: How will I get across?

HERACLES: In a tiny boat—so big—an aged salt
Rows people over for two bits a head.

DIONYSUS: Aha! Good old two bits will get you anywhere!
   How did they get down *there?*
HERACLES: Theseus, of course.
   Next, you will see big snakes and dreadful beasts
   Past counting.
DIONYSUS: Don't you try to frighten me.
   You cannot scare me out of it.
HERACLES: Then, mud,
   Masses of mud, and streams of muck, in which
   Is every man who ever wronged a guest,
   Or beat his ma or slapped his father's face,
   Or took a girl to bed and wouldn't pay,
   Or swore an oath he knew he couldn't keep,
   Or copied out some lines by Morsimus.
DIONYSUS: And likewise everyone, I hope, who danced
   That Pyrrhic number by Cinesias!
HERACLES: Then flutes will breathe sweet music through the
     air,
   A light as brilliant as the sun will shine,
   And myrtle groves and blissful throngs appear
   Of men and women clapping their hands for joy.
DIONYSUS: Who *are* they?
HERACLES: Those who have entered into Bliss.
XANTHIAS: And I'm the ass they tie outside the gate!
   Damned if I tote this stuff another yard!
HERACLES: And they will tell you all you need to know.
   Their happy homes are yonder by the road,
   Close to the very doors of Pluto's house.
   And now good-bye, dear brother.
DIONYSUS: Same to you.
   Keep well. (*To* XANTHIAS, *as* HERACLES *retires.*) And you
   pick up your pack again.
XANTHIAS: Before I've set it down?
DIONYSUS: Get going, there!
XANTHIAS: Oh please. . . . Why don't you hire another boy—
   Some dead man coming from his funeral?
DIONYSUS: Suppose I cannot find one.
XANTHIAS: Then take me.
DIONYSUS: All right. . . . Yonder's a bier approaching now.
   (*Enter a* CORPSE *with* BEARERS.)
   Hey, you! —Not *you*. . . . I'm talking to the corpse.
   Look, will you carry a small pack for me?
CORPSE: *How* small?

DIONYSUS: This here.
CORPSE: A dollar, shall we say?
DIONYSUS: Too much!
CORPSE (*to* BEARERS): We might as well be getting on.
DIONYSUS: Wait, my good man. I'm sure we can agree.
CORPSE: One dollar, cash, or not another word!
DIONYSUS: Six bits!
CORPSE: I'd sooner come to life again!
XANTHIAS: Stuck up, now, ain't he? Shucks! Be damned to
     him!
     I'll go, sir.
DIONYSUS: Spoken like a gentleman!
     Let's find the boat.
          (CHARON *is heard offstage.*)
CHARON: Avast! Bring her ashore.
XANTHIAS: What's that I see?
DIONYSUS: What's what? . . . Oh, that? . . . A lake—
     The one he told us of. And look—a boat!
XANTHIAS: Yes, by Poseidon, yes . . . and Charon too!
DIONYSUS: *Ahoy there, Charon!*
XANTHIAS: *Hi there, Cap!*
DIONYSUS: }
XANTHIAS: }   *Ahoy!*
CHARON: All passengers for the Land of Sweet Repose,
     Bound for Oblivion, or Ass's Locks,
     The Doghouse, Hell, or Taenarum—*Aboard!*
DIONYSUS: Here's *one.*
CHARON: Then get aboard. Step lively, please!
DIONYSUS: You really go to Hell?
CHARON: For *you* we will!
     Get *in!*
DIONYSUS: Come, boy.
CHARON: Sorry, no slaves allowed,
     Unless they fought to free their carcasses.
XANTHIAS: I couldn't—had the pink-eye . . . just my luck!
CHARON: Then you will have to run around the lake.
XANTHIAS: Where shall I meet you?
CHARON: Rest-in-Peace Hotel,
     At Tombstone Point.
DIONYSUS: You understand?
XANTHIAS: Too well!
     What evil omen crossed my path this day?

CHARON (*to* DIONYSUS): You take an oar. —Time's up, now.
   All aboard!
   What do you think you're doing?
DIONYSUS: What you said—
   Told me to take an oar ... I *took* an oar!
CHARON: Sit *down* there, Fatty, on that bench!
DIONYSUS: All right.
CHARON: Stretch out your arms ... full length.
DIONYSUS: Well, there you are.
CHARON: Now stop this silly clowning. Brace your legs
   And row ... row like a good one.
DIONYSUS: Never learned—
   Complete landlubber ... *most* unnautical.
   How *can* I row?
CHARON: Easily. You will hear,
   Once you have started, lovely songs ...
DIONYSUS: By whom?
CHARON: Our minstrel frogs ... wonderful!
DIONYSUS: Give me the count.
CHARON: Stroke. ... Stroke. ...
   (*The* CHORUS OF FROGS *is heard offstage, croaking in
   rhythm with the* OARSMEN.)

CHORUS: *Brekekekex ko-ax ko-ax*
             Brekekekex ko-ax ko-ax
           From marsh and mere
              Sound again
              Your fair refrain
             Deep and clear,
             O humid race,
           Booming the bass
              Cadenza
             Ko-ax ko-ax.
            In sweet accord
             Thus we laud
          Divine Dionysus, when,
       Beside his temple in the Fen,
      Townsmen and villagers journey,
      Tankards replete for the Tourney,
        So tipsily reeling around
          My hallowed ground.
         Brekekekex ko-ax ko-ax.
DIONYSUS: My poor behind begins to ache.

                Ko-ax yourself, for heaven's sake!
                But *you* don't care, you maniacs.

CHORUS: *Brekekekex ko-ax ko-ax.*
DIONYSUS: Be damned to you, *ko-ax* and all!
                Ko-ax and nothing else you bawl!
CHORUS: 'Tis our right and proper chorus,
                Meddlesome wight.
             For the lyric Nine adore us,
      As doth goat-footed Pan, who merrily
      Plays his pipes on hillock, in hollow,
          And the Harpist, Lord Apollo,
    Rendering thanks for the reed that I verily
    Nurse for the lyre in swampy lands.
             Brekekekex ko-ax ko-ax.
DIONYSUS: I'm raising blisters on my hands;
             My rump is in a fearful stew,
           And soon he'll up and say to you . . .
CHORUS: *Brekekekex ko-ax ko-ax.*
DIONYSUS: O tuneful breed,
              Pray give o'er!
CHORUS: Nay, nay! Indeed
            All the more
           Shall we chant,
           If e'er before
        On a sunlit morn we capered
     Where the flags and rushes tapered,
        Trilling arias ecstatic
      Suited to our sports aquatic,
     Or, in flight from rainy weather,
     Danced in wat'ry regions nether,
       Brightly caroling together
    Many a bubble-and-spray gavotte . . .
DIONYSUS: *Brekekekex ko-ax ko-ax—*
             I beat you that time, did I not?
CHORUS: Fearsome fate for me to suffer!
DIONYSUS: Mine will certainly be tougher
             If I row until I split!
CHORUS: *Brekekekex ko-ax ko-ax.*
DIONYSUS: Do *I* care, damn you? Not a bit!
CHORUS: 'Tis our song. We'll not forsake it—
         Never, as long as throat can take it—
           Crying loudly through the day . . .
DIONYSUS: *Brekekekex ko-ax ko-ax.*

You cannot win in this affray!

CHORUS: Nor can *you* put *us* to rout, sir!

DIONYSUS: Nor can *you!* With conqu'ring might

Will I lift my voice and shout, sir,

Be there need, into the night,

          Brekekekex ko-ax ko-ax.

And press the fight

Until I out-*ko-ax* you, son.

   (*Belligerently.*)

          Brekekekex ko-ax ko-ax.

   (*Silence from the* FROGS.)

          Well, was I right?

Not one *ko-ax* I hear. . . . You're done!

CHARON: Slow up, there! . . . Easy! . . . Bring her in! . . .

   Now, then,

Ashore! . . . All tickets, please!

DIONYSUS: Here's mine—two bits.

Hey, Xanthias! . . . Where are you, Xanthy? . . . Hi!

XANTHIAS: Yoo-hoo!

DIONYSUS: Come over here! . . .

XANTHIAS: How are you, boss?

DIONYSUS: What is it like out yonder?

XANTHIAS: Darkness . . . Mud . . .

DIONYSUS: You saw the parricides and perjurers

He told us of?

XANTHIAS: Certainly. Didn't you?

DIONYSUS: Oh yes, I saw them . . .

                              And I see them *now!* . . .

All right, what next?

XANTHIAS: We'd better move along.—

This is the place in which he said we'd find

Those awful animals.

DIONYSUS: To hell with him—

A showoff, telling tales to frighten me.

He's jealous of my well-known fortitude.

Nothing is haughtier than . . . Heracles!

I only wish I *could* meet one of them,

And win a trophy worthy of my tour.

XANTHIAS: What's that? . . . I hear a funny kind of noise.

DIONYSUS: Which way?

XANTHIAS: Back yonder.

DIONYSUS: Walk behind me, then.

XANTHIAS: No, it's in front.

DIONYSUS: Then go ahead of me.

XANTHIAS: I see it now. I see a great beast!

DIONYSUS: Wh-what sort?

XANTHIAS: Ghastly. . . . Never stays the same—
A bull, first . . . then a mule . . . and now a *girl* . . .
Good looker, too.

DIONYSUS: Where? Lemme get to her!

XANTHIAS: She isn't there. She's turned into a bitch.

DIONYSUS: Empusa!

XANTHIAS: Maybe. Her face is all ablaze
With fire.

DIONYSUS: And has she got one leg of brass?

XANTHIAS: By George, she has! and the other one's pure *gall!*

DIONYSUS: I want to go away from here.

XANTHIAS: Me too.

DIONYSUS (*appealing to his priest in the audience*): Save me
Your Eminence—till suppertime!

XANTHIAS: May Heracles preserve us!

DIONYSUS: Stop it, man!
For heaven's sake, don't speak my name out loud!

XANTHIAS: Well, Dionysus, then.

DIONYSUS: That's even worse! . . .
Now get along with you.

XANTHIAS: Here, Master, here!

DIONYSUS: What is it?

XANTHIAS: Calm yourself. Fair Fortune smiles.
We now may say, *à la* Hegelochus,
The storm is spent. The ocean is a tease.
Empusa's gone.

DIONYSUS: You swear?

XANTHIAS: Honest to God!

DIONYSUS: You cross your heart?

XANTHIAS: Yes.

DIONYSUS: Hope you may die?

XANTHIAS: I do.—
I must admit she turned me green with fright . . .
And you turned yellow. . . . Look, you're yellow still!

DIONYSUS: What brought these miseries upon my head?
Who up in heaven wants to ruin me?

XANTHIAS: *Aether, God's Tenement? . . . The tread of Time?*
(*Sound of music offstage.*)

DIONYSUS: Hey!

XANTHIAS: What's the matter?

DIONYSUS: Didn't you hear it?
XANTHIAS: What?
DIONYSUS: That *breath of flutes*.
XANTHIAS: Yes, and another breath,
  The mystic scent of torches, comes to me.
DIONYSUS: Let's squat down here and listen silently.
CHORUS: All hail, hail, Iacchus!
              All hail, hail, Iacchus!
XANTHIAS: That's who it is—the Saved, the Blessed Ones
  He told us of, in joyful song nearby . . .
  The very same they sing in the Agora.
DIONYSUS: You're right, I do believe. In any case
  We'd best keep quiet till we know for sure.
    (*Enter the* CHORUS *of* MYSTICS.)
CHORUS: Divine Babe, here residing
      In a fane built for thy biding,
      All hail, hail, Iacchus!
        Join our throng,
          Ever by us
        In the dance song
         Of the pious
      Through the moorland;
    On thy fair forehead, the gleaming
    Of a wreath with berries teeming,
    Set aquiver by the measure
  That with bold foot thou dost beat
  In a bold rite, and replete
  With a pure, a holy pleasure
  And the sweet charm of the graces
      That are meet
  For the Mystics' hallowed paces.
XANTHIAS: O great and glorious Persephone,
  How redolent, that song, of barbecue!
DIONYSUS: Be still, then, if you want some sausage too!
CHORUS: The firebrand must awaken;
    For our Day-Star is uptaken—
      All hail, hail, Iacchus!—
        Doth arise,
        And a splendor
        In the dark skies
        Doth engender
      Through the meadow
    Where the aged limb is leaping,

And our woes away are creeping,
And the sore burden is lightened
Of the years' wearisome pain
By the dance thou dost ordain
In a vale with blossoms brightened.
Mid the torch glow that is o'er us
Lead amain,
Blessed Youth, a youthful chorus!

Be silent. Attend. Let no one offend by his presence our ritual dances,

Whose taste is impure, nor knows the lure of the Word, the art that entrances;

Nor shared the delights of the elegant rites of the Muse, the Mistress of Glamour;

Nor deeply the wine has imbibed of Cratinus, the dauntless Bull of the Drama;

Nor feels malaise at a scene that displays a malapropos vulgarity;

Nor seeks to quiet political riot by preaching and practicing charity,

But quite unashamedly fans the flame to further his private ambitions;

Or, mid the unrest of a country distressed, takes gold from corrupt politicians

A ship or a fort to betray, to export from Aegina a contraband cargo—

Thus aping Thoricion, that blackguard official of *five per cent, or embargo!*—

The contents of which—sails, oarlocks, pitch—Epidaurus will have in an hour;

Or cash would entreat for the enemy's fleet from a certain imperial power;

Or, while he's rehearsing his chorus, perversely gives Hecate's precinct a shower;

Or nibbles away at the dramatists' pay—some demagogue fain to attack us

Because we had twitted the fellow a bit in accord with the rubrics of Bacchus:

All these do I warn, *Begone, begone! Avaunt!* is my stern exhortation.

Make way for the mystic, the pure, the artistic, who, roused by a holy elation,

Will dance till the dawn and will rest in the morn, as is
meet for this fair celebration.

> March onward, all ye blessèd,
> By pasture bloom caressèd,
> Your step firm and lithesome,
> 'Mid quip and jest
> And mocking banter blithesome—
> Though lunch was none too good, at best!
> Stride on. The Maid applaud ye,
> Our Virgin Savior laud ye;
> Her praise hymn forever,
> Who guards this spot,
> And vows to fail us never—
> Although Thoricion likes it not!

Now raise ye another refrain for the Mother, the Queen of
the Harvest to honor,
Adorning with beauty of voice and of flute Demeter, our
Holy Madonna.

> O Mistress of this solemn rite,
> Stand thou beside me in the fight,
> And lead thy graceful choir aright,
> To utter naught that in thy sight
>   Is stupid or immoral!
> O grant me witty things to say,
> And earnest things in a witty way,
> All worthy of thy festal day,
> That I may win the merry fray
>   And wear the victor's laurel!

> Now hear ye!
Call forth the Holy Child with song; summon the Babe
Iacchus,
That he may join our pilgrim throng, votaries of Bacchus,
> Thou who the fairest of festal music inspirèd,
> Come seek with us, O Infant ever desirèd,
>   Thy Mother's fane,
>   And prove thee able to sustain
>   The toilsome course untirèd.
Iacchus, lover of song and dance, lead thou me on.

> This tattered tunic here, let none misjudge it;
> This battered shoe I wear, let none begrudge it;

'Tis thy decree,
As aiding in our jollity—
And balancing the budget!
Iacchus, lover of song and dance, lead thou me on.

A comely maid beside us, thanks to you, sir,
Afforded me a stimulating view, sir,
When from her shirt
One little bosom like a flirt
Peeped out and said *How-do, sir!*
Iacchus, lover of song and dance, lead thou me on.

DIONYSUS: Processions I could never eschew.
A whirl with yonder girlie
I'd simply love—I mean that peekaboo!
XANTHIAS: Me too!
CHORUS: Methinks it would beseem us
To jeer at Archidemus,
The snaggle-tooth Bicuspidorian,
Who nowadays, God love us,
Commands the dead above us,
Top villain of the hyphenated clan.

Young Cleisthenes, the queerie,
Intones a *miserere*
For sweet Sebinus, prostrate in despair.
His manly features mauling,
Incontinently bawling,
He beats his breast and plucks his bottom bare.

And Callias, the fearless,
In navel battles peerless,
Engaged the foe bedight in pussy skin.
DIONYSUS: Could any of you tell us
Where Pluto lives? From Hellas'
Shores we only recently got in.
CHORUS: It is not far away, sir;
Nor ask again, I pray, sir.
Behind yon very portal he doth dwell.
DIONYSUS: Then bring the baggage, fellow.
XANTHIAS: The old refrain—how mellow!
But toting baggage is no bagatelle!

CHORUS: Now onward,
To enter the Deity's holy ground, tread its carpet of
flowers,

Glad partners in a solemn round dear to Potent Powers.
And I will bear the torch to light blessed maids and matrons
Who through the night in darkling rite laud our Heavenly
    Patrons.

>   Aye, onward to the meadows bright
>   With asphodel and roses,
>   To dance in our native way
>   That beauteous dance and gay.
>   For thus on this happy day
>   Fair Fortune disposes.

>   On us alone the sun doth smile
>   With face benign—stout yeomen,
>   True Saints of the Mystic Band,
>   Who greet with a guileless hand
>   All friends from an alien land,
>   All . . . parvenu showmen!

(DIONYSUS *and* XANTHIAS *approach the palace of*
    PLUTO.)

DIONYSUS: Well, I suppose I ought to knock. But how?
    I wonder how they do it hereabouts.

XANTHIAS: Quit dawdling. Go and have a try at it.
    The *mood* of Heracles should match his *mode!*

DIONYSUS (*knocking*): Hello!

    (AEACUS *appears.*)

AEACUS: Who's there?

DIONYSUS (*striking a pose*): The valiant Heracles!

AEACUS: You reckless rogue, you barefaced good-for-naught,
    You scamp, you utter scamp, you . . . scalawag!
    Our watchdog Cerberus, my special care,
    First luring from his post, you seized and choked,
    And off you ran with him. But now you're caught,
    Hemmed in by yon blackhearted Stygian peak,
    Acheron's canyon that with gore doth reek,
    Cocytus' wanton bitches, swift and sleek!
    Echidna's fivescore mouths thy veins will tear;
    Bloodsuckers of Tartessus will not spare
    Thy severed lungs, Teithrasian Gorgon hags
    Thy very vitals ripping into rags,
    Thy entrails mangling to a scarlet shred!
    To summon them I presently am sped.

                                (*Exit* AEACUS.)

    (DIONYSUS *collapses.*)

XANTHIAS: I say, what *have* you done? . . . Ridiculous!

DIONYSUS: *Propissiation for my shins. Amen.*

XANTHIAS: Get up! Somebody'll *see* you!

DIONYSUS: I am faint.
   Water! A sponge, to press upon my heart!

XANTHIAS: Well, here's one. . . . Take it.

DIONYSUS: Where?

XANTHIAS: Ye golden gods!
   That's where you keep your heart?

DIONYSUS: It got so scared
   It went into a tailspin, so to speak!

XANTHIAS: Of all the cowards, human or divine . . . !

DIONYSUS: A coward, eh? I asked you for a sponge,
   When anybody else would have . . .

XANTHIAS: Done what?

DIONYSUS: Just lain there, stinko—any *coward* would.
  But I got up, and wiped myself besides!

XANTHIAS: God, what a *man!*

DIONYSUS: Exactly what *I* think.
   Weren't *you* afraid, when all that hell broke loose?

XANTHIAS: Why no, I never even thought of it.

DIONYSUS: All right, then, since you are a dauntless soul,
   With such a hero complex, *you* be *me.*
   Put on the lionskin and take the club,
   And I will tote the baggage for a change.

XANTHIAS: No sooner said than done. Your word is law.—
   Well, look me over—Xanthias—Heracles!
   You'll see a better brand of spunk than yours.

DIONYSUS: What *I* see is the Melitean *punk!*
   But first, to get this luggage on my back.
    (*A* HOUSEMAID *appears.*)

HOUSEMAID: Heracles! Darling! Here at last! . . . Come in.
   My mistress, learning you'd arrived, at once
   Put loaves into the oven, made pea soup—
   Oh, pots and pots of it—and cakes and rolls,
   And barbecued an ox. . . . But do come in!

XANTHIAS: No, thank you very much, but . . .

HOUSEMAID: I insist!
   I simply cannot let you go like this.
   Roast chicken, and delectable desserts,
   And wines the sweetest ever. Come with me.

XANTHIAS: I'm much obliged, but . . .

HOUSEMAID: Don't be silly, now.
   You've *got* to! Think of all those lovely girls

We have, to play the flute and dance for you—
A half a dozen of them!

XANTHIAS: How's that? *Girls?*

HOUSEMAID: The cutest things—so young and soft and smooth.
Now hurry. Cook was taking off the fish
When I came out, ready to send it in.

XANTHIAS: Oh very well, then. You may run ahead
And tell the girls that I am on the way.—
Up with the baggage, boy, and follow me.

DIONYSUS: Hey, *wait* a minute! You aren't *serious?*
Dressing you up like that was just a joke!
Now stop this foolishness at once, my lad.
Pick up these bundles here and be yourself.

XANTHIAS: You don't intend to rob me of this rig
You *gave* me?

DIONYSUS: Not at all. . . . I'm *doing* it!
Remove that lionskin, sir.

XANTHIAS: I protest!
I call upon the gods to . . .

DIONYSUS: *What* gods? . . . *Me?*
How vain, how stupid, to suppose that you,
A common slave, could be Alcmena's son!

XANTHIAS: Here, take it, by all means. But some fine day
Perhaps you'll need me yet—God grant you may!

CHORUS: 'Tis the mark of one sagacious,
            Practical and perspicacious,
                Who hath sailed the seven seas,
            That he roll across to larboard
            If it's stormy on the starboard—
                Not immobile, if you please,
            As a graven image, never
            Shifting in a smart endeavor
                To secure a softer breeze.
            Such a man is jolly clever—
                Aye, a born Theramenes!

DIONYSUS: Would it not have been diverting
            If old Xanthias, while flirting
                With a maiden minus clothes,
            Had declared an intermission
            For a privy expedition;
                Whereupon I, on my toes,
            Seeing what was up, had darted
            In to finish what he started;

But he peppered me with blows,
Knocking out—the lionhearted—
From my kisser both front rows!

(*Enter* LANDLADY *and* PLATHANE.)

LANDLADY: Here, Plathane, look yonder. . . . That's the scamp
Who came—remember?—to my boardinghouse
And ate up sixteen loaves of bread . . .

PLATHANE: It is—
The very same!

XANTHIAS: Bad news for *somebody!*

LANDLADY: And twenty portions of roast beef besides,
At four bits *per* . . .

XANTHIAS: Somebody's in for it!

LANDLADY: And nearly all my garlic . . .

DIONYSUS: Nonsense, madam.
Surely you cannot mean that . . .

LANDLADY: So? You thought
I wouldn't know you in those fancy shoes?
And *fish*—I haven't even mentioned that!

PLATHANE: Nor yet, dear me, the elegant fresh cheese
That he devoured, drying cloth and all!

LANDLADY: And then, when I informed him what he owed,
He glared at me and bellowed like a bull . . .

XANTHIAS: Quite typical. That's how he always acts.

LANDLADY: And drew his dagger, like a crazy man.

PLATHANE: Oh heavens, yes!

LANDLADY: We, horrified, of course,
Went scrambling up the ladder to the loft.
But out he rushed—and took my pallet, too!

XANTHIAS: He would. Just like him.

PLATHANE: Something must be *done.*

LANDLADY: Go get my lawyer, Cleon. Bring him here.

DIONYSUS (*to* XANTHIAS): You go and find, for *me,* Hyperbolus!

LANDLADY: I'll have revenge!—You greedy gullet, you!
Oh how I'd love to take a stone and crack
Those grinders that cleaned up my pantry shelves!

XANTHIAS: *I'd* love to fling him on the city dump!

PLATHANE: Or take a scythe and slice right off his neck
The throat that gobbled my delicious tripe!
I'm going after Cleon, who this day
Will serve a writ and wind the business up.

(*Exeunt* LANDLADY *and* PLATHANE.)

DIONYSUS: Damme if I don't love my Xanthias!

XANTHIAS: I know what *that* means! . . . Not another word!
I *won't* be Heracles . . . I *won't!*

DIONYSUS: Now, Xanthy,
Please do not talk like that!

XANTHIAS: But how could I,
A common slave, become Alcmena's son?

DIONYSUS: *I* know, *I* know. . . . You're mad. . . . You've a
right to be.
I wouldn't blame you if you slapped my face.
If ever I rob you of the role again,
A curse on me, my spouse, my little brood . . .
And Archidemus of the bleary eye!

XANTHIAS: That does it! I accept. It's worth a try!

CHORUS: Now that you once more are wearing
                An investiture so daring,
            'Tis your task with might and main
            To renew your youth, acquiring
                An expression awe-inspiring,
            Mindful of the brawn and brain
            Of your great heroic model.
            For if, prone to silly twaddle,
                You emit one word inane,
            'Tis your destiny to toddle
                'Round beneath that load again.

XANTHIAS: Good advice, my friends; but, queerly,
It just happens that I really
    Thought of it myself, by chance.
True, when things are looking better,
He will rob me, and forget a
    Promise made me in advance.
Nonetheless you shall behold a
Man of spirit even bolder,
    And with mustard in his glance.—
Hark! . . . I'll need, before I'm older,
    'Twould appear, all vigilance.
        (*Enter* AEACUS *with* POLICEMEN.)

AEACUS: Arrest this dog thief here without delay.
We'll show him! Quick!

DIONYSUS: Bad news for *somebody!*

XANTHIAS: To hell with you! Stand back!

AEACUS: Resisting, eh?
What ho! Ditylas, Pardocus, Sceblyas,

Come out and help us overcome this rogue!

DIONYSUS: Isn't it terrible—a thief like him
  Assaulting an officer?

AEACUS: Monstrous, indeed!

DIONYSUS: Outrageous . . . oh dear me!

XANTHIAS: I hope to die,
  If ever I came near this place before,
  Or stole a cent's worth of your property!
  Now here's a sporting offer, freely made:
  You give this slave of mine the third degree,
  And if you prove me guilty, kill me dead!

AEACUS: What may we do to him?

XANTHIAS: Why, anything!
  The rack, the wheel, the whip. . . . Skin him alive . . .
  Vinegar up his nose . . . bricks on his chest . . .
  Or hang him by his thumbs . . . what have you. . . . *But*
  No lashing with a leek or onion top!

AEACUS: That's fair enough. And if I lame the boy
  In any way, you shall be reimbursed.

XANTHIAS: Not I! Just take him off and torture him.

AEACUS: Here, rather. Let him say it to your face.—
  Put down your pack. . . . No lies, now! Understand?

DIONYSUS: To whom it may concern I give due warning:
  I'm an Immortal. If you torture *me*,
  You'll have yourself to blame.

AEACUS: What did you say?

DIONYSUS: That I am Dionysus, son of Zeus.
  This person is my slave.

AEACUS (*to* XANTHIAS): Hear that?

XANTHIAS: I do.
  All the more reason, then, to torture him . . .
  Won't even feel it, if he is a god!

DIONYSUS: *You* claim to be a god too—Heracles.
  So shouldn't *you* be beaten, just as much?

XANTHIAS: Sounds logical.—Whichever one of us
  Shows that he minds it, or lets fall a tear,
  You may be certain he is not a god.

AEACUS: I must admit that you're a gentleman—
  Completely fair and square. —Take off your coats.

XANTHIAS: But how can *you* be fair?

AEACUS: Oh easily—
  A blow for you, a blow for him.

XANTHIAS: All right.

(AEACUS *strikes him.*)

Well, go ahead. And watch whether I flinch.

AEACUS: But I've already *hit* you!

XANTHIAS: No-o-o! You swear?

AEACUS: I'll go and hit the other fellow.

(*He strikes* DIONYSUS.)

DIONYSUS: When?

AEACUS: Just *did* it!

DIONYSUS: Wouldn't you think I'd *sneeze* or something?

AEACUS: Funny . . . I'll try this other chap again.

XANTHIAS: What are you waiting for, then?

(AEACUS *strikes him.*)

                                    Oh!

AEACUS: Why "Oh"?

It didn't *hurt* you?

XANTHIAS: No. . . . Suddenly thought

'Twas time my Diomean rites were held!

AEACUS: The man's a marvell! . . . Now back over here.

(*Strikes* DIONYSUS.)

DIONYSUS: Hey!

AEACUS: *What?*

DIONYSUS: Hey look! Yonder's the cavalry!

AEACUS: Why *weep* about it?

DIONYSUS: Onions. . . . Can't you smell?

AEACUS: No *pain,* by any chance?

DIONYSUS: Not in the least!

AEACUS: I'll step across and take a crack at *him.*

XANTHIAS: Golly!

AEACUS: You mean . . . ?

XANTHIAS: My foot. . . . A blasted thorn!

AEACUS: Now what the deuce . . . ? Well, back again we go.

DIONYSUS: O Lord! . . . *of Delphi and of Delos fair!*

XANTHIAS: Aha! *That* stung him! Did you hear?

DIONYSUS: Not me!

Just trying to recall Hipponax' words.

XANTHIAS: You're getting nowhere. Crack him in the ribs.

AEACUS: Ribs nothing! Stand up. . . . Stick your belly out.

DIONYSUS: Great God! . . .

XANTHIAS: He felt it *that* time!

DIONYSUS: . . . *whose realm, far beneath Aegean's silver sea,*
                Monarch of headland heights . . .

AEACUS: I give it up! I simply cannot tell

Which of you is a god! —But let's go in.

My Master and his Queen, Persephone,
Will surely know, for they are gods themselves.
DIONYSUS: Right, but I wish it had occurred to you
Before you tried to beat me black and blue!

(Exeunt.)

CHORUS: Lead us, O Muse, in the maze
         Of a dance, of a song
         To enrapture thy heart.
         Lift thy gaze
         Over this throng
         Of the gallant—
         Numberless lovers of art,
         Famed for wit and talent,
         More avid of hon-
         Or than great Cleophon,
         Whose babbling, bilingualist lips
         Sudden anxiety grips.
         Lo, a Thracian swallow
         Hath perched on his tongue—
         That barbarous bloom—
         And hath plaintively sung
         A cadenza of gloom:
         Though the jury be hung,
         My *hanging soon will follow!*

'Tis indeed the bounden duty of this consecrated band
That they offer worthy counsel to the people of this land.
First, let all our folk be equal, and be free from civic fear.
If, with Phrynichus entangled, one was thrown upon his ear,
Slipping into grievous error, barking painfully his shins,
True confession and repentance should absolve his former sins.
Furthermore, no son of Athens ever ought to lose his vote.
Why, a slave who manned a trireme in a certain scrap of note,
Straightway was a good . . . Plataean—his own master overnight.
Not that I would want to argue that this action wasn't right;
'Twas the only deed of wisdom you have done, it seems to me.

But the men who've fought your battles o'er and o'er upon
  the sea,
As their fathers did before them, men of pure Athenian
  stock,
Surely ought to be forgiven if just once they ran amok.
Let us put away resentment, let us use our native wit,
Welcoming into our household for the common benefit
Every loyal friend and neighbor who has battled at our
  side.
For if we persist in showing such a vain and snobbish pride
When our Ship of State is struggling *in the billows' wild
  caress,*
History will not be likely to applaud our cleverness!

> *If into life I have looked,*
> *Into man and the heart*
> *Of a man . . .* 'ittlekin's doom,
> *One* is booked
> Soon to depart,
> And doth fidget,
> Pestilent ape, in his gloom—
> Cleigenes the Midget—
> That niggardly Knight
> Of the Baths, downright
> Dictator, who forced us to buy
> Soap that was nothing but lye
> Mixed with gritty gravel!
> No pacifist, he.
> For he's sorely afraid
> That when off on a spree
> He'll be bashed on the head,
> And will impotent be
> Without his trusty *gavel!*

It appears to us that Athens shows the selfsame attitude
To the fairest and the purest and the noblest of her brood,
As toward our silver coinage and the later wartime gold,
Both of which are out of fashion, though their worth has
  been extolled
As the finest ever minted. All men everywhere agree
That their weight and sterling soundness are unique in
  currency,
Whether here at home in Hellas or abroad. But recently

We ourselves no longer like them, and prefer to use for
  cash
A debased, barbaric tender—this new-fangled copper trash!
So, too, *men* of weight and substance, Hellenes to the
  manner born,
Men of rounded education and of sterling worth, we scorn.
Aye, a gentleman, a sportsman, and the cream of Athens'
  crop
We reject for something trashy, for a half-breed carrot top!
In the old days we were chary of preferment for a scamp,
Nor would rashly put in office persons of a shabby stamp;
And not even as a scapegoat did we use a common tramp!
Pick *deserving* public servants, as of old, my foolish friends,
And once more you'll seem to merit any luck that Fortune
  sends;
While, despite your reformation if you meet adversity,
You'll escape the shame of hanging from a *sour* apple tree!
    (*Enter* AEACUS *and* XANTHIAS.)

AEACUS: By Jove, your master is a splendid chap—
  A perfect gentleman!
XANTHIAS: Of course he is—
  Knows how to drink and wench . . . and nothing else!
AEACUS: Proved you had been impersonating him,
  And didn't even whip you. Think of it!
XANTHIAS: He'd better *not* have!
AEACUS: *That's* the talk, my boy!
  Below-stairs lingo. . . . How I love the sound!
XANTHIAS: Really? You do?
AEACUS: Why, I'm in paradise
  When I can damn the boss behind his back.
XANTHIAS: And grumble at him when you're safe outside,
  After a licking?
AEACUS: It delights my soul!
XANTHIAS: And meddling in his business?
AEACUS: Can't be beat!
XANTHIAS: My twin! My long-lost twin! . . . Eavesdropping,
  now,
  On private conversation?
AEACUS: Ravishing!
XANTHIAS: And blabbing to the parlor maids?
AEACUS: Oh God!
  At that point, brother, I ejaculate!
XANTHIAS: Then put it there! . . . The old fraternal grip!

Blest be the tie that binds the servants' hall!
Let me enfold you in a fond embrace.—
I say, what's all the rumpus? What goes on—
A row?
AEACUS: Aeschylus and Euripides—
At it again. We've had a great to-do
Down here—amounts to a civil war, in fact.
XANTHIAS: What caused it?
AEACUS: There's a statute on our books
That the most skillful craftsman in each art—
I mean the fine arts, poetry and such—
Be asked to dinner in the City Hall,
And have a chair by Pluto's side . . .
XANTHIAS: I see.
AEACUS: Until a better artist in that line
Appears among us. Then he has to move.
XANTHIAS: But why should this have worried Aeschylus?
AEACUS: The Tragic Throne was naturally his,
As being master of his trade.
XANTHIAS: Who else?
AEACUS: Well, when Euripides appeared, of course
He started showing off to the underworld.
Pickpockets, gangsters, burglars, parricides—
And we've a lot of them around—went wild
Over his fancy footwork in debate,
And cheered him as the champ. That turned his head,
And thereupon he claimed the right to sit
Where Aeschylus had sat.
XANTHIAS: Wasn't he lynched?
AEACUS: Oh no, the mob kept yelling for a trial,
To prove which poet really was the best.
XANTHIAS: That convict crowd?
AEACUS: Aye, screaming to the skies.
XANTHIAS: But weren't there others backing Aeschylus?
AEACUS: Few *decent* people anywhere—just look!
XANTHIAS: Well, what are Pluto's plans? What will he do?
AEACUS: He'll hold a competition, here and now—
A contest in poetic skill.
XANTHIAS: But, say,
Why hasn't Sophocles put in a claim?
AEACUS: Not he! Look what he did the day he came—
Gave Aeschylus a hug and shook his hand,
And tacitly conceded him the throne.

Now he intends, Clidemides reports,
 To watch from the sidelines, and if Aeschylus wins,
 He'll stay there. But if Aeschylus should lose,
 He's ready to take on Euripides.

XANTHIAS: It's really coming off?

AEACUS: Oh yes, quite soon.
 And when it does, you'll see strange goings-on:
 Poetry will be measured by the pound . . .

XANTHIAS: What? Weighed in scales like so much butcher's
  meat?

AEACUS: Yardsticks and rulers will be put to work,
 Rectangular forms . . .

XANTHIAS: Who's making any brick?

AEACUS: Wedges and miter squares. Euripides
 Will overhaul each drama verse by verse.

XANTHIAS: I dare say Aeschylus resents all this?

AEACUS: *'Neath pendent brows he glowered like a bull.*

XANTHIAS: Who'll judge the case?

AEACUS: Difficult question, that.
 They found a dearth of qualified referees.
 Aeschylus balked at an Athenian . . .

XANTHIAS: Too many crooks, no doubt!

AEACUS: Yet all the rest,
 As judges of poetic genius, were,
 To him, a joke. So finally they chose
 An expert in dramatic art—your boss.—
 But come. *When masters are on business bent,*
 Tears are the wages of the indolent.

             (*Exeunt.*)

CHORUS: Wrath, dread wrath will be his whose voice is as
  thunder,
 While his antagonist whets his tusk—that voluble wonder!
    Ah, what a terrible frenzy will torture his soul—
         Yea,
      How his angry orbs will roll!

 Strife, dire strife will ensue, as verse that is helmeted,
  plumèd,
 Battles with splinters and shavings that fall from a style
  that is groomèd,
    Fending itself from the prancing phrases designed—
         Yea,
      Fathered by a matchless mind.

Lo, yon mane that does stream from the neck of the cham-
    pion bristles.
Fury does furrow his brow. With a roar he hurls his mis-
    siles—
        Riveted timbers of verbiage ripped from the stage—
                Aye,
        Heavèd with a giant's rage.

Then will the tongue *précieuse,* suave master of arts belle-
    tristic,
Smoothly uncoiling its length, give rein to a rancor phlogistic,
      Mincing the mightiest words into fragments of naught—
              Aye,
        Words by toil of Titan wrought.
    (*Enter* DIONYSUS, EURIPIDES, *and* AESCHYLUS.)

EURIPIDES: I'll *not* renounce my claim. Don't ask me to.
    For I'm a better dramatist than he.
DIONYSUS: You hear his statement, Aeschylus? . . . Speak up!
EURIPIDES: Too proud to speak. The same old *silence* gambit,
    Used to create an awesome atmosphere.
DIONYSUS: Now, now, sir! Easy does it. Draw it mild!
EURIPIDES: I know the fellow—know him through and
    through—
    Arrogant, wanton savage that he is,
    Of speech unbridled, passionate, unfenced,
    A ranting, pompous portmantologist!
AESCHYLUS: *What, scion of the Mistress of the Peas?*
    You scoff at *me,* cliché anthologist,
    Maker of ragamuffin manikins?
    You'll rue the day that . . .
DIONYSUS: Come come, Aeschylus,
    Heat not thy heart with vengeful bitterness.
AESCHYLUS: Nay, I must show this cripple puppeteer
    Just who he *is,* to be so impudent!
DIONYSUS: A lamb, a *black* lamb, bring me here forthwith!
    A monstrous storm is threatening to burst.
AESCHYLUS: Importing lovesick monodies from Crete,
    Vile, godless passions that degrade our Art!
DIONYSUS: One moment, pray, most noble Aeschylus.—
    My poor Euripides, be sensible,
    Take cover from this blizzard for the nonce.
    Some headlong hailstone, sir, may smite your brow
    And smash to smithereens your . . . Telephus!—

Now calm down, Aeschylus, and let us have
A quiet give-and-take, without abuse.
Poets should not be fishwives, gentlemen.
(*To* AESCHYLUS.) You come out roaring like a forest fire!

EURIPIDES: I'll face him in the cockpit any time,
To peck and claw—and let him claw *me* first—
Dialogue, lyrics—tear them limb from limb
And rip them up the back—*Meleager, Peleus,
Aeolus,* even *Telephus,* by God!

DIONYSUS: Well, what do *you* think, Aeschylus? Speak up.

AESCHYLUS: To hold a contest here was not my wish,
For I should be at a disadvantage.

DIONYSUS: How?

AESCHYLUS: Because my dramas did not die with me . . .
His did, and are available for use.
If you approve, however, I concur.

DIONYSUS: Some incense, and an altar! I would make,
Before this war of wits begins, a plea
That I may judge their art with artistry.—
You sing to the Muses while I pray to them.

CHORUS: Heavenly Nine, pure Maids everlasting,
Rapt spectators of bouts between critical minds magistratic,
Wrestlers in bitter dispute, sagacious, trenchant, Socratic,
Crafty contortionists, fain to exhibit a skill acrobatic,
Hark to a duel 'twixt power and guile.
Here is a genius at blinding and blasting;
There, an adept at the saw and the file.
Haste ye! This trial of talents contrasting
Neareth heights dramatic.

DIONYSUS (*to* AESCHYLUS *and* EURIPIDES): You too should
pray, before you speak your lines.

AESCHYLUS: Demeter, nurse and mother of my art,
Let me be worthy of thy Mysteries.

DIONYSUS: And now it's your turn.

EURIPIDES: No, I thank you. No.
The gods *I* worship are of another stamp.

DIONYSUS: Your own? You have a private mint?

EURIPIDES: Quite so.

DIONYSUS: Rank amateurs, at best! . . . Well, pray to them.

EURIPIDES: Aether, my Bread of Life, O vibrant Tongue,
O Mother Wit, O Nose fastidious,
Grant that I neatly pin him to the mat!

CHORUS: Right eager are we to behold these twain

> Militant rounds of Logic dancing,
> Tripping amain—
> How entrancing!—
> *Treading the way of war*. 'Tis plain,
> Frenzied is the tongue, advancing
> To attack, the spirit prancing
> In its pride, alert the brain.
> This one doubtless will endeavor
> To be eminently clever—
> Polished, pointed, and urbane.
> On will rush his foe, refuting
> And disputing,
> Massive verbiage uprooting,
> Till he wrecks the whole terrain.

DIONYSUS: Begin. . . . And plead your case with wit—no cheap forensic shoddy—

The sort of thing that we may hear from almost anybody!

EURIPIDES: Postponing to the end discussion—which indeed I owe you—

Of *my* achievements as a playwright, first I wish to show you

The kind of mountebank *he* was, and how he fascinated

The simple folk whom Phrynichus had newly graduated.

To start with, up there on the stage some creature he would set out—

Achilles, say, or Niobe—who, muffled as all-get-out,

Was Tragedy incarnate, but no word, no sound, would let out.

DIONYSUS: No, not a peep!

EURIPIDES: The Chorus, meanwhile, duty never shunning,

Assailed that silent figure with a string of odes hand-running,

But got no answer.

DIONYSUS: Good! I liked it . . . found it far more pleasant

Than all this modern talky-talk.

EURIPIDES: The viewpoint of a peasant!

DIONYSUS: No doubt. . . . But why did what's-his-name *do* that, whereas at present . . . ?

EURIPIDES: A faker's trick, to keep the house on tenterhooks, uncertain

If Niobe would *ever* speak. . . . And then, down came the curtain!

DIONYSUS: The old rapscallion! How he fooled me! Un-
    ashamed hijackery!—
    Why squirm and twist, my man?
EURIPIDES: Because I'm showing up his quackery.—
    And when the play was halfway done, with all this fiddle-
    faddle,
    He'd spout a stream of beefy words, gigantic forms astrad-
    dle
    Great steeds with beetling brows and crests—a literary diet
    That Athens never ate before!
AESCHYLUS: Oh oh! I cannot . . .
DIONYSUS: Quiet!
EURIPIDES: *Nothing* a chap could *understand!*
DIONYSUS (*to* AESCHYLUS): No use to grit your grinders!
EURIPIDES: *Scamander* this, *Scamander* that. . . . Such moun-
    tainous spellbinders
    As *griffin-eagles* built of *bronze*—a *shield,* in *his* cryptology.
    But how was anyone to *know?*
DIONYSUS: As to his ornithology,
    Through weary watches of the night I've thought on what
    in thunder
    That *gilded centaur-chanticleer* could be . . . and *still* I
    wonder!
AESCHYLUS: A figurehead upon a ship, you dullard!
DIONYSUS: Always foxin' us!
    I fancied 'twas the gilded jockey fathered by Philoxenus!
EURIPIDES: And after all, in tragedy, why introduce a *rooster?*
AESCHYLUS: Think of the monsters in *your* works that we
    are introduced to!
EURIPIDES: No horse-cocks, anyway, or goat-stags—heathen
    hyphenations
    Less fitting in Greek dramas than in Persian decorations!
    When you bequeathed to me this Art, she was a curiosity—
    Swollen with bombast, corpulent with verbal ponderosity.
    Well, first of all, a slenderizing regimen I gave 'er
    Of beet juice, exercises, verse of light and pleasant flavor,
    A broth of bookish hand-me-downs from my immense col-
    lection;
    Then built her up on monodies.
DIONYSUS: Cephisophon's confection?
EURIPIDES: My prologues never were confused, abrupt, and
    desultory,

But gave at once the pedigree, the outline of the story.

DIONYSUS: Good thing they went no further. . . . *Yours* is
    not so hunky-dory!

EURIPIDES: My characters were kept at work right through
    to the finale;

    The prince, the pauper, young or old—no one could dilly-
    dally;

    Servants and masters, women, men, were equally loqua-
    cious.

AESCHYLUS: And shouldn't you have hung for it?

EURIPIDES: For what?
    Why, goodness gracious,
    It is the democratic way!

DIONYSUS: I'd stop, if I were you, sir.
    Discourse upon *that* topic you had better not pursue, sir!

EURIPIDES: I taught these people how to use their tongues . . .

AESCHYLUS: A frightful blunder!
    And, ere you made it, I could wish that you had burst
    asunder!

EURIPIDES: And eyes and heads—to comprehend, to dodge
    and weave, to wrangle,

    To gauge a style with nicety and test its every angle,

    Prove all things and suspect the worst.

AESCHYLUS: You did, and I
    could strangle . . . !

EURIPIDES: By choosing themes that were concerned with
    everyday reality,

    I taught them how to criticize a play with rationality,

    Their sober reason undisturbed by mere theatricality,

    Like tinkling-brass-accoutered-colts cavorting to amaze them,

    A Cycnus or a Memnon flashing foreign arms to daze them.

    My true alumni you can tell from those of this word heaver:

    His are Megaenetus the Wop, Phormisius the Beaver—

    Mustachioed swashbucklers both, and frolicsome Pine
    Benders;

    Theramenes and Cleitophon, *my* graduate defenders.

DIONYSUS: Theramenes? Now there's a chap that's clever in
    the clinches.

    When trouble gets him in its grip, the fellow never
    flinches—

    He throws a lucky flip-flop and escapes defeat by inches!

EURIPIDES: These wholesome habits, then, of thought
    To this democracy I taught:

I showed them logic on the stage
Till logic now is all the rage.
They reason, they discriminate,
And everything investigate.
Their homes they manage better, too:
What goes on here? they ask. *Hey, you!*
Where's so-and-so? Who took my new . . . ?

DIONYSUS: I grant you that, by God! They do!
As soon as they are past the door,
They have the servants in, and roar
What's happened to the soup tureen?
Who bit the head off this sardine?
That handsome bowl I bought last year
Has gone to glory—'tisn't here!
And where is Sunday's garlic, pray?
Who nibbled at this olive, eh?
Time was when they were stupid clods,
Mere Simple Simon noddynods
          And lazy mollycoddles!

CHORUS (*to* AESCHYLUS):
          Thou seest the hazard, illustrious thane.
               How wilt thou answer a charge so black, sir?
                    Prithee maintain
                    Care lest passion seize the rein,
               Sweeping thee beyond the track, sir.
               Calmly meet this dread attack, sir;
                    Wrath, my noble prince, restrain,
                    Nor indulge in bitter censure.
               Reef thy sails before thou venture
                    Out upon the stormy main.
               Watch the angry winds, awaiting
                    Their abating;
               Then, with caution navigating,
               Launch with vigor thy campaign.

DIONYSUS (*to* AESCHYLUS): Thou first to impart to theat-
     rical art a style as sublime as the mountains,
     With lofty disdain for the flat and the plain, release thy
     rhetorical fountains.

AESCHYLUS: That I should be forced to reply to this person
     arouses my deep indignation;
     Yet, lest he assert that I haven't the means of disproving
     his bold accusation,

(*To* Euripides.) What gifts do you hold that a poet should
   have, to be worthy of men's admiration?

Euripides: Superlative artistry, craftsmanship, and the skill
   of a talented teacher

To make men better by counsel sage.

Aeschylus: And if, as a teacher—
   or preacher—

You've failed, and have turned into villainous rogues sound
   youngsters, the pride of our city,

What punishment ought you to suffer?

Dionysus: Ask *me*: to be hung,
   sans mercy or pity!

Aeschylus: Consider the audience I had bequeathed him:
   cowardly loafers and laggards?

Degenerate scamps like the youth of today, who are naught
   but promising blackguards?

No! Fine six-footers with courage so sturdy that nothing
   could ever o'erwhelm it,

Each breathing the spirit of spear, of lance, of the pure
   white plume of the helmet,

Hearts booted and spurred for the rout of the foe, that
   highest and noblest of missions.

Dionysus: Hey, stop it! Enough of your helmets and spears.
   I am sick unto death of *munitions!*

Euripides: Just what did you do that another did not, to de-
   velop this spirit, I pray you?

Dionysus: Speak out! Why stand there preening yourself
   and nursing your dudgeon? . . . What say you?

Aeschylus: By writing a drama *instinct with Mars.*

Dionysus: What drama?

Aeschylus: The
   Seven, which fired

In every spectator a passion for war and for deeds of daring
   inspired.

Dionysus: 'Twas the *Thebans* you taught to be daring, and
   they have in this very war been pursuing

The principles given by you to their sires—and you ought
   to be flogged for so doing!

Aeschylus: Those lessons you too might have learned, but
   you wanted your ease, all hardship eschewing.—

And again, by producing my *Persians,* this aim was
   achieved once more—to enamor

Our youth of a yearning for victory won by a feat of illustrious glamour.

DIONYSUS: I was charmed when Darius emerged from his
coffin and published the doom of his nation,

The chorus wringing their hands, meanwhile, indulging in
loud lamentation!

AESCHYLUS: For such are the paths that a poet should tread.
Our earliest civilization

We owe to the poets, who helped us escape from the laws
of barbaric society.

'Twas Orpheus who taught us to reverence life, a religion
of mystical piety;

Musaeus who brought us oracular wisdom, and magical
methods of healing;

And Hesiod told of the tillage of earth, her opulent beauty
revealing;

The fame of the godlike Homer was won by the lessons he
gave to our heroes:

Good discipline, courage, the wearing of arms . . .

DIONYSUS: Well,
Pantacles' marks were all zeros!

While puffing along in a recent parade, poor chap—he's a
bit on the stout side—

His helmet agleam on his head, he was trying to fasten the
plume from the *out*side!

AESCHYLUS: But many another, like masterful Lamachus,
learned what Homer imparted;

And his was the matrix from which I have molded the
forms of my own *lionhearted*

Patroclus and Teucer, whose valor, I trusted, would arouse
Athenian yeomen

To rival their deeds at the sound of the trumpet and van-
quish the finest of foemen.

This further: loose women I never created—no Phaedras,
no Stheneboeas.

And who can assert that in dramas of mine any lovelorn
lady appears?

EURIPIDES: Ah no! Aphrodite had left you untouched, with
none of her graces endowered.

AESCHYLUS: Thank heaven! On you and on yours, I am
told, her charms in such volume were showered

That wreckage and ruin were brought to your home.

DIONYSUS (*to* EURIPIDES):   *Touché!* By
  Jove, it is true, sir:
The things you had written of other men's wives, your
  own inflicted on you, sir!
EURIPIDES: My poor Stheneboeas! What harm has been done
  to the world by their tragic romances?
AESCHYLUS: Why, virtuous spouses of virtuous husbands, ap-
  palled by their brazen advances,
Drink hemlock, feeling vicarious shame at their lurid Bel-
  lerophon fancies.
EURIPIDES: And Phaedra . . . you think that her story is false,
  imagined by *me,* a mere fiction?
AESCHYLUS: Unhappily, no. She is real. But a poet should
  seek to avoid the depiction
Of evil—should hide it, not drag into view its ugly and
  odious features.
For children have tutors to guide them aright; young man-
  hood has poets for teachers.
And so we must write of the fair and the good.
EURIPIDES: In language
  to dwarf Lycabettus?
In words to outweigh the Parnassian cliffs? Quite frankly,
  where does it get us,
As teachers, to talk in a tongue superhuman?
AESCHYLUS: Pedestrian
  spirit, in *my* style
Great words are begotten to match great thoughts. Sub-
  limity speaks in the high style.
Then too it is right that a hero of drama should use words
  larger than ours,
When even the costume he wears is designed to reflect his
  superior powers.
These noble devices of mine you spoiled.
EURIPIDES: Just how? By
  what indiscretion?
AESCHYLUS: By wrapping your princes in beggarly rags, to
  produce a pathetic impression
Of woe that would soften the hearts of their hearers.
EURIPIDES: Was
  that so dire a transgression?
AESCHYLUS: A plutocrat, chosen to captain a trireme, swears
  that he hasn't a dollar,

Tricked out as a tatterdemalion Telephus living in absolute
  squalor.
DIONYSUS: And sporting a *tunic* of elegant wool! If he wins
  a reprieve by his fakery,
He's sure to pop up next morning in market, ready to buy
  out a bakery!
AESCHYLUS: Besides, you are guilty of training our youth in
  the art of sophistical gabble.
The playgrounds are empty; our athletes sit on their well-
  worn haunches and babble.
Our prize bluejackets today, I am told, are bandying words
  with the skipper.
In *my* time, none of them *knew* any, even aboard our fan-
  ciest clipper.
Ahoy! he could bellow, *Avast! Aye aye, sir,* and shout for
  his "grub" from the steward . . .
DIONYSUS: And, firing a jet from his ample exhaust, asphyxi-
  ate all to the leeward!
The menacing mucker would then go ashore for thieving
  and raising a rumpus.
                  Now they argue and never row
                  And let the ship a-bobbing go.
AESCHYLUS: Of what ills is Euripides *not* the cause?
Pimps he brings on in defiance of laws,
A woman in a temple becoming a mother,
A woman lying with her own brother,
No-life equals life asserting,
Our whole city thus subverting,
Filling it with clowns of diverse shapes,
Half-educated demagogue apes,
Whose study it is the people to debauch.
None can now carry the relay-race torch
For none works out in the gymnasium.
DIONYSUS: I near died laughing at the Panathenaeum!
A stooped-over fellow, short, fat, and pale
Was puffing along at the race's tail;
At the Ceramicus gate folk thwacked his flanks,
His belly, his rump, his sides, his shanks.
The beating caused his wind to fan:
Out blew the torch and away he ran.
CHORUS: Sharp the strife, violent the collision,
  Difficult 'twill be to reach a decision.

The one will press with energy immense, the
Other dodge with footwork fancy.
Keep not always the same stance:
Attack however there's a chance.
Bring all your resources into play;
Wrangle, tangle, be flayed and flay.
Draw arguments old from out your store,
Venture subtleties never used before.
If you fear your audience uninitiate,
Unable profundities to penetrate,
Rest easy; out of fashion is naivete.
Veteran campaigners of many a fray,
The spectators come well-girt:
Each has book in hand, each has wits alert.
You've a sage and clever audience;
There's naught to fear, take heart, advance!

EURIPIDES: To your prologues I'll address myself first. I'll test
The opening lines of this able playwright's work.
His statement of subject is opaque.

DIONYSUS: Which will you choose for examination?

EURIPIDES: Many, but first give me the opening of the
Oresteia.

DIONYSUS: Silence, everyone! Speak, Aeschylus!

AESCHYLUS: *Hermes of the nether world who surveys paternal power,*
Be savior and ally at my supplication:
I come to this land, here I return.

DIONYSUS: Do you find any fault in these lines?

EURIPIDES: More than a dozen.

DIONYSUS: But there are only three lines in all.

EURIPIDES: And twenty slips in each.

DIONYSUS: Aeschylus, I beg you, do be quiet. If you don't
You'll be more than three lines short.

AESCHYLUS: Me be quiet for *him?*

DIONYSUS: If you take my advice.

EURIPIDES: Right away he blundered sky-high.

AESCHYLUS: You see, Dionysus, how foolish your advice?

DIONYSUS: I don't much care.

AESCHYLUS: What blunder are you referring to?

EURIPIDES: The opening again, please.

AESCHYLUS: *Hermes of the nether world who surveys paternal power——*

EURIPIDES: Is it Orestes speaking at the grave of his murdered father?

AESCHYLUS: Precisely.

EURIPIDES: Would a man whose father had been treacherously murdered

By a woman's intrigue speak of Hermes as *surveying?*

AESCHYLUS: Not that Hermes, but Hermes the Helper, as he demonstrated

By assigning paternal surveillance.

EURIPIDES: A worse fault than I thought. If he held nether paternal surveillance——

DIONYSUS: He would be a grave robber at his father's bidding.

AESCHYLUS: Dionysus, the wine you drink is flat.

DIONYSUS: Recite another line, and you, Euripides, keep an eye out for mistakes.

AESCHYLUS: *Be savior and ally at my supplication:*
I come to this land, here I return.

EURIPIDES: Our sage Aeschylus gives us the same thing twice.

DIONYSUS: How twice?

EURIPIDES: Look at the text and I'll explain. *I come to this land,*

Says he, *and I return,* the meaning's the same.

DIONYSUS: By Zeus, it is—as if a man said to his neighbor
Lend me your skillet, your frying pan lend me.

AESCHYLUS: Not at all the same, you hairsplitter; the words are right.

DIONYSUS: How so? Tell me what you mean.

AESCHYLUS: A man who has a country and happens to arrive *comes;*

An exile *comes* and *returns.*

DIONYSUS: Good, by Apollo. And what do you say, Euripides?

EURIPIDES: I say that Orestes never *returned.* He sneaked in, surreptitiously.

DIONYSUS: Good, by Hermes. —What it means I haven't a notion.

EURIPIDES: Continue with another line, please.

DIONYSUS: You, Aeschylus, continue at once. And you look for mistakes.

AESCHYLUS: *At the tomb's edge I invoke my father: hear, hearken!*

EURIPIDES: Again the same thing twice, most obviously: *hear, hearken*.

DIONYSUS: But it's to the dead he's speaking, rascal; they can't hear

Even if we call them three times.

AESCHYLUS: And how do you make *your* prologues?

EURIPIDES: I'll tell you, and if you find repetition or padding, spit on me.

DIONYSUS: Speak, I'm eager to hear the perfection of your prologues.

EURIPIDES: *Oedipus was a lucky man at first.*

AESCHYLUS: Never, by Zeus, but most unlucky from the start. Before he was born

Apollo predicted he'd murder his father. How could he be
A lucky man at first?

EURIPIDES: *Then he became the wretchedest of mortals.*

AESCHYLUS: Zeus, no! He never stopped being. As a babe newborn, and in winter,

They put him out in a crock, not to grow up to murder his father;

Then with swollen feet he hobbles off to Polybus, then he marries

An old woman, and his mother to boot, then blinds himself.

DIONYSUS: Blindness would be lucky if he served with Erasinides.

EURIPIDES: Bosh! I make *good* prologues.

AESCHYLUS: I'll not maul your text word by word, but with heaven's help,

I'll smash them all with an oilcan.

EURIPIDES: My prologues with an oilcan?

AESCHYLUS: With just one. Such are your iambics that an afghan

Or reticule or oilcan can be fitted in.

I'll demonstrate.

EURIPIDES: You say you'll demonstrate?

AESCHYLUS: I do.

DIONYSUS: Time to speak.

EURIPIDES: *Aegyptus, according to the prevalent story,*
Touching at Argos with fifty sons——

AESCHYLUS: Lost his oilcan.

EURIPIDES: What's that oilcan? Damn it!

DIONYSUS: Give him another prologue; the point will be clearer.

EURIPIDES: *Dionysus in fawn-skins clad, with thyrsus and torch*
Bounding and dancing——

AESCHYLUS: Lost his oilcan.

DIONYSUS: Ah, I am smitten once more—by the oilcan.

EURIPIDES: No matter. You'll not be able to fit your oilcan to this:
No man is in all respects happy. One nobly poor is needy,
Another, of low birth——

AESCHYLUS: Lost his oilcan.

DIONYSUS: Euripides!

EURIPIDES: What is it?

DIONYSUS: Better reef your sails; that little can will blow a gale.

EURIPIDES: I'm not worried, by Demeter. I'll smash it in his hand.

DIONYSUS: Recite another, then, but beware the oilcan.

EURIPIDES: *Upon leaving Sidon's town Agenor's son Cadmus——*

AESCHYLUS: Lost his oilcan.

DIONYSUS: Better buy that oilcan, friend: he'll chip away all your prologues.

EURIPIDES: What, I buy of him?

DIONYSUS: If you take my advice.

EURIPIDES: Never. I can produce many prologues to which he cannot fix his oilcan.
Tantalid Pelops faring to Pisa with swift mares——

AESCHYLUS: Lost his oilcan.

DIONYSUS: D'you see? He did tack the oilcan on. Buy it, do;
You can get it good as new for an obol.

EURIPIDES: Not yet; I still have plenty. *In his field one day Oeneus——*

AESCHYLUS: Lost his oilcan.

EURIPIDES: Do let me finish the whole line. *In his field one day Oeneus*
After reaping an abundant harvest, while offering first fruits——

AESCHYLUS: Lost his oilcan.

DIONYSUS: In the midst of sacrifice? Who stole it?

EURIPIDES: Let be, mister. Let him try this one. *Zeus as Truth hath said——*

DIONYSUS: He'll ruin you; he'll say *Lost his oilcan.* On your prologues

That oilcan grows like sties on eyes. In heaven's name,
Turn now to his melodies.

EURIPIDES: I can prove he's a bad melody maker: he makes
them all alike.

CHORUS: What new action in this fray?
What charge, I wonder, can he lay
Against our age's master tragic,
Most melodious, most prolific?
How will he fault our Bacchic lord?
I tremble for the lesser bard.

EURIPIDES: Marvelous tunes indeed! You'll see through him
soon.
I'll cut all his lines down to one.

DIONYSUS: And I'll get some pebbles to keep score.
(*Flute music offstage.*)

EURIPIDES: *Phthian Achilles, why, hearing the man smiter*
Hah, come you not to the rescue, striking?
Ancestor Hermes, whom we by the lakeside revere,
Hah, come you not to the rescue, striking?

DIONYSUS: That's two strikes, Aeschylus.

AESCHYLUS: *Noblest of Achaeans, wide-ruling son of Atreus,*
hear me:
Hah, come you not to the rescue, striking?

DIONYSUS: Strike three, Aeschylus.

EURIPIDES: *Hush! Soon will the Bee keepers open Artemis'*
house:
Hah, come you not to the rescue, striking?
Mine the right to utter the heroes' auspices:
Hah, come you not to the rescue, striking?

DIONYSUS: Royal Zeus, what a heap of strikes; I must to the
bath:
Those strikes have inflamed my kidneys.

EURIPIDES: Not till you have heard the other sheaf,
Worked from music for the lyre.

DIONYSUS: Go on, then; but not another strike, please.

EURIPIDES: *Twin-throned power of Achaeans, flower of*
Hellas,
Phlattothrattophlattothrat.
Send baneful Sphinx, the presiding bitch
Phlattothrattophlattothrat,
With spear and avenging hand that stalwart bird
Phlattothrattophlattothrat,
Vouchsafes the stark air-faring fowl

Phlattothrattophlattothrat,
The onset against Ajax,
Phlattothrattophlattothrat.

DIONYSUS: What's that *phlattothrattophlattothrat?* Where
   did you get that chanty?

From Marathon? From rope twisters?

AESCHYLUS: From a noble source I took it and to noble use
   applied it;

I would not be seen culling flowers like Phrynichus' in the
   Muses' meadow.

He from all that's meretricious draws his ditties, catches

Of Meletus, Carian flutings, dirges, dances. Proof is forth-
   coming;

Bring a lyre, someone. But why a lyre for this—where's the
   tambourine girl

With her castanets? Hither, Muse of Euripides! For such
   songs

She is proper patroness.

   (*Enter a* WANTON, *swaying and clashing castanets.*)

DIONYSUS: The muse a Lesbian? No!

AESCHYLUS: *Halcyons ever twittering*
   By the billowing spume
   With dewy droplets glittering
   On every moistened plume.
   Intricate, dainty webs of lace
   Spiders weave with fingers nimble
   In every nook and crannied place
   Plying their shuttle like a cymbal.
   Wantons the dolphin flute-loving
   Before men-o'-war dark-prowed,
   Oracular patterns proving
   Or racing before a crowd.
   Flowering spiral of fragrant vine,
   Cluster of care-banishing grape:
   Child, twine your arms in mine.
   Do you see this foot's shape?

DIONYSUS: I do.

AESCHYLUS: So. And this one's?

DIONYSUS: I see it.

AESCHYLUS: Who writes knavery so prolix
   Filled with a dozen whorish tricks,
   Shall he dare my odes to spurn?
   So much for odes. Now I turn

The fashion of his solos to transfix.
Darkness of shadowy Night,
What dire dream to affright
Sendest thou, Hades' queen,
From abyss unplumbed, unseen—
A horrible, shuddering sprite
In cerement's black bedight,
Portending slaughter in eye and maw
And in prodigious rending claw.
The lanterns, my maidens, be kindling,
Draw river-dew up in your pail;
The water boil till it's bubbling,
I'll slosh off that Vision's bale.
Busy at my task was I, poor soul,
My spindle full, making a hank
To sell at dawn at a market stall,
But up that rooster did soar and bank,
Spreading the tips of his agile wings,
To me bequeathing sorrow sore.
For the great grief disaster brings
I weep and shall weep forevermore.
Ye constables from Crete, Ida's band,
Limber your limbs, dance round the house,
Fly to the rescue, bows in hand.
Come too, Dictynna, your hounds arouse,
Maid Artemis come, the chambers rummage.
And you, O Hecate, child of Zeus,
Cast torches bright on Glyce's cottage,
Make the culprit pay back her dues.

DIONYSUS: Music enough, from both of you.

AESCHYLUS: Enough for me. I'd like now to bring him to the
    scales:
    That's the only way to assay our poetry; that will
    Prove whose verses are weightiest.

DIONYSUS: Step up, then, if I must apply the cheese-selling
    technique
    To poetic operations.
        (*A large pair of scales is brought in.*)

CHORUS: These clever men, how diligent!
    Here's another brand-new portent,
    Beyond the ordinary man's capacity;
    If told I'd doubt the teller's veracity
    And scorn the simpleton's naivete.

DIONYSUS: Come, stand by the scales, both.

AESCHYLUS: } Here!
EURIPIDES:

DIONYSUS: Each hold it and recite a verse, and don't let go
Till I cry *Cuckoo!*

AESCHYLUS: } We've got it.
EURIPIDES:

DIONYSUS: Now speak your line into the scale.

EURIPIDES: *Would that Argo had never winged its way—*

AESCHYLUS: *River Spercheius, cattle-grazing haunts—*

DIONYSUS: Cuckoo! Let go! Aeschylus' sinks way down.

EURIPIDES: What's the reason?

DIONYSUS: Because he injected a river, like a wool merchant
Wetting his ware to make it weigh more. You put wings on
yours.

EURIPIDES: Make him recite another verse and stand by it.

DIONYSUS: To the scales again!

AESCHYLUS: } Here!
EURIPIDES:

DIONYSUS: Speak.

EURIPIDES: *Persuasion's sole sanctuary is eloquence—*

AESCHYLUS: *Alone of the gods Death is no lover of gifts—*

DIONYSUS: Let go, let go! Again Aeschylus' is down.
He injected Death, the heaviest of all ills.

EURIPIDES: And I *Persuasion,* a word fine to speak.

DIONYSUS: Persuasion's a light and feather-brained thing.
Think
Of something heavier to depress your scale, something big
and strong.

EURIPIDES: Where have I got one, where?

DIONYSUS: I'll tell you: *Achilles threw deuce and four.*
Speak up now; this is the last lap.

EURIPIDES: *An iron-studded club in his right hand he seized—*

AESCHYLUS: *Chariot upon chariot, and upon corpse corpse—*

DIONYSUS: He's foiled you again, Euripides.

EURIPIDES: How?

DIONYSUS: Two chariots and two corpses he heaved in.
A hundred gypsies couldn't hoist them.

AESCHYLUS: No more line for line. Let him get into the scale,
With his children, his wife, Cephisophon, and himself
Holding all his books; I need but two of my lines.

DIONYSUS: Both are my friends, and I cannot play judge.
Neither

Would I have my enemy. One I think clever, the other delights me.

PLUTO: Then you won't accomplish your errand.

DIONYSUS: And if I decide?

PLUTO: You can take whichever you decide with you, and your trip
Will not be footless.

DIONYSUS: Bless you! You know, it was for a poet I came.

PLUTO: With what motive?

DIONYSUS: So the city saved may keep its choral festivals.
'chever is likely to advise the city well, him
I intend to take back. First about Alcibiades. What
Is your opinion? The city is still in heavy labor.

EURIPIDES: What is its feeling about Alcibiades?

DIONYSUS: What? Yearning, hatred, desire. But what of you two?
Say what you think about him.

EURIPIDES: I hate a citizen slow to help his country, swift to harm it.
Ingenious for himself, for the state feckless.

DIONYSUS: Well put, by Poseidon. And you, Aeschylus, what is your opinion?

AESCHYLUS: Best it is never to rear a lion in the city; but if reared
It has been, 'tis best to yield to its ways.

DIONYSUS: Savior Zeus, what a hard decision! One speaks cleverly,
The other clearly. Give us, each, one other response.
How think you the state may be saved?

EURIPIDES: Hitch wings to Cinesias and Cleocritus, so that breezes
Might waft them over the watery main.

DIONYSUS: A comical spectacle—but what's the idea?

EURIPIDES: In naval engagements supply vinegar to squirt in enemy eyes.
I know something I want to tell.

DIONYSUS: Say on.

EURIPIDES: When we hold the mistrusted trustworthy, and the trustworthy mistrust.

DIONYSUS: How's that? I don't understand. Less profundity, please,
And more clarity.

EURIPIDES: If citizens we now trust we mistrust, and employ those

We do not now employ, we shall be saved. If disastrous

Our present course, surely its opposite must bring salvation.

DIONYSUS: Well done, Palamedes! What a genius! This invention—

Is it yours or Cephisophon's?

EURIPIDES: All mine. The vinegar idea was Cephisophon's.

DIONYSUS: What about you, Aeschylus? What do you say?

AESCHYLUS: Tell me first whom the city employs. The good?

DIONYSUS: What a notion! It hates them worst of all.

AESCHYLUS: But likes the bad?

DIONYSUS: Not really, but uses them perforce.

AESCHYLUS: How save a city which likes neither cape nor coat?

DIONYSUS: Do find some solution if you go up again.

AESCHYLUS: There I may speak; here I will not.

DIONYSUS: No, please; send the good things up from here.

AESCHLUS: When they come to regard enemy land as their own

And their own as the enemy's, their ships as true wealth

And their wealth a cipher.

DIONYSUS: Good enough, but the juries devour it all.

PLUTO: Make your decision.

DIONYSUS: As between these two, him I choose in whom my soul delights.

EURIPIDES: Remember the gods by whom you swore you'd take me

Home again; choose your friends!

DIONYSUS: *'Tis my tongue that swore*—'tis Aeschylus I choose.

EURIPIDES: What have you done, vile creature?

DIONYSUS: Me? Judged Aeschylus victor. Why not?

EURIPIDES: And after conduct so shameful you dare face me?

DIONYSUS: *What's shameful if spectators do not so regard it?*

EURIPIDES: Cruel! Will you ignore me when I'm dead?

DIONYSUS: Who knows whether to live is to die, to breathe to dine,

To sleep a fuzzy blanket?

PLUTO: Come inside now, Dionysus.

DIONYSUS: What for?

PLUTO: We'll entertain you two before you embark.
DIONYSUS: Thanks, by Zeus; it's no trouble at all.
                    (PLUTO *and* AESCHYLUS *withdraw*.)
CHORUS: Happy is the man of intellect keen—
    In cases many is this principle seen.
    Proven to possess an intelligent brain,
    Aeschylus goes back home again,
    To his fellow citizens to be a boon,
    A boon likewise unto his own
    Kith and kin—all for his sagacity.
    Better it is to eschew loquacity,
    Following in the Socratic train,
    Rejecting music with high disdain,
    Abandoning with foolish equanimity
    Noble tragedy's lofty sublimity.
    To make your study grandiloquence
    And busy quibbling devoid of sense
    Argues an empty mind and sick,
    In point of fact a lunatic.
PLUTO: Fare you well, Aeschylus, go and save
    Our hard-pressed city by your precepts grave.
    School the silly; their kind is numerous.
    This rope to Cleophon take, this to Nicomachus,
    This to the gang that the revenue collects,
    This to Archenomus, this to Myrmex.
    Tell them all what I have to say:
    Come to me here with no delay.
    If they dawdle, I swear by Apollo,
    Branded and fettered down they go
    With Adeimantus, Leucolophus' son
    To lowest darkness every one.
AESCHYLUS: Your bidding I'll do. To this my chair
    I make genial Sophocles my heir,
    Till I return to guard and possess,
    For he comes second to my success.
    Never shall *that* impostor base
    Occupy my rightful place—
    That lying rogue, that low buffoon,
    Will he nill he, late or soon.
PLUTO: Light, mystic throng, his upward way
    As your holy torches glitter and sway.
    Escort him with his own sweet chants,
    Glorify him with song and dance.

CHORUS: First, ye deities of the world below,
Grant a happy journey to the poet who will go
To the light above. Next to our nation
Grant counsels sound to work salvation,
Surcease swift from all that harms,
Respite from foul war's alarms.
Cleophon may fight, and others that will,
In distant fields which foreigners till.

(*Exeunt.*)

DISCOVER
THE DRAMA OF LIFE
IN THE LIFE OF DRAMA

☐	13434	**CYRANO DE BERGERAC** Rostand	$1.75
☐	12204	**FOUR GREAT PLAYS** Ibsen	$1.95
☐	13615	**COMP. PLAYS SOPHOCLES**	$2.95
☐	11936	**FOUR GREAT PLAYS BY CHEKHOV** Anton Chekhov	$1.75
☐	13001	**THE NIGHT THOREAU SPENT IN JAIL** Jerome Lawrence and Robert E. Lee	$1.95
☐	13390	**RUNAWAYS** Elizabeth Swados	$2.50
☐	12832	**THE PRICE** Arthur Miller	$1.95
☐	13363	**BRIAN'S SONG** Blinn	$1.95
☐	12548	**THE EFFECTS OF GAMMA RAYS ON** **MAN-IN-THE-MOON MARIGOLDS** Paul Zindel	$1.95
☐	14161	**50 GREAT SCENES FOR STUDENT ACTORS** Lewy Olfson, ed.	$2.50
☐	12917	**INHERIT THE WIND** Lawrence & Lee	$1.75
☐	13102	**TEN PLAYS BY EURIPIDES** Hadas	$2.50
☐	13902	**THE CRUCIBLE** Arthur Miller	$2.25
☐	13527	**THE MIRACLE WORKER** Gibson	$1.95
☐	14101	**AFTER THE FALL** Arthur Miller	$2.50

Buy them at your local bookstore or use this handy coupon for ordering:

THE NAMES THAT SPELL GREAT LITERATURE

Choose from today's most renowned world authors—every one an important addition to your personal library.

Hermann Hesse

☐	13956	MAGISTER LUDI	$2.95
☐	13523	DEMIAN	$2.25
☐	11978	THE JOURNEY TO THE EAST	$1.95
☐	12529	SIDDHARTHA	$2.25
☐	12758	BENEATH THE WHEEL	$2.25
☐	12509	NARCISSUS AND GOLDMUND	$2.50
☐	13174	STEPPENWOLF	$2.25
☐	11510	ROSSHALDE	$1.95

Alexander Solzhenitsyn

☐	10111	THE FIRST CIRCLE	$2.50
☐	13441	ONE DAY IN THE LIFE OF IVAN DENISOVICH	$2.50
☐	2997	AUGUST 1914	$2.50
☐	13720	CANCER WARD	$3.95

Jerzy Kosinski

☐	14117	STEPS	$2.50
☐	13619	THE PAINTED BIRD	$2.50
☐	2613	COCKPIT	$2.25
☐	11899	BLIND DATE	$2.50
☐	13843	BEING THERE	$2.50

Doris Lessing

☐	13433	THE SUMMER BEFORE THE DARK	$2.95
☐	13675	THE GOLDEN NOTEBOOK	$3.95
☐	13967	THE FOUR-GATED CITY	$3.95
☐	11717	BRIEFING FOR A DESCENT INTO HELL	$2.25

André Schwarz-Bart

☐	12510	THE LAST OF THE JUST	$2.95

Buy them at your local bookstore or use this handy coupon for ordering:

Bantam Book Catalog

Here's your up-to-the-minute listing of over 1,400 titles by your favorite authors.

This illustrated, large format catalog gives a description of each title. For your convenience, it is divided into categories in fiction and non-fiction—gothics, science fiction, westerns, mysteries, cookbooks, mysticism and occult, biographies, history, family living, health, psychology, art.

So don't delay—take advantage of this special opportunity to increase your reading pleasure.

Just send us your name and address and 50¢ (to help defray postage and handling costs).